Ingenious Trade

Ingenious Trade recovers the intricate stories of the young women who came to London in the late seventeenth century to earn their own living, most often with the needle, and the mistresses who set up shops and supervised their apprenticeships. Tracking women through city archives, it reveals the extent and complexity of their contracts, training and skills, from adolescence to old age. In contrast to the informal, unstructured and marginalised aspects of women's work, this book uses legal records and guild archives to reconstruct women's negotiations with city regulations and bureaucracy. It shows single women, wives and widows establishing themselves in guilds both alongside and separate to men, in a network that extended from elites to paupers and around the country. Through an intensive and creative archival reconstruction, Laura Gowing recovers the significance of apprenticeship in the lives of girls and women, and puts women's work at the heart of the revolution in worldly goods.

Laura Gowing is Professor of Early Modern History at King's College London, specialising in the history of early modern women, gender, and the body. She is the author of *Domestic Dangers* (1996) and *Common Bodies* (2003) which won prizes from the Society for the Study of Early Modern Women and the American Historical Association (Joan Kelly prize) respectively. She is an editor of *History Workshop Journal*.

Ingenious Trade

Women and Work in Seventeenth-Century London

Laura Gowing
King's College London

CAMBRIDGE
UNIVERSITY PRESS

University Printing House, Cambridge CB2 8BS, United Kingdom

One Liberty Plaza, 20th Floor, New York, NY 10006, USA

477 Williamstown Road, Port Melbourne, VIC 3207, Australia

314–321, 3rd Floor, Plot 3, Splendor Forum, Jasola District Centre, New Delhi – 110025, India

103 Penang Road, #05–06/07, Visioncrest Commercial, Singapore 238467

Cambridge University Press is part of the University of Cambridge.

It furthers the University's mission by disseminating knowledge in the pursuit of education, learning, and research at the highest international levels of excellence.

www.cambridge.org
Information on this title: www.cambridge.org/9781108486385
DOI: 10.1017/9781108639323

© Laura Gowing 2022

This publication is in copyright. Subject to statutory exception and to the provisions of relevant collective licensing agreements, no reproduction of any part may take place without the written permission of Cambridge University Press.

First published 2022

Printed in the United Kingdom by TJ Books Limited, Padstow Cornwall

A catalogue record for this publication is available from the British Library.

ISBN 978-1-108-48638-5 Hardback

Cambridge University Press has no responsibility for the persistence or accuracy of URLs for external or third-party internet websites referred to in this publication and does not guarantee that any content on such websites is, or will remain, accurate or appropriate.

Contents

List of Figures	*page*	vi
List of Tables		vii
Acknowledgements		viii
	Introduction	1
1	Bred in the Exchange: Seamstresses and Shopkeepers	11
2	Girls as Apprentices	55
3	Managing the Trade: Women as Mistresses	99
4	What Girls Learned	137
5	Making Havoc: Discipline, Demeanour and Resistance	178
6	Freedoms and Customs	209
	Conclusion	243
	Appendix: Who's Who	251
	Bibliography	254
	Index	269

Figures

1.1	Wenceslaus Hollar, *Winter* (1643–4)	*page* 15
1.2	Sites of the shopping galleries	17
1.3	Robert White, *The Royal Exchange* (1671)	19
1.4	Abraham Bosse, *La Galerie du Palais* (1637–38)	20
1.5	Detail of Ogilby and Morgan's 1676 map of London, showing the Royal Exchange and Gresham College	24
1.6	Schematic plan of the layout of the first floor of the Royal Exchange after the Fire	27
1.7	Women's connections in the Exchange	43
2.1	Ann Evans's indenture	56
2.2	Lucy Maes's indenture	70
2.3	Numbers of female apprenticeships	79
2.4	Characteristics of female apprentices, 1660–1700	85
2.5	Goldsmiths' Company Apprenticeship	86
3.1	Indenture of Mary Toft to Elizabeth Fazakerley	106
3.2	Richard Court's indenture	107
3.3	Mary and William Hull's apprentices	113
3.4	Elizabeth and Thomas Bromhall's apprentices	113
3.5	Frances and John Spillett's apprentices and children	116
3.6	Alice Guidot's apprentices	119
3.7	Rachel Erskine's apprentices	124
3.8	Elizabeth Kingsman's apprentices	125
4.1	Named occupations in girls' apprenticeships	144
5.1	F. Shepherd, *Sir Paul Pindar's House* (1812)	196
6.1	Patrimony form for Anne Allison	227
6.2	Mary Spark's petition	228

Tables

2.1	Proportions of female apprentices	*page* 88
3.1	Mistresses of female apprentices, 1640–1700	111
3.2	Numbers of apprentices to married couples taking boys and girls	111
3.3	Girls apprenticed to single women	123
3.4	Apprenticeships and their outcomes, 1640–1700	123
3.5	Mistresses and their female apprentices, 1640–1700	124
4.1	Gendered occupations	147
4.2	Valuing seamstresses	167
4.3	Costs of shop goods	167

Acknowledgements

This book has taken longer than an apprenticeship, for many reasons, and I'm very grateful to all the people and institutions who supported it. Research and writing were generously funded by a Leverhulme Trust Research Fellowship in 2016. At Johns Hopkins University, the stimulating luxury of a Hinkley Visiting Professorship in 2010 nurtured the start of the book. King's College London granted me two sabbatical terms at critical moments. Mark Merry, Olwen Myhill, Michael Scott and Patrick Wallis kindly shared the digitised guild and tax data which made it possible to find and count women in London's livery companies. My interest in the London Mayor's Court developed many years ago with a fortuitous dip into the card index of the old Corporation of London Record Office; since then I've benefitted greatly from the expertise of archivists at the London Metropolitan Archives, Guildhall Library and several City of London Companies, especially Jessica Collins, Penny Fussell, Jane Muncaster and Charlie Turpie. Many friends and colleagues have discussed ideas and answered odd questions. I want to thank in particular Sarah Bendall, Judith Bennett, Sarah Birt, Esther Brot, Kate Chedgzoy, Molly Corlett, Hannah Dawson, James Daybell, James Fisher, Mary Fissell, Amy Froide, Anne Goldgar, Julie Hardwick, Karen Harvey, Cynthia Herrup, Tracey Hill, Kate Hodgkin, Ann Hughes, Margaret Hunt, Cathy McClive, Angela McShane, John Marshall, Jonah Miller, Hannah Murphy, Maggie Pelling, Sara Pennell, Sophie Pitman, Lyndal Roper, Isabella Rosner, Michael Scott, Pam Sharpe, Alex Shepard, Deb Simonton, Hilda Smith, Craig Spence, Naomi Tadmor, Alice Taylor, Barbara Todd, Sonia Tycko, Brodie Waddell, Tim Wales, Patrick Wallis, Rachel Weil, Evelyn Welch, Jane Whittle and Andy Wood. Seminar and conference audiences in Cambridge, Durham, Exeter, Kent, London, New York Uppsala and on Zoom all contributed to the work's final form. Working with King's students on the archives of early modern women has always raised new questions. Catherine Hinchliff and Mark Jenner thought of me when they found indentures, and Charlie Berry, Lucy Munro and

Tim Reinke-Williams kindly pinged other references into my inbox. Amy Erickson's acute comments have been an enormous help. At Cambridge University Press, I'm very grateful to Liz Friend-Smith, Atifa Jiwa and Melissa Ward for their enthusiastic support and to the anonymous readers for the Press. Deepest thanks, and no responsibility, go to the friends and colleagues who gave their time and expertise, at a time of great pressure, to comment so perceptively on sections of the manuscript: Hannah Dawson, Mary Fissell, Amy Froide, Julie Hardwick and Hannah Murphy. From picket line to pandemic, colleagues at King's have offered the best-humoured solidarity as well as intellectual companionship. And at home, Louise Gray's partnership and editorial eyes, enlivened by Nic, supported the project from start to finish: my heartfelt thanks.

Sections of Chapter 5 appeared in an earlier form in Laura Gowing, '"The Manner of Submission": Gender and Demeanour in Seventeenth-Century London' in *Cultural and Social History* ©The Social History Society, reprinted by permission of Informa UK Limited, trading as Taylor & Francis Group, www.tandfonline.com on behalf of The Social History Society.

Introduction

In 1668, Frances Angell, an apprentice seamstress, lost her temper with her mistress Apollonia Maddox. She stormed out of the house and refused to return, saying 'she could maintain herself well enough' without her. She meant, as a witness explained, 'she had attained to so good skill and instrucon in hir arte of a sempstress as she was able thereby to gett hir living'. Frances Angell and her father sued Maddox and her husband to get back the premium that had been paid for Frances's training. The Maddoxes resisted, claiming Frances was idle, stubborn and wasteful; disobedient to both her mistress and her father; and 'a slattern in her clothes'.[1]

Frances was one of a generation of young women who, in their mid-teens, were bound as apprentices to learn to make a living. The path of trained apprenticeship for young women featured almost nowhere in printed literature, in advice to girls, in ballads or in plays. But it was a well-established route to independent work, practised in parishes and towns around the country as well as in guilds like those of the City of London and drawing in girls from the poorest to the gentry, as well as the women who ran successful businesses and those who laboured sewing for them, making lace or buttons, washing and starching, making cakes and selling fruit. This book uncovers their stories, and the networks of labour, credit and skill that gave working women their place in the early modern city.

Girls and women who maintained themselves, we will see, were ordinary, familiar figures in early modern cities. Domestic service through the later teenage years was characteristic of the life cycle of women in Northwestern Europe, where marriage was typically delayed till the mid-twenties. But other aspects of women's occupational training and artisanal life cycle are under-recorded both in formal archives and in the historiography. The guilds in London and elsewhere through which

---

[1] LMA, CLA/024/05/249 (1669).

many girls were apprenticed adopted ambivalent attitudes to their labour, and the formulaic records of apprenticeship minimise women's roles. Court cases like Frances Angell's; wills, tax lists and other administrative records; and record digitisation make it possible to find women in guilds and fill out the picture of their lives.[2] The chapters that follow examine how girls and women in late seventeenth-century London trained to earn a living and incorporated themselves into the institutions of apprenticeship and guilds, and the foundations this laid for the community of working women.

The 'ingenious trade' of the title described the work of one of London's seamstresses, Margaret Reeves. A friend looking to place an apprentice with her in 1694 described her as 'the best & most Ingenious of her tread makes & draws all her own patterns works only to people of the greatest quality'.[3] London's fashion market was teeming with ready-made goods, from shifts and aprons to coifs and gowns. Seamstresses acquired patterns to cut out garments with economy and style, and specialised needlewomen used patterns for embroidery or drew their own. The phrase also stands for the necessary ingenuity of making a career in a City regulated by London's livery companies, the guilds, and pressed by the forces of commerce and patriarchal regulation. 'Ingenious' connoted mastery of a craft, talent matched with technique, but also a kind of cunning in outwitting limits, or contriving an elegant effect with hidden means.[4] It suggested, often, an accomplished male virtuoso; to find it used of a woman's trade illuminates the skills and techniques that went with the seventeenth-century needle and shop.

The ubiquity of seamstress work in early modern cities makes it a fertile ground for tracing gendered conflicts over occupational identity and revealing female agency in the face of the obstacles to women's economic autonomy.[5] London's special place in those conflicts was shaped by the resources and strategies of the women who came to work

---

[2] Critical here is the searchable guild data on ROLLCO, www.londonroll.org. The London Apprenticeship Abstracts by Cliff Webb and the Freedoms of the City of London are available commercially on www.findmypast.co.uk and www.ancestry.co.uk, respectively.

[3] Bristol University Special Collections, Pinney Papers, Red Box 2 folder VII, Mary Pinney to Hester Pinney, 7 February 1695. This encounter is discussed further in Chapter 3. "Tread" = trade - or possibly, thread.

[4] Alexander Marr et al., *Logodaedalus: Word Histories of Ingenuity in Early Modern Europe* (University of Pittsburgh Press, 2018), introduction.

[5] See, for example, Clare Haru Crowston, 'Engendering the Guilds: Seamstresses, Tailors, and the Clash of Corporate Identities in Old Regime France', *French Historical Studies* 23, no. 2 (2000): 339–71; Mary Prior, 'Women in the Urban Economy', in *Women in English Society 1500–1800*, ed. Mary Prior (London: Methuen, 1985), 147–72; Deborah Simonton, '"Sister to the Tailor": Guilds, Gender and the Needle Trades in Eighteenth-Century Europe', in *Early Professional Women in Northern Europe,*

there, and also by the peculiarities of City custom. By the seventeenth century, the livery companies that functioned as guilds were losing their power to regulate their own trades so that seamstresses, like other artisans, could join most companies, could train apprentices and could gain the benefits of City freedom through their husbands, through the patrimonial right of their fathers and through their own apprenticeships.[6] Women's careers were often short or interrupted but laid the grounds for a future working life in which both sewing and trading were likely to be useful resources. Some worked for much longer, setting up shops and businesses that ran for years and taking on a series of apprentices who did the same.

Women's work in the textile trades of early modern London was critical to the expansion of those trades in the service of new patterns of consumption, which included quicker, cheaper fashion, often bought off the peg, with numerous ready-made accessories, alongside more disposable household goods. Shopping, so often portrayed as leisure, was also unpaid work, and learning to distinguish the increasingly varied goods of the seventeenth-century marketplace and shopfront involved expertise and touch. The households of urban tradespeople were the leaders in purchasing mirrors, curtains and goods for entertainment; they probably also led in displaying the clothes they sold.[7] Apprentices learned to make and sell clothes and also to want more or better for themselves. The women of this book lived in this world of shops as consumers, but also as workers and as businesswomen. Learning and teaching sewing put women behind the counter in the consumer revolution, alongside the asset management and economic decision-making that were typical of women's roles in business and merchant households.[8] They learned to make, trim, appraise and sell, and established a place in the world of new shops and shopping galleries like the Royal Exchange. The labour of

---

c. 1650–1850, ed. Johanna Ilmakunnas, Marjatta Rahikainen and Kirsi Vainio-Korhonen (Abingdon: Taylor & Francis, 2017).

[6] Amy Louise Erickson, 'Eleanor Mosley and Other Milliners in the City of London Companies 1700–1750', *History Workshop Journal* 71 (2011): 147–72 illuminates the significance of female apprenticeship in early modern London.

[7] Lorna Weatherill, *Consumer Behaviour and Material Culture in Britain, 1660–1760* (Brighton: Psychology Press, 1996).

[8] Alexandra Shepard. 'Crediting Women in the Early Modern English Economy', *History Workshop Journal* 78 (2015): 1–24; Lorna Weatherill, 'A Possession of One's Own: Women and Consumer Behavior in England, 1660–1740', *Journal of British Studies* 25, no. 2 (1986): 131–56; Margaret Hunt, *The Middling Sort: Commerce, Gender, and the Family in England, 1680–1780* (Berkeley: University of California Press, 1996); Jan de Vries, *The Industrious Revolution: Consumer Behavior and the Household Economy, 1650 to the Present* (Cambridge University Press, 2008).

apprentice girls and their mistresses helped shape the new world of consumption.

Their work was an integral part of an expanding urban economy, sustained by a trade boom and a transatlantic trading empire which made luxury textiles and foods cheaper and more readily available. As in cities across Europe, women migrants came in such numbers, often as servants, that they outnumbered men in the population by 3:2. Textile work – the largest sector of women's employment – was increasingly specialised, involving women of all ages and marital statuses in different roles. Evidence from legal records shows married women working widely independently from their husbands, largely in sewing, provisioning and the service sector.[9] Single women, too, were establishing more opportunities to hold shops and trade in their own name and the number of never-married women reached a peak in the mid-seventeenth century. Tax lists in 1693 show around 16 per cent of London's households headed by women and 26 per cent in the dockside hamlet of Ratcliff, London's Sailortown.[10] While Jan de Vries saw in the long eighteenth century an 'industrious revolution' which expanded women's orientation towards the market, Alexandra Shepard has suggested that what women were doing may simply have become more visible in these specialised urban contexts.[11] While sewing, making clothes and accessories and textile manufacture were the most prominent trades in London female apprenticeship, it extended to pastry-making, pin-making and numerous other trades.

In the bigger picture of women's work, continuity of inequality underpins significant economic and social shifts. Over a century ago, the first extensive study of early modern women's work, Alice Clark's *Working Women in Seventeenth-Century England* organised an exhaustive archival investigation around a transition from domestic and family industry to capitalist production, which effectively marginalised women's productive participation in the economy.[12] Both the chronology and the terms of her

---

[9] Amy Louise Erickson, 'Married Women's Occupations in Eighteenth-Century London', *Continuity and Change* 23, no. 2 (2008): 267–307; Peter Earle, 'The Female Labour Market in London in the Late Seventeenth and Early Eighteenth Centuries', *Economic History Review* 42, no. 3 (1989): 328–53.

[10] Craig Spence, *London in the 1690s: A Social Atlas* (London: Centre for Metropolitan History, 2000), 75.

[11] De Vries, *The Industrious Revolution*; Alexandra Shepard, *Accounting for Oneself: Worth, Status, and the Social Order in Early Modern England* (Oxford University Press, 2015), 30.

[12] Alice Clark, *Working Life of Women in the Seventeenth Century*, ed. Amy Louise Erickson (London: Routledge, 1992); Clark's material includes substantial references to women in urban crafts guilds, though it is often not clear what trade they were actually practising.

Introduction   5

argument have been substantially modified. The earlier period was no golden age: a relatively free labour market after the population loss of the Black Death was followed by a reduction in the scope of and reward for women's work in the sixteenth century. In the seventeenth century, the growing wage economy and the move of production outside households still involved significant, rewarding participation from both married and single women.[13] A continuing profile of low reward and poor esteem kept the 'patriarchal equilibrium' in place.[14] Recent large-scale archival projects have pioneered the analysis of legal records, with their extensive details about daily life, to create a time-use analysis of gendered work, noting who was doing what, for how long, and when, and reaching a fuller range of gendered labour by including all work that could be paid for.[15] One of the revealing findings of Jane Whittle and Mark Hailwood's investigation of women's work using this method is that women's work is systematically under-reported in witness statements, which were more often than not made by men.[16] The depositions used in this study, similarly, often reflect different stresses on the part of young women, male apprentices, interested neighbours and families. The stories of apprentices, mistresses and freewomen testify to the place of work in women's lives and to the structural system that underpinned their training. They reveal work at the centre of adolescent life, training for work as part of the plans by and for a wide spectrum of young women, and the role of a mistress as a particular and unique aspect of urban women's married and single lives.

The stories that record these roles are contested ones. At the common-law jurisdiction of the Mayor's Court, dissatisfied apprentices 'sued out' their indentures, dissolving their contracts. In the flexible system of apprenticeship, interrupted contracts were more common than completed ones and were mostly managed outside the courts, but the litigation guaranteed a closure of the obligation on both sides.[17] A small

---

[13] Jan de Vries, 'The Industrial Revolution and the Industrious Revolution', *Journal of Economic History* 54, no. 2 (1994): 249–70; Shepard, *Accounting for Oneself*.
[14] Judith M. Bennett, *History Matters: Patriarchy and the Challenge of Feminism* (Philadelphia: University of Pennsylvania Press, 2006), chapter 4.
[15] Sheilagh Ogilvie, 'How Does Social Capital Affect Women? Guilds and Communities in Early Modern Germany', *American Historical Review* 109, no. 2 (2004): 325–59; Maria Ågren, ed., *Making a Living, Making a Difference: Gender and Work in Early Modern European Society* (Oxford University Press, 2017).
[16] Jane Whittle and Mark Hailwood, 'The Gender Division of Labour in Early Modern England', *Economic History Review* 73, no. 1 (2020): 11. Both sexes were less likely to report work done by the opposite sex.
[17] Patrick Wallis, 'Labor, Law, and Training in Early Modern London: Apprenticeship and the City's Institutions', *Journal of British Studies* 51, no. 4 (2012): 791–819.

number of families went on to use the equity side of the Mayor's Court to try to recoup the premium they had paid for training, litigation which could involve substantial costs and which was mostly concluded with the repayment of a proportion of the premium which reflected the court's judgement on how badly each side had failed to perform their duty. Accounts were often wildly divergent, though not irreconcilable. Apprentices and their parents brought witnesses to drudgery, poor food, bad training and violence. Mistresses, hoping to have to pay back as little as possible, complained of poor work, unauthorised absences, idleness, theft and rudeness but reiterated their willingness to continue the contract. While both sides, guided by attorneys, structured their complaints around predictable grounds based on the apprenticeship contract, their narratives and the gaps between them provide a view into a world that has been largely invisible. Moreover, the use that women made of the Mayor's Court system reveals the integration of a set of expectations around women's work into an extensive wider system for managing training through customary norms and institutional mediation.

Over the last thirty years, historians have worked out methods of reading court records as sources for social history. Their narratives are constructed around memories, mediations, truths and fictions; the whole idea of truth in law is historically specific. Fictions woven for court cases tend to reveal fantasies that had real power over people's minds, and the power of the plausible means that fictionalised, exaggerated versions can be as useful to historians as strict truths. Alongside the key contested events, most testimonies include significant extraneous detail that reveals who was doing what, where and when. From the answers witnesses gave to leading questions, a landscape of daily life can be reconstituted alongside an attention to the fantasies and fictions people wove around their daily lives. The Mayor's Court cases come late in the bloom of legal activity that characterised the early modern period. They were pursued by gentry families, City traders and artisans and witnessed by their servants, apprentices, family and neighbours, with the aim of reaching a financial resolution based on the principles of equity. Many of these people had substantial social capital and literacy and were experienced in using the law. Other equity jurisdictions have been shown to be particularly open to women, but at the Mayor's Court, held at the Guildhall with a fixed team of attorneys, fathers or male guardians rather than mothers typically represented their daughters, perhaps reflecting the culture of the City and the guilds. Mayor's Court litigants and many of their witnesses were knowledgeable navigators of their generally privileged world, and they testified accordingly. The degree to which apprentices could or should partake of that privilege was one of the points of

Introduction

stress in their households. These testimonies were given in private and written up by a clerk; cases that were contested involved attorney advice as well. Witnesses responded to explicit and often fulsome libels framed by litigants. All this makes them feel quite practised. London's shopkeepers were interested in manners, politeness and civility, and so it is not surprising that the cases attend particularly to the ways of the body and to the performances of work and respect. Sixteenth and early seventeenth-century church court depositions – fodder for much rich social history of sex and marriage in the period – often echo popular stories, jokes and play plots, especially in London. The stories from the Mayor's Court of the late seventeenth century, with less raw human drama to them and pursuing a financial judgement, tend to have a different psychological dimension. They try to read character, to judge laziness or hard work alongside its appearance; their argumentative working women and men, preoccupied with status, appearance and worldly goods, are characters from an age of epistolary novels with an interest in personality development.

The fullest evidence survives for litigation over expensive apprenticeships. The premiums paid by the women who sued at the Mayor's Court ranged up to £50, representative of three or five times a labourer's average annual income, and a significant outlay for citizens or gentry. This kind of investment has important implications for women's work but represented a tiny minority of female apprentices. Most guild apprentices paid nothing like this, nor did the vast number of arrangements made outside the remit of the City of London and its companies, by families and intermediaries, by institutions like Christ's Hospital and by parishes making plans for their orphans and pauper children. Those apprenticeships went wrong too but were unlikely to reach public attention unless violence or significant debt was involved. Eve Salmon's case was one such problem. Apprenticed to housewifery in Hackney in 1686, she petitioned to be released after four years. Her master and mistress accused her of deserting, purloining goods, frequenting 'debauch't houses' and contracting venereal disease; Eve said she was driven to it by a want of food and clothes. Like Frances Angell, but in very different circumstances, Eve claimed she could provide for herself 'without being a charge to any person'.[18] Glimpses of apprentices' lives come from a variety of records, most of which leave only basic details, but there are enough to put together a rich profile of the households who trained young women of all statuses in the early modern city. Guild records

---

[18] LMA, MJ/SP 1691/02/11 and MJ/SP 1691/02/012.

and tax listings make it possible to reconstruct the quantitative contours of that world, showing up patterns within different companies, differences of marital and social status and sometimes the long life cycles of women's shop and craft work. Wills and indentures reveal the family and kin structures behind apprenticeship, showing us the informal networks that sustained women's work in the metropolis and reaching out into the provinces.

Apprenticeship for girls was a potentially radical business. The paperwork of apprenticeship reflects the impulse, apparent across London's livery companies as in guilds elsewhere, to celebrate male artisanship and repress the place of women. The records of guilds, unlike those of the courts, used conventions that concealed women's' and girls' roles, speaking of masters rather than mistresses and boys rather than girls, until they were forced to write them in. Keeping women's part in apprenticeship under cover tacitly enhanced the masculine ideal of corporate and civic life and the ideal life cycle of male artisans. Apprenticing girls subverted the apparently overwhelming masculinisation of artisanal labour in towns and cities and their guilds. In the late seventeenth century, London's seamstresses often lived in dyads of single mistresses and apprentices, a quite different model of work to that of the artisanal household. Even without the outright conflicts between women seamstresses and male tailors that characterised places like Oxford and York, or Rouen and Paris, women in London's guilds were changing the system to which they were attached.

Histories of women's work customarily frame it as under-recognised, informal, flexible and unregulated. Apprenticeship was different: it contracted women to each other with binding, legally significant expectations. The profiles of apprentices and mistresses in the chapters that follow reveal a system of formal training, based on reciprocal contracts, that was a familiar part of women's work lives in early modern England. The path of apprenticeship was an increasingly familiar choice for the gentry and middling sort and for artisanal families across the social spectrum. It extended down to the very poorest: the contract of training was not strikingly different from that given, with much less choice, to those bound by parish officers as a result of the provisions of the Poor Laws. Arranged, often, without paperwork that survives, frequently unrecorded by guilds, the apprenticeship of young women nevertheless represents a formal recognition of skills and an articulation of the costs and benefits of training that reshapes the idea of women's work as outside the realms of skill, training and measurable reward. The constraints and assets of a contract between an apprentice and her employer, often in the context of a guild, provided both disciplinary structure and a

Introduction 9

recognised place in the business world of the early modern city. More widely, the system of apprenticeship for girls created a capillary network of girls, women and skills across the country.

To take apprenticeship and mistresshood seriously means rethinking the place of work in women's minds and manners. Being trained, earning money, and doing work that could be rewarded or substituted with pay was a normal experience for seventeenth-century women, and for many it helped shape their sense of who they were and who they might become. The social history of later seventeenth-century women is still underdeveloped. By the 1660s, the verbal, spiritual and popular political authority that women had claimed in the Civil Wars and the English Revolution functioned as much as a reminder of the dangers of the world turned upside down, as an example of what women could do; the return of a court in which women's roles were highly sexualised reinvented patriarchal order in a different vein. A nominally universalising political language came to signify the practical exclusion of women and the identification of political agency as masculine.[19] In the realm of political theory, social contract shifted the marital relationship and women's role out of politics and into the world of nature. The naturalisation of the politically resonant patriarchal household made marriage, paradoxically, less public and perhaps less open to debate.[20]

At the same time, a new model of politeness structured behavioural norms for women around inward modesty: the outward performance was meant to demonstrate the inner virtue. A rhetorical bifurcation of male and female worlds functioned as an insistent backdrop to women's agency in economic, political and print worlds. In the context of metropolitan life before and after the Fire, as trade, housing, social life, work and manners underwent rapid change, young women who came to the City made identities as workers and consumers, seamstresses and shopkeepers, single women and wives. In the closely written legal records, a new language of sensibility traces what they learned and the challenges of their social, domestic and labour relations. The seamstress's life had its own power dynamics: conflicts of words and violence between apprentices and their mistresses, the pressure to fit women's work into family economies and the trade-offs between exploitation and autonomy that characterised learning to sew in the metropolitan market. The chapters

---

[19] Hilda L. Smith, *All Men and Both Sexes: Gender, Politics, and the False Universal in England, 1640–1832* (University Park: Pennsylvania State University Press, 2002).

[20] The classic statement of this development is Carole Pateman, *The Sexual Contract* (Stanford University Press, 1988); see also Rachel Weil, *Political Passions: Gender, the Family, and Political Argument in England, 1680–1714* (Manchester University Press, 1999).

that follow trace the possibilities and the limits this brought for individual women and the networks of work, interest and credit that connected them. In the stories of apprenticeships that worked out and those that did not, from those of paupers to those of gentry daughters, we will see pragmatism, determination, calculation, childish fantasy and rebellion.

The course of the book follows the careers of girls and women in and around London's guilds, the places they worked, the skills and manners they learned and their place in the changing city. It begins in the shops where they worked and moves through their careers as apprentices, mistresses and freewomen. Each chapter begins with a case study from the legal archive. Chapter 1 starts the story in the shops of the Royal Exchange, reconstructing its particular, feminised shopping space and the working lives of its shopkeepers. Chapter 2 goes back to apprentice training, using guild and court records to uncover the extent and nature of female apprenticeship in London and reconstructing a moment of transformation in the 1650s when girls started to join London's companies. Chapter 3 turns to mistresses and shows how skills were transmitted through networks of women, how marital status shaped work life and how guilds and contracts constrained and enabled women's work. Chapter 4 explores how, and what, girls learnt in apprenticeship, using legal records to recover in new detail the occupations, mostly textile-related, in which women trained and the skills and teaching that established girls in the sewing trade. Chapter 5 looks at the other side of apprenticeship: the behaviour that made girls into appropriate workwomen and the battles that marked their adolescence. Here, the language of legal records, attentive to subtle shades of gesture and character, presents apprenticeship as a mode of manners and a window into the social dynamics of shops and working households. The final chapter looks at the longer relationships women made with City Companies over their lifetimes: claiming the freedom, using their fathers' patrimonies, and petitioning for the right to trade, making themselves, to some degree, citizens. Petitions and the diverse documentation of freedoms reveal the paths by which women negotiated a formalized place in the civic community. As in many contexts of women's public lives, they trod a tautly balanced line between exclusion and acceptance, initiative and compromise.

1   Bred in the Exchange: Seamstresses and Shopkeepers

Ann Gray and Sarah Frost

In the late seventeenth century, the shops of the Royal Exchange housed many of the apprentice seamstresses in London's companies. One of them was Ann Gray, whose mistress, Sarah Cleave, drove a 'considerable trade' in her shop in the Royal Exchange in 'costly laces and other things'. Sarah Cleave was a single woman who had earned the freedom of London after her own apprenticeship, and Ann was her second apprentice. Seamstresses and shopkeepers like these worked in shops, stalls and houses across the City and Westminster and in the shopping galleries of the Royal Exchange, whose small, prestigious shops proved particularly attractive to the middling and gentry women who joined the City companies in the late seventeenth century. Even with an interrupted training, young women like Ann Gray readily went on to make a living at sewing, but their apprenticeships, work and subsequent lives have left little record, and the story of London's consumption revolution has focused more on goods and shoppers than their female makers and sellers. Litigation like that brought by Ann's family to recoup the costs of her abandoned apprenticeship is a rare and eloquent source.

Sarah Cleave's flourishing business in the Exchange looked promising to her new apprentice, Ann Gray, until Cleave made plans to marry a scrivener, William Frost, and the Grays lost faith that her business would carry on. Ann's brother George Gray claimed that Sarah's trade was reduced. She was dealing in gauze and bone lace but not in point and 'other costly laces', 'nor doth she drive soe considerable a trade as she did before her intermarriage … but doth decline the same very much & not mind her shop at all'. She had scarcely any goods, he claimed, to run a business. George confronted William Frost, asking how he planned to provide for his wife-to-be's apprentice: he received the non-committal reply that 'he would provide for her as he thought fit'. Ann Gray offered her services instead to another Exchange seamstress, Katherine Bobart, and left the Frosts two years into her contract. Sarah and William Frost continued to take a few apprentices, male and female, over the next thirteen years, suggesting that Exchange business waxed and waned with trade conditions as much as marital choices.[1] Their negotiations illuminate the female-dominated retail world of the Royal Exchange in the late seventeenth century and the interpersonal and spatial connections that governed its trade.

At the Mayor's Court, witnesses described Ann Gray's transgressions of the apprentice code. The Frosts alleged that Ann, working in Sarah's shop, had allowed customers to buy on credit and had either kept the money or not pursued the debt. Katherine Bobart came to explain that she had refused to take Ann on herself. Although she believed Ann to be already a capable worker, worth being paid wages as well as diet and lodging, she had heard that her brother was 'a contentious person' and that Ann 'owed money to several persons on the Exchange', as well as to Katherine herself and her servant. Ann's dubious transactions, and her brother's contentiousness, established a reputation for them 'on the Exchange'.

Two other young women came to testify about Ann Gray's misdealings. Elizabeth Spencer, a twenty-one-year-old servant to a threadman, described Ann's misuse of credit. Visiting Sarah's shop in the upper galleries of the Exchange, Elizabeth Spencer had bought 'a gauze pass for the head', an elaborately woven head covering, from Ann for 14 pence on credit. Evidently, strolling in the Exchange did not require ready cash. Elizabeth returned to the shop subsequently and told Sarah Frost she would repay her debt later; but when, on a third visit to the Exchange, she saw Ann Gray, she decided to pay her only 2 pence, because Ann already owed her a shilling (12 pence). Ann argued, because she had been sick and did not have a shilling to pay her mistress herself, and she kept the transaction secret. It emerged, of course, when Elizabeth saw Sarah Frost again, asked if the apprentice had paid her and discovered Sarah had had none of the money. This was one of the breaches of trust of which Sarah complained. Credit, in this transaction, was contested; Ann's use of it as an apprentice was dubious, nor was she entrusted to give credit to customers. The repeated encounters of the protagonists, circulating around the tightly packed space of the Exchange, made discovery inevitable. Others went further: Sarah Stables, another shopkeeper, had Ann Gray arrested for debt for buying things on credit and never paying. Visiting Ann in the 'prison house', presumably in the hope of getting the debt settled before formal proceedings began, Sarah found Ann's master, William Frost, also there, confronting Ann with a bill he produced from his pocket. He told Ann to

---

[1] ROLLCO, Sarah Cleeve, William Frost.

read it, but she refused. Sarah read it for her 'and seeing one particular therein being a sute of French Colebertine asked the Complainant [Ann], What she had to doe with any such sort of thing?' 'Is that there?' parried Ann and told her it was paid for.² Colbertine was the fashionable lace made at the royal lace enterprise, instigated by Colbert, at Alençon, its name featuring in the 'Fop's Dictionary' and Congreve's *Way of the World*.³ Its trimming on a suit of clothes was not what an apprentice, however aspirational, should have been wearing, though it epitomised Exchange fashion.

Ann's acquisition on credit of the Colbertine suit was part of a series of transactions between the apprentice, her associates and shopkeepers on the Exchange, which indicates how apprentices might become enmeshed in the micro-economy of credit there. Women were heavily represented in London debtors' prisons, reflecting the prominent role of single and married women in London's business world; a quarter of the prisoners of the late seventeenth-century Sheriff's Court were female.⁴ As part of her induction into the world of trade, Ann Gray was at risk of abusing credit both as a customer and as a shopkeeper. The majority of transactions in seventeenth-century shops involved credit, and the capacity to judge it was central to a shopkeeper's skills. Here, the rules of engagement in consumption were being crafted between shopkeepers and shoppers, and the Royal Exchange – a hub of prestigious leisure shopping – was developing rules of its own.

The Royal Exchange was itself a forum for credit, a place where business relationships were brokered. Sarah Frost's shop was upstairs, in the rows of tiny shops that lined the upper gallery. Downstairs, merchants met to trade in the Exchange's open quadrangle. They dealt in luxury goods from abroad, but sometimes also with stocks and bills of exchange, stigmatised by Defoe and others as fundamentally untrustworthy.⁵ In the upstairs shops, too, women's shopkeeping activity was part of a metropolitan circulation of money, credit, goods and reputation, centring women as consumers and workers.

---

² LMA, CLA/024/05/493 (1689). On the wider role of women in providing credit, see Judith Spicksley, '"Fly with a Duck in Thy Mouth": Single Women as Sources of Credit in Seventeenth Century England', *Social History* 32, no. 2 (2007): 187–207 and Craig Muldrew, *The Economy of Obligation: The Culture of Credit and Social Relations in Early Modern England* (London: Palgrave Macmillan, 1998).
³ Fanny Bury Palliser, *A History of Lace* (London: Sampson Low, Marston, Low & Searle, 1875), 303; Samuel Johnson, *A Dictionary of the English Language* (London: Longman, Rees, Orme, 1827).
⁴ Craig Muldrew, '"A Mutual Assent of Her Mind"? Women, Debt, Litigation and Contract in Early Modern England', *History Workshop Journal* 55 (2003): 56.
⁵ Natasha Glaisyer, *The Culture of Commerce in England, 1660–1720* (Woodbridge: Boydell & Brewer, 2006), 57.

The dispute over Ann Gray's abandoned apprenticeship exposes contests in the Exchange over credit, shopkeeping conduct, City custom and married women's work. This chapter examines those issues through the spatial arrangements of the Exchange and its networks of business and credit, drawing on the Gresham Repertories which recorded Exchange business, litigation and tax records. The Exchange was laden with spatial and symbolic significance, both for merchants and for female shopkeepers and shoppers: looking at its people and transactions more closely will enable us to connect new practices of consumption with the daily experience of women as workers and shoppers. More broadly, Ann Gray and Sarah Cleave are exemplars of the women who made a network of apprenticeship for seventeenth-century London. They laid the groundwork for a new sort of consumerism. Their apprenticeships trained them for the productive working lives that were characteristic of seventeenth-century women from a range of social origins. Around them, in London's variety of shops and housing, were girls from poverty to gentry, sewing for a living. This book starts with the shops in which girls and women were 'bred in the Exchange'.

Building the Royal Exchange

In Wenceslaus Hollar's set of four seasonal images of English women, a fantasy of 'Winter' poses in front of a City backdrop, dressed in robes, fur, high heels, hood and a half-mask to protect the complexion (Figure 1.1). Her clothes reflect the luxury shops of mid-seventeenth-century London; everything she wore could be bought nearby. Pictured at the corner of Cheapside and Cornhill, she is flanked on the left-hand side by the established style of shop, with front shutters that folded down to display the goods inside, and doors for public access. On her right, the Royal Exchange, with its tower and facade, offers a different model: a merchants' exchange in a quadrangle below and galleries of tiny stalls surrounding it above. Shopping galleries like this were pivotal in the development of women's businesses in late seventeenth-century London.

The Royal Exchange was not only the original Stock Exchange but the first of London's shopping galleries.[6] It followed the Exchanges of Paris, Amsterdam and Antwerp, where purpose-built, covered walkways of small shops sat alongside law courts and stock exchanges, and it was meant to put London on the mercantile map with an equivalently protected trading centre. The shop part upstairs, the 'pawn' (after the Dutch

---

[6] William C. Baer, 'Early Retailing: London's Shopping Exchanges, 1550–1700', *Business History* 49, no. 1 (2007): 29–51.

Bred in the Exchange: Seamstresses and Shopkeepers

Figure 1.1 Wenceslaus Hollar, *Winter* (1643–4). 26 × 18 cm.
Metropolitan Museum of Art, NY, CC.

baan, for pathway), was built on a model also used in Westminster Hall, the New Exchange on the Strand and the Middle and Exeter Exchanges, with stalls, 'boxes' or booths along a walk where shoppers could browse in comfort. They were an attraction in themselves, picked out in guidebooks and drama as the epitome of urban style, consumption and sociability. While the buildings were grand and lavishly decorated, the shops themselves were simple wooden structures: all the originality and excitement were in the exotic and fashionable goods they sold.[7] Contemporary satire also marked the role of women as both shoppers and shopkeepers, and from the mid-seventeenth century, the 'exchangewoman' featured as a focus of sexualised denigration in plays and satires. Hollar's *Winter* endorses the sexualisation of consumption: beneath her rosetted shoe, lines read, 'The cold, not cruelty makes her weare / In Winter, furrs and Wild beasts haire / For a smoother skinn at night / Embraceth her with more delight'. The verse alludes glancingly both to the erotics of fur and folk tales of shrewish women subdued by being beaten and wrapped in salted animal skins.[8] Along with the four other shopping galleries of late seventeenth-century London, the Exchange represented a new, specialised marketplace, to which the fashions, desires and labours of women were central.

Each Exchange had its own character. Westminster Hall's shops, laid out around the outside of the formal space occupied by law courts, sold books, legal supplies, lozenges for the attorneys' and MP's voices, and millinery. The three clustered around the Strand (Figure 1.2) were the most associated with sexual transactions in satire if not in actuality; Strype's *Survey of London* described the short-lived Middle Exchange as a 'Whores-Nest'.[9] There, the dynamics of class, appearance and sexual libertinage combined to undermine reputations. A pamphlet exchange dramatised the question of whether the 'ape-gentlewomen' shopkeepers of the New Exchange were 'really' gentry or whether their descent into trade, from displaced clergy parents or dislocated county gentry, left them irretrievably damaged.[10] The issue of women's shopkeeping at this

---

[7] Claire Walsh, 'Social Meaning and Social Space in the Shopping Galleries of Early Modern London', in *A Nation of Shopkeepers: Five Centuries of British Retailing*, ed. John Benson and Laura Ugolini (London: I. B. Tauris, 2003), 52–79.

[8] See, for example, Joannes Bramis, *Here Begynneth a Merry Ieste of a Shrewde and Curste Wyfe, Lapped in Morrelles Skin, for Her Good Behauyour* (1580); for more on Hollar's furs, see Julia V. Emberley, *Venus and Furs: The Cultural Politics of Fur* (London: I. B. Tauris, 1998), 110–23. The verse is anonymous.

[9] John Strype, *Survey of London* (1720), book 4, chapter 7.

[10] *Ape-Gentle-Woman, or, The Character of an Exchange-Wench* (1675); *An Answer to the Character of an Exchange-Wench, or, A Vindication of an Exchange-Woman* (1675); Will

Figure 1.2 Sites of the shopping galleries. Left to right: Westminster Hall, New Exchange, Middle Exchange, Exeter Exchange and Royal Exchange.
Map: Morgan, *London Actually Surveyed* (1682), London Topographic Society 1904. Wikicommons/Library of Congress (annotations added).

juncture and in this place touched a nerve because it involved gentility and professional aspirations.

The location of the Royal Exchange, in contrast, connected it to merchants, guilds and apprenticeship. Natasha Glaisyer's analysis of England's late seventeenth-century culture of commerce puts the Exchange at the heart of London's self-image, particularly as it was renovated after the Fire.[11] The intellectual community of the city also interwove mercantile interest with cultural exchanges. While most historical attention to the Exchange has examined the role it played for the merchants who used its downstairs, this chapter argues for the significance of its upper galleries, where women worked and shopped, and, in doing so, it rewrites the Exchange and its surroundings to include its community of female work.[12] The shops of the upper pawn were key to the development of female apprenticeship amongst gentry and middling girls and the enterprise of mistresses, and they also illuminate the whole

---

Pritchard, *Outward Appearances: The Female Exterior in Restoration London* (Lewisburg: Bucknell University Press, 2008), chapter 5.

[11] Glaisyer, *Culture of Commerce*.

[12] Amy Louise Erickson, 'Eleanor Mosley and Other Milliners in the City of London Companies 1700–1750', *History Workshop Journal* 71 (2011): 147–72, discusses women at the eighteenth-century Exchange.

issue of gender and consumption from a different angle – that of the shopkeeper. The name 'exchangewoman' appears both in the satires of the New Exchange and in the tax records of the Royal Exchange: its satirical exploitation should not be allowed to undermine the real significance of shop work.[13] Rather, the Exchange's critical location in the middle of the City placed women's business in the heart of mainstream mercantile exchange, enabling stallholders to represent themselves as respectable and elite businesswomen. Across eighteenth-century towns and cities, Deborah Simonton argues, the elite end of the needle trade constituted a profession, supported by strategic shop locations at the heart of Edinburgh, Bath and Colchester, as well as London.[14] The Royal Exchange, established before shops moved away from the City to the West End, helped inaugurate this model of women's shops.

At the Exchange's heart, both before and after the Fire, was the trading floor where merchants met, an irregular quadrangle framed by an arcaded entrance, carved staircases and statuary, with a number of shops along the sides (Figure 1.3). Less attention has been paid to the shops on the upper storey.[15] However, they were crucial to the Exchange's economy: the building's upkeep depended on the rents of milliners and linen drapers. Spatially, too, the shops were part of the Exchange's daily life. Visitors to the shops crossed the trading floor to reach the stairs. The most desirable shops looked out and down onto it, and balconies on the inner side allowed shoppers to look down onto those below. The twice-daily bells to signal trading time, and the four different tunes played by the clock after the Fire, rang through the pawns as well as the piazza. The shops were there to make profits to keep the building going. The women who tenanted them and shopped there were not segregated from the downstairs merchants but shared on unequal terms in the Exchange's project.

The upper pawn, where the majority of women kept their shops in the late seventeenth century, consisted of rows of small shops arranged around passageways that surrounded the central quadrangle, with the

---

[13] James Grantham Turner, '"News from the New Exchange": Commodity, Erotic Fantasy and the Female Entrepreneur', in *The Consumption of Culture 1600–1800: Image, Object, Text*, ed. Ann Bermingham and John Brewer (Abingdon: Routledge, 1995), 419–39.

[14] Deborah Simonton, '"Sister to the Tailor": Guilds, Gender and the Needle Trades in Eighteenth-Century Europe', in *Early Professional Women in Northern Europe, c. 1650–1850*, ed. Johanna Ilmakunnas, Marjatta Rahikainen and Kirsi Vainio-Korhonen (Abingdon: Taylor & Francis, 2017), 137–57; Elizabeth Sanderson, *Women and Work in Eighteenth-Century Edinburgh* (Basingstoke: Macmillan, 1996).

[15] This neglect was first addressed by Jane Muncaster, '"Six Foote of Shop Roome": Women as Subjects in the Records of the Royal Exchange in the 1690s' (MA thesis, Birkbeck: University of London, 2003).

Figure 1.3 Robert White, *The Royal Exchange* (1671). 46 × 57 cm. The south portico with the chiming clock tower faces onto Cornhill. The upper pawn was on the top storey, lit by skylights.
London Metropolitan Archives (City of London).

idea that shoppers would walk the length of the circuit of shops. They were identified by the signs of animals or other names, such as the Orange Tree, the address given for the widowed seamstress Elizabeth Eardley when she took an apprentice in 1671.[16] The layout encouraged browsing without commitment, as the shops were open, and goods could be seen when passing by (Figure 1.4). At the same time, the narrow walks and the small shops made for intimate encounters. The Exchange shops were tiny, measured before the Fire as 5 feet wide and 7½ feet deep, and not much larger afterwards, with 8 foot the standard width in 1670. They were often leased in multiples, with tenants taking double shops, or a

---

[16] Michael Scott, ed., *Apprenticeship Disputes in the Lord Mayor's Court of London, 1573–1723* (London: British Record Society, 2016); on the Exchange building, see Ann Saunders, ed., *The Royal Exchange* (London: London Topographical Society, 1997).

Figure 1.4 Abraham Bosse, *La Galerie du Palais* (1637–38). 25 × 32 cm. A Parisian counterpart to the Royal Exchange shopping galleries, showing collars, gloves and fans on sale as well as books. Musée Carnavalet (public domain).

shop and a half.[17] Moveable partitions could be adjusted to suit shopkeepers' business; some deliberately encroached into the windows between the outer shops, blocking the light that showcased their neighbours' goods, or even cut into the Exchange walls to get more room.[18] This versatility was, as Craig Spence has suggested, peculiarly suited to women's business.[19] Jane Muncaster found that single women typically took smaller shops, though some continued with those same small spaces for years. Men also often took up small shops, perhaps as supplementary or initial enterprises. Widows and married women and men tended to

---

[17] Ann Saunders, 'The Organisation of the Exchange', in Saunders, *The Royal Exchange*, 85–98.
[18] Mercers' Company, Gresham Repertories (henceforth MC, GR) 1669–78, p. 230.
[19] Craig Spence, *London in the 1690s: A Social Atlas* (London: Centre for Metropolitan History, 2000), 127.

hold larger shops.[20] Shopboards were provided to lock them up and to serve as counters for display and selling. Hanging signs before the Fire were replaced later with signs set into a frieze above the shops. In these narrow spaces, shopkeepers worked alone or in pairs, sometimes with an apprentice or servant, though some had enough room for a chair for a customer to sit on. Goods, customers and shopkeepers were pressed close together, and some shopkeepers in the later seventeenth century pressed for the stairways to be opened out and corner shops removed to make more spacious, handsome quadrangles.[21]

The emergence of consumer culture in the eighteenth century has been strongly identified with the performance of gender, with the retail sphere described as a female space, and shopping as an act of identity formation. As recent work has shown, shopping was hardly universally feminised. If plebeian and middling women were more likely than men to use the practical skills of assessing ripe food, the luxurious fantasies of clothes shopping were part of masculine as well as feminine leisure. The spaces of shopping likewise varied in their gender dimensions; the New Exchange's association with women sat alongside its grand spaciousness, while Westminster Hall's closeness to the political hub and law courts might give it a more masculine tone, but female and male shoppers used both.[22] The Royal Exchange's unique location in the heart of the City gave it another character. Claire Walsh points out how effectively consumers extended the use of the galleries beyond their intended design, making them a place of social life. Shopping could be seen as a reflection less of individualistic identity than interpersonal activity, shaped by the perceived needs of others and the desire to impress and create narratives of self in a collective context; the social space of the Exchange loaded its transactions with social values and messages about status.[23] Apprentices and mistresses were as significant as consumers in making these meanings.

The Exchange was also a place of rich literary fantasy. Like all urban spaces, its meaning was configured by the human relations that took place there, and those relations were also staged against the way it figured

---

[20] Muncaster, '"Six Foote of Shop Roome"', 31–3.   [21] MC, GR 1669–78, p. 120.
[22] Claire Walsh, 'Shops, Shopping and the Art of Decision-Making in Eighteenth-Century England', in *Gender, Taste, and Material Culture in Britain and North America, 1700–1830*, ed. John Styles and Amanda Vickery (New Haven, CT: Yale Center for British Art, 2006), 151–77; Amanda Vickery, 'Women and the World of Goods: A Lancashire Consumer and Her Possessions, 1751–81', in *Consumption and the World of Goods*, ed. John Brewer and Roy Porter (London: Psychology Press, 1994), 274–303; Lorna Weatherill, 'A Possession of One's Own: Women and Consumer Behavior in England, 1660–1740', *Journal of British Studies* 25, no. 2 (1986): 131–56.
[23] Walsh, 'Social Meaning and Social Space'.

in satire and cheap print. In the series of pamphlets lauding, and appealing to, the Royal Exchange, the figure of the female shopper was prominent. *London's-Nonsuch; or, the Glory of the Royal Exchange* depicted two sisters walking upstairs and downstairs, through hosiers and glovers' shops to those of goldsmiths and booksellers; it was presented as an advertisement of 'what Trades the Ladies and Gentelwomen may there finde'.[24] Like most discussion of women in the Exchange, the text portrayed women as hunting not just for goods but for men. The coat-seller 'takes ladies by the waste'; the silk and prunella wool in the mercers' shops are sold by 'handsome fellows'. In the linen and lace shops, women are behind the counter, selling lace and bands and talking 'so wittily' to the men who come to see them that they 'allure / Their moneys from them, by their tongue'. As they turn to descend the stairs, the sisters praise the Gresham Committee for 'placing all the trades in view at once / So that we may not here and there Along the streets so wide / Run to and fro, for Trades, when here / We have them by our side'. Women's shopping, long established as integral to their domestic role as the spenders of what men gained, was easily read as gadding; the Exchange is imagined as a containing solution. Other texts made it sound more like a brothel, depicting the labour of shopping as sexualised exchange. Ned Ward's satirical romp through the Exchange buildings in 1699 presented the visitor as besieged first by 'swarthy buggerantoes' and 'bumfirking Italians' on the ground floor, then upstairs by the linen-sellers and milliners calling their custom into his ear.[25] None of this was new; the sexualised critique of women's consumption had deep roots.[26] The fantasy of flirtation ran parallel to the concrete exchange of material goods in the passageways of the Exchange, and in some cases, it actually interrupted women's labour. Women's work at the Exchange was not confined to its shops. The fruit sellers who worked at its doors were a perpetual focus of civic complaint in the sixteenth and seventeenth

---

[24] Ehver Kind, *London's-Nonsuch; or, the Glory of the Royal Exchange* (1668).
[25] Ned Ward, *The London Spy Compleat* (1703), 66.
[26] On London's shops in this period, see Claire Walsh, 'Shopping in Early-Modern London c. 1660–1800' (PhD dissertation, European University Institute, 2001); Vanessa Harding, 'Shops, Markets and Retailers in London's Cheapside, c. 1500–1700', in *Buyers & Sellers: Retail Circuits and Practices in Medieval and Early Modern Europe*, ed. Ilja van Damme et al. (Turnhout: Brepols, 2007), 155–70. On England, Hoh-cheung Mui and Lorna H. Mui, *Shops and Shopkeeping in Eighteenth-Century England* (Montreal: McGill-Queen's University Press, 1989); Jon Stobart, Andrew Hann and Victoria Morgan, *Spaces of Consumption: Leisure and Shopping in the English Town, c. 1680–1830* (London: Routledge, 2007). The intersection of sex and shopping is explored by Elizabeth Kowaleski-Wallace, *Consuming Subjects: Women, Shopping, and Business in the Eighteenth Century* (New York: Columbia University Press, 1997).

centuries; the Exchange was a centre of the female-dominated world of street food selling.[27]

The Exchange, noted for the elegance of its shops, was also a place of bawdry. As a centre of information and advertisement, rude signs were hung up on its walls alongside the more prosaic notices; in 1660, Pepys heard of a picture hung up there of the naval officer John Lawson, who had cooperated with the Restoration of Charles II, with 'a great pair of buttocks shitting of a turd into Lawsons mouth, and over it was writ "The thanks of the House"'.[28] Ned Ward described a rampant display of medical advertisements and crowds of hawkers selling glass eyes, ivory teeth and corn cures.[29] These polar opposites of images of elegance and decay helped structure this space of fashion, playing into the tropes of deceit and cheating that were associated with consumption and providing the backdrop to the strenuous efforts at civility and gentility that were expected of mistresses and apprentices.

Twenty years after Hollar's print, the landscape it depicts was largely burnt to the ground by the Fire of 1666. Most of the shops where City seamstresses and milliners worked were destroyed, along with the Exchange and its stalls; businesses relocated to the suburbs, and residents took refuge in the fields. The Fire's destruction of the Exchange had a symbolic power. To the clergyman Thomas Vincent, reflecting later on God's vengeance on the City, its fall heralded the final evacuation of citizens, their wives ('some from their childbed') and children. He saw the Exchange, 'the glory of the merchants, invaded with much violence; and when once the fire was entered, how quickly did it run round the galleries, filling them with flames; then descendeth the stairs, compasseth the walks, giving forth flaming volleys, and filled the court with sheets of fire'.[30] The flames ran round the galleries just as the genteel shoppers had.

Women came to the fore of the Exchange when the post-Fire renovations shook up shop leases. In the short term, St Bartholomew's Hospital rehoused the tenants of shops on their City lands in the hospital cloisters; the Royal Exchange, which was not rebuilt until 1671, relocated to the Mercers' other principal building, Gresham College on Bishopsgate, and

---

[27] Laura Gowing, '"The Freedom of the Streets": Women and Social Space, 1560–1640', in *Londinopolis: Essays in the Cultural and Social History of Early Modern London*, ed. Mark S. R. Jenner and Paul Griffiths (Manchester University Press, 2000), 130–53.
[28] *The Diary of Samuel Pepys: A New and Complete Transcription*, ed. Robert Latham and William Matthews (London: Harper Collins, 1995), vol. I, 45; Lawson had previously been a republican.
[29] Ward, *London Spy*, 67.
[30] Thomas Vincent, *God's Terrible Voice in the City* (1667), 61.

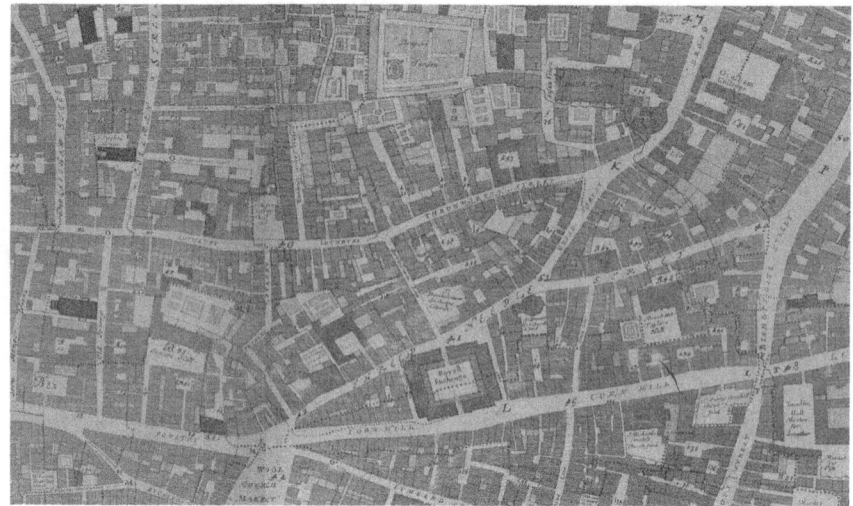

Figure 1.5 Detail of Ogilby and Morgan's 1676 map of London, showing the Royal Exchange (lower centre) and Gresham College (top right).
British Library (public domain).

leased space to shopholders there at reduced rents (Figure 1.5). Committee reports record a certain amount of chaos, as shops were crammed in alongside the meetings of the Royal Society and in the hayloft, cellar, quadrangle and galleries, with places accorded to people according to 'seniority' and a latrine built hastily when the nearby dunghill became 'noisome'.[31] In the longer term, the City's efforts to encourage trade back in included offering the Freedom without charge to anyone taking a shop lease, and this may have encouraged women into the City's shops.[32] Crisis, as at other moments, created opportunities for women.

The businesses rehoused in Gresham College already included some women. Anne Whitter, who had served an apprenticeship in the Merchant Taylors, was described as 'milliner de Gresham Colledg' when she took on her sister as an apprentice in 1670.[33] Other women petitioned for places there on grounds of financial need. Widow Oliver was one: she had 'long kept a linen shop over against the Great Conduit in

---

[31] Saunders, *The Royal Exchange*, 126.
[32] J. R. Kellett, 'The Breakdown of Gild and Corporation Control over the Handicraft and Retail Trade in London', *Economic History Review* 10, no. 3 (1958): 381–94.
[33] GL, MS 34038/16, 40.

Cheapside and hath eight children'.[34] As the new pawn was planned, women's past occupation of the Exchange gave them a claim to places in the new building. Mary Wimbush's request received favour, and the minutes recorded: 'Ordered that Mary Wimbush who was formerly bred in the Exchange be accommodated with a shop there and that her name be placed in shop next to Mrs Jane Kellway in the southwest corner'. There was apparently an actual paper plan on hand, and shortly afterwards Mary Wimbush's name was ordered to be erased again when the committee planned a large shop in the corner, with a promise 'to be preferred over any stranger'.[35] To be 'bred in the Exchange' denoted a loyalty to which the management would attend, as well as a suggestion of training and perhaps a set of Exchange-specific manners and expertises.

The rebuilding project of the decade after the Fire created more open shops on Cheapside, encouraging a different mode of shopping. It also reconfigured the galleries of the Royal Exchange. One of the side effects was a noticeable increase in the number of women leaseholders. By the 1670s, when the Royal Exchange reopened for business, lease applications show that women held around half the stalls in the upper galleries and they continued to do so through the ups and downs of the Exchange in subsequent decades. Particularly in the City companies associated with the Exchange, the Haberdashers' and the Merchant Taylors', urban women used the Exchange to build their trades, and female apprentices worked with them. Tax and company records use 'exchangewoman' as an occupation, as for Elizabeth Hebborn, a maltster's daughter from Henley on Thames apprenticed to Winifred Cervington, 'exchangewoman' in the Drapers, in 1656.[36]

As the Exchange was rebuilt, applications began to come in for the new shops. The investment that citizens had in the building's shape and success is indicated by the extensive discussions, reverberating into print, over the post-Fire layout. A balance had to be struck between high numbers of shops to maximise rents and too much competition for existing trade, as well as cramped conditions for the shops. As the first floor was planned, the Gresham committee and representatives of the tenants discussed the relative merits of a 'double pawn' of many small shops, which, some argued, risked ruin and 'a Disreputacon upon the Place'.[37] Henry Duke printed pamphlets arguing for a balance between a double pawn of smaller shops on two sides of the Exchange and deeper

---

[34] MC, GR 1626–69, p. 249.   [35] MC, GR 1669–76, pp. 40–1.   [36] ROLLCO.
[37] MC, GR 1626–69, p. 256; 1669–78, p. 1.

shops with warehouses on the east and west.[38] Duke was a shopkeeper himself and also the master of an apprentice who took up her own shop in the 1690s and continued it into the eighteenth century: Bethiah Paradise, from a wool draper's family in Devizes.[39] In the end, the Gresham Committee settled for a double pawn all round, with the maximum number of small shops, which proved difficult to fill, particularly on the darker side. In 1712, there were 160 of them, but the land tax records of 1693 and 1703 show only around 50 tenants. The shops were laid out in two corridors, arranged around the quadrangle so as to feed visitors all the way around (Figure 1.6); the courtyard downstairs remained visible at the centre of the quadrangle of shops, with skylights above. Locations were described minutely as, for example, 'the western side of the south outward pawn'. Some shops were set into arches or by windows. The minutes of the Gresham committee show each part accruing its own reputation, relating particularly to its aspect, with its stallholders participating in the decision-making by means of representatives who were generally male. At one point, petitioners for changes to the layout were sent off to canvass the views of the other stallholders in their respective pawns. The 'innermost pawn', which had a view from balconies onto the trade in the quadrangle below, was the most popular, and the shops most expensive. The outermost pawn had windows but was felt to be short of light. In the southwest corner of the outer pawn in 1688, the roof was leaking, shops were suffering from 'dead trade' and being too far from the stairs. The East India Company's habit of sifting pepper by the cellar stairs annoyed the nearby tenants.[40] Behind these negotiations was a network of businesswomen.

Exchangewomen and Their Networks

The management of shop leases at the Exchange shows women making their place in the passages of the upper pawn. Shopkeepers at the Exchange held long leases on their small shops, often subletting them to others. Before the Fire, women held a smaller proportion of leases than men, and many were subletting to others, often men; the shops were a useful source of income rather than employment. Increasingly, the committee took against this form of business and prioritised those who

---

[38] Kind, *London's-Nonsuch*; see also T. P., *A Brief Memorial Wherein the Present Case of the Antient Leasees, the Inward Pawn Sub-Tenants, and the Outward Pawn Present Tenants, of the Royal Exchange [Is] ... Stated* (1674).
[39] LMA, COL/CHD/FR/02 138/78; LMA, MS 11316/13 (1703).
[40] MC, GR 1626–69, p. 216.

Bred in the Exchange: Seamstresses and Shopkeepers

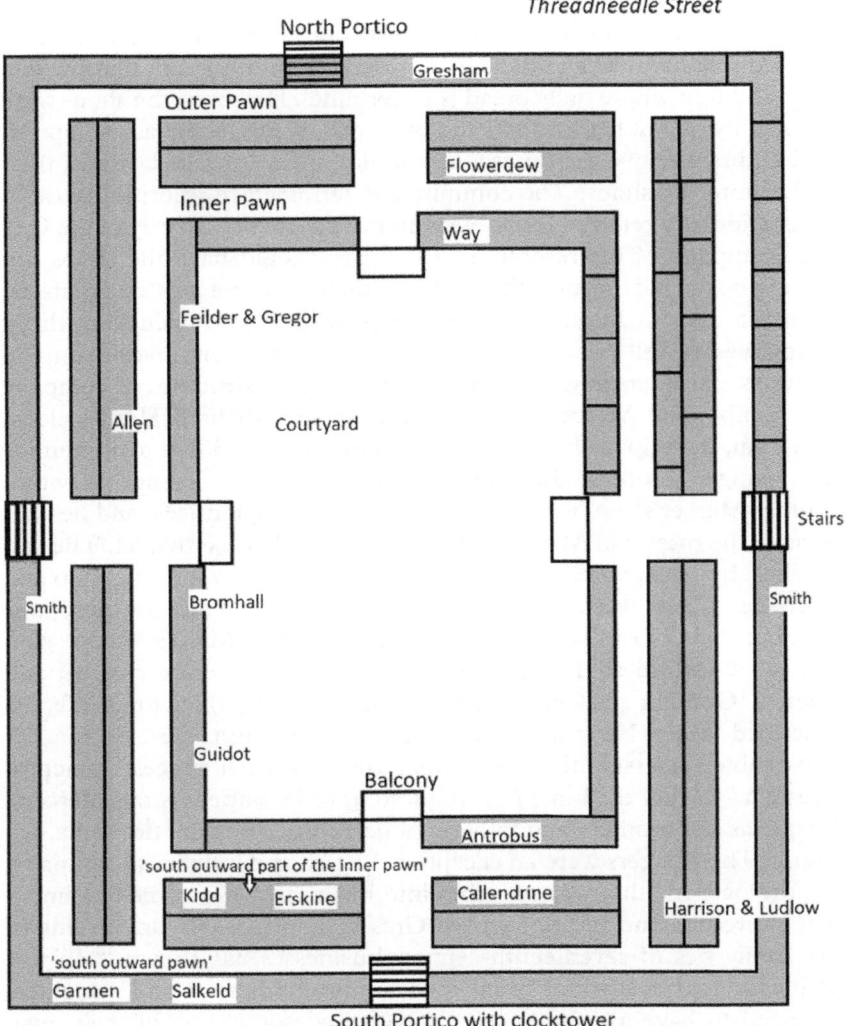

Figure 1.6 Schematic plan of the layout of the first floor of the Royal Exchange after the Fire. Tenants from the 1680s and 1690s.
Based on information in Gresham Repertories.

would occupy the shops themselves. The last petitions heard by the Gresham Committee before the Fire raised this issue. Mary Newton, née Hunt, came to request leases for two shops on the south side of the Exchange known by the signs of 'The Ring-Dove' and 'The Griffin', which had previously been held by her father, a mercer; the estates he had left his children had suffered confiscations at the Restoration. Mary pleaded that her husband had lost thousands of pounds and that she had 'nine children whose daily bread is uncertain'. However, the shops were claimed by one of her brothers too, who had worked there as an apprentice, and by the two men presently running them, who had 'drawn their trades' into the shops. The committee determined to prioritise those in occupation and referred Mary Newton instead to 'the Charity of the City and Company'. This resolution that 'none should have the shops but those who would occupy the same in their own persons' suggests an approach that might have helped prompt women into occupying shops themselves as well as taking up leases. Mary's own story reveals some of the ways a woman might fit into the patrimonial structure of company and family. The Mercers' records indicate that Richard Hunt's eldest son, John, took up his freedom by patrimony and used that to apprentice his younger brother, Benjamin. Mary's husband, Henry Newton, another Mercer's son, was another of Richard's apprentices, and he later became the master of Mary Hunt's younger brother, Nathaniel. The two families, by 1666, were woven together by the ties of apprenticeship and marriage. They were also scholars: another brother, Richard, was appointed the Gresham Professor of Rhetoric. Mary's eldest son, Henry, at Oxford at the time of her petition, became a diplomat, and when a German professor later recounted Henry Newton's life, he described Mary Newton as 'distinguished amongst her sex for her remarkable understanding': his Latin word *prudentia* suggests practical foresight.[41] Mary died in 1714, requesting to be buried in the Mercers' Chapel as her brothers and father had been: the company ties remained strong. The Mercers were an exceptionally rich and influential company, but the patterns that wove kinship into business, with women as linchpins, were not unusual as Richard Grassby's meticulous unravelling of the family ties of seventeenth-century businesses has shown.[42] In this politically and academically inclined family, both sons and daughters expected to have a stake in the Exchange, if not a shop of their own. The business family, Grassby argues, had an economic identity of its own, and every business had a familial structure. In families like these,

---

[41] Stuart Handley, 'Newton, Sir Henry (1650–1715)', *Oxford Dictionary of National Biography*, www.oxforddnb.com (2008); John Ward, *The Lives of the Professors of Gresham College* (1740), 319; Georg Christian Gebauer, *Narration de Henrico Brenkman ... et vita Henrici Newtoni* (Gottingen, 1764), 216, whose Latin phrase is 'matronam ob insignem prudentiam inter alias sui sexus eminentem'.

[42] Richard Grassby, *Kinship and Capitalism: Marriage, Family, and Business in the English-Speaking World, 1580–1740* (Cambridge University Press, 2001), 413.

the world of the narrow shops was connected through inheritance, investment and sales to the expanding empire. It sat above a quadrangle in which traders apparently clustered by nationality, a microcosm of the global economy. Contemporary prints represent Ottoman Turkish merchants in traditional dress squatting round the outside, alongside many other nationalities.[43] The gentry origins and family wealth of many of the women Exchange shopkeepers rooted them firmly in London's growing global market. Women's part in the financial revolution of the late seventeenth century is increasingly well documented: they invested in government stocks, which could escape the rules of coverture, and had long been invested in the Virginia and East India Companies. Women with property were expected to defend familial and personal interests, often through petitions and legal actions.[44]

In the years before the Fire, twice as many men as women were requesting leases, but the shops may well have included more women trading: an increase in women traders was noted in the 1640s, a time at which companies were also beginning to see female apprentices.[45] When the shops were reallocated after the Fire, both women and men applied for them, but the male applicants were more likely to have a history in the Exchange. In 1670, rights to the new leases were allotted first to those who formerly kept shop in the old Exchange, in the order of 'seniority'; the rest, from the time they respectively had the right to the Freedom of the City.[46] This may have kept new unfree women out, but in fact there was only a short period in which there were no vacancies, and, by the 1680s, the more significant issue was the quality of shops in use. Men continued to outnumber women in the leases overall after the Fire, but in the upper pawn, as opposed to the downstairs shops, the gender ratio was close to equal. This balance laid the foundations for the roughly 50:50 ratio of men and women in the upper-pawn shops of the late seventeenth century.[47]

---

[43] Wenceslaus Hollar, 'The Royal Exchange' (1644).
[44] Barbara Todd, 'Fiscal Citizens: Female Investors in Public Finance before the South Sea Bubble', in *Challenging Orthodoxies: The Social and Cultural Worlds of Early Modern Women: Essays Presented to Hilda L. Smith*, ed. Sigrun Haude and Melinda S. Zook (London: Ashgate, 2014), 53–74; Misha Ewen, 'Women Investors and the Virginia Company in the Early Seventeenth Century', *Historical Journal* 62, no. 4 (2019): 853–74; Pamela Sharpe, 'Gender at Sea: Women and the East India Company in Seventeenth-Century London', in *Women, Work and Wages in England, 1600–1850*, ed. K. D. M. Snell, Penelope Lane and Neil Raven (Woodbridge: Boydell & Brewer, 2004), 47–67.
[45] Saunders, *The Royal Exchange*. [46] MC, GR 1669–76, p. 36.
[47] The fullest list of leases is in LMA, CLA/062/04/16. Another record of inhabitants of shops (not all of whom were necessarily the leaseholders) is in the Land Tax records of 1693 and 1703.

...ere often granted to those already in occupation as ...change may not represent a dramatic increase of women ...but it does reflect a formal recognition of women as ...f permanence and substance. At the same time, numbers ...rentices in guilds were steadily increasing from 1667. Some ...tually joined mistresses working in the Exchange, like ...arker, a London merchant tailor's daughter apprenticed in ...izabeth Deadman, a widow in the Haberdashers working in the ...of the Exchange, but more broadly they were part of an environ-...which more daughters of artisans and gentry were moving into ...hes trade.[48] Alongside those who came in from apprenticeship ...idows carrying on a shop trade, or starting a new one, and married ...n running independent shops. The widespread use of 'Mrs' [mis-...] to denote a businesswoman makes it hard to determine marital ...us, though research into the female tenants of the late seventeenth ...tury indicates a high proportion of single women and widows.[49]

The first woman recorded as receiving a lease after the Fire was Elizabeth Athey, a widowed periwig-maker, who, in June 1670, was given a 10-foot shop downstairs, on the easterly side under the north portico, to hold for eleven years for £30.[50] On 13 August 1670, when Mary Wimbish along with Mr Debnam, Mr Hudson, Mrs Lloyd and Mr Dudley all requested shops in the new pawn, they were told that they would be granted shops 'in case there happen to be surplusage of shop room above that will satisfie those bred in the Exchange'. Mary Lloyd, who lived on Little Tower Hill, had already asked in April and had been told that the committee doubted they would have a surplus; she was still asking in October, by which time she was promised first choice.[51] Records of another 'ancient' leaseholder, Alice Salkeld, reveal the way credit and favour operated in shop allocations over a period when the popularity of exchange shops was very variable. Salkeld complained in October 1670 that Hester Sheppard, 'a stranger there', had been given the choice of a shop before her. The committee accepted her point and ordered that Sheppard's name be removed from the shop on the south side where she had been placed, Salkeld's put there instead and Sheppard reallocated to Salkeld's inferior position. In 1671, Salkeld was told, with two other women, 'to expect the favour of the

---

[48] Scott, *Apprenticeship Disputes*.
[49] Muncaster, '"Six Foote of Shop Roome"'. On the meaning of 'Mrs', see Amy Louise Erickson, 'Mistresses and Marriage: Or, a Short History of the Mrs', *History Workshop Journal* 78 (2014): 39–57.
[50] MC, GR 1669–76, p. 14. [51] MC, GR 1669–76, pp. 11, 28, 32.

little shop in the Exchange was part of a transatlantic estate, which, by the time of her son's death, also included at least two slaves, named in his will.[63] Jane Clarke surrendered all her leases after the Fire but maintained a right in the Exchange, the committee promising that her relative would have preferential right to a place near his previous occupancy. Elizabeth Eardley enterprisingly took over her bankrupt brother's shop in the Exchange in 1668, before the new building was ready; she planned to install her sister in it to dispose of his goods. Her husband Richard's inventory indicates that before his death in 1663, they had run a shop dealing in children's clothes, laces and ribbons; perhaps she continued it afterwards and expanded into the Exchange. By 1670, she was holding a shop in her own name in the rebuilt Exchange. Her deceased husband's freedom of the Haberdashers enabled her to take on a company apprentice for a few years, but the contract broke down, and by 1682 Eardley was 'broke and gone'.[64]

As prominent as marital ties were those between other family members, particularly sisters and mothers and daughters. As in apprenticeship arrangements, kinship ties between women helped promote them into desirable shop places. In 1670, Mary Hebb, who leased a window shop on the east side of the inner pawn, came to ask if the committee would accommodate her daughter with a shop on the south side of the outward pawn; the committee agreed, because she was already short of shop space. Susanna and Rebecca Way, described as spinster sisters, took over a shop and a quarter in 1679 on the north inner pawn, promising to pay £7 next Michaelmas. Rebecca was a member of the Salters' Company, probably by patrimonial right; she is cited on the back of another woman's freedom in the Barber-Surgeons' in 1690.[65] Naomi Slany, a widow £30 in arrears in the ill-fated east outward pawn, had so many losses that she could not keep her shop, but her daughter came to pay her last quarter's rent before she left, and she was discharged £30 of arrears. The widowed Alice Guidot held a 10-foot shop in the inner pawn with the merchant Joseph Alder, her son-in-law; her father and son also had shops.[66] Other shops were passed between friends or trading connections. Katherine and Herbert Allen held a shop 'at the sign of the

---

[63] John Frederick Dorman, ed., *Genealogies of Virginia Families: From Tyler's Quarterly Historical and Genealogical Magazine*, vol. 1 (Baltimore: Genealogical Publishing Co., 1981), 542–3; John Bennett Boddie, *Seventeenth Century Isle of Wight County, Virginia* (Baltimore: Genealogical Publishing Co., 1973), 681.
[64] MC, GR 1678–1722, pp. 82, 99; LMA, CLA/002/02/01/0276, f. 24b.
[65] LMA, COL/CHD/FR/02/0036, no. 52; MC, GR 1678–1722, p. 16.
[66] LMA, P69/MRY7/A/002/MS04997 (10 December 1681), Joseph Alder/Margaret Guidott; MC, GR 1678–1722, p. 210.

Parrot', on the west side, in the 1660s. Herbert died while the Exchange was closed after the Fire, and Katherine re-opened it when the pawn was rebuilt, trading until 1690 when she passed on her 8 foot of shop room to William Barton and his wife, Mary, a milliner.[67] Both Katherine and Mary had been pursued in the Mayor's Court by their recalcitrant apprentices. Bonds between women, as Amy Froide has shown with respect to single women's wills, were critical to women's economic independence.[68]

Despite the apparent demand for leases, some parts of the new Exchange seem never to have become successfully established. The outward pawn was particularly problematic, without benefit of the light and activity of the courtyard below. Mr and Mrs Smith, linen-sellers who had taken out leases for shops in both the west and east outward pawns, found they could not find tenants for them and so were released from their obligations. The south outward pawn was still unbuilt when tenants were moving back into the rest of the building, and those who had been given leases there found they still had no functioning shops. Mary Browne was one of them: she petitioned in 1679 that she had been persuaded, 'for the service of the City', to exchange her lease of a valuable shop in the inner pawn for a larger one in the south outward pawn. Those shops, she said, remained 'wholly desolate ... for the most part'.[69] The committee reduced her arrears from £71 to £22 to represent the lesser value of her new position.

By 1682, several female tenants were described as in 'desperate arrears'. Requests for abatement included one from Mrs Hoard, a married woman with 'many children' who complained that 'trading hath been and still continues very low'; she was still in arrears in 1687.[70] Mary Goddard was let off the rent for her shop as she had left it when the shops 'went to ruin', though Elizabeth Goddard continued paying for her 9 foot of shop room in the inner pawn, at £22 for two years. In at least some parts of the building, the leases' costs were too heavy for the shops' profits. In 1684, 'the widow Miles' countered a demand for her £26 arrears with a plea that she had paid £5 for a shop she had never had and another £6 towards the general rebuilding; the committee reached a compromise with her. Elizabeth Foster refused to pay her quarter's rent because she had left her shop, and her husband was in debt. At the same time, though, the court continued to charge extremely highly for leases,

---

[67] MC, GR 1678–1722, p. 222.
[68] Amy M. Froide, *Never Married: Singlewomen in Early Modern England* (Oxford University Press, 2005).
[69] MC, GR 1669–77, p. 153.   [70] MC, GR 1678–1722, pp. 20, 172.

even in the unpopular areas: Elizabeth Harrison, citizen and joiner, paid £25 for a year's rent of 10 foot of shop room in the east outer pawn in 1687 – half the average house rent in Cornhill.[71] Other shops in the City rented for an average of only £9 a year.[72] Petitions in 1688 crystallised the complaints of the outward pawn shopkeepers: deadness of trade, distance and narrowness of the passage from the stairs to the shops; annoyance from the workmen repairing the roof; and shops standing empty to the 'great discouragement of the place which daily grows worse'.[73] High rents and lease premiums marked the place's continuing prestige, whilst gathering arrears made it possible for businesswomen to continue in the face of failing trade or low profits.

Who were the exchangewomen? Both 'exchangewoman' and 'exchangeman' were occupational titles, given in tax listings in the 1690s, but many of those who were listed that way have left no other record in the accounts of the Exchange itself. Those who worked on the stalls were not always the leaseholders. But enough survives to suggest an emerging profile of exchangewomen with distinctive social, domestic and economic features.

Those who leave the best evidence are connected to gentry and merchant families; they were the likeliest to be able to make the substantial investment in leases, and apprenticeship and freedom to a guaranteed trade could be an inheritance in itself. Some were from London families. Anne Gosfreight, whose name is in the 1702 list of stallholders, was the daughter of longstanding stallholder Solomon Gosfreight. Her father had left her a half-share of his estate in 1700, having, as his will explained, already advanced her brother and one of her sisters; another sister had forfeited her inheritance by joining a Benedictine convent in Paris, from where she petitioned the queen for the protection of her brother as a merchant banker in Alicante.[74] Lucy Maes, one of the many apprentices of John and Frances Spillett, was the daughter of a gentleman from St Andrew Holborn. At his death in 1682, his estate was divided between his wife and three daughters. The eldest, Mary, received a pearl necklace and £40 extra as well; Lucy, the youngest, was apprenticed to the Spilletts and became free in 1692. In another case, apprenticeship in the Exchange, like the removal of fines, was offered as charity to a needy woman. Margaret Lendale, the daughter of a captain, received royal charity to set up as an apprentice specifically in the Exchange, indicating its status as a reliable career for girls. First she was apprenticed to a

---

[71] MC, GR 1678–1722, p. 185. [72] Spence, *London in the 1690s*, 125, 176.
[73] MC, GR 1678–1722, p. 189.
[74] *Calendar of the Stuart Papers* (London: HMSO, 1902), 181.

haberdasher in the Royal Exchange in 1660, her premium paid by royal gift. When her time ran out, she petitioned, pleading that 'the said Trade being to Sell all Sorts of Rich Laces and other things of great value requireing a Considerable Stock; for want thereof, yor Petitioner (who is destitute of Friends and all other meanes of subsistance) can not sett up ye same, without yor Majesties Espetiall Grace and favor be further extended'. She received £200 in royal bounty to set up her shop.[75] Other apprentices came from provincial gentry or mercantile families, often with London connections. Rowley Grevill, who held three quarters of a shop in the 1690s, inherited the estate of her namesake, a spinster aunt. Both of them had been christened Raleigh Grevill; the elder was the daughter of Richard Grevill, a cousin of the poet Fulke Grevill, who christened his children Fulke and Raleigh in memory of his friendship with Walter Raleigh. London made them into Rowley or Rawley, the name given in the Exchange records and both their wills.[76]

Exchangewomen were meant to be free of the City in order to trade there, and many of them had the freedom in their own right or through their husbands or fathers. Unlike men, they were rarely described as citizens. Rather, the phrase 'of London' was used to indicate the freedom. Ann Gregor had been a gentry apprentice from Cornwall: once free, she took an Exchange shop and became in the Gresham records 'spinster of London'.[77] Elizabeth Harrison was unusual in claiming, or being given, the title 'citizen and joiner', yet plenty of exchangewomen had the freedom after apprenticeship. Agnes Blennerhassett's short Exchange career exemplifies one route. Apprenticed in 1686 to John and Frances Spillett, who had two shops in the upper pawn, she became free in 1692 and took out a lease of her own, giving her 8 feet of shop room on the 'inner part of the east inner pawn', previously held by Mrs Clarke, for eleven years at £20 a quarter. She held the shop until the end of 1695, when she married a goldsmith.[78] Several freewomen took their sisters into apprenticeship and, presumably, into their Exchange shops. Sarah Bonwick, who ended up in arrears in the 1680s, had been apprenticed in 1669 and become free of the Drapers' Company in 1676. She took her sister Mary as an apprentice in 1680.[79] Sarah's path of freedom

---

[75] LMA, CLC/L/HA/C/011/MS 15860/006, 84; TNA, SP 29/281A f. 84; *Calendar of Treasury Books, vol. 2, 1667–1668*, ed. William A. Shaw (London: HMSO, 1905), 605.
[76] TNA, PROB 11/384/256; GL, MS 9172/102, no. 247.
[77] Muncaster, "'Six Feet of Shop Room'".
[78] GR 1678–1722, p. 278; *England, Essex Parish Registers, 1538–1900* (Salt Lake City, UT: FamilySearch, 2013); Ambrose Heal, *The London Goldsmiths* (Cambridge University Press, 1935), 89.
[79] ROLLCO (Sarah Bonwick).

before shopkeeping was not universal; other exchangewomen seem to have become free after they had begun trading, which may suggest some pressure was applied.

The fullest information about an exchangewoman we have, though, comes from Hester Pinney, a lace seller from Bristol who worked with her sister in the New Exchange on the south side of the Strand just below Covent Garden. As Pamela Sharpe has shown, the Pinney women and particularly Hester built an independent working life from the family lace trade, drawing on connections that came from family ties and their own enterprise.[80] Letters to Hester show her lodging in various places, including with Mrs Janeway, for which she records paying £8 10s a year. Others were addressed to her at 'the Seven Stars in the inner row below stayres of the New Exchange in the Strand', or 'Mr Carr's against the Rose Coffee House in Covent Garden', and sometimes in taverns, where she also met other tradeswomen and later conducted her administrative and financial business.[81] In 1687, her father, an ejected Presbyterian minister, was writing to her from Dublin, asking querulously 'to what purpose you would furnish a room in London, where you have no business I do not at all understand'. Hester's mother refused to send her a bed, since they did not want her to live there. Two months later, John Pinney wrote again to say he was 'not satisfied with your living in a taverne a place of so many temptations and dangers', urging her to return to live with him: 'if debts remain let your sister get them in & be accountable to you for them'.[82] Hester spent most of the rest of her life in London, moving from her Exchange work into managing investments and maintaining amicable, amatory and professional relations with gentlemen and merchants.

The take-up of shops by recently freed gentry apprentices like Ann Gregor from Cornwall and Bridget Flowerdew from Norfolk suggests that as well as having, probably, substantial premiums to start off their apprenticeships, they were also able to command the money to begin and continue leases: Bridget Flowerdew began an eleven-year lease in 1690, in a shop she was already occupying, paying an £18 fine and £18 a quarter. Bridget had been apprenticed to Ann Flowerdew, probably her aunt, in 1679, became free ten years later and was still taking apprentices

---

[80] Pamela Sharpe, 'Dealing with Love: The Ambiguous Independence of the Single Woman in Early Modern England', *Gender & History* 11, no. 2 (1999): 209–32; on Pinney as investor, see Amy M. Froide, *Silent Partners: Women as Public Investors during Britain's Financial Revolution, 1690–1750* (Oxford University Press, 2016), 186–95.
[81] Bristol University Special Collections, Pinney Papers.
[82] Geoffrey Nuttall, ed., *Letters of John Pinney, 1679–1699* (Oxford University Press, 1939), 51.

in 1711.[83] Other women seem to have used taking apprentices as a means to establish those expensive shops. The high premiums paid by some gentry apprentices reversed the usual economics of apprenticeship: in cases like Ann Gray's, the relationship began with an apprentice putting in a premium that far exceeded the cost of their training or keep, enabling their mistress to establish herself in a prestigious location with a good display of goods. The gains were not just the skills of sewing and selling but the credit that was provided by experience in a city shop with the shelter of a mistress's household; clothes came into the bargain too. When Gray sued for the return of her £40 premium after two years, she got back £30 of it: her witnesses had argued both that she had not acquired the requisite skills but that the £24 worth of clothes provided by her friends had been 'for the most part worne out and spoyled'.[84]

The shops of the pawn worked well for women because they were flexible and small, but also, it seems, because over the years, a special set of customs had evolved to suit its apprentices. The Exchange was treated as a place with its own rules. No paperwork laid these down, but a number of references in both legal cases and petitions make clear that by the later seventeenth century, 'exchange-maids' expected a particular, abbreviated apprenticeship, for fewer years (typically five, rather than the standard seven) and higher premiums (as high as £50). Katherine and Herbert Allen, whose several apprentices worked in their Exchange shop, regularly bound their female apprentices for five years. When one of their apprentices went to court, bringing the contract into question, Francis Hunlock testified in support of Katherine Allen that 'it is usuall with persons keeping shopps in the Royall exchange London to take maiden apprentices for noe longer time then 5 yeares' and also 'it is not usuall with persons keeping shopps in the exchang to find or provide their mayden Apprentices with any manner of apparell or necessaries of that kinde but that ye same are usualy provided & given unto them by their frends during their Apprenticeship there'.[85] Exchange-maids followed their own rules. Whether intentionally or not, this meant that those who graduated from these contracts were not entitled to be free, because they had not served the seven-year term that custom required: one of them, Hester Wright, kept her shop in her brother's name for this reason.[86]

---

[83] MC, GR 1678–1722, p. 205; LMA, COL/CHD/FR/02/24, nos. 46, 146; COL/CHD/FR/02/0171, no. 34; COL/CHD/FR/02/0394, no. 9 (Flowerdew, Hall, Stamper).
[84] Patrick Wallis, 'Apprenticeship and Training in Premodern England', *Journal of Economic History* 68, no. 3 (2008): 832–61, where the 'standard account of apprenticeship' diagram is reproduced. Gray's case is LMA CLA/024/05/493.
[85] LMA, CLA/024/05/131B (1662). [86] LMA, CLA/024/05/131B (1662).

Francis Hunlock's testimony reflected an Exchange expertise, which he shared with his female relatives. A wealthy Painter-Stainer, he had a shop in the Exchange from at least 1668. His wife, Martha Osbaldeston, had inherited from her father, when she was twenty-five, a shop lease at 'Britain's Burse', the New Exchange in the Strand, which was temporarily sublet to another woman. Her sisters and sisters-in-law inherited books, but Martha was the only one still single when her father made the will, and a shop was a flexible, useful inheritance.[87] After her husband Francis's death in 1679, Martha took up a lease of her own in the Royal Exchange. She took at least one girl as an apprentice milliner, in 1687. She still held the shop in 1690, when she died in Clapham, and she bequeathed it to another widow who lived near the Exchange: Mary Stalman, who was taxed at £25 in 1692 for 'all her houses in Maidenhead Court and Grubb Street', at the heart of the cheap print trade.[88] Both their wills offer glimpses of wealthy women working and planning in the late seventeenth-century city. Martha Hunlock, with several surviving adult children, one of whom had moved to New England, left careful sums to each of them, many derived from existing loans to the children or from goods of hers that were already in their possession. That she left the shop away from them might indicate that she did not expect, or trust, them to use it, or that her bond of friendship or business with Mary Stalman took priority. In fact, the bequest to Mary Stalman seems to have fallen away, for, a year later, the Gresham Committee were discussing the Hunlock children's request to use the shop, which had earlier been sublet to another tenant, themselves. Mary Stalman, the intended inheritor of the Hunlock shop, also left a revealing will. Widowed with three children in 1679, her will in 1696 mentioned none of them but instead left her estate to the under-age daughter of another woman with no evident ties of kinship. The bequest included those standbys of late seventeenth-century widows, an Exchequer tally (an interest-bearing loan) which paid £14 a year for ninety-six years, and six lottery tickets which paid a minimum of 26s each for sixteen years.[89]

Within the Exchange, a web of connections sustained the trading community, many of them between spinsters and widows living and working together. The list of tenants in the Land Tax of 1693, of whom half were women, records a series of traders who were connected by

---

[87] Henry F. Waters, *Genealogical Gleanings in England* (Boston: New England Historic Genealogical Society, 1901), part 2, 1043–5.

[88] Scott, *Apprenticeship Disputes*. The apprentice, Sarah Wavell, sued for the return of her premium after Martha's death. MC, GR 1669–76, p. 82; TNA, PROB 11/403/137 (1691/2); LMA, CLC/525/MS11316/003 (Cripplegate Without, 1692).

[89] Froide, *Silent Partners*, 31–4.

kinship, business, apprenticeship and domestic arrangements. Rachel Erskine had held a stall since 1676.[90] Next to her in the tax list was Elizabeth Kidd, whose sister had a stall as well. In the corner shop, Mary Ludlow and Elizabeth Harrison, both spinsters with the freedom of the Girdlers' and Joiners' Company, respectively, shared 'a shop and a quarter', though by the next quarter's payment that had reduced to '3/4 of a shop'. Harrison had earlier joined Ludlow to her first shop's lease in 1687, and the two lived together in the parish of St Margaret Lothbury with two young women apprentices and one servant.[91] Jane Fielder rented a shop on the west inner pawn in 1689 and soon afterwards requested to have Ann Gregor join her. Gregor, daughter of a Cornish landowner and merchant, had been apprenticed to a goldsmith and had been made free three years before. In 1694, she and Fielder were lodging together in the household of Walter and Ann Holt, along with Lucy Maes, who had been an apprentice of the Spilletts and moved on to work on her own. Her sister was living there too. When Ann Gregor died in 1704, another Fielder woman was one of the witnesses to her will.[92] The other women in the house were also living with relatives, in one case as a servant.[93] Mary Barton was another central figure, with a shop on the 'outward part of the west inner pawn' from the 1680s. She and her husband, running a millinery business, took over the shop of Katherine Allen in 1690 when she left the Exchange after thirty years of shopholding. In 1688, Barton also took over the apprentice Frances Bickley when she broke away from her mistress. The Bartons' shop was close to the Spilletts' two shops, where Lucy Maes, Agnes Blennerhassett and their other apprentices would have worked.[94] Six months after being freed, Agnes Blennerhassett leased her own Exchange shop.[95] Anne Vanderspritt was in a shop leased by her husband in 1689 after becoming free of the Painter-Stainers. The shops and houses constituted a community of interconnected tenants and apprentices, drawing on long-standing bonds of kinship, obligation and shared occupation and moving flexibly between apprenticeship, shops and houses.

Other records reveal more of apprentices' and shopkeepers' living arrangements. The Exchange separated residential apprenticeship from shopkeeping, but often not by much distance. The tenants of the upper pawn lived predominantly within a few minutes' walk of the building. Of

---

[90] GL, MS 34042, p. 38.   [91] LMA, COL/CHD/LA/04/049, p. 41.
[92] LMA, CLC/525/MS11316/008; ROLLCO, Anne Gregor; MC, GR 1678–1722, p. 182; TNA, PROB 11/474/432 (1704).
[93] LMA, COL/CHD/LA/04/20, p. 3.
[94] ROLLCO, John Spillett; LMA, CLA/024/05/509.   [95] MC, GR 1678–1722, p. 208.

the forty-three traceable tenants of the upper Exchange tax list in 1693, nine lived in the same parish and another twenty-four in adjacent parishes. The tax records of the nearby parishes also include others listed as 'exchangemen' or 'exchangewomen'. Both men and women clearly needed shops and homes to be close together, and some may have had shops in their houses as well as in the Exchange. There is a suggestive difference by gender: men who did not live near the Exchange tended to live west of it, towards Holborn and St Paul's, while women tended to live east of it, towards the river and the poorer eastern suburbs. A more marked difference amongst the Exchange tenants is between male shopkeepers as householders in their own right and female shopkeepers as lodgers. Where their status is traceable, in the early 1690s, male shopkeepers were twice as likely as female ones to be householders, often with substantial stocks worth more than £50.[96] Nearly all the shopkeepers living in lodgings, in contrast, were women. The same pattern held for men and women working as seamstresses, tailors and milliners elsewhere. In general, women describing themselves as seamstresses were mostly living in lodgings, with no stocks on which to be taxed. Milliners and tailors were overwhelmingly male, and often householders, holding taxable shop stocks; the handful of women milliners in the poll tax lists were also householders. The very few female tailors listed were widows. Inside and outside the Exchange, men and (single) women were engaged in quite different shopkeeping enterprises.

Lodgers' housing arrangements demonstrate the particular lifestyles of working women, which were very different from the old model of residential apprenticeship. Home and work were separate, though they sometimes involved the same people. Twenty-six-year-old Charity Needler, who had requested a lease at the Exchange when she was twenty-three, lodged with her sister and brother-in-law, a gentry couple in St Mildred, Poultry, along with their son and four servants. She was not free of the City, but she took up the freedom of her father's company, the Innholders, by patrimony in 1697, perhaps realising the uses of company membership.[97] The household of Elias Pledger, an apothecary, and his wife, Elizabeth, included their children, his sister, four female 'servants' (of which at least two were actually apprentices who went on to become free and take a shop together) and three 'lodgers', one of whom, Anne Towse, held an 11-foot shop.[98] These were the kind of non-nuclear families and complex households that nurtured City trade.

---

[96] Poll Tax 1692.
[97] LMA, COL/CHD/LA/04/081, p. 2, Higgins family; LMA, COL/CHD/FR/02/113, no. 97, names a Higgins as 'guardian' on Needler's patrimony application.
[98] COL/CHD/LA/04/02/81/16. Bethiah Paradise, one of the apprentices, had been turned over from Henry Duke.

In multiple occupancy lodgings close to the Exchange, shared housing was a mark of convenience rather than poverty. Rachel Erskine, free in the Merchant Taylors' after her own apprenticeship, was a householder, with rent assessed at £20 and goods at £50. She held a shop 'at the Scotch Arms' in the 1670s, was the under-tenant of a 7-foot shop leased by Mrs Hunt in May 1682 and took out her own lease in the 1690s and kept it up for a further twenty years. Erskine shared her house in St Mary Abchurch, near the Exchange, with Frances Antrobus, a twice-widowed Exchange shopkeeper; Frances's daughter, Hester; an apprentice; and two other female servants. Erskine took a series of apprentices and died in 1715 with a good stock of annuities to bequeath.[99] The Exchange was the ideal place to combine investment and shopkeeping.[100] Frances Antrobus herself had begun in the Exchange as 'Widow Hulse', marrying the merchant tailor Robert Antrobus during her time as a shopkeeper. She might have been the cousin Frances mentioned in Rachel Erskine's will. Katherine Sommerfield, another wealthy householder and exchangewoman in St Margaret Lothbury, held stock valued at a minimum of £150. Her household included two female servants (who may have been apprentices or helped in the shop), a family who lodged with her and two other unidentified women. Elizabeth Brewer, another widowed exchangewoman, lived close by, with three children and three servants or apprentices.[101] The houses of exchangewomen were densely populated and connected like the upper pawn itself. The old pattern of residential apprenticeship had developed a new form, in which the spatial layout of a gallery of shops reflected the networked relations of mistresses, apprentices and journeywomen.

One way of illustrating this is through social network analysis, tracking the bonds between shopwomen. Figure 1.7 illustrates some of the social and contractual bonds that ran alongside the Exchange's shop passages. It foregrounds women and includes shopkeepers and their apprentices but does not include the many tenants for whom no connections have been traced. Most of the bonds are of apprenticeship, because these are the most visible, and it is these which connect a large portion of the tenants to each other. Digitally mapping the ties between people reveals a set of women who act as foci, training several apprentices and creating other connections. Rachel Erskine is at the hub of one series of apprentices, indicating the longevity of her tenure. Ties of executorship added

---

[99] GL, MS 34042, p. 38; MC, GR 1669–77, pp. 91, 146; MC, GR 1678–1722, p. 205; COL/CHD/LA/04 /58, p. 10.
[100] On women's investment strategies, see Froide, *Silent Partners*.
[101] LMA, COL/CHD/LA/04/049, p. 4; 1692 Poll Tax.

Bred in the Exchange: Seamstresses and Shopkeepers

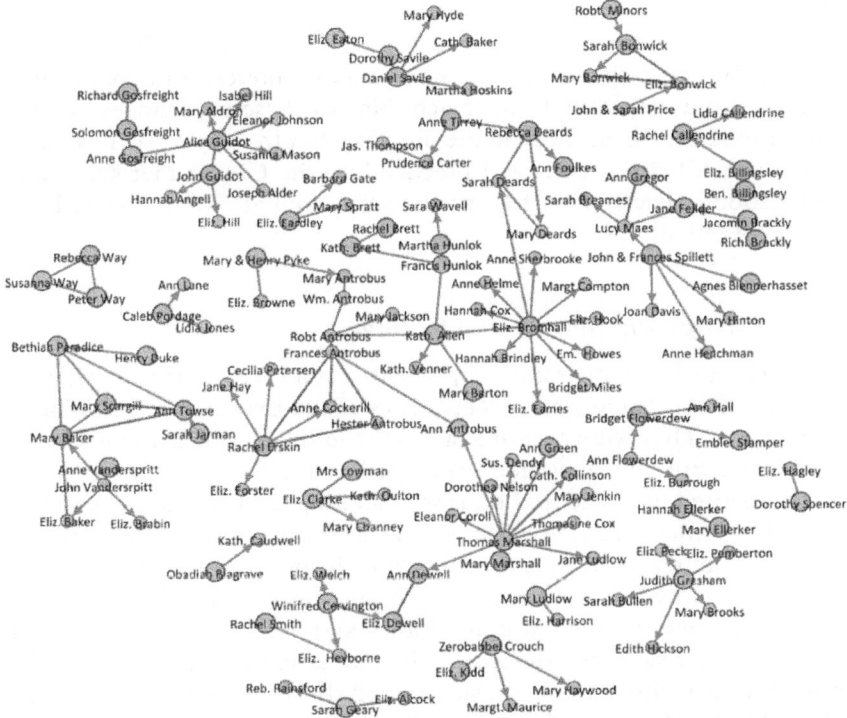

Figure 1.7 Women's connections in the Exchange. Arrows point from mistress to apprentice; larger nodes are shopholders; others are connections without (known) shops. Connections include kin, marriage, housing, shop-sharing and executorship.
Produced with Gephi.

another web of usefulness: Katherine Allen's husband's executors connected her to the Bromhall and Antrobus families. Two networks of four women reflect the shared households near the Exchange: one of four stallholders and apprentices living together, another of four stallholders lodging with an apothecary household. Other clusters represent families of stallholders (Peter Way and his two spinster daughters all held shops), and women who took kin as apprentices, like the Callendrine sisters where the older was apprenticed to Elizabeth Billingsley and the younger to the older. Family ties and business ties are not easily distinguishable.

The dense network indicates the work that apprenticeship did for the business community: it was part of a set of reciprocal ties that bound stallholders and their connections together, providing credit and expertise on which to draw, as well as political affiliations like the Bromhalls' Dissenting activities (discussed in Chapter 3): the Exchange was surely better than a guild for sociability, interest and connection. This is also a map of outward reach. Not all these apprentices became free or took their own shops in the building, but the upper pawn acted as a hub which fed out skills and practice into the City's other shops and connections back to the provincial families who aspired to City apprenticeships.

Shopping, Sewing and Selling

Returning to Ann Gray's inappropriate lace suit takes us back to what the milliners, linen drapers and seamstresses of the Exchange were doing in their shops. They were part of a fashion revolution. The garments of the sixteenth century were predominantly tailored to fit, lasted for years and were inherited or resold and remade. Tailoring, across Europe, was cast as male; women's sewing work was meant to be confined to garments without boning, or inner garments, though the extent of these varied. During the seventeenth century, outfitting came to involve more garments and new fashions in both clothes and accessories. The growing availability of ready-made garments (first for armies, with fixed sizes); the symbolically white linen shirts, sleeves and shifts; changeable accessories like ruffs, hoods and coifs; and comfortable or resizable loose coats for women and children all depended on seamstresses' work.[102] Childbed linen was another important market. The introduction of the mantua from the 1670s, a one-piece untailored gown that could be made by seamstresses rather than tailors, evolving later into a formal dress that could be arranged over a bodice and petticoat, was once seen as the key to women's growing place in the clothes trade.[103] It now looks like just one part of women's role in sewing innerwear and, increasingly, outerwear. The dissemination, formal and informal, of specialised sewing skills was part of a broader shift in clothes-making from a culture of tailoring, which was largely male, to one which included and showcased the work of women as seamstresses and, later, milliners. Recent research by Sarah Birt on women in the Merchant Taylors' company reveals the

[102] Beverley Lemire, *Dress, Culture and Commerce: The English Clothing Trade before the Factory, 1660–1800* (Basingstoke: Palgrave Macmillan, 1997), chapter 2.
[103] Clare Haru Crowston, *Fabricating Women: The Seamstresses of Old Regime France, 1675–1791* (Durham, NC: Duke University Press, 2001), 36. Examples of the variety of mantuas, from loose kimono-type jackets to more formal gowns, can be seen in 'Lady Clapham's Mantua' in the V&A collections, and the late seventeenth-century mantua at the Metropolitan Museum of Art, accession no. 33.54 a–c.

extent to which women were present and working alongside tailors, apprenticed to their wives and working in their shops.[104]

Exact details of what the Exchange shops sold, and particularly the occupations of female stallholders, are rarely recorded. In the upper pawn, shops selling clothes, headwear and other accessories predominated, though the Exchange made strenuous efforts to attract other trades; there was a particular concern amongst shopholders in hard times that too many shops were overlapping. Alongside the many seamstresses and milliners worked Mrs Smith, a linen-seller, and Elizabeth Jenkinson, a spinster who sold spectacles 'and other glasses'. A number of exchangewomen signed a petition of 1696, submitted to the House of Lords in concern about a plan to ban the trade in calico and Bengal silks in London. The trade was managed through the East India Company, and other evidence reveals women's participation in the EIC as stockholders, voters, provisioners and workers on shore, as well as antagonists in property disputes.[105] The petition described the shopkeepers, male and female, as 'bred in the trade and thereby provided for themselves and families': as Aske Brock and Misha Ewen point out, the expansive global trade of the late seventeenth century brought new opportunities and challenges for women in business, as they chased their money and goods across the widening world.

Exchange shops were small, and girls worked closely with their mistresses, progressing to being left on their own, where their responsibilities for goods and transactions could be daunting. Both tailors and seamstresses worked directly with clients and with proxy shoppers commissioning gowns or buying aprons and handkerchiefs for their sisters, daughters, wives and mothers in the country. Letters, discussions and close observation gave both male and female London shoppers the know-how to buy for their families.[106] The scale of some stallholders' stock suggests they had bigger shops elsewhere, but many women's shops seem to have been their only one. Although small, shops could be elaborately fitted. Abraham Dudley, who sold Indian chintz nightgowns, claimed to have spent 'near £200' in fitting up his shop to make it 'an ornament to

---

[104] Sarah Birt, 'Women, Guilds and the Tailoring Trades: The Occupational Training of Merchant Taylors' Company Apprentices in Early Modern London', *The London Journal* 46, no. 2 (May 2021): 146–64.

[105] Sharpe, 'Gender at Sea'; Aske Laursen Brock and Misha Ewen, 'Women's Public Lives: Navigating the East India Company, Parliament and Courts in Early Modern England', *Gender & History* 33, no 1 (March 2021): 3–23.

[106] Danae Tankard, *Clothing in 17th-Century Provincial England* (London: Bloomsbury, 2019), chapter 6.

the Exchange'.[107] Testimony about a theft from another Exchange shop indicates that it had room for customers to sit down while they shopped. Elizabeth Jones had been sitting in a chair in Mrs Bassett's shop, bargaining for £10 worth of bone lace to make sleeves, and tried to conceal it under her petticoat. When she got up, the lace caught around her legs and made her theft obvious; she got away but was caught nearby in Castle Alley.[108] The small size and ready surveillance of Royal Exchange shops, as well as the long route from shop to exit, seem to have made them less vulnerable to the habit of shoplifting that drove shopkeepers to lobby for an Act against it in 1699. Rather, their shops ran heavily on credit or partial credit, as indicated by the considerable debts in the inventories and wills of stallholders; the wealthier Royal Exchange customers had other ways of shopping without paying.[109]

Bargaining looms large in the numerous shoplifting cases in the Old Bailey: 'cheapening' provided cover for dragging out a purchase. It was evidently critical to the skills of both shopper and shopkeeper.[110] Ann Gray's troubles with credit, and the accusations levelled at other Exchange girls, where transactions were short of pence and sixpences, were individually recognisable and also reflect the shortage of ready cash in late seventeenth-century London. Shopkeepers often used their own tokens to replace it. An epidemic of coin clipping (in which women were heavily involved) meant, too, that silver coins no longer represented their value. The 1696 Recoinage Act demanded that legal currency be punched with a hole to mark it as unclipped, giving rise to bawdy ballads fantasising about lusty girls rushing to be 'punched'.[111] At the same time, shops ran on credit and kept large tabs running for their credit customers; the difference between shoplifters and credit shoppers was not always obvious. Cash transactions could be tricky, and managing them meant shopkeepers and apprentices navigating the line between credit, cheating and theft.

In 1678, an anonymous woman authored *Advice to the Women and Maidens of London*, a women's guide to accounting, printed by Benjamin Billingsley, a stationer with a shop by the Exchange. Billingsley's wife, Deborah, sold medicines and had, it was said, sufficient expertise to keep

---

[107] MC, GR 1678–1722, p. 4.
[108] *Old Bailey Proceedings Online* (www.oldbaileyonline.org), 30 August 1694, t16940830-4.
[109] Jonah Miller, 'Review of Shoplifting in Eighteenth-Century England', *Reviews in History*, no. 2329, www.reviews.history.ac.uk; Shelley Tickell, *Shoplifting in Eighteenth-Century England* (Woodbridge: Boydell & Brewer, 2018).
[110] Helen Berry, '"Polite Consumption": Shopping in Eighteenth-Century England'. *Transactions of the Royal Historical Society* 12 (2002): 375–94.
[111] Lili Loufborrow, 'The Punching-Office: Where 17th-Century Ladies Go for Sex', www.thehairpin.com/2011/04/the-punching-office-where-17th-century-ladies-go-for-sex/.

Bred in the Exchange: Seamstresses and Shopkeepers

her husband's shop going in his absence.¹¹² His sister, Elizabeth, was a seamstress in the Scriveners' Company, who took her own apprentices, including Rachel Callendrine, who then became free and opened her own shop in the Royal Exchange. Perhaps one of these women wrote the *Advice*.¹¹³ The book reconstructs typical shop debts and credits in minute detail, demonstrating how double-entry bookkeeping could keep track of the kind of long, transferrable debts that shopkeepers were apt to live and die with. The reader is asked to 'Imagine an Exchange-Woman, Shop-keeper, or the like, newly entring upon Trade'. First, she draws up an inventory of her estate: £60 in ready money, £8 of black alamode (a thin, plain-woven lustred silk used for scarfs and hoods), twenty dozen women's gloves worth £16 and a debt of £20 from Mrs Martha Thorpe. That debt from Mrs Thorpe is then augmented by her taking another £35 worth of gloves; when our shopkeeper buys 60 ells of Bag-Holland (fine quality linen) and four pieces of cambric for a total of £23 from James Jones, she pays him £12 10s in cash and assigns him £10 10s of Mrs Thorpe's debt. She has the linen cut up and made into handkerchiefs, cravats and cuffs, paying the seamstress £2 10s for her work. She meets a merchant going to Barbados, who offers two hogsheads of sugar in exchange for half her stock of linen. The slave trade was only one step away from the Exchange shops, its transactions worked out on the Exchange floor and in Cornhill's coffee houses.¹¹⁴ Our exchange-woman's trade is enabled by the demand for luxury goods and more disposable fashion, connecting the transatlantic forces of commerce and investment with Londoners and provincial customers. On a smaller scale, the whole business of debt management and accounting was a critical skill for shopkeepers, and here it also overlaps with apparently pre-existing debts between women; the micro-economies of provincial England were sustained by such loans, with single women and widows prominent in them.¹¹⁵

---

[112] Elizabeth Lane Furdell, *Publishing and Medicine in Early Modern England* (University of Rochester Press, 2002), 109. The report is from John Dunton.
[113] LMA, COL/CHD/FR/02/2, no. 31; Rachel Callendrine's indenture to Elizabeth Billingsley in 1674 was witnessed by Benjamin Billingsley. Deborah Billingsley is a likelier potential author, as the text refers to managing her father's household when she grew up, while Elizabeth's father died before she was eleven.
[114] *Advice to the Women and Maidens of London Shewing, That Instead of Their Usual Pastime, and Education in Needlework ... It Were Far More Necessary and Profitable to Apply Themselves to the Right Understanding and Practice of the Method of Keeping Books of Account ... by One of That Sex* (London: Benjamin Billingsley, 1678), 21–2. This book is discussed further in Chapter 3.
[115] Muldrew, *Economy of Obligation*.

The contents of London shops have left some record in accounts and probate inventories. A chancery case at the end of the seventeenth century included as evidence the account book of a Miss Goreing, a rural gentlewoman living in London. In the second half of 1697, she bought flannel and dimity for petticoats; 'Bengall' for two frocks; muslin for lining; six pairs of shoes; two sarsnet hoods; an Indian satin gown 'lyned with Pertian' for 15s; fine holland to make shifts, pins and tape; and fans, ribbons and gloves. She had two coats made and spent £5 on rich silk. Silk loomed large in her spending, and she also paid a dancing master, but more ordinary purchases involved muslin and holland, and hoods, ribbons and gloves, as well as mourning for herself and two servants when her uncle died. Her maid's wages for the half-year were £1.[116] A more precise picture of shop contents can be found in the probate inventory of Herbert Allen, the haberdasher who, with his wife Katherine, took a series of apprentices, boys and girls, to work in their Exchange shop in the 1660s. Allen's inventory was drawn up in 1668, seemingly while the shop was relocated at the New Exchange after the Fire. It records an extensive list of ready-made goods, worth over £1,000, 'in the shop on the Exchange known by the sign of the Parrett'. There was £300 worth of various kinds of lace and numerous bundles of holland, lawn and cambric; alamode and lutestring silks; and 40 ells of yellow birdseye, a cheaper patterned wool which sold at 1s 6d an ell. The Allens were also selling ready-made clothes: laced, linen or plain suits (14s to 52s); waistcoats and undergarments, including parcels of 'old fashioned' linen for women; 'childbed linen' (£3) and children's linen. There were countless accessories too: women's sleeves, twenty dozen children's caps, aprons, fans, neckcloths and masks.[117]

Apprentices working in such a shop would need a thorough knowledge of the range of goods and the cost of different weights and classes of textiles, as well as how to navigate its doubtless crammed shelves and parcels of goods. Herbert Allen's appraisers, Robert Antrobus and Thomas Bromhall, were themselves skilled and knowledgeable men of the Exchange and its goods. Debts were enormous too: Allen had over £2,000 of outstanding debts, including sums from several regular customers, the Duke of Buckingham and the Countess of Bedford, one of the 'Beauties' of Charles II's court. The Allens' shop, with its series of gentry apprentices, was at the forefront of elite shopping in the Exchange.

The last item on Herbert Allen's shop inventory was £5 12s worth of 'holland fabric in the hands of work women to make up', reflecting, like

[116] TNA, C 114/182.
[117] LMA, CLA/002/02/01/0570 (3 October 1668). An ell was just over a yard.

Advice to Women, the degree to which Exchange shops and milliners depended on seamstresses working elsewhere. The putting-out system employed an invisible number of women in supplying shops, at rates which were dropping; apprenticeship as a seamstress offered the potential of moving to the upper end of the system, supplying customers directly or running a shop. One of Hester Pinney's letters from her sister-in-law Mary describes 'the baggarly working to the Change which is now grown very low and Contemptible'.[118] Mary Pinney may have been referring to all the Exchanges, or just the New Exchange where she and Hester Pinney worked; her assessment indicates the growing autonomy of the seamstresses outside the City, around Covent Garden, Charing Cross and the Strand, where several of the women in the Merchant Taylors' Company had their shops and which may have provided longer careers as well as better rewards than the small Exchange shops.

The Royal Exchange had also long been a centre for portrait painters. In the later seventeenth century, several members of the Painter-Stainers' Company held shops there, including the portraitists John Vandersprit and Daniel Savile, who drew Pepys. Their wives had shops too and they took female apprentices, some of whom went on to start their own shops. Women did train painter-stainers, as well as practising as painters: Helen Draper's examination of the painting trade in seventeenth-century London reveals at least one who took male apprentices.[119] In the Exchange, though, the evidence shows millinery and drapery running alongside the painting trade. The interface between husbands' and wives' businesses remains opaque. Daniel Savile took six apprentices, the first two boys and the rest girls; he requested a lease in the Royal Exchange in 1689, and his wife, Dorothy, held a shop there in the 1690s, jointly with Elizabeth Eaton.[120] Daniel and Dorothy's final apprentice, Elizabeth Calverley, completed her apprenticeship after Daniel's death, became free and, in 1703, was holding an Exchange shop with Samuel Dudley. All the signs are that Dorothy, more than Daniel, was the active employer here, and her shop was in the upper Exchange alongside milliners and haberdashers. The Painter-Stainers were tied into the Exchange network of social and business contacts, suggesting a shared trade amongst the

---

[118] Bristol University Special Collections, Pinney Letters, Red Box 2 folder VII, Mary Pinney to Hester Pinney, 7/2/1694/5.
[119] Helen Draper, 'Mary Beale and Art's Lost Laborers: Women Painter Stainers', *Early Modern Women* 10, no. 1 (2015): 141–51.
[120] Kate Loveman, 'Samuel Pepys's First Portrait Painter: Daniel Savile and Portraiture for the Middling Sort in Restoration London', *Journal of the Warburg and Courtauld Institutes* 81 (2018): 269–79; MC, GR 1678–1722, p. 208.

wives. Other couples in the same company followed the same route, in varying proportions. John Vanderspritt and his wife, Elizabeth, took two girls and two boys between 1688 and 1693: first a boy, then a boy and a girl, then another girl. His sister Anne had a shop in the Exchange as well. Francis and Martha Hunlok took three female apprentices between 1668 and 1675, and Martha took another one in her widowhood, a gentleman's daughter from London, at which point her trade is described as milliner. Judith Gresham, another widow taking apprentices, was also in the Painter-Stainers'; her own two daughters, Mary and Judith, remained single and described themselves in their wills as 'spinster and trader'. Thomas Marshall and his wife, Mary, took eighteen apprentices from 1676 to 1712, where all but four of them were girls.[121]

The last of Thomas and Mary Marshall's apprentices left extensive evidence of her career and connections. Ann Dewell was the daughter of a gentleman from Worcester, apprenticed in 1699; her two sisters were also apprenticed to London guilds. Alongside Ann Dewell in the Marshall business worked Mary Dix, another gentry daughter from Liverpool, who was apprenticed a few years later in 1704. By this time the Marshalls had a shop on the upper floor of the Royal Exchange, and when Ann Dewell completed her apprenticeship and became free, she took a shop herself, with Mary Dix as partner.[122] The Exchange was a stronghold of female business partnerships. Some such relationships were flexible, others lasted years; one advantage was to allow women without the freedom to draw on the privileges of those with it. In contrast to trading with a husband, it allowed equitable sharing of responsibility as well as debts, and while some partners were single, others kept up business partnerships alongside their marriages, enjoying with them a protection from the constraints of coverture.[123] In the case of Dewell and Dix, Mary Dix died young in 1718 and left details of their partnership in the will she wrote when she became ill. It partook of the riskiest features of Exchange shops, accumulating considerable debts:

and whereas my partner Mrs Anne Dewell and myself had sundry debts due and owing from severall persons to us at Christmas 1717 amounting in the whole to 1017 pounds by the accompt of our debts then taken appears a good part of which are yet standing out And whereas since taking the said accompt of the said debts other fresh debts have become due to us and fresh credit must be given soe long as we carry on our joint trade.[124]

[121] LAA. [122] LMA, CLC/525/MS11316/016.
[123] Alexandra Shepard, 'Minding Their Own Business: Married Women and Credit in Early Eighteenth-Century London', *Transactions of the Royal Historical Society* 25 (December 2015): 53–74.
[124] TNA, PROB 11/365/519 (1718); PROB 11/818/476 (1755).

Ann Dewell went on trading and took her own apprentices: her much younger sister, Rebecca, in 1725; Oriana Michell; and Carolina Banson, a clerk's daughter from London who took an apprentice herself and then married. Ann Dewell's will indicates the networks that these years of business generated: she had her will proved by Henry Marshall, Thomas and Mary's son, who was just completing his own apprenticeship with his father as Anne arrived in 1699, and left money to a Mrs Marshall (perhaps Henry's sister, or wife) and to Mrs Banson, probably her own ex-apprentice.

The Exchange, then, offered an ideal forum for the honing of appearance and self-presentation that both portraiture and millinery provided; in these working households, studios and shops, the overlap between painting, drawing and sewing was surely a benefit to gentry girls in service.

Daniel Defoe's nostalgic vision of 1727 saw the present as characterised the 'squandering of trade' in the City; his seventeenth century, by contrast, was the time of 'the two great Centers of the Women Merchants ... The Royal Exchange, and the new-Exchange in the Strand'. Once full of 'flourishing milliners', they had become warehouses and insurance offices.[125] By the second quarter of the eighteenth century, the place of trade in the City seemed to be disappearing. Women merchants are an addendum to Defoe, at the very end of his long parade of City trades, but his sense of the Exchanges as a centre of female trade is important. For a hundred years, the location of the Royal Exchange put its shops at the heart of other City businesses and brought guilds and women merchants, shopping and investing, intimately together.

The shopwomen of the Exchanges were subject to sexualisation in both print and person. A number of late seventeenth-century pamphlets represented the barter of shopkeeping in sexual terms. James Turner has acutely summed up the commodification of female entrepreneurs in libertine satire: 'the sites of women's agency are interchangeable in the libertine imagination', and all female enterprise could be interpreted as cover for the sale of women themselves.[126] The Strand Exchanges were most heavily appropriated, but the idea of shopping galleries as sexual may have cast a rhetorical shadow over the rest too. Pepys's accounts of his trips to Westminster Hall, the New and the Royal Exchanges record the variety of business he transacted at each, a combination of meetings, shopping, and leaving and collecting Elizabeth, his wife. At the New Exchange, where they spent the most shopping time,

---

[125] Daniel Defoe, *The Complete English Tradesman: In Familiar Letters* (1727), 166.
[126] Turner, '"News from the New Exchange"', 419–39.

Samuel sometimes left her to shop while he walked up and down talking; on other occasions he shopped alone, or they went together. At Westminster Hall, he made a particular habit of visiting the shops of his 'sweethearts', sometimes taking them off to drink elsewhere. Amongst them was Betty Martin, who held a draper's stall; visiting her there in early 1666, he was relieved to discover her child was to be named Charles, meaning he was not to be the godfather and freeing him from the suspicion of paternity.[127] At the Royal Exchange, nearer home, Samuel targeted Mary Batelier, who he first encountered in April 1665, when buying a pair of cotton stockings at the shop of her brother, who he took to be her husband:

At noon to the Change, and then went up to the Change to buy a pair of cotton stockings, which I did at the husband's shop of the most pretty woman there, who did also invite me to buy some linen of her; and I was glad of the occasion and bespoke some bands of her, entending to make her my seamstress – she being one of the prettiest and most modest-looked women that ever I did see.

On another occasion, he came back to see if she was there, 'poor pretty woman', and 'saluted her over her counter in the open Exchange above'.[128] Mary Batelier's 'invitation' gives a hint of the social intercourse expected of women in the Exchange, another kind of work that seems comparable to the 'emotional labour' traced by Arlie Hochschild in modern coffee shops and service industries.[129] More precisely, it was a sexualised labour, where working at a certain look – amplified in the depositions that underline the need for tidiness and good dress – might also involve calling out and calling attention to both human and linen goods.[130] Several later commentaries describe women in the Exchange calling out to their customers; in the *Spectator* in 1712, Addison described how 'the dear Creatures called to me to ask what I wanted, when I could not answer, only *To look at* you'.[131] Alongside the sexualisation of seamstresses, though, we should consider also the actual emotional and sexualised labour, the work of the look, that women were expected to put in. Pepys's other references to Mary Batelier give a glimpse of her life outside the shop. The family lived at Crutched Friars, close enough to the Navy Office where the Pepyses lived to talk

---

[127] Pepys, *Diary*, 9 March 1665/6. [128] Pepys, *Diary*, 2 April and 20 December 1665.
[129] Arlie Russell Hochschild, *The Managed Heart: Commercialization of Human Feeling* (Berkeley: University of California Press, 2003).
[130] Chris Warhurst and Dennis Nickson, '"Who's Got the Look?" Emotional, Aesthetic and Sexualized Labour in Interactive Services', *Gender, Work & Organization* 16, no. 3 (2009): 385–404.
[131] Saunders, *The Royal Exchange*, 207.

to them across the roof leads where the Pepyses had made a balcony.[132] Mary visited Mrs Pepys, came with her brother to play cards and have supper, recommended a controversial sermon and was a bridesmaid at Pepys's maid Jane's wedding in 1669.[133] That, as a sister of a stallholder, she does not appear in the Exchange records is a reminder of how many other women worked in the shops.

This feminine and feminised shop world sat in the midst of the mercantile city. Its most obvious counterpart, apart from the downstairs Exchange, was the coffee-house, another point of contact for politicians and merchants. By the late seventeenth century, the Exchange was surrounded by coffee-houses, differentiated by political and religious affiliation and treated, by both contemporaries and historians, as the stage for masculine political conversation.[134] The coffee-house world provided, too, a place where brokers and jobbers could connect. In contrast to the coffee house's masculinised sphere, the Exchange offered heterosociality, female trade and easy interchange between the exchanges of financial trading and those of millinery. Coffee-houses too were run by women: at least eleven women are listed as coffee-house keepers in the Poll Tax list of 1692, along with twenty-two 'coffee-women' who sold coffee in stalls or on the streets. But their clientele appears to have been predominantly, if not entirely, male. This is not to oppose shops and politics or containment and free movement. The Whig connections of some Exchange tenants suggest that, like coffee houses, it might also have reflected Whig dominance in City government and the Nonconformist merchants' interests of the 1670s and 1680s. Likewise, while coffee-house culture has been neatly mapped onto the normative masculine public sphere, the Exchange was also seen as a place of loose talk. The actual spatial range of late seventeenth-century London women seem to have been at least as broad as that of their male peers, as they travelled through the metropolis for work and leisure.[135] Rather, the Exchange complicates the distinction of public/private yet again. The Exchange/coffee-house matrix also suggests a way to think about racially marked products in the market of late seventeenth-century London.

---

[132] Pepys, *Diary*, vol VII, 15 n. 4.
[133] Pepys, *Diary*, 14 February 1665/6; 18 January 1666/7; 27 March 1669.
[134] Brian Cowan, 'What Was Masculine about the Public Sphere? Gender and the Coffeehouse Milieu in Post-Restoration England', *History Workshop Journal* 51 (2001): 127–57; Joseph Monteyne, *The Printed Image in Early Modern London: Urban Space, Visual Representation, and Social Exchange* (Aldershot: Ashgate, 2007), 36.
[135] Robert Shoemaker, 'Gendered Spaces: Patterns of Mobility and Perceptions of London's Geography, 1660–1750', in *Imagining Early Modern London: Perceptions and Portrayals of the City from Stow to Strype, 1598–1720*, ed. J. F. Merritt (Cambridge University Press, 2001).

Exchangewomen sold white linen to (largely) white customers, some of whom traded in and benefitted from slavery; meanwhile, the blackness of coffee was fantasised as contagious to English stomachs (and, by extension, the dissent of the coffee house a risk to loyalism) and the regular image of the Turk's Head that was used to sell it offered a persistent exotic other to the London consumer.[136] Alongside such images, black workers were integrated into London households: William Batelier, Mary's brother, had two black servants, one of whom, Doll, regularly dressed the Pepyses' meat and danced jigs with other guests at a family wedding.[137]

The Exchange women were not typical of women's work in seventeenth-century London, or even of seamstresses, milliners and linen-sellers. They were subject to, and sometimes mistresses of, a spatially and economically particular set of power dynamics, in which they laid claim to the rights of the City to work in a circumscribed yet influential place. The skills of sewing and selling that were shared there had reverberations through London's fashion economy. The spatial organisation of their labour and social lives adds a key dimension not only to the Exchange world but to the notions of male, female and mixed space that were in the process of being established in the late seventeenth-century city. That space was created through consumption and labour. At its heart was an economy of credit: earned through trust, bartered between women and accumulated by women's management of shops, goods and debts.

---

[136] Monteyne, *Printed Image*, chapter 1.   [137] Pepys, *Diary*, 5 April 1669.

2 Girls as Apprentices

Margaret Kirkam and Ann Evans

Girls' apprenticeships began with the indentures that bound them to their mistresses. The smudges on Ann Evans's indenture (Figure 2.1) betray the ambiguity of women's place in the guild bureaucracy. Indentures came in identical pairs, divided on the serrated (indented) line on the upper edge. Signed by each party, they were the proof of a period of service that could, if completed, qualify the apprentice to become free of the company and the City. Pre-printed forms like this one were based on a long-established form of words, designed for the archetypal male apprentice and adapted for a girl and her mistress. Charles Hargrave, the company clerk, has laboured to make the document work, inserting 'S' to alter the pronouns and rubbing the print off the parchment to turn 'Master' into 'Mistris'. Small, easily stored and meant to last, indentures were printed on parchment as a continuation of older manuscript traditions, but, paradoxically, ink was easier to remove from parchment than paper. So the form itself, a fortuitous hybrid, made it possible to include women.

This indenture was made in 1696 between Ann Evans, daughter of a gentleman from Monmouth in Wales, and Margaret Kirkam, a milliner who, by London's peculiar custom, was a member of the Barber-Surgeons' Company. Like thousands of other young people in the towns, cities and craft guilds of early modern Europe, Ann was bound as an apprentice, with the right to become free of the city of London and to practice her trade when she completed her term. Companies like the Barber-Surgeons were the guilds that regulated economic life, and apprenticeship was the social and economic institution that underpinned artisanal economies and life cycles. It shaped untaught young people into skilled journeymen and women who could work for wages and become masters or mistresses themselves. Evans's indenture survives because she completed her seven years' contract and was made free of her company, after which she brought her half to the City Chamberlain and paid the fee to gain the freedom of the City, giving her the right to trade there and train her own apprentices.

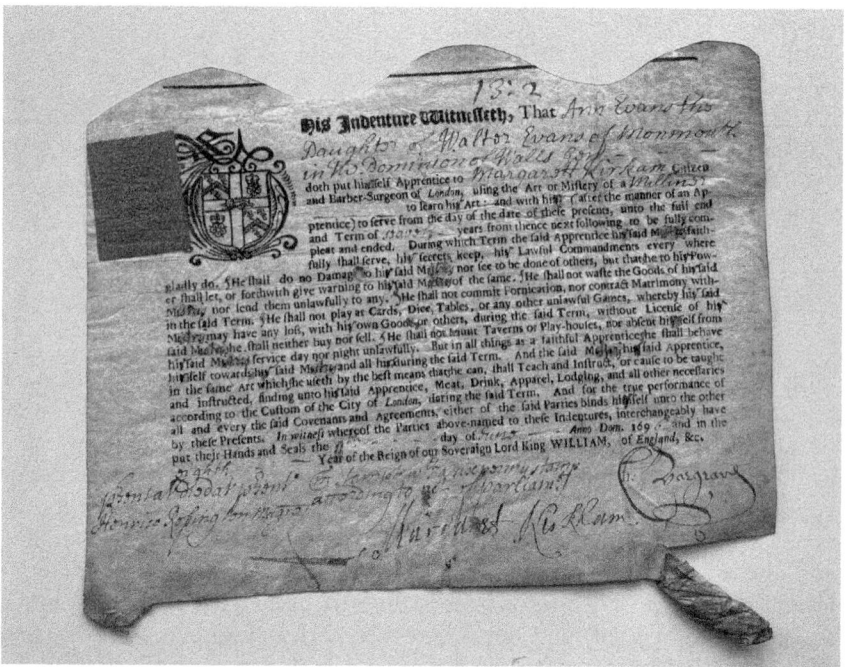

Figure 2.1 Ann Evans's indenture. Parchment. 15 × 12 cm.
London Metropolitan Archives (City of London).

When an apprenticeship was agreed, each party signed one part before witnesses and kept it safe as a necessary record. Indentures like this were provided by the companies, printed in bulk by stationers who specialised in the growing mass of forms required by early modern bureaucracy.[1] Other girls were given different paperwork. Many were apprenticed with manuscript documents copying, or slightly adapting, the standard form of words. The Drapers' and the Merchant Taylors' Companies had forms printed specially for girls, with 'she' and 'her' printed in; this was

---

[1] On similar indentures, see Urvashi Chakravarty, 'Bound to Serve: Apprenticeship Indentures at the Folger', The Collation, 5 January 2018, http://collation.folger.edu/2018/01/indentures/ and Derek Dunne, 'Sign Here Please: _____ Blank Forms from the Folger Collection', The Collation, 30 March 2017, http://collation.folger.edu/2017/03/sign-here-please/. See also Peter Stallybrass, '"Little Jobs": Broadsides and the Printing Revolution', in *Agent of Change: Print Culture Studies after Elizabeth L. Eisenstein*, ed. Sabrina Alcorn Baron, Eric N. Lindquist, and Eleanor F. Shevlin (Amherst: University of Massachusetts Press, 2007), 315–41; Naomi Tadmor, 'The Settlement of the Poor and the Rise of the Form in England, c. 1662–1780', *Past & Present* 236 (2017): 43–97.

an easy change to make for stationers, but it required companies to command it. Jobbing stationers also produced forms with simple City arms and female pronouns, to suit any company that needed them. Similar forms were sold at the Royal Exchange.² The Haberdashers' Company, another company with increasing numbers of girls, used perhaps the most radical option: a form that had gaps rather than gendered pronouns, conveying the impression that apprenticeship was genuinely gender-neutral. Only girls seem to have used them; boys still used forms with the male forms printed in. So the attempt to make paperwork more flexible still preserved normative masculinity. Girls were still using adapted boys' forms at the end of the eighteenth century.

Ann Evans's roughly adapted indenture is also a reminder that, in a bureaucratising culture, paperwork mattered. Another apprentice, Anne Howard, lost her indenture, and in its place the freedom archive includes a laborious note on a scrap of paper provided by her mistress, Huldah Lyford, dated 18 September [16]99:

> This is to satisfy the master of this honorall Company of Weevers that this pearson Mrs Anne Howard was bound prentice to my husband Mr Richard Lyford and to me his wife in the year 89 but Cane not find her indentor this is to Sattisfey you that Mrs Anne Howard did prove her Sellf a Honnest Servant tharfor humbly desir she may have her freedom
>
> Your servant
>
> Huldah Lyford³

This proof, the rough hand of Huldah Lyford a suggestive contrast to the status connoted by 'Mrs', was accepted. City officers, mistresses and apprentices worked together to bind girls into and around the guild's bureaucracy.

From the mid-seventeenth century onwards, the companies of London enrolled girls into formal apprenticeship with married couples and single women, most of them learning not to practice the trade of the guild but to sew. Like their male peers, they were apprenticed around the age of fourteen to sixteen and finished their contracts three to seven years later. Their enrolment may have been useful at a time when the guild system was under considerable political and economic stress and the London economy was vulnerable to the effects of war, plague and fire. It also gave a formal structure to the training and education of young women from a wide range of social backgrounds, establishing the route to a short- or long-term career in the urban marketplace. The institutional backing of

---

² Sonia Tycko, 'Bound and Filed: A Seventeenth-Century Service Indenture from a Scattered Archive', *Early American Studies* 19, no. 1 (2021): 185.
³ LMA, COL/CHD/FR/02/145 no. 24.

the companies provided a framework for women's substantial part in the textile economy, and women, like men, used apprenticeship to build networks of patronage and favour. Ann Evans's mistress, Margaret Kirkam, had been apprenticed herself, in 1688, to a man who came from her hometown in Gloucestershire.[4] She was probably trained by his wife. Her sister had taken the same route five years earlier, apprenticed to a merchant tailor who took a series of five female apprentices.[5]

Apprenticeship was also an intimate relationship. Apprentices and their mistresses were likely to be ten or fifteen years apart in age; as with servants, they lived on close terms in household and shop, with an expectation of discipline, education and good behaviour. Occasionally, their conflicts produced prolix complaints which are some of the sources for this book. This chapter argues that Margaret Kirkam and Ann Evans's experiences, from the awkward negotiation of paperwork to the life of their working household, were more common than we have known. In and outside the guilds, apprenticeship was a regular part of girls' and women's experience in the seventeenth century. It shaped the nature of women's working lives, offering more structure and contractual obligations than are generally associated with women's work; it provided intimate training and financial investment for women's businesses; it created formal, conditional relationships between women and city institutions; it was part of household and family; and it was supported by a lattice of connections between businesswomen, shopkeepers and their extended families and friends, which reached from London to the provinces and back. Indentures reflect the balance of inclusion and contingency that characterised women's relationship with the institution of apprenticeship.

The paperwork of apprenticeship enshrined, and sometimes challenged, implicit and explicit gender rules. This was not always intentional. Companies ordered their own indentures, but manuscript ones were generally created by apprentice and assistant scriveners, following formulae they had learned, and sometimes including particular clauses that mattered to families.[6] As institutional and personal documents, though, they reflected the way that early modern guilds were a prime site for regulations and contests about women's work. Despite all the uncertainties of the expanding urban economy of the late seventeenth

---

[4] LMA, COL/CHD/FR/02/103/50; *Oxford University Alumni 1500–1714*, vol. 3.
[5] LMA, GL MS 43038/17 (Sarah Kirkham).
[6] James Fisher's recent description of indentures as 'modular' is useful here: Fisher, 'Inventing a New Form of Labour: Early Indentures for Parish Apprentices, 1598–1630', *University of Exeter History of Economy Research Blog* (January 2021).

century, guild customs structured work and politics. Central to City administration, to urban politics and to labour organisation, their statutes and practices prescribed an artisanal life cycle for boys and men, to which women were necessary but marginal. Freedom also constituted the entrance to citizenship, the keystone of urban political identity, and despite the limits on women's political participation, women did sometimes call themselves citizens.

Women, Work and Guilds

Guilds were the key organising structure of urban artisans, and the nature of their impact on women's economic role has been discussed at least since the researches of Alice Clark and Dorothy George in the early twentieth century.[7] Clark saw medieval guilds as generally positive for women's work, supporting their place in an economically productive household; the seventeenth-century shift towards the market undercut the family as unit of production and edged women out. The picture across Europe has emerged, through several decades of research, as complex and variable, with the guild household as fundamentally hierarchical and unequal and women's work marginalised by guild restrictions.[8] Within the family workshop, guilds often sought to limit the tasks open to women, defining gender roles as they did so: baking small cakes, working with watches but not clocks, making sausages.[9] Ogilvie's study of the guilds of the Black Forest, who controlled agricultural as well as artisanal labour, pay and training, reveals both the full range of women's working activity and the extensive means by which guildsmen blocked their access to training, wages and licenses.[10] Guilds, Ogilvie argues, were social networks that facilitated both exclusion and exploitation. The cultural side of guild power mattered too: the integral place of the male life cycle to the artisanal ideal made the guild the civic heartland of

---

[7] Alice Clark, *Working Life of Women in the Seventeenth Century*, ed. Amy Louise Erickson (London: Routledge, 1992, first edition 1912). George's contribution to Clark's work is discussed in Tim Stretton, 'Alice Clark's Critique of Capitalism', in *Generations of Women Historians – Within and Beyond the Academy*, ed. Hilda Smith and Melinda S. Zook (London: Palgrave Macmillan, 2018). Clare Crowston's 'Women, Gender, and Guilds in Early Modern Europe: An Overview of Recent Research', *International Review of Social History* 53, supplement S16 (2008): 19–44, provides an extensive review of the field.
[8] Merry E. Wiesner, *Working Women in Renaissance Germany* (New Brunswick: Rutgers University Press, 1986).
[9] Olwen H. Hufton, *The Prospect before Her: 1500–1800* (London: Harper Collins, 1996), 92.
[10] Sheilagh Ogilvie, 'How Does Social Capital Affect Women? Guilds and Communities in Early Modern Germany', *The American Historical Review* 109, no. 2 (2004): 325–59.

male bonding. In this context, female labour could be represented as dishonourable.[11] The Dutch Republic provides an example of more flexible regulation, which did not significantly block women's significant contribution to the flourishing economy, though their work might be pushed into the informal economy.[12] In some French towns, guild privileges were specifically opened to women: Clare Crowston and Daryl Hafter have argued that the guild privileges of the old regime gave significant opportunities to women in sewing, drapery and silk work.[13]

London's guilds, in the form of livery companies, drew on many aspects of the various guild cultures of Europe, but by 1650, in a much enlarged metropolis, their power to regulate was significantly constrained. As in other towns and cities, through the early modern period, a high proportion of the male population were citizens and guild members. Most had gained the freedom of the City, and the right to trade in it, through apprenticeship in a guild. Apprenticeship lasted seven years, and at its end the apprentice was entitled to become free of both the company and the City. Some became masters who could take on their own apprentices, while others remained journeymen working for wages. All these options were, in principle, open to women, but very few girls were recorded as apprentices or became free, though widows practising as masters were much more numerous. Most of those apprenticed in guilds seem to have been sewing, making clothes and accessories or producing and finishing textiles; a few were working with food, particularly as fruiterers, one as a pastry chef. The other major areas of women's urban work – nursing, midwifery, street-selling, laundry and catering – were unlikely to come within the remit of apprenticeship.

---

[11] Merry E. Wiesner, 'Guilds, Male Bonding and Women's Work in Early Modern Germany', *Gender & History* 1, no. 2 (1989): 125–37; Jean H. Quataert, 'The Shaping of Women's Work in Manufacturing: Guilds, Households, and the State in Central Europe, 1648–1870', *American Historical Review* 90, no. 5 (1985): 1122–48; Lyndal Roper, *The Holy Household: Women and Morals in Reformation Augsburg* (Oxford University Press, 1991).

[12] Sheilagh Ogilvie, *A Bitter Living: Women, Markets, and Social Capital in Early Modern Germany* (Oxford University Press, 2003); Ariadne Schmidt, 'Women and Guilds: Corporations and Female Labour Market Participation in Early Modern Holland', *Gender & History* 21, no. 1 (2009): 170–89. Danielle van der Heuvel, 'Guilds, Gender Policies and Economic Opportunities for Women in Early Modern Dutch Towns', in *Female Agency in the Urban Economy: Gender in European Towns, 1640–1830*, ed. Anne Montenach and Deborah Simonton (New York: Routledge, 2013), 116–33.

[13] Clare Haru Crowston, *Fabricating Women: The Seamstresses of Old Regime France, 1675–1791* (Durham, NC: Duke University Press, 2001); Daryl M. Hafter, *Women at Work in Preindustrial France* (University Park: Pennsylvania State University Press, 2007).

By the late seventeenth century, apprenticeship rates were falling, and, partly because of the metropolis's expansion far beyond the City walls and also the difficulties of controlling crafts and trades, citizenship was less significant and necessary. Participation in City politics and governance continued to require company membership, but many companies had lost the capacity to control the trades whose name they bore.[14] Instead, the 'custom of London' required traders to have the freedom of the City through *any* company so Clothworkers could be cabinet-makers or flax-dressers. Hence, Margaret Kirkam is described as a member of the Barber-Surgeons' Company, who practised as a milliner. Her own master had been a Barber-Surgeon, but he could have been practising any trade, perhaps millinery with his wife. This disjuncture meant that while women could be blocked from practising weaving or tailoring, they were not excluded from the companies of that name. Access to company membership through apprenticeship, marriage and patrimony meant London women escaped some of the confrontations with guild authority that female artisans encountered in other European urban contexts, whilst keeping them within the restricted political and economic context of City custom. Guilds' basic treatment of women, both married and single, as different kinds of workers than men, with more fragile entitlements to guild protection, was still part of their corporate identity. Pragmatically, they responded to female initiatives and accommodated them, but they retained a communal tradition of deliberate marginalisation of women's work and reinforcement of patriarchal family structures. The City custom of the freedom, too, was premised on careful restriction of women's rights to trading privileges and political participation. Single women could earn it by apprenticeship, married women could use their husbands' freedom, but only men could bestow the right of freedom by patrimony to their children, or by marriage to their wives.

Across Europe, sewing was one of the crafts where guilds used symbolic and actual distinctions to exclude women. While much women's work nursing, midwifery, street-selling, victualing, laundry, catering – operated outside guilds, manufacturing textiles and making clothes was a major sector of female labour, and this was very evident in

---

[14] On London's guilds: Ian Gadd and Patrick Wallis, eds., *Guilds, Society and Economy in London 1450–1800* (London: Centre for Metropolitan History, 2002); Steve Rappaport, *Worlds within Worlds: Structures of Life in Sixteenth-Century London* (Cambridge University Press, 2002); Joseph P. Ward, *Metropolitan Communities: Trade Guilds, Identity and Change in Early Modern London* (Stanford University Press, 1997); Ian Archer, *The Pursuit of Stability: Social Relations in Elizabethan London* (Cambridge University Press, 1991).

London.[15] Seamstresses everywhere were working outside guilds and running into conflict with tailors. In early modern Istanbul, as in Wurttemberg and London, women who sewed were being told they had no place in guilds, though they persisted in asking.[16] As guilds' power and membership waned, some became more flexible. In Paris and Rouen, seamstresses established their own guilds, as did flower sellers; from 1675, Louis XIV's minister of finance, Colbert, supported seamstresses' independent organisation as a means of managing their surplus labour. In Bologna, textile guilds tried to bring previously excluded women in, hoping for membership fees and a means of labour control, but many resisted inclusion, finding marginality useful.[17] The tailors' guild of Oxford allowed widows to trade but blocked their membership when they posed a threat. In early eighteenth-century York, women joined the Merchant Tailors' Company in large numbers, composing 30 per cent of the new members.[18] There, as in Oxford, women mantua-makers and milliners were using the guild, in the words of Mary Prior, to 'insert themselves in the interstices of the changing occupational structure'.[19] In London, they were already well established in those interstices; from the mid-seventeenth century, the wives of freemen across a variety of companies, many with textile and tailoring associations, were using their husbands' freedoms to train girls to sew. While London's guild records almost invariably describe women as seamstresses and tailors like men, a few women did describe themselves as tailors, and many more, as Sarah Birt's recent research has shown, used the benefits of being in their company to establish skills and female networks.[20]

[15] Amy Louise Erickson, 'Married Women's Occupations in Eighteenth-Century London', *Continuity and Change* 23, no. 2 (2008): 267–307; Peter Earle, 'The Female Labour Market in London in the Late Seventeenth and Early Eighteenth Centuries', *Economic History Review* 42, no. 3 (1989): 328–53.
[16] Haim Gerber, 'Social and Economic Position of Women in an Ottoman City, Bursa, 1600–1700', *International Journal of Middle East Studies* 12, no. 3 (1980): 231–44.
[17] Dora Dumont, 'Women and Guilds in Bologna: The Ambiguities of "Marginality"', *Radical History Review* 70 (1998): 5–25. See also Harald Declauer and Bibi Panhuysen, 'Dressed to Work: A Gendered Comparison of the Tailoring Trades in the Northern and Southern Netherlands, 16th to 18th Centuries', in *Craft Guilds in the Early Modern Low Countries: Work, Power and Representation*, ed. Catharina Lis et al. (London: Routledge, 2017), 133–56.
[18] S. D. Smith, 'Women's Admission to Guilds in Early-Modern England: The Case of the York Merchant Tailors' Company, 1693–1776', *Gender & History* 17, no. 1 (2005): 99–126.
[19] Mary Prior, 'Women in the Urban Economy', in *Women in English Society 1500–1800*, ed. Mary Prior (London: Methuen, 1985), 147–72.
[20] Sarah Birt, 'Women, Guilds and the Tailoring Trades: The Occupational Training of Merchant Taylors' Company Apprentices in Early Modern London', *The London Journal* 46, no. 2 (2020): 146–64.

Late seventeenth-century guilds continued to assert the symbolic meanings of artisanal identity, now endorsed by Enlightenment ideas about nature and sensibility. 'Masculine sex', opined the German lawyer Adrian Beier in 1685, 'is one of the indispensable preconditions for admission to a guild. The entire social order ... is based upon each sex taking on those tasks which are most fitting to its nature'.[21] Women's responses contributed too. One petition from French seamstresses in the late eighteenth century proclaimed, 'For a long time the vulgar hands of men have held the delicate waist of a woman in order to measure it, and to cover her with elaborate clothing; for a long time modesty has been compelled to suffer the prying gaze that prolongs its regard under the pretext of a greater exactitude.'[22] The tasks of sewing could bring the division of labour into the realm of honour and modesty.

The ultimate effect of guilds' move from exclusion to conditional incorporation is, it has been argued, the increased participation of women in the labour market of the proto-industrial and industrial economy.[23] But the other side of that journey was one of constrained reward. It was increasingly hard to make a good living at sewing where large parts of the industry were becoming essentially sweated labour, nor was it easy to live off many of the other kinds of occupations in which women were clustered.

The inclusion of women in guilds had implications for the corporate identity that underpinned early modern urban communities, where a citizen was typically a freeman of a guild. The women's guilds of some French cities and towns offered an alternative to masculine corporate identity. When the Revolutionary economy threatened the seamstress guilds with abolition, campaigning writers proclaimed them the saviours of female independence and the protectors of women against the 'patrimony of weakness'. London women made no guilds of their own, nor did they engage in public conflict over tailoring and trade. Rather, companies offered them a conditional accommodation. Yet the underlying issue was the same: in Cynthia Truant's words, 'the existence of guilds*women* created a category that was both like and unlike that constructed by their male counterparts'.[24] The French comparison also brings up another

---

[21] Ogilvie, *A Bitter Living*, 97.
[22] Judith G. Coffin, 'Gender and the Guild Order: The Garment Trades in Eighteenth-Century Paris', *Journal of Economic History* 54, no. 4 (1994): 783.
[23] Ogilvie, *A Bitter Living*.
[24] Cynthia Maria Truant, 'Parisian Guildswomen and the (Sexual) Politics of Privilege: Defending Their Patrimonies in Print', in *Going Public: Women and Publishing in Early Modern France*, ed. Elizabeth C. Goldsmith and Dena Goodman (Ithaca, NY: Cornell University Press, 1995), 45–61.

point, elucidated by the work of Clare Crowston: a new model of women's work was competing with the family-based ideal of the sixteenth-century guild. This understanding of women's place in guilds as markedly different to men's represents a new approach to guild history, one that illuminates gender in the making. Crowston argues that 'women's experience in female corporations helped to propagate the notion of gender itself and the use of gender as a tool of social organization throughout the eighteenth century'.[25] The English system had no female corporations, but the relationship between guilds and their members was equally part of the apparatus of gender. The customs of London, the culture of guilds and the established institution of apprenticeship came together to form city women's specific occupational identity, and all this helped constitute what it meant to be a woman in the late seventeenth century.

The power of early modern guilds lay not only in their capacity to regulate their members but in the control they exercised over the whole world of work. Looking in more depth at two companies engaged in this project reveals the gendered control of craft in practice. While a good deal of women's sewing and textile work went unregulated in early modern London, and most London companies had lost a good deal of their capacity to regulate the crafts whose name they carried, a few companies still controlled the exercise of their craft and continued to organise searches of workshops, managed by company officials, to find and eliminate those working in the trade without guild membership or with poor workmanship. Offenders were summoned to the company court and given fines or, where craftsmanship was concerned, had their work destroyed. These were rituals that allowed plenty of room for reconciliation and pardoning; only a small proportion of fines were actually paid. Patrick Wallis, examining the search procedure in the early seventeenth century, describes these responses to illicit trading as ultimately reconciliatory, aimed at reinforcing the bonds of fraternity by re-integrating workers into the structure of discipline. That model also works well for those companies who continued their right to search in the later seventeenth century. However, it also involved a performance of exemplary justice.[26]

---

[25] Clare Haru Crowston, 'Engendering the Guilds: Seamstresses, Tailors, and the Clash of Corporate Identities in Old Regime France', *French Historical Studies* 23, no. 2 (2000): 339–71.

[26] Patrick Wallis, 'Search and Reconciliation in the Early Modern Livery Companies' in *Guilds, Society and Economy*.

Girls as Apprentices

The Weavers' Company had a long-running concern with women workers. Earlier seventeenth-century court minutes ordered women weaving to pull down their looms; by the 1660s, orders focused more on male weavers employing girls and women. Edward Sudbury appeared in 1667, confessing that he had employed a girl for seven years: he 'supposed he might do so' because she was a weaver's daughter. He was fined 3s 6d to the poor box. In the same year, Robert Harper confessed to working with two women: one 'a Sawyer's widow and a freeman of this company' and the other 'a free Weaver's wife'.[27] Despite both having some right to the freedom, both were disallowed, and he was ordered to discharge them. At the same time, the company allowed, if not encouraged, girls into apprenticeship with wives and single women: 125 were indentured between 1664 and 1706.[28] In the last twenty years of the century, at least ten women members of the Weavers' Company became free by servitude. Several went on to become free and take their own apprentices – not in weaving but in other textile occupations: the masters and mistresses of girls in the company who came to the Mayor's Court gave occupations including silk stocking seller, sempstress, periwig maker and spinner of worsted. Companies' attempts to control women's work in their own trade was, it seems, quite separate from their willingness to enrol girls into their guild, as long as they were not actually on the looms.

The Broderers' Company exerted a more direct control over women workers. Most of them still practised embroidery, and even after the Restoration, the company retained the right to search the workshops of embroiderers outside their company, insisting on company membership and fines and penalising poor workmanship in the guild tradition of public rituals of destruction. The company by-laws had forbidden female apprentices in 1609, but girls were being apprenticed to the company by at least the later seventeenth century, and the Mayor's Court occupational listings suggest most were working in embroidery rather than other crafts.[29]

A good half of those caught up in the search of workshops in the 1680s were female, working with other men or women. They included Anne Tires, caught working illicitly 'at her mother's at the Punchenello in Hedge Lane': she was then admitted into the company as a journeywoman at the cost of £1 17s. Several women had actually been apprenticed in the company and were still working at the trade. However,

---

[27] GL, MS 4655/4 ff. 31v, 36, 40. [28] Ward, *Metropolitan Communities*, 136.
[29] Christopher Holford, *A Chat about the Broderers' Company* (London: G. Allen, 1910), 271.

even when they were married to Broderers, the court required evidence of their apprenticeships to allow them to practice. Dorothy Holmes was caught by searchers in 1689, 'found at work on a Cap, not being sworn'; the cap was removed, her husband appeared at court on her behalf and alleged she had served an apprenticeship, but since she could not prove it, she was fined 40s for unlawful working. Here, having the evidence of an apprenticeship was critical. Mary Rons 'alleged she served an Apprenticeship to Joseph Slovey of this company but not being able to make it appear was fined for unlawful working 40s'. Mary Ingley, wife of a pinmaker in Playhouse Yard, Whitecross Street, 'made it appear by certificate and otherwise that shee had served her time': she paid 17s for her oath and the spoon that marked her company membership, and a fine of 6s 6d because she had not been bound at Broderers' Hall. Three years later, she was examined for keeping a work house without being qualified, and paid more fines to be allowed to employ other workers.[30] Grace Smith, wife of a cloth-drawer and Broderer in Leather Lane, convinced the court that she had served an apprenticeship, and paid 17s to be allowed to work, another 8s to be admitted to run a work house and 20s in lieu of providing the traditional masterpiece, the evidence of craftsmanship demanded of masters. The court also ordered that her daughter Mary be bound to her as an apprentice. This investment established Smith in her trade, and a few years later she appeared again, her husband now dead, taking another Broderer's daughter as an apprentice.[31] In this case it seems that Grace Smith's husband, a cloth-drawer, was not embroidering, but she took up the trade under the mantle of his company affiliation. At the lower end of the scale of participation in the trade, another woman accused of unlawful working confessed that she was 'Apprentice to the Apprentice of Mary Wade sempstresse who did not worke imbrodery'. She had only done one piece of work and promised to bring her husband to be bound over on oath that she would not work at the trade again.[32]

Most London companies had ceased attempting to control the practice of their trade, but the Broderers, like the Merchant Taylors, were making serious endeavours to continue their monopoly. Their acceptance of women's separate trades was accompanied by a routine incorporation of husbands' joint responsibility and their capacity to provide a company affiliation for their wives. Some women also pleaded to be let into the Broderers after apprenticeship in other companies, suggesting that this

---

[30] GL Ms 14657/1, 7 September 1686; 3 September 1689. These work houses involved clusters of journeyers working under a supervisor and were common amongst pinmakers as well.
[31] GL Ms 14657/1, 7 September 1686; 13 July 1690. [32] GL Ms 14657/1, 29 July 1686.

was one of the companies for whom membership served an important purpose for women in the trade as well as a qualification to work. In 1681, Anne Mathew had been apprenticed to Thomas Blair and his wife in the Cooks' Company, which she had duly completed; in 1692, she petitioned that she was a broderer by trade and requested to be admitted to the freedom of the Broderers, 'paying a small fine she being very poor, and can scarce maintain herself'. It seems likely that Thomas Blair's wife had trained her apprentice in embroidery.[33] The company let in a number of seamstresses in the 1690s alongside Mathew, suggesting that embroidery was sometimes part of the seamstress trade.

Other women drew on their fathers' company membership to gain permission to work: William Rawson, a girdler in the company, appeared at the court with his wife, Elizabeth, who was sworn in on the basis of being the daughter of a broderer.[34] The numbers of women who had no evidence of their apprenticeship (the Broderers kept good records themselves) or who had been sworn outside from the Hall indicate the potential extent of unrecorded female apprenticeship, which considerably expands the numbers in guild records.

At issue for the Broderers was both unlawful working and poor craftsmanship, and women were accused of both. At one point a group of women who had already been granted the right to work as journeywomen were questioned again for the quality of their work, the issue eventually settled by a court resolution.[35] The ultimate sanction for poor workmanship was a long-established guild tradition of ritualised destruction. By the late seventeenth century, this was unusual but still held over transgressors as a threat, and the details indicate some of the goods on which women were working. In a search in 1689, a stomacher was removed from Elizabeth Penneer and 'cut and defaced'; a holster cap, part of an embroidered saddle, that Elizabeth Vandallen was working on suffered the same fate. Elizabeth Dodson, also working on saddlewear in Paul's Alley, by the Cathedral, had 'a housing and two crowns' judged as bad. The embroidery of the housing was defaced, but the velvet and crowns were returned to her undamaged 'in charity'. Charity was part of the company's power.[36] In 1681, the widowed Margaret Wadding had 'two pieces of Brodered works for petticoats' confiscated in a search judged 'insufficiently wrought'. They were ordered to be cut and burnt, but upon her 'humble request' and 'promise not to worke any more (being an unlawfull worker)', the court contented itself with fining her 2s 6d and

---

[33] LMA, COL/CA/05/01/0004 (1694).
[34] GL, Ms 14657/1, 7 September 1686.
[35] GL, Ms 14657/1, 12 March 1687/8.
[36] GL, Ms 14657/1, 3 September 1689.

returning her work.[37] Elizabeth Coleman, less fortunate, had her work destroyed and was fined 40 shillings for being 'one who imployed and taught persons to work being not quallified or authorised by the Ordinances of the Company'.[38]

The process of confiscation, assessment, being summoned and dealt with deployed a visceral, material damage to expensive fabric and labour, and it brought women to the Broderers' Hall to reiterate a responsibility for regulation that in most guilds by this point was fictive. In the eighteenth century, embroidery emerged as a craft of gentility and, eventually, a mark of femininity.[39] But in the late seventeenth century, women were working as supervisors of the trade and labouring in the work houses that produced, amongst other goods, the very emblems of the guilds. For City women, embroidering was a marketable skill, the stuff of work houses as well as parlours. The endeavours of the company to regulate women's use of it provide a significant contrast to the apparently easier integration of women into other companies where they practised a craft distinct from the company name. Searching and punishment can be seen as integrative rituals, and, as such, they performed an important task for gendered labour relations, asserting that women's work could be legitimised and insisting on the importance of guild regulation for them. At the same time, women were apparently especially likely to fall foul of searches, suggesting that embroidery was one of the contested areas in which women were working without formal training. The nature and location of women's work made it particularly vulnerable to the disruption and humiliation of a search and destruction, reinforcing precarity.

London's guilds operated so distinctively that their history offers no straightforward contribution to the debate over the gains and losses of guild regulation for women's work. But their distinction between the property of being a guild member, and the occupation of practising a craft, can help us unpick the layers of exclusion and marginalisation that determined women's experience of artisanal work. London companies became particularly accustomed to keeping women out of artisanal crafts whilst allowing them into the guilds to practice the few acceptable occupations allowed to them. The custom of London meant company membership functioned as a gateway to city life: women could achieve it through marriage, apprenticeship or patrimony. But both practice and paperwork problematised their relationship to the freedom and to companies.

---

[37] GL, Ms 14657/1, 25 October 1681.   [38] GL, Ms 14657/1, 31 December 1681.
[39] Rozsika Parker, *The Subversive Stitch: Embroidery and the Making of the Feminine* (London: I. B. Tauris, 2012).

London's Female Apprentices

Tracing London's female apprentices is an archival challenge. Despite the London livery companies' reputation as a haven for male exclusivity, women's part in company life has been long established, but it has been obscured partly by the habitual erasure of women's work, as well as the masculine identity elevated by guild clerks and masters.[40] Much historical work on London's guilds tends either to champion the narrative of a particular company or to pursue a global economic history of the effects and extent of the regulative powers that waxed and waned in guilds' hands between the medieval and the modern period. Recent work on apprenticeship as training provides a more socio-economic context, which makes a good comparison for the profiles of girls in apprenticeship.[41]

Guild records themselves abet the project of suppression. Guilds and companies were deeply self-conscious record keepers; their archives were part of their culture, and the routine inscriptions as well as the marginalia and doodles helped constitute the world of each company, bound up with self-representation, with the exclusion of the marginal and illicit and with the celebration of predictable routines and solid history. The story that women were 'illegal workers' was part of the fable that guilds told themselves and the City, increasingly so in the seventeenth century as their capacity to regulate waned. Married women shared in their husbands' freedom, taking apprentices both through their name in marriage and on their own, as 'consorts' in widowhood. They attended some ceremonies and feasts; the Drapers' Company ordered a 'handsome fretwork ceiling' for the room called the Ladies' Chamber.[42] But in many guild records, the evidence of women's active roles is hidden. Young women feature purely symbolically, in rituals and imagery. The Mercers' Maiden, played in their pageants by a young girl, was modelled in stone and wood inside and outside their properties, her face still present in

---

[40] On apprenticeship generally: Peter Earle, *The Making of the English Middle Class: Business, Society, and Family Life in London, 1660–1730* (London: Methuen, 1989), 85–105; Joan Lane, *Apprenticeship in England, 1600–1914* (London: Routledge, 1996); Christopher Brooks, 'Apprenticeship, Social Mobility and the Middling Sort, 1550–1800', in *The Middling Sort of People*, ed. Christopher Brooks and Jonathan Barry, (London: Macmillan, 1994), 52–83.

[41] Ruben Schalk et al., 'Failure or Flexibility? Apprenticeship Training in Premodern Europe', *The Journal of Interdisciplinary History* 48, no. 2 (August 2017): 131–58; Chris Minns and Patrick Wallis, 'Rules and Reality: Quantifying the Practice of Apprenticeship in Early Modern England', *Economic History Review* 65, no. 2 (2012): 556–79.

[42] Drapers' Company, MB 15 f.22v.

Figure 2.2 Lucy Maes's indenture. The adaptations to this engraved form have been made more gracefully than in Figure 2.1.
London Metropolitan Archives (City of London).

corners of the City, and she was engraved on their most elaborate indentures (Figure 2.2). The Barber-Surgeons' Company regularly paid 'young maids' 30 shillings to strew flowers on the way to church on the day their company officials were elected.[43]

Recent work has taken a productively forensic approach to recontextualising women in London guilds. Helen Smith for the sixteenth century and Paula McDowell for the seventeenth and eighteenth have reconstructed the quotidian roles of women in the Stationers' Company.[44] The established custom of widows taking over businesses after their husbands' deaths suggests a less obvious history of trades that might be jointly run through the marriage. Wives, mothers and daughters were

---

[43] Sidney Young, *The Annals of the Barber-Surgeons of London* (London: Blades, East & Blades, 1890), 416.

[44] Helen Smith, *'Grossly Material Things': Women and Book Production in Early Modern England* (Oxford University Press, 2012); Paula McDowell, *The Women of Grub Street: Press, Politics, and Gender in the London Literary Marketplace 1678–1730* (Oxford University Press, 1998).

part of the community of Stationers. Women's work, Smith argues, sustained the guild and constituted a 'material subtext' to printed books. It was core to the social reproduction that civic ritual involved: women attended corporate banquets, paid towards livery dinners, cleaned the hall and its tableware and left bequests to the company. As recipients of pensions and charitable gifts, they provided testament to corporate generosity.[45] This illuminating focus on the paperwork of the guild provides a means of excavating not just the visible traces of women but the less visible labour that they contributed to households and workshops.

Beside the symbolic image of the Mercers' Maiden on Lucy Maes's indenture (Figure 2.2) lay the evidence of a more active female role: a girl who apprenticed herself and later became free of the City, taking her own apprentice. One hundred years earlier, company officials professed themselves unsure whether such an arrangement was possible. The Draper's Minute book for 14 March 1569 recorded a discussion about it, after a meeting at which the wardens and masters were viewing the company lands and dining at the Bishop's Head in Lombard Street, along with the assistants and the auditors of the accounts. 'Before they went to dynner', the clerk noted, 'a question was moved to Mr Dummer whether a mayden servannt willing to be bounde apprentice to a master and mistres for terme of yeres might not be presented in our hall and also inrolled in the Chamber of London as other apprentices ar and thereby to enjoye also the fredome of the Cytie'. William Dummer, whose wife was a silkwoman, confirmed it was possible; there were precedents going back more than 100 years, and girls should take the same oath as boys and receive the same indentures, including the clause forbidding marriage. (In later years, this clause was often deleted in girls' indentures.) However, the man who had tried to bind a girl, Mr Calverley, had already been refused, for the master and wardens 'had not seen the Lyke heretofore'.[46]

If this forgetting looks ideological, it may also reflect a reality in sixteenth-century practice. Between 1480 and 1600, many London guilds recorded no female apprentices at all. Earlier records suggest higher numbers: between 1350 and 1480, around 10 per cent of the apprentices in administrative records were female.[47] The most

---

[45] Smith, '*Grossly Material Things*', chapter 3.
[46] Drapers' Company, MB VIII, f. 97, also explored in Lena Cowen Orlin, *Locating Privacy in Tudor London* (Oxford University Press, 2010), 294.
[47] Stephanie R. Hovland, 'Girls as Apprentices in Later Medieval London', in *London and the Kingdom: Essays in Honour of Caroline M Barron*, eds. Matthew Davies and Andrew Prescott (Donington: Shaun Tyas, 2008), 179–94. It is not clear that all these apprentices are in guilds.

convincing explanation offered for this apparent collapse is the shift in labour supply caused by the Black Death in the late fourteenth century. In the immediate aftermath, with a decimated labour force, girls had more economic heft and autonomy, but once the labour market recovered, they were no longer encouraged into artisanal apprenticeships, losing access to the relative economic power that came with a marketable skill.[48] Even in this relative 'golden age', though, apprenticeship offered women a modicum of economic status but no political power. The most organised of medieval London's female workers, the silkwomen, flourished outside, not within, the guild system, repeatedly petitioning for protection from competition but never becoming a guild.[49] Well before the end of the sixteenth century, the silk trade was largely out of women's hands.

From 1600, there are a few more records of girls being apprenticed in the larger guilds, but the real increase there comes in the era that saw guilds moving away from tight occupational control, enabling both male members and their wives to practice not just different trades to their company title but also separate ones. At the same time, many guilds were still largely identified with the occupational categories of processing textiles, making clothes and selling them. Where occupations are listed, most female apprentices in companies were bound to men involved in making and selling clothes, and their wives were likely to be working in the same or a related trade. They would always have trained girls: what changed in the seventeenth century was a gradual and piecemeal move towards the use of formal apprenticeship.

While London's leading companies were slow to enrol girls, in the sixteenth century, girls were being apprenticed in other English and Scottish towns, and in London on the margins of the companies. Urban guilds like that of Bristol recorded small numbers of girls, where they were around 3 per cent of apprentices in the mid to late sixteenth century. Many were apprenticed to both domestic service and textile or clothing work. They were distinguished from boys by having their bindings recorded in full in the town apprenticeship books: as in London later, there was a separate routine for girls.[50]

---

[48] Caroline Barron, 'The "Golden Age" of Women in Medieval London', *Reading Medieval Studies* 15 (1989): 35–58.

[49] Maryanne Kowaleski and Judith M. Bennett, 'Crafts, Gilds, and Women in the Middle Ages: Fifty Years after Marian K. Dale', *Signs* 14, no. 2 (1989): 474–501, and more on silkwomen in Orlin, *Locating Privacy*.

[50] Ilana Krausman Ben-Amos, 'Women Apprentices in the Trade and Crafts of Early Modern Bristol', *Continuity and Change* 6, no. 2 (1991): 227–52; Susan E. James,

From the 1650s, female apprenticeship appeared more regularly in London's livery companies. The dislocations following the Civil War may have prompted clergy and artisan parents to find training opportunities for their daughters as well as their sons. The Clothworkers had already been registering girls as apprentices through the 1630s and 1640s, as had the Merchant Taylors; the Drapers and Goldsmiths now joined them, with girls such as Martha Lancashere, a clergy's daughter from Loughborough, in 1655, and Hester Sneade and her sister, daughters of a Bristol draper.[51] Notably, the clerk recording the first girl apprenticed in the Drapers' Company, in 1635, described her as 'filius' (son) before amending the word to 'filia' (daughter). Many of this first generation were the children of artisans in the textile and tailoring trade themselves, though their connections were not company-driven: very few girls were apprenticed into their fathers' companies, though a few were bound apprentice to their own mothers. Between 1650 and 1700, the Drapers' Company listed ninety-four new female apprentices, the Clothworkers seventy-three and the Goldsmiths fifty-three. Very few of those girls, though, became free at the end of their contracts – only one in nine of the Drapers' apprentices were freed, compared to an average of around one in three of male apprentices. In the Mercers' Company, closely tied to the Royal Exchange where many women ran shops, the pattern was different: at least five of the nineteen girls who were recorded as apprentices between 1670 and 1700 took the freedom.

Already this suggests widely varying career patterns for apprentices. Some of this reflected their backgrounds. By the 1650s, England's apprenticeship market attracted the middling sort and gentry, as well as aspiring rural and artisanal youth, particularly in the grand London companies.[52] Young women from gentry and clergy backgrounds were part of this trend; their move into occupational training reflected a general shift in the social identity of gentry families, whose impact on girls has yet to be observed. The money their parents derived from land was used to invest in training them for the market and providing a productive skill as well as a means of making a good living inside or, increasingly, outside marriage. For the girls in the Mercers, around 40 per cent of whom had fathers described as gentry or clergy, apprenticeship in a City company also had a good chance of leading to full company membership as freewomen. Numbers of girls were still minute compared to boys. In most companies, percentages of registered

---

Women's Voices in Tudor Wills, 1485–1603: Authority, Influence and Material Culture (Abingdon: Routledge, 2015), 107–10.

[51] Jessica Collins, 'Jane Holt, Milliner, and Other Women in Business: Apprentices, Freewomen and Mistresses in The Clothworkers' Company, 1606–1800', *Textile History*, 44, no. 1 (2013): 72–94.

[52] Brooks, 'Apprenticeship, Social Mobility and the Middling Sort, 1550–1800'.

female apprentices hovered at less than 1 per cent in the second half of the seventeenth century but increased in the 1680s and 1690s to 2–5 per cent: the increase in female apprenticeship was small but noticeable, and it was very sharply linked to the particular circumstances of the 1680s onwards. It was particularly marked in two larger companies associated with tailoring and clothes-making: the Merchant Taylors and the Haberdashers. Here the proportion of girls in lists of apprentices stood at 4–5 per cent in the 1680s and 1690s, increasing steadily from the 1660s, with the size of the company meaning that twenty to twenty-five girls were apprenticed in a year. In the Broderers, a similar pattern prevailed, though here the parents of the female apprentices were much more likely to be gentry than those of the boys. In companies like these, female apprenticeship was attracting gentry and clergy daughters, who accounted for nearly half of the intake, alongside urban and provincial artisans' and yeomen's daughters.

Alongside these girls, there were two guilds with a strikingly different pattern, where girls and boys took up apprenticeships in equal numbers: the Glovers and the Pinmakers. These take us into the world of lower-status labouring women. Pinmakers were at the bottom end of the labour market, where wages and premiums were low and goods were laborious to produce. The Pinmakers' Company was also relatively new, having been established in 1636; there was no impetus to control the entry of girls. Pinmaker apprentices, at the end of their contracts, did not take the freedom but were explicitly admitted as journeywomen, working for masters or mistresses. They represent an entirely different world from those who became Drapers or Clothworkers. None were the daughters of gentry, and two-thirds of them came from the riverside south London parishes, Southwark and Bermondsey, where pinmakers' workshops were located. Premiums were universally low, typically 5 shillings. Apprenticeship for these girls may have been residential, but it was unlikely to involve migration: they worked near their birthplaces.

The Glovers, who also had high numbers of female apprentices at least in the late seventeenth century, had a different pattern again. The limited apprentice records that survive show that over half the apprentices of the late seventeenth century were female, increasing to 60 per cent by the end of the 1670s; about ten were enrolled annually but three or more times that were not enrolled. In the rural southwest of England, glovemaking seems to have been women's work.[53] In London, the girls apprenticed often went on to practice the trade as journeywomen and seem to have retained a firmer link to it than the boys, who sometimes

---

[53] Jane Whittle and Mark Hailwood, 'The Gender Division of Labour in Early Modern England', *Economic History Review* 73, no. 1 (2020): 3–32.

became free and went on to practice other occupations. By the eighteenth century, the girls have disappeared from the apprenticeship lists: women's glovemaking had moved out of the company realm. Gloving has a long history of gender division, with men cutting and women sewing the glove together, but this distinction seems not to have been in place in the seventeenth century. In the London workshops listed in the quarterage records, women and men worked together in groups of between two and twenty workers: in April 1676, Mrs Katherine Clowes had working for her Kaleb Anton, Oliver Platt, Widdow Legg and Margarett Turner.[54]

Girls in the Glovers were socially a step above those in the Pinmakers. Like the pinmakers, they were often Londoners, with 60 per cent coming from London or Middlesex, but more of them (partly because they were based in the City) had fathers who were citizens – 18 per cent – and a few, 4 per cent, had gentry origins. Like the pinmakers, many later became journeywomen, and while some men became masters, almost no women took the freedom and became mistresses in their own right, though some widows did. A journeywoman's career could last through her marriage. Elizabeth Crawley was bound in 1668 to John Greene, completed her apprenticeship and married Jonas Tyler. She was eventually admitted as a journeywoman in 1679. By then, her master had died, his wife had remarried and then died, and Elizabeth's apprenticeship had to be certified by the surviving widower of her mistress.[55]

Companies like this with a continuing occupational identity might have a very distinctive gender profile, quite different from the companies which apprenticed girls as seamstresses with no reference to the company name. This was particularly marked in the late seventeenth century, when female apprenticeship was emerging as an option at both ends of the occupational spectrum. The potential for apprenticing daughters was increasingly part of the perspectives of gentry, yeomen, tradesmen and artisans alike. Some of these gentry daughters were apprenticed to couples who themselves had origins in the provincial gentry, clergy or professions. Others went to London artisans whose roots were in the City. In the shifting social landscape of the later seventeenth century, work for women with training and recognition was one of the many strands of gentry and middling social identity and family strategy.[56]

---

[54] GL, MS 4591/1, p. 41.   [55] GL, MS 4591/1, p. 183.
[56] Brooks, 'Apprenticeship, Social Mobility and the Middling Sort, 1550–1800', 52–83; Craig Muldrew, 'The "Middling Sort": An Emergent Cultural Identity' and Henry French, 'Gentlemen: Remaking the English Ruling Class' in *A Social History of England, 1500–1750*, ed. Keith Wrightson (Cambridge University Press, 2017), 290–309 and 269–89.

The Glovers and the Pinmakers also reveal the importance of training for plebeian London girls, who would graduate not to being free but to being waged journeywomen.

So far, these estimates of the scale of female apprenticeship in London's companies have been drawn entirely from the company registers. But there is other evidence, which suggests those records are strikingly incomplete even for company apprentices. In the Mayor's Court archive, nearly 200 suits to dissolve girls' apprenticeships survive from the late sixteenth and seventeenth centuries. This, too, is an incomplete record, but it is exceptionally revealing. Nearly all the female apprentices at the Mayor's Court were indentured to members of City companies, but many of them made no appearance in the company registers. Most cases were sued on the grounds of non-enrolment, the failure to register the apprenticeship with the City Chamberlain, suggesting that they were always intended to be a somewhat flexible arrangement, or that enrolment was strategically delayed, but most boys were at least in the company membership books, while the girls were not. Seventy-five per cent of the male apprentices who used the Mayor's Court to sue out their indentures were listed in the company archives. For girls, the opposite was true: 80 per cent of the young women whose apprenticeships were dissolved through law do not appear at all in the records of the appropriate company, and without this archive, their apprenticeships would have left no record at all.[57]

It is unsurprising that girls were less likely to reach the formal record than boys. London and guild custom imposed limits on apprentices per master, and since freemen's wives had to take apprentices in their husbands' names, their apprentices might reduce the husband's capacity to take more boys; however, very few of the masters here took apprentices in such numbers. In some cases, masters registered their male apprentices and not the female ones who may have been working with their wives in a related or separate trade, suggesting a further distance between married women and the company as institution. In many cases, though, the unrecorded girls were apprenticed to households who never took or recorded male apprentices either: in households like this, women had an apprenticeship business, while their husbands did not. None of the Drapers' female litigants were registered with the company, and none

---

[57] Michael Scott, ed., *Apprenticeship Disputes in the Lord Mayor's Court of London, 1573–1723* (London: British Record Society, 2016), using the project's underlying data kindly shared by the authors. Of 103 girls who appear in the Mayor's Court litigation to dissolve their contracts, and whose companies have searchable records, 79 are not recorded in the registers, across companies including the Clothworkers, the Drapers, the Goldsmiths, the Grocers, the Haberdashers and the Plaisterers.

were enrolled with the City as they should have been; they were working with mistresses in millinery, sempstry, upholstery and silver spinning. One master in the Drapers' Company, Ferdinand Gunter, had a male apprentice registered but not the two girls who sued for their premiums. The Haberdashers' Company, strongly associated with female apprenticeship, was better at recording girls, with a third of those who sued at the Mayor's Court appearing in the apprenticeship registers. Goldsmiths, and further down the company ranks Grocers and Stationers, were likewise poor at recording their female apprentices, much better at recording boys.

This omission from the record has significant implications for girls' use of the freedom: if they were not enrolled, they could not become free, trade in their own right and be mistresses themselves. The failure to enrol was meaningful in itself, suggesting girls were marginal to paperwork and formal procedures. It was precisely this question that was raised at the Drapers' Company dinner. The issue was not simply whether a girl could be an apprentice to a freeman and his wife, but also whether she 'might not be presented in our hall and also inrolled inth Chamber of London'. It was these two steps, being presented at the hall and enrolled with the Chamberlain, that were missing for the vast majority of apprenticed girls in the late sixteenth and early seventeenth centuries. Thus, they could be trained, or part-trained, but they could be easily released from their contracts – an advantage if marriage was on the cards – and they did not have the privilege of freedom that a properly enrolled apprentice would have had.

The Mayor's Court archive does not allow us to extend this picture back to the earlier sixteenth century, but this habit of apprenticing girls outside the company may also mean that the drop in female apprenticeship after the medieval 'golden age' has been exaggerated. The records for every available sample are incomplete; what we learn from the seventeenth century is that the chancy relation between apprenticeship and its record is distinctly gendered. This returns us to the persistent issue of the erasure of women's work from the record. Economic coverture had the result of concealing not just wives' work but a whole other structure of training.

The evidence of the Mayor's Court transforms the broader landscape of female apprenticeship. Many of its lawsuits are missing from the archive. Those that do survive add a considerable number to the formal lists. Since Mayor's Court cases involved failed contracts that led to litigation, they are only a small proportion of the girls who started apprenticeships. Of the girls who *were* recorded in company records, 3.3 per cent also appear in the Mayor's Court, and a similar proportion applies to boys; if we assume that proportion is replicated amongst *all* female apprentices, it gives us an overall figure of a minimum of 140 girls taking up apprenticeships in the City each year. It also increases the proportion of girls being apprenticed to freemen and women in particular companies. The Mayor's Court cases have a slightly higher proportion of female apprentices (2 per cent) than company records generally, and individual companies have markedly different profiles. The ratio of girls to boys in the court records is noticeably higher for the Haberdashers' and the Drapers' Company than it is in the company records.[58] Young women may be over-represented in litigation to dissolve contracts, or there may just have been many more girls than were registered.

The Mayor's Court girls, that cohort who was typically left out of company registers, had distinctive demographic characteristics. More of them – around half, compared to a third in companies – came from London and Middlesex. Nearly 40 per cent alone were from the City. The same was not true of boys, where London-born apprentices were equally represented across both sets of data. Conversely, the Mayor's Court girls were less likely to come of gentry parents.[59] The parents of London girls were butchers, weavers, tobacco pipe makers, mariners and cabinet makers; those from outside London were clerks, yeomen, husbandmen and tradesmen. The purpose of the court process at this level was to achieve a conclusive dissolution of apprenticeship: perhaps Londoners were more likely to ensure that both parties were formally freed from their obligations. The difference in figures is so considerable that it suggests a whole missing cohort of London apprentice girls. These are, of course, only the ones whose apprenticeships terminated early, their contracts lasting between three and five years before being dissolved and resolved through the court. Like the girls in company lists, most were involved in making and selling clothes, but the Mayor's Court records provide a much fuller sense of mistresses' occupations, and their details suggest that this is what the girls were actually learning: of 150 women with their own named occupations, there were 35 sempstresses, 14 button-makers, 9 fruiterers, 8 milliners, 8 lace-makers of various kinds, flax-dressers, coat-sellers, fringe-makers, a coney-wool cutter and a physic-herbwoman. Patrick Wallis has shown that apprenticeships were intentionally flexible, and girls' absence from the formal record despite

---

[58] Nearly four times as many for the Haberdashers and twice as many for the Drapers from 1650 to 1700.

[59] Company figures come from the companies whose data is digitised on ROLLCO and from Cliff Webb's London Apprentice Abstracts digitised on www.findmypast.co.uk. 16 per cent of the Mayor's Court girls had gentry parents compared to 23 per cent in ROLLCO and LAA.

Girls as Apprentices

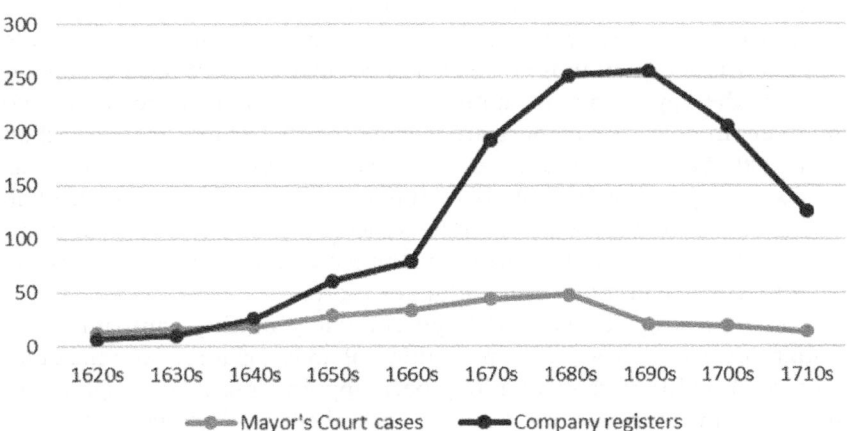

Figure 2.3 Numbers of female apprenticeships. Data as previously, excluding companies with partial coverage. Note the Mayor's Court cases represent failed contracts only.

being bound under the custom of the City suggests contracts that were both binding and somewhat unofficial.

Finally, the Mayor's Court offers a different chronology for the growth in female apprentices. Companies' records suggest female apprenticeship rose somewhat in the 1640s, doubled in the 1660s and leapt between 1670 and 1700, falling again in the 1710s and collapsing in the 1780s (Figure 2.3). The Mayor's Court records, including those girls who were not enrolled with companies, suggest a broader, longer context for girls' apprenticeship. In contrast to the sharp increase in girls in the company records, it received a steady flow of lawsuits through the seventeenth century, tripling after the mid-century. In the first half of the seventeenth century, there were as many girls in court over female apprenticeships from all the companies as there were in the ten company registers that have been digitised. In the guild records, there are very few girls at all before 1640, but at the Mayor's Court, they constitute around 2 per cent of apprentices suing to dissolve their indentures both before and after 1640. There was a history of girls apprenticed to company women long before the later seventeenth century; they were simply not being enrolled in company records.

In companies such as the Clothworkers' and Drapers', between 1600 and 1640, none of the apprentices who dissolved their contracts at the Mayor's Court were recorded in the appropriate guild records, suggesting a whole missing sector of girls apprenticed to freemen and their wives but not recorded by the company. By the mid-century, there is some overlap between the two, and the Mayor's Court figures include a small percentage of those recorded in company lists. What's changing, then, is the appearance of apprenticed girls in company records. The numbers in company records are volatile, partly because they are small and partly because of the influence of livery company culture and networks amongst company members. It may be that the Mayor's Court line on the graph in Figure 2.3 is more reflective of the actual changes in female apprenticeship than the company records: it triples in the 1660s–1670s, rather than increasing tenfold or more.

This data suggests that girls' apprenticeship in City companies was both more extensive and less intermittent than is apparent from the guild records. London parents had long been apprenticing their daughters to women and couples with company membership, but without being enrolled or registered they would not have been entitled to become free in their own right. Apprenticeship for these girls was a training that led them to become journeywomen or to bring their skills into marriage. The Haberdashers', Clothworkers' and Merchant Taylors' Companies look particularly significant; one of the earliest girls whose case appears in the surviving Mayor's Court archive was Millicent Pickard, a goldsmith's daughter who was apprenticed to John and Elizabeth Waules in the Haberdashers' Company in 1574, leaving four years later.[60] The Clothworkers' Company recorded only one girl in its pre-1645 apprenticeship records, but between 1611 and 1644, eleven girls apprenticed to clothworkers appeared in the Mayor's Court to dissolve their contracts. Assuming that only a small proportion used the court to end their contracts, as was the case later in the century, the actual numbers of apprentices in the company might have been around seven times that number. Between 1600 and 1640, forty-nine cases from girls survive in the (incomplete) Mayor's Court records. Over half were from London and Middlesex; only three were the children of gentry. All were registered to couples, and their occupations were mostly seamstresses, bonelace makers and button-makers.[61] In the artisanal and citizen families of early modern London, apprenticeship for girls was already familiar; it was the companies who were ignoring it. Other records of apprentices support this evidence of a wider practice of apprenticeship amongst citizens and their wives that was not recorded by guilds. A scrivener's waste book from early seventeenth-century London lists notes of at least

[60] Scott, *Apprenticeship Disputes*. [61] Scott, *Apprenticeship Disputes*.

fifteen girls for whom indentures were drawn up between 1614 and 1617. They included apprentices to citizens, yeomen and artisans, both inside and outside the City, bound for between five and twelve years. All were apprenticed to couples, some with specific direction to be taught by the wife; the most specific was for Suzan Stallard to a Stationer's wife to be taught to sew, make bands and learn the art of a spinster for eight years. The contract was not recorded in the Stationers' records.[62] The longest contract was for twelve years, in which Joyce Clark, a husbandsman's daughter from Walthamstow, was apprenticed to Richard and Alice Fox in the Drapers' Company. They were to provide meat, drink and clothes, but this was an exceptionally long, and apparently poor value, apprenticeship.

Several of these girls were contracted to be paid wages that increased over the apprenticeship. Margaret Stone, apprenticed for eight years to a cook (though this may not be what she learned) was to be paid from 20 shillings the first year up to 30 shillings for the last five.[63] From the start, they were expected to provide more labour than they gained value from their mistresses' teaching. None paid premiums to learn, though some had contracts which prescribed their parents to provide the first two or three years' worth of their clothes. Critically, despite their mistresses having the right to the freedom through their husbands, they did not themselves have the potential to become free because they were not registered with companies or the City. These apprenticeships were not meant to be a route to independent shopkeeping in the City, unless young women went on to marry freemen. But they did offer the security of guaranteed employment for several years, and young women without the freedom could trade outside the City, in Westminster and elsewhere in Middlesex.

Over the course of the seventeenth century, more girls were apprenticed and more girls were formally recorded by guilds. Very few of these contracts survive, and there is no detail of whether they paid premiums or were given wages. The shift, after 1640, towards enrolling them into City companies seems to have come from a particular confluence of factors. The first was the Civil War. Between 1640 and 1650, there is a slight increase in girls being apprenticed, both at the Mayor's Court and in the guild records. The 1640s are the first decade where the guild registers record girls entering apprenticeship in any noticeable numbers. No one company led the way; between 1644 and 1650, where there are records, girls can be found in the Brewers, Cooks, Fishmongers, Blacksmiths,

[62] TNA, Ward 9/351 (12 September 1614), with thanks to Lucy Munro.
[63] TNA, Ward 9/351 (April 1615).

Drapers, Grocers, Clothworkers, Mercers, Turners, Skinners, Tallow Chandlers and Fruiterers. A third of these girls came from London, the daughters of artisans and citizens in lesser companies. Most of the rest were the daughters of yeomen or of provincial tradesmen ranging from a waggoner to a brewer. None were explicitly apprenticed to train as seamstresses; their mistresses and masters' occupations are only occasionally recorded and include spinning, flaxwoman, broderer, buttonmakers, silver and gold spinners and a confectioner. The effects of civil war in London shrank the economy, affecting trade and consumer spending; apprenticeship overall was down by a third.[64] In this climate, it seems likely that women were encouraged to initiate new businesses and to take or become apprentices.

The next factor bringing girls into City apprenticeships was probably the aftermath of the Plague and Fire in 1666. Plague deaths hit London and its suburbs heavily; the Fire emptied the City. The City of London responded by offering freedoms free of charge to those who tenanted the empty shops. It was from the 1660s, too, that the Royal Exchange shops, rebuilt, drew in more female tenants. Both the legal records and the guild records show female apprentices doubling between the 1640s and the 1660s. These new entrants came increasingly from gentry backgrounds, a shift from the girls of the earlier era and from clergy families. For provincial gentry, apprenticeship was an increasingly popular family strategy, which brought their sons into the urban hierarchy. The girls who became apprentices seem to have been part of the same plan; some had brothers apprenticed around the same time.[65] A quarter of the girls apprenticed in the larger companies from 1660 to 1700 had gentry parents, twice as many as their male peers. In all companies, the majority of girls were the children of provincial and urban artisans, farmers, sailors and yeomen. A quarter came from London, and another large portion from the south east. While the connections that brought young people to London are hard to trace, the proportions of gentry parents are noticeably higher for those from further away, like Cornwall and Yorkshire; these are parents who probably already had London connections. As well, as gentry proportions increased and the textile trade developed, shopkeeping was more frequently referenced in the record, with occupations such as 'exchangewoman' and 'sempster' appearing long before the development of mantua-making brought more women into fashionable sewing. The expansion of the market for accessories and ready-made

---

[64] Ben Coates, *The Impact of the English Civil War on the Economy of London, 1642–50* (Aldershot: Routledge, 2004).
[65] Brooks, 'Apprenticeship, Social Mobility and the Middling Sort, 1550–1800'.

garments brought more women into company apprenticeships, many of them connected to the Exchange: 'exchangewoman' was an occupational category in itself. Apprenticeship extended into the lower end of fashion work, too: Elizabeth Burgis, daughter of a ship's carpenter in Wapping, was apprenticed to a fringe-maker in 1679.[66]

The increase in entrants to apprenticeship and the increasing chances that they would be registered with a company marked a shift in aspirations: girls who were formally enrolled by the companies, unlike those with unofficial apprenticeships, had a chance of becoming free by their servitude, giving them the right to trade in the City in their own names. Many did not do so, but the opportunity was there. Freedom was not noticeably correlated to status: gentry girls were no likelier to take it up than those from other backgrounds. Rather, this shift was a cumulative development. Girls were apprenticed in clusters, sometimes with several in one year or at one company court meeting. Word of mouth helped make female apprenticeship popular and presumably also ensured that it was increasingly properly recorded. The peak in freedoms came around the same time as that in apprenticeships, with double the numbers freed in the 1680s compared to the 1670s. The 1700s saw a fall again, suggesting that the move of the dress trade away from the City, the collapse of the Royal Exchange shops and the waning power of guilds made freedoms for seamstresses less necessary.

The expansion of female apprenticeship and the move towards freedom also reflected another change: a few apprenticed girls were becoming free and taking apprentices themselves, continuing to work as single women. The generation who matured in the 1640s were likelier than their elders to never marry, and the growth and growing visibility of single women, able to take apprentices, in the later seventeenth century may well be another factor in the development of female apprenticeship in the companies, as it seems to have been in some French guilds.[67] Two of the first single women to graduate from apprenticeship into freedom, apprenticed in the late 1660s, were Sarah Bonwick, daughter of a Surrey gentleman freed in 1676, and Rebecca Deards, a grocer's daughter from Bedfordshire freed in 1679. Both took their own sisters as their first apprentices, suggestive of the incorporation of family networks into the structures of apprenticeship. This was the beginning of longer careers: ten years later, both were running shops in the Royal Exchange. In less prestigious companies, women like Elizabeth Harris in the Weavers' Company, the daughter of a gardener, were also taking the freedom.

[66] Scott, *Apprenticeship Disputes*.   [67] Crowston, *Fabricating Women*.

The bigger increase came in the 1680s and is apparent both in livery companies and at the Mayor's Court. The growth of the Exchange, many of whose shopkeepers were company members, was one influence here; across London, too, seamstresses were extensively employed in sewing the expanding range of accessories and headwear, as well as, eventually, mantuas. Girls' apprenticeship peaked in the 1680s and the 1690s, before dropping in the 1710s. By this point, more of the Mayor's Court girls were properly registered in companies, suggesting that more were joining formally with the chance of freedom and shopkeeping. Those girls who were properly enrolled were markedly more likely to come from gentry backgrounds: around a quarter of those in guilds, compared to 11 per cent of the largely unrecorded girls at the Mayor's Court. Gentry birth, and to a lesser extent a birthplace outside London, was directly linked to a greater likelihood of formal registration with a guild, although not noticeably with becoming free. A simultaneous decrease in male apprenticeship across most companies may have made them keener to have girls enrolled and paying fees. By the end of the century, as we will see in Chapter 6, a number of women were petitioning to be allowed to trade as freewomen despite having improper indentures or not being enrolled with the City. At the same time, the numbers of male apprentices were dropping; companies were probably keener to incorporate all apprentices and their fees. The fall in female apprenticeship in the 1700s reflects the clothes business generally shifting towards the West End and Covent Garden, where company membership was not needed; however, throughout the eighteenth century, a steady stream of young women continued to join the companies, and the take-up of freedoms actually increased in the mid-eighteenth century.[68] The late seventeenth century was an exceptional moment for companies: it re-established a foundation of apprenticeship and freedom for girls, which persisted into the nineteenth century and underpinned the indentures of the oldest trained seamstresses today.[69]

The relationship of female apprentices to companies thus had two strands to it: artisanal identity and company association. The two overlapped but were far from identical. Companies with large numbers of practising tailors, drapers or coat-makers had more female apprentices, but other companies, such as the Goldsmiths, also had particular associations with female apprentices and mistresses. Girls, like boys and men,

---

[68] Figures based on ROLLCO.
[69] I'm grateful to members of the audience of a talk at Guildhall Library for sharing memories of their own indentures.

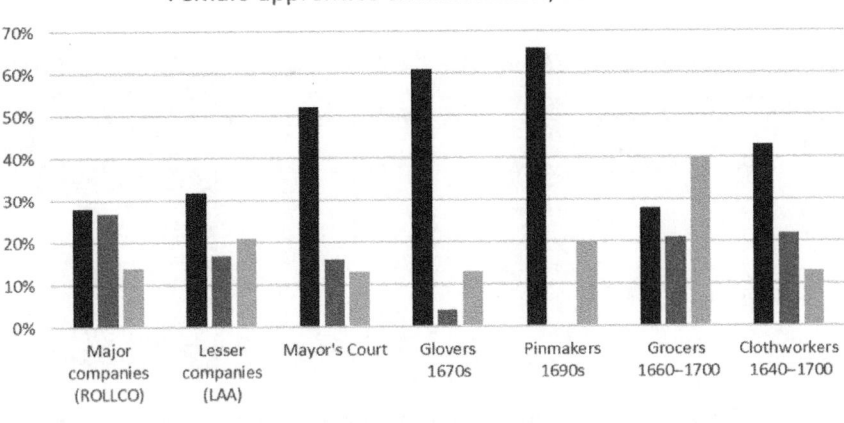

Figure 2.4 Characteristics of female apprentices, 1660–1700.

were acquiring the habit of a company property – an affiliation to a livery company that reflected status and networks, not their trade.

Figure 2.4 shows some of the features of girls recorded in different companies and contexts. The two largest groups of girls came from gentry families across England and from artisanal backgrounds in greater London and the City. There was a marked difference between those recorded in company records and those who were recorded only in lawsuits; we have already noted that the latter were more likely to be Londoners, suggesting an established tradition of London girls who had not been indentured through the company. In most companies, though, the majority of girls had migrated from elsewhere in England. The home counties of Kent, Buckinghamshire, Hertfordshire and Essex accounted for many; others came from further away, such as Oxfordshire or Leicestershire. Nearly as many came from Yorkshire as from Essex, both from villages and from towns like Leeds, Bristol or York, which had their own seamstress opportunities. London had its own pull. For many girls, this journey was a long and lasting trip away from their birthplaces. Others, from gentry families with property or legal reasons to be in London, had not left their parents and siblings so far away.

Social backgrounds differed across companies. The lesser companies had a lower proportion of gentry parents, who seem to have aimed for the Mercers, Drapers and similar; correspondingly, they had a slightly higher proportion of London artisans. Companies differed in the proportion of single mistresses taking female apprentices, but with little relationship to

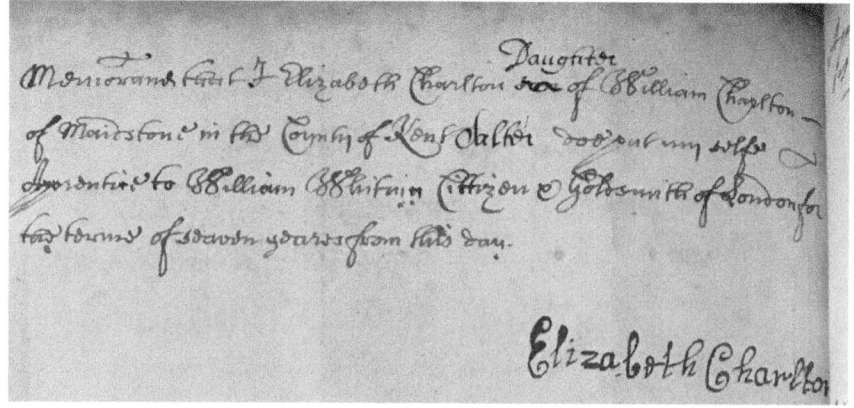

Figure 2.5 Goldsmiths' Company Apprenticeship Book 3, p. 193.
By permission of the Goldsmiths' Company.

their status: in both the elite Grocers and the plebeian Pinmakers, large proportions of their girls were apprenticed to single women. Most were able to sign their names. Margaret Kirkam was typical in signing clearly when she was apprenticed, as well as when she became a mistress to Ann Evans. In the Goldsmiths' Company, where apprentices signed their entries in the membership books, most of the girls joining in the late seventeenth century signed, some with particular elegance. Elizabeth Charlton, apprenticed in March 1691 (Figure 2.5), gave a studied signature that contrasted with the error of the Goldsmiths' clerk who, out of habit, had written son rather than daughter.

Amongst those apprentices who were from artisanal backgrounds, while there are very few guild links between parents and their daughters' mistresses, there is some evidence of connections between parental trades and the decision to apprentice a daughter into sewing. About a third of daughters had parents in the clothing trades; however, this was reflective of occupational patterns as a whole. The Haberdashers and Merchant Taylors were especially well Represented. Less predictably, the Barber-Surgeons were too. Here, the likelihood that wives would be practising a separate trade to their medical husbands might have encouraged them to apprentice their daughters, but barber-surgeons also needed to know how to stitch.

The strength of guilds was in their potential for networking and patronage, but for women the connections that established and furthered their working lives were often found elsewhere. William Whiting and his wife took five girls and no boys as apprentices; two came from Kent, but the first, in 1667, was a cousin. The most obvious ties were those of sisters. Turning sibling ties into apprenticeship contracts offered both a training to the younger and a means for both girls eventually to work together with freedoms of their own, through the company link originally established by the elder's apprenticeship. Miriam Colman, daughter of a Hertfordshire yeoman, was apprenticed to Ann Simpkins in the Drapers' Company in 1671. In 1682, she took her sister Anna as an apprentice, and three years later another young woman: sisters were typically the first apprentice. Apprentices themselves also might be indentured alongside their sisters, occasionally to the same person but rarely or never to different people in the same company. Mary and Deborah Chamberlain, daughters of a Hertfordshire gentleman, were apprenticed to a Grocer and a Broderer in 1693 and 1700. Rebecca, Sarah and Mary Deards were apprenticed in turn from 1670: Rebecca to Anne Terry, Mary to Rebecca and Sarah to Thomas Bromhall.[70] The ties that bound apprentices were those of kinship, family and friendship; guild membership was largely incidental.

Despite this apparent lack of company affiliation, different guilds do seem to have encouraged different patterns. Table 2.1 shows the differences between individual companies, both in the proportions of female apprentices and their careers. Everywhere except the Pinmakers and the Glovers, girls were fewer than 7 per cent of the apprenticeship cohort, but in most companies their numbers increased in the last two decades of the century. The proportions that went on to take the freedom varied more noticeably. The differences between companies are compounded by the numbers of masters and mistresses who took multiple apprentices so that what looks like a trend may only be three or four prolific households. In the Drapers, although only two or three female apprentices were recorded annually, one in seven took the freedom; comparable figures for boys were around one in three. The Mercers, with still fewer apprenticed girls, had six of twenty-one becoming free, but fourteen of them were bound to just three masters, and the freedoms were clustered amongst them. By the 1680s, a third of the single mistresses taking on girls in those companies had been apprenticed themselves. Perhaps relatedly, very few of their apprentices appeared in the Mayor's Court over broken contracts. In other companies, like the Clothworkers and the Goldsmiths, fewer than five of the fifty or so apprentices over the last twenty years of the seventeenth century became free. The most decisive factor in encouraging take-up of the freedom seems, not surprisingly, to

[70] All in ROLLCO.

Table 2.1. Proportions of female apprentices

Company	Number of female apprentices	Percentage of female apprentices	Girls apprenticed to masters/mistresses who took more than one girl	Apprentices freed (min)	Girls apprenticed to mistresses
Major Companies (Drapers, Mercers, Clothworkers, Goldsmiths and six other companies) 1650–1700	372	1.45	140 (37%)	30 (8%)	81 (22%)
Mayor's Court cases 1640–1700	194	2.16	n/a	n/a	25 (13%)
Goldsmiths 1680–1700	41	2.2	26 (63%)	2 (5%)	10 (24%)
Salters 1680–1700	28	3	16 (52%)	1	5 (17%)
Drapers 1680–1700	42	2.6	14 (67%)	6 (14%)	10 (22%)
Clothworkers 1650–1700	73	0.79	21 (28%)	3 (4%)	17 (23%)
Haberdashers 1660–1700	265	3 (estimate)	5/50 (10%)	27 (10%)	9/50 (18%)
Broderers 1679–1700	27	5.71	11 (41%)	0	5 (18%)
Merchant Taylors 1674–96	185	5 (estimate)	74 (40%)	6 (2.7%)	41 (22%)
Glovers 1675–79	105	52	29 (27%)	0	13 (12.76%)
Pinmakers 1690–1700	54	43	16 (29%)	0	12 (22.2%)
Grocers 1680–1700	73	2	38 (52%)	3 (4%)	30 (40%)

have been the footing that the Mercers and Drapers had in the City's drapers and milliners' shops, especially at the Royal Exchange. Mistresses in the Clothworkers, whose occupational listings are amongst the most detailed, included embroiderers, button-makers, periwig-makers and fruiterers, along with seamstresses and milliners, but their apprentices seem to have gone on to work either for wages or outside the City, and they did not have the same large, leading apprentice-taking households as the Drapers.

For the provincial gentry who made up such a strong constituency of apprentice parents, family strategy was a key factor in determining girls' careers. William and Mary Hulls took a series of apprentices, including two with a long connection with them: Deborah and Ann Whinnick were two of the eight children of William Hulls's uncle, Robert Whinnick, a Westminster victualler who had died in 1685 when they were small children. Robert Whinnick's will planned for all his children 'as they grow up and capable of service' to be 'placed out apprentices to such decent trades such as their genius leads them or to such as my Executors shall think fitt and convenient'. The costs of binding and placing them out, along with their education and maintenance, were to come from rents from the property he requested his investors to buy with £700 raised from his estate. Another £50 each was to be put towards setting them up in business when their apprenticeships were out. No distinction was made between the three boys and five girls, and there was no mention of marriage portions. Robert's widow received £15 a year as long as she remained unmarried. William Hulls was one of his executors, and this must have led seamlessly to taking the girls as apprentices twelve years later; he left money to one of them, and to her brother, in his own will in 1708.[71]

Other families made more explicit plans for apprenticeship for their daughters. William Dugdale, Warwickshire antiquarian and royal herald, did so using the connections that brought him frequently to the City, where he used the Tower of London archive and wrote a history of St Paul's. His wife and children's parts in the deliberations are less visible. Dugdale's first son was apprenticed to a surgeon. Around 1656, his daughter Helen started a London apprenticeship with the Exchange shopkeepers Katherine and Herbert Allen, becoming free of the Haberdashers' Company in 1663. He bound another daughter, Lettice, to their London kinswoman Judith Dugdale, who had completed her own apprenticeship in the Girdlers' Company, and Lettice took her

---

[71] TNA, PROB 11/381/169 (1685); PROB 11/504/279 (1708).

freedom in 1669 and took a shop in the Royal Exchange. Helen, Lettice and two other daughters married men of the New or Royal Exchange: apprenticeship helped bind them into City networks. It was not, in Dugdale's view, a successful choice. In his will, he described Helen's husband as 'one Fitzpatrick an Irishman woorth nothing': nonetheless, he charged his older grandson to supply her with her needs if she was 'in great want', taking advice from Helen's older sisters. Lettice had married Bruyn Radford after her apprenticeship, but she too was regarded as shiftless: £20 a year was to be employed for her maintenance, 'provided allwayes that shee shall have noe power to challenge any parte thereof ... lest trusting to her owne management thereof shee should through improvidence wastfully consume it'. William Dugdale provided for Lettice's children too, recollecting that he had been 'at noe small charge' in their breeding and education, 'and have already placed the two elder of them [a boy and a girl] out to apprentice'. He also provided for the last girl, Anne, and finally for his other granddaughter Margery,

> that when shee comes of age whereby she may be fitly put out to apprentice if in my life time she be not soe disposed of that shee be placed to some sufficient seamstresse in the City of London for the term of seaven years and so much money given with her as shall be requisite for her Instruction in that trade and maintenance with food and rayment and all other necessaryes during that terms.[72]

Apprenticeship may have advanced Dugdale's daughters, but marriage put them back; still, he retained faith in a seamstress's training, or perhaps saw no better option, for his granddaughters.

Apprenticeship was not an alternative to marriage, but it helped lay the foundation for adult life when marriage was typically late and a high proportion of women remained single. The decrease in female apprenticeship in the later eighteenth century coincided with a fall in marriage ages and a lower proportion of women never marrying.[73] At the same time, it is increasingly clear that marriage itself was a gateway to a wider variety of work, particularly in areas with specialised industries.[74] Training in sewing and running a shop was as likely to be useful for wives as well as for single women.

---

[72] TNA, PROB 11/382/415 (1686), Will of William Dugdale; *Le Neve's Pedigrees of the Knights* (London: Harleian Society, 1873), 319; Mercers' Company, Gresham Repertories 1669–76, p. 5 (1670).

[73] K. D. M. Snell, *Annals of the Labouring Poor: Social Change and Agrarian England, 1660–1900* (Cambridge University Press, 1987), 311.

[74] Alexandra Shepard, *Accounting for Oneself: Worth, Status, and the Social Order in Early Modern England* (Oxford University Press, 2015), 13.

Girls as Apprentices

The minutiae of apprenticeship contracts reflected this. For urban boys, apprenticeship and freedom was the route to becoming a master and a husband, and their indentures included a clause forbidding 'fornication or matrimony', keeping them single until their training was done. Those who married inappropriately early were fined, might have their contracts dissolved and could not become free without petitioning the Aldermen.[75] The barrier to marriage was economic dependency. Girls' indentures treated the ban differently, either deleting the clause or, in handwritten ones, leaving it out. The result was a contract that was not invalidated by having sex or marrying early. This was not so much a suggestion that marriage (or fornication!) during apprenticeship was acceptable, as a recognition that the prohibition had different meanings for girls. Marrying in service would, in theory, put a girl under two masters. 'Our law freeth a maidservant when she is married from her master's covenant', noted William Gouge in 1622.[76] In New World servitude, as Jennifer Morgan shows, colonial authorities argued that a woman who married under indenture had two masters and punished the women who became pregnant whilst indenturing their children. The marriage ban long established in apprenticeship, extended to women, thus became a gateway to the exploitation of indentured and enslaved women's 'dual labours', reproductive and manual.[77]

Contemporaries were well aware of the differential impact of such rules on young men and women. In 1602, a barrister, recording London customs, noted, 'If a man prentice in London marry, he shall be forced to serve of his time, and yet loose his freedome. But yf a woman prentice marry, shee shall onely forfayte hir libertie, but shall not be forced to serve.'[78] Male apprentices were forbidden from marrying on penalty of losing their freedom; women marrying while in apprenticeship lost their access to the freedom but could not be forced to complete their contract. At this point, almost no girls were recorded in London companies' apprenticeship registers, yet the customs applying to apprenticeship in the city more broadly were understood as affecting both sexes. Removing the matrimony clause encouraged girls and their parents to see apprenticeship as no obstacle to marriage, and it suggested that prioritising apprenticeship over marriage was wrong for girls and right for boys.

---

[75] Lane, *Apprenticeship in England, 1600–1914*, 170.
[76] William Gouge, *Of Domesticall Duties: Eight Treatises* (1622), 664.
[77] Jennifer L. Morgan, *Laboring Women: Reproduction and Gender in New World Slavery* (Philadelphia: University of Pennsylvania Press, 2011), 76.
[78] *Diary of John Manningham: Of the Middle Temple, and of Bradbourne, Kent, Barrister-at-Law, 1602–1603*, ed. John Bruce (London: J. B. Nichols & Sons, 1868), 12.

Like the matrimony clause, the habit of apprenticing seamstresses (particularly those at the Royal Exchange) for five rather than seven years created a separate model for girls. In this case, it apparently cut young women off from access to the freedom, prioritising shorter terms of service (often with correspondingly more costly premiums), perhaps reflecting less time needed for skills acquisition and an expectation of earlier liberation for marriage or more independent work. One young apprentice, Hester Hudson, apparently insisted she would not be bound for more than three or four years.[79] There were ways around the freedom's rules. When Katherine Venner and her master and mistress, Herbert and Katherine Allen, went to arbitration over her broken apprenticeship in 1662, Katherine's representative (a gentleman from her home county of Warwickshire) said she intended to 'take a shop and deal for herself'. Leonard Bates, a City scrivener speaking for the mistress, replied, 'she could not do so, her time being not out ... nor being free of this city'; Venner's representative said she had planned to trade in someone else's name. Katherine Venner had already gone to work with Hester Wright as partner, but Hester had had a five-year contract herself and was not free, so the shop was in her brother's name. Her deposition explained,

Katherine is in the shopp with her this deponent as her freind to assist her in the managment of her trade of a sempstrice in the royall exchange London but ... is not there in hir owne right either as proprietor of the shopp or goodes or any parte or parcell thereof nor hath she any manner of interest or propriety in the said trade & stock either as partner or otherwise howsoever but that the same shopp stock & trade ... doth solely & properly belong & perteine to this deponent's Brother.[80]

The word 'brother' was inserted at the end. Freedom was somewhat negotiable, and short contracts had advantages for both sides, but the result was that just as women were establishing themselves in shops, girls were being encouraged to contract themselves under conditions that disqualified them from the freedom that would enable them to trade in their own name.

Outside the guilds, rules were somewhat looser but predicated on some basic understandings of labour, reward and discipline. Even in London, not all apprentices had even a nominal relationship to the guild system, and in the wider area of the metropolis, where guild membership was not necessary to trade, apprentices were bound through private arrangements. Both the West End and the poorer dockside areas of

---

[79] LMA, CLA/024/05/72 (1654).   [80] LMA, CLA/024/05/131A (1662).

East London had girls apprenticed as seamstresses, button-makers and, at the poorer end, pipemakers. The fullest evidence for these apprenticeships comes from petitions to the Middlesex and Westminster sessions. Their apprenticeships often followed the same rule of seven years, though contracts of four and five years were also common. The prominence of mothers in their petitions suggests many young women had been propelled into apprenticeship by the loss of their fathers, indicating the fragility of female-headed households as well as the potential of apprenticeship to offer a future. The apprenticeship system brokered by Christ's Hospital, which catered for the children of freemen, offered a similar set of opportunities, placing girls almost entirely with mistresses, half of them single and the other half married but working, often, in their own occupations.[81] Apprenticeship offered a route for poorer girls out of the precarity of losing a male parent, and it did so through connecting girls to a wider world of working women. But orphanhood was not the primary push into apprenticeship. In London's companies, the majority of apprentices in companies had fathers who were still alive. In companies from the Glovers to the Drapers, and from farmers' and artisans' daughters to gentlemen's daughters, fewer than a quarter had fathers recorded as 'deceased'. The prompt for apprenticeship came from elsewhere: even gentry girls did not, it seems, require the death of a father to need to train to earn their own living.

The tax records of the late seventeenth-century City make it possible to fill out this picture of young women's work and domestic lives. So far we have looked only at guilds, but the economy of apprenticeship was a much wider one, in London as well as outside it. Girls, like boys, were apprenticed by parishes (where their numbers were equal to those of male apprentices, unlike in guilds) and privately to masters and mistresses with no guild membership. Tax lists include a much wider range of apprentices, and the majority of girls described on them as apprentice are not in company records. Across the range of households and social ranks, girls in apprenticeship were part of a common system whose understanding of girls as contracted workers in training is important for our understanding of what it meant to be female in the City.

In 1695, assessors for the newly introduced Marriage Duty listed the taxable inhabitants of every parish, grouped by house. The returns for London provide a unique seventeenth-century record of houses and their inhabitants. For all their flaws and inconsistencies, they offer us an image

---

[81] Erickson, 'Married Women's Occupations'.

of living households, better described as housefuls.⁸² Brackets, lines and gaps offer at least a partial picture of the various 'units' that composed a houseful: married couples, their children, servants and apprentices; lodgers; other relatives; and other families. The size and flexibility of London houses offered a variety of settings for residential apprenticeship, and girls' living arrangements fell into some clear patterns. Some of these houses were also shops, but many women were sewing for shops elsewhere or working in shops apart from their houses. Their apprentices must have gone with them, so residential apprenticeship was a base rather than a contained workshop.

The household listings are predictably inconsistent in recording apprentices and servants, reflecting the subjective concerns of the inhabitants who took on the task of making the list. Some parishes do not list them; others give their names but no status; many do not distinguish between servants and apprentices. Parishes with more detailed records can convey some sense of the scale of female apprenticeship. The large parish of Christ Church by Newgate, on the edge of the City, listed 169 male apprentices and 15 female apprentices. This already gives a proportion of girls much higher than those in companies – more like 8–9 per cent than the 1–5 per cent in company records. Female apprentices are still demonstrably under-recorded. Martha Sherrock, daughter of Richard Sherrock of Newgate Street, had been apprenticed to Thomas Raban, a barber-surgeon, in 1691. In 1693, she was living with Thomas and Susanna Raban, their two children, another apprentice named Henry Cheney and two other men, probably lodgers. The Rabans had had their children in the 1680s and started taking apprentices afterwards. In 1701, three years out of apprenticeship, Martha Sherrock took up the freedom of the City.⁸³ Her family must have been nearby while she trained in Raban's household, unlike the other apprentice in the house who was from Cambridgeshire. The Rabans' own son became an apothecary, but Martha was probably learning to sew from Susanna, as was the case with other barber-surgeons' wives. The connection between surgery and seamstry would fit well with Sandra Cavallo's picture of the clusters of 'body-work' occupations in early modern Italy.⁸⁴ Henry Cheney was

---

[82] Mark Merry and Philip Baker, '"For the House Her Self and One Servant": Family and Household in Late Seventeenth-Century London', *The London Journal* 34, no. 3 (November 2009): 205–32.
[83] LMA, COL/CHD/LA/04/09, p. 45; COL/CHD/FR/02/163, no. 105.
[84] LMA, COL/CHD/FR/02/172, no. 22 (Henry Cheyney); TNA PROB 11/583/233, will of Thomas Raban; the 1692 Poll Tax describes Raban as a barber. Sandra Cavallo, *Artisans of the Body in Early Modern Italy: Identities, Families and Masculinities* (Manchester University Press, 2007).

listed as an apprentice, but Martha was not. Both had been indentured with the same types of document, and both took the freedom, but perhaps the assessor's eye was fixed on the barber-surgeon's apprentice and not the business of his wife. Other apprentices in the parish of Christ Church were better recorded. Martha Cottage was the apprentice of Mary Southin, lodgers in a house with a large family and two other single women; Lidia Weatherfeild, a twenty-one-year-old Londoner, was apprenticed to a married couple who also lived with another single woman, perhaps a servant; and Martha Jones was apprenticed to a widow, with whom she lived alone.[85]

These young women reflected the variety of forms of apprenticeship that characterised early modern England. Skilled apprenticeships attracted premiums and were used by families entering, or already part of, the middling sort: gentry, yeomen, clergy and citizens with membership in trade and craft guilds. Some girls were apprenticed through guilds, and many more were indentured privately with a wide range of premiums. Paupers and orphans were bound by the parish or by hospitals with minimal premiums and learning housewifery and a variety of textile crafts. The parishioners appointed as assessors made no differentiation between types of apprentice. They treated it, rather, as a status that defined both life stage and work identity, and this is a useful insight for the idea of apprenticeship, from paupers to gentry, as a national and metropolitan system. The numbers of female apprentices in the household listings suggest that the apprenticeship of girls was familiar and well established in the city. Girls at work were not only domestic servants but craftspeople in training.

The household listings of 1695 reveal some distinctive patterns of girls' living arrangements. Most male and female apprentices lived in relatively large households, with a mean total inhabitants (including children) of eight; the average size of all households was between four and five. London households had a distinctive pattern, well established by demographic historians: they had fewer children than those outside the city and often included lodgers; their mean number of inhabitants was noticeably larger than elsewhere, reflecting the way that houses could contain multiple families and units, many with no obvious 'head of household'.[86] Within these households, girls in apprenticeship tended to live either in medium-size family units, with a couple and often one or two other apprentices or servants, or, in a pattern unique to girls, alone

---

[85] LMA, COL/CHD/LA/04/9, p. 17, 65.
[86] D. V. Glass, *London Inhabitants within the Walls 1695* (London: London Record Society, 1966); Merry and Baker, '"For the House Her Self and One Servant"'.

with a single mistress. The experience of apprenticeship was not necessarily, as it was almost always for boys, one of learning to fit into an artisanal or mercantile household run by a married couple: it also exposed girls to the more diverse, non-nuclear living arrangements of the single women who headed 15 per cent of the city's households.

The female apprentices recorded in the 1695 tax listings lived in household units that ranged in size from just two people to fourteen. At the small end, eight of the eighty-two girls identifiable as apprentices lived alone with a mistress, either in one house or as lodgers in a bigger houseful. These mistress–servant dyads mostly involved women with no known company affiliations; freewomen tended to have larger households, as wives or sometimes with other single women. One in three of the female apprentices of 1695 were the only apprentices or servants in their household. This solitary service was typical of girls with female mistresses, common for girls apprenticed to married couples. In contrast, boys are never found in households with single men, whose living and working arrangements did not generally have room for an apprentice. Female apprenticeship, with the premiums and labour it brought in, actively supported the autonomy and survival of spinsters in the City.

Most girls lived in bigger households, with couples or single mistresses, alongside other apprentices and servants. At the other end of the scale in the same parish, Mary Mapleton lived with a wealthy merchant couple, their four children and eight other servants, apprentices or lodgers. A more modest but equally extensive houseful included the apprentice Anne Wallin, two married couples with their children, two pensioner widows with children, another widow, a woman servant and a male lodger. It's not clear which of them was Anne Wallin's mistress.[87] Company records show mistresses and couples taking on female apprentices infrequently and alone; household records of the wider range of apprenticeship show a context in which female apprenticeship was more common and more companionable.

Another sharp distinction marked the living arrangements of girls and boys in apprenticeship. Male apprentices generally lived in households that also employed female domestic servants; female apprentices often did not. In the Cheapside parish of St Margaret Lothbury, a small, wealthy community, all but five of the sixty-six households with apprentices (male or female) had servants as well. Only one of the girls identifiable as company apprentices lived in a household with no servant: generally, skilled apprentices with premiums were well protected from

[87] LMA, COL/CHD/LA/04/9/2,3.

domestic labour. Company apprentices also tended to live in bigger households with a variety of other servants and apprentices. Hannah Kelsey was apprenticed to a chandler's widow, and they lived with her son, a maidservant and three bachelor lodgers. Jane Child lived with her merchant master and his wife, their four children and two other girls who may have been servants or apprentices. James and Abigail Allen, members of the Skinners' Company, headed a household including a manservant and three girls described as maids, of whom at least one was actually a company apprentice. They lived in the same house as a physician, his wife and their two servants, in the parish of St Mary Woolchurch. Another composite household in St Mary-le-Bow included Samuel Blanckley, a barber, and his wife, Katherine; Elizabeth Wood, Mary Dracott and John Peddyham, apprentices; a lighterman and his wife; a coal-seller and his wife, Jacob and Lettis Mold; and Mary Cole, a maidservant, who, by all appearances, was serving the whole house.[88]

The majority of female apprentices' household units were less well served than this. Two-thirds had no servant alongside the apprentice, suggesting they were either apprenticed into housewifery or, as in Bristol, expected to do housework as well as learning a craft. This was particularly marked in the generally poorer parishes outside the City walls, where fewer than one in five units with female apprentices had servants listed as well; these were households, often outside the remit of the custom of London, that were less likely to be supporting company apprentices. Some of these units were lodgers in larger housefuls, but in others there is no sign of a servant.[89] In the Redcross Street precinct of St Giles without Cripplegate, just outside the walls, none of the discrete households with female apprentices had servants as well. Amongst them, Anne Todd and Elizabeth Miners lived with the Pawling family, Hannah Corner with the Ridgelys and Rachel Calver with Elizabeth Clarke. Some of these girls were paupers, like Elizabeth Alphage, named after her parish.[90] There is less evidence for these apprentices that they were learning to sew: Elizabeth Hunt, for example, apprenticed to a victualler and his wife alongside a cookmaid, might have been engaged in cooking.[91] Recent research has shown how far female servants' work ranged outside the domestic; here we see an opposing trend, of

---

[88] LMA, COL/CHD/LA/04/19/31; 61/4; 70/3; 62/3.
[89] Profiles calculated from LMA, COL/CHD/LA/04 and Philip Baker, Mark Merry and Gill Newton, *People in Place: Families, Households, and Housing in London, 1550–1720* [data collection]. UK Data Service. SN: 5791.
[90] LMA, COL/CHD/ LA04/107D.   [91] LMA, COL/CHD/ LA04/73/13.

apprentice girls being expected to practice both commercial production skills and domestic labour.[92]

Their households are a reminder, too, of the city's diversity. No black apprentices are recorded, but black women had already worked with and as seamstresses in London. One of them was Mary Fillis, from Morocco, servant to a seamstress in East Smithfield at the end of the sixteenth century.[93] In 1731, an ordinance from the Lord Mayor prohibited 'Negroes or other Blacks' from being bound apprentices in City Companies, suggesting either anticipatory prejudice or that black apprentices had indeed been enrolled with freemen to learn trades. Company apprentices were not likely to be immigrants, parish apprentices perhaps more so, but they lived alongside adults and children from diverse backgrounds, noted in passing. Elizabeth Griffen was apprenticed to Charles and Katherine Daniel, who also cared for 'Nunis a jews child' in Carr Yard, by Grub Street. In St Botolph without Aldgate, Francis and Katherine Wood's family shared their house with 'A blackmoore woman her husband at sea' and 'Sarah her child'. The casual erosion of proper names for these London inhabitants leaves only a hint of the nature of neighbourly relations: did the man who recorded his parish's population really not know the black woman's name, and what understanding of belonging persuaded him that noting her as black was more important than providing her name? The two 'Jamaica girls' in one household were the white daughters of the island's chief justice: their origins, perhaps evident in clothes, manners or voice, were noted in the same way as skin colour and religion.[94]

---

[92] Charmian Mansell, 'Beyond the Home: Experiences of Female Service in Early Modern England', *Gender and History* 33, no. 1 (2021): 24–49.

[93] Miranda Kaufmann, *Black Tudors: The Untold Story* (London: Simon & Schuster, 2017), 6.

[94] LMA, COL/CHD/ LA04/103/136, 62/6. Other 'Negroes' are listed in Glass, *London Inhabitants within the Walls*, 332.

3   Managing the Trade: Women as Mistresses

Ann Bell and Dorothy Stable

In the seventeenth century, the prefix 'Mrs' in manuscript and print documents stood for Mistress. It denoted not necessarily a wife but an established woman of means, skilled or a manager of servants or apprentices.[1] In a society with extensive life-cycle service, managing employees was typically part of adult women's life experience. That role has social and relational implications, as well as economic and labour significance. The relations between mistresses and servants offer revealing insight into the power dynamics between women in a patriarchal system.[2] In the world of apprenticeship, though, we encounter a set of unusually formal contracts between adult and adolescent women, which structured their social and economic relations, and a mode of being a mistress which was entirely different to the masters in guilds and companies.

In the records of seventeenth-century guilds, it is rare to be able to trace a woman's career from apprentice to mistress herself. Most women who trained girls had not been formally apprenticed, and there is rarely any record of what happened to apprentices after their time was out. Ann Kent was an exception. Daughter of a yeoman couple from Newport Pagnell, Ann came to London in 1681 and was apprenticed to a widow of the Clothworkers' Company. She started to train as a seamstress, but within a year, she left her position, with the flexibility that was common amongst early modern apprentices, and married. Her husband, Giles Bell, also a yeoman's child, had just become free of the Goldsmiths' Company, and with his freedom both of them could trade freely in the

---

[1] Amy Louise Erickson, 'Mistresses and Marriage: Or, a Short History of the Mrs', *History Workshop Journal* 78 (2014): 39–57. 'Mrs' was also used for young women of means.
[2] Marisa J. Fuentes, *Dispossessed Lives: Enslaved Women, Violence, and the Archive* (Philadelphia: University of Pennsylvania Press, 2016); Laura Gowing, 'The Haunting of Susan Lay: Servants and Mistresses in Seventeenth-Century England', *Gender & History* 14, no. 2 (2002): 183–201.

City, taking apprentices in his name. With the foundations of a household of his own on the horizon, he signed up his first apprentice, Isaac Finch, two weeks before marrying Ann.[3] Eight months later, in March 1683, Ann and Giles Bell took another apprentice, this time a girl whom Ann would teach to sew: Dorothy Stable, one of the older daughters of an alderman from Pontefract. Her father was a gentleman, and the apprenticeship register recorded her, unusually, as 'spinster', possibly suggesting her social status was worth noting. A family friend, Ann Huetson, an old friend of the Stable family, helped make the contract. Dorothy brought with her a premium of £20. Ann Bell was already pregnant, and four months later she gave birth to a daughter, who died at just two days old.[4] The suspicion of pregnancy evidently had not impeded Ann's plans to train a seamstress; perhaps she anticipated a young woman's labour being useful in the newly established household.

Less than two years later, Ann Bell died too, a victim of the high mortality of married women in the years of childbearing. Ann's single sister, Frances Kent, stepped in to take over the shop. She reported that she

> did take up the said trade there & did manage & carry on the same And did doe hir best endeavour to teach and instruct the said Dorothy in the said trade and did further hir therein all she could & put hir upon buying and selling of goodes in the shopp and gave her full direccons touching the same. Insomuch that the said Complainant Dorothy was for hir time as well taught & instructed therein as any of the trade & as able to manage & performe the same.

Dorothy's father claimed that her training had been a failure, and the widowed Giles had driven her out; the family ended up suing for the return of her premiums. Supporting Giles's defence, Frances Kent claimed that Dorothy was so well trained that she was ready to work on her own: 'she hath heard the said complainant Dorothy since hir departure from the defendant's service hath followed & managed the said trade for hir selfe & hir owne peculiar profitt and hath made inquiry for a servant or Apprentice to serve hir in the said trade.' Further testimony came from another apprentice from Southwark, Frances Fletcher, apprenticed to a potter's wife, who signed only with a circle. Frances reported that her mistress, Eleanor Sligh, had heard that Dorothy 'did carry on and manage the said trade of a sempstriz for hirselfe and was able to teach and instruct an Apprentice therein'. Having a girl 'to put forth', Eleanor sent Frances to Dorothy to ask if she would take the girl as an apprentice, and Dorothy said she needed an apprentice and would

---

[3] ROLLCO, Giles Bell.
[4] St Mary Colechurch parish registers, 29 July and 1 August 1683, *England, Births and Christenings, 1538–1975*, www.ancestry.co.uk.

take her if she liked her, 'upon some such terms as they could agree'.[5] Dorothy Stable, it seems, was negotiating to become a mistress even before her own terms were dissolved.

The lawsuit Dorothy Stable's parents brought against her master produced a rare set of detailed testimonies about the life cycle and aspirations of young women training to be seamstresses. The careful analysis of Dorothy's capacity to work 'for herself' defines the central aim of her apprenticeship: independence. Dorothy, it was alleged, had been given a special kind of contract, which limited her term of service and fast-tracked her to the role of a mistress running her own shop. Her father claimed, and witnesses agreed, that he had taken a bond from her master for £100 guaranteeing that although she was bound for seven years, she would only have to serve for five. 'And that at the end of the said five years the said complainant Dorothy should act and trade for herselfe and for her owne peculiar proffitt without any molestacon or disturbance of or from the said Defendant'. This phrase – 'peculiar profit' – hinted at the profit sharing that would otherwise be expected in a partnership; without this guarantee, Dorothy's labour would still be bound to her mistress and the profits she made due to her. It was a clause that undercut the custom of London which required seven years' servitude before the freedom could be granted, as well as Dorothy's entry in the Goldsmiths' Apprenticeship Book. Dorothy's aspirations to take her own apprentices were part of a new understanding of apprenticeship for women, in which truncated contracts and private agreements were meant to circumvent established City custom.

This chapter recreates the work of women like Ann Bell and her sister, Frances Kent, who came to be mistresses through a number of routes: their own apprenticeships, leading to freedom; marriage to freemen; and widowhood, leaving them with the right to their husbands' freedom privileges. Frances Kent was a single woman who had become free and a mistress in her own right; women like her had a distinctive career pattern. In contrast, most married mistresses had reached that position simply by virtue of marrying a freeman. While married and single women demonstrated quite different patterns of taking apprentices, Ann Bell's position as both ex-apprentice and freeman's wife indicates the overlap of married and single women's careers. Becoming a mistress involved, in many cases, a parallel world of skills transmission to that of men in guilds, which brought into play connections of kin and patronage, shared origins and a common understanding of expertise and its worth. The

---

[5] LMA, CLA/024/05/449 (1685).

chapter begins by making visible the mistresses concealed in the paperwork of apprenticeship. It then draws on the data of company records and tax lists to present a profile of mistresses' working lives which demonstrates stark differences based on marital status and a distinctive role for single women. Lastly, the chapter examines the networks and connections through which contracts between mistresses and apprentices were made. Mistresshood, I argue, provides a new perspective on women's work. While guilds and laws constrained and marginalised, married couples established collaborative workshops, single women created their own artisanal generations and networks of kin and friendship laid the foundations for binding contracts.

Making Mistresses Visible

By the mid-eighteenth century, trades directories were marking out for parents and young people which trades could establish a girl as a mistress. Hoop-petticoat maker was one: 'about £20 will make a mistress of her'. For mantua-makers, a trade which 'belongs entirely to the Women': 'to make a mistress, there is little else wanting than a clever knack at cutting out and fitting, handsome Carriage, and a good set of Acquaintance'.[6] Connections and carriage were the necessary accompaniment to the skills of scissor and needle. The apprentices and mistresses of the seventeenth century were the forerunners of these mantua-makers, and the balance of manners and skill is played out in disputes at the Mayor's Court; but the realm of the mistress was one which had a much broader significance for the working women of early modern London.

Across Europe, while some seamstresses were working out how to break into the guild world, others were operating in a parallel structure, outside the family workshop. The limited inclusion of London women in guilds meant that they too had their own work world. Those who had earned the freedom through apprenticeship, who had married free men or who had bought the freedom by patrimony still did not hold the civic, political or even artisanal meanings of freedom that were associated with masters. Instead, London's mistresses found the peculiar liberties of City custom flexible enough to allow them to build their own networks. Frances Kent's takeover of her sister's apprentice was typical of the importance of sibling bonds, buttressed by networked migration patterns. Typical, too, of London mistresses was the ease with which some

---

[6] *A General Description of All Trades, Digested in Alphabetical Order* (1747).

apprentices, particularly the well born, moved on with confidence into their own businesses. Mistresses are often absent from the apprenticeship record, but the role transforms our understanding of women's labour, showing them as managers, as independent supervisors of workshops and businesses and as partners working alongside their husbands.

Legally, English wives were peculiarly constrained, barred through coverture from contracting debts or trading in their own right. Apprenticeship custom proscribed married women from appearing in indentures: their apprentices were to be bound to their husbands. Under coverture, they should not have even been able to buy on credit except as their husbands' agents. But the custom of London, as in other borough towns, allowed married women to trade as if they were single, as 'feme sole traders'.[7] It was on this basis that married women ran their own businesses, their husbands' credit protected against their debts and vice versa. Around 1700, Amy Erickson finds, 'total economic partnership was unusual' for married couples.[8]

Over the last four decades, research on the implications of coverture in practice has fleshed out early modern women's economic roles, revealing extensive agency, autonomy and capacity to manage economic life within and outside the rules of the common law.[9] The strictures of coverture had a wide range of practical implications, and many manoeuvres around it. Equity and other legal jurisdictions allowed married women more equality. The common law itself contained a series of legal devices allowing women's agency, restricting women whilst integrating them into commercial and property activities.[10] Feme sole trader status was widely understood and defended in law. It allowed married women to trade and buy independently, but, more significantly, it offered protection to their husbands and to trading families more generally. Over the course of the eighteenth century, common law's grip on married women's status seems to have grown firmer, and coverture was increasingly defended

---

[7] Mary Bateson, *Borough Customs*, vol. 1 (London: Selden Society, 1904), 229.
[8] Amy Louise Erickson, 'Married Women's Occupations in Eighteenth-Century London', *Continuity and Change* 23, no. 2 (2008): 267–307.
[9] See, for example, Tim Stretton and K. J. Kesselring, eds., *Married Women and the Law: Coverture in England and the Common Law World* (Montreal: McGill–Queen's University Press, 2014).
[10] Amy Louise Erickson, 'Common Law versus Common Practice: The Use of Marriage Settlements in Early Modern England', *Economic History Review* 43 (1990): 21–39; Joanne Bailey, 'Favoured or Oppressed? Married Women, Property and "Coverture" in England, 1660–1800', *Continuity and Change* 17, no. 3 (2002): 351–72; Margot Finn, 'Women, Consumption and Coverture in England, c. 1760–1860', *Historical Journal* 39, no. 3 (1996): 703–22.

against local customs.[11] Everyday marital life and economic exchange often differed sharply from the letter of the common law, as Margaret Hunt has shown for married women's property rights in eighteenth-century London.[12]

Legal constraints had a prescriptive power, but daily practice could undermine them, and a pluralistic legal system offered certain benefits to married women's enterprise. Lawsuits reveal some of the manoeuvres wives were expected to carry out, counselled by friends and relatives. In 1662 Grace Powell's widower went to court over her estate, claiming that after their marriage, they had fallen out (Grace's sister said he was unthrifty), and Grace had got him pressed into Cromwell's army in Ireland. While he was away, she 'did drive her trade of a clothdrawer' in a house she leased from the Skinners' Company in Basing Lane. According to her sister, Grace then relinquished the lease to her husband's brother: 'her friends having advised her that they conceived that it would be more safe and secure in his hands and more for her benefit and comoditie'.[13] The expertise of managing coverture was part of the work of family and kinship.

Research on the business families of the long eighteenth century has shown how critical married women's work was to the new middle class. Family and commerce were intimately connected, family businesses drawing on women's work and investments. Economic participation did not necessarily bring reward or status. Margaret Hunt argues that the business roles of middle-class women in the eighteenth century kept girls and women in the least remunerative trades and their expectations geared towards emotional, more than financial, reward.[14] Richard Grassby's picture is similar: marriage undermined women's limited chance at occupational identity, and businesswomen tended to enter trade through their husbands.[15] Alexandra Shepard has qualified these findings, arguing that marriage could be a gateway to a wider range of types of work; married women in court often described supporting

---

[11] Nicola Phillips, *Women in Business, 1700–1850* (Woodbridge: Boydell & Brewer, 2006), chapter 2; Susan Staves, *Married Women's Separate Property in England, 1660–1833* (Cambridge, MA: Harvard University Press, 1990).

[12] Margaret Hunt, 'Wives and Marital "Rights" in the Court of Exchequer in the Early Eighteenth Century', in *Londinopolis: Essays in the Social and Cultural History of Early Modern London*, ed. Mark S. R. Jenner and Paul Griffiths (Manchester University Press, 2000), 107–29.

[13] LMA, CLA 024/05/127.

[14] Margaret R. Hunt, *The Middling Sort: Commerce, Gender, and the Family in England, 1680–1780* (Berkeley: University of California Press, 1996).

[15] Richard Grassby, *Kinship and Capitalism: Marriage, Family, and Business in the English-Speaking World, 1580–1740* (Cambridge University Press, 2001), chapter 8.

themselves, though only sometimes with a named occupation.[16] The evidence gives a fuller picture of the economic cycles of married women's work in shops and crafts, catching them at the moments where they left an imprint on official records through indentures or shop leases. It also suggests the potential apprenticeship offered for careers that might be short, long or interrupted: women like Ann Bell graduated, as masters did, from apprentice to mistress when they married, while others returned in widowhood to the skills of their youth. In the ambitions and competences of mistresses and their apprentices, late seventeenth-century London's economic and legal landscape made it a hub of women's enterprise.

The history of women as mistresses was also an interpersonal one. The success of a working relationship depended on the effective transmission of skills, discipline and behaviour. The same was true for domestic servants, but they were not bound by contract; apprentices and mistresses had an unusually specific set of rules, designed around a masculine model of workshop and mastery but readily adapted to govern a working relationship between women. Some of the bonds forged in apprenticeship later became partnerships in shops; they also involved competition in a crowded market, and the social lives of mistresses and apprentices sometimes brought envy, suspicion and power struggles into house and shop.

The paperwork of apprenticeship often conceals the part that women played in training girls. Typically, both the two-part indentures that masters, parents and children signed, and the company registers where some but not all the contracts were later recorded, recorded married mistresses under the name of their husbands. The records of Dorothy Stable's apprenticeship to Ann Bell in 1683 named only her master, Giles Bell, who seems in practice to have had no involvement in her training.[17] Giles Bell took male apprentices too, but his incapacity to manage Dorothy Stable after his wife's death suggests that wives were critical to training. Indeed, this seems to have been true for male apprentices too: no tax listings record single men with apprentices.

Widows and single women, on the other hand, were mistresses of apprentices in their own right. Some indentures, like that made out for an apprentice to Elizabeth Fazakerley, a shopkeeper in the Drapers' Company, 1694, used forms printed for a mistress, which describe her as a 'Citizen and Draper': this was one of the rare moments in which a

---

[16] Alexandra Shepard, 'Crediting Women in the Early Modern English Economy', *History Workshop Journal* 78 (2015): 1–24.
[17] Goldsmiths' Company, Apprenticeship Book 3, p. 126 (28 March 1683).

Figure 3.1 Indenture of Mary Toft to Elizabeth Fazakerley.
London Metropolitan Archives (City of London)

woman was described as citizen (Figure 3.1). The word 'citizen' may simply have been left unchanged from the male version of the form, but the rest of it reflects a need for a single woman's role as mistress, like a girl's place in apprenticeship, to be accurately recorded.

The erasure of the married mistress's role was consistent with the patriarchalism of guilds, and it was also typical of English custom, which led the way in coverture. It was perceived as legal necessity, and, in 1699, Constance Downes, a Stationer's widow, petitioned the Lord Mayor to complain that her daughter Margaret's apprenticeship to Sarah Bulley, a seamstress and milliner, with £25 was 'absolutely void in law' because the indenture was for only three years and made out to a wife.[18] In France, 'marchande publique' status meant that women members of guilds, whether married or single, could take apprentices in their own right. The Parisian seamstresses' guild, established in 1675, ordered its own standardised contracts using 'mistress' and the female form of

---

[18] LMA, City of London Sessions Papers (14 October 1699), *London Lives* LMSLPS150100114.

Managing the Trade: Women as Mistresses 107

Figure 3.2 Richard Court's indenture.
London Metropolitan Archives (City of London)

'apprentice'.[19] In England, despite the existence of feme sole trader status, apprenticeship paperwork, particularly that of guilds, generally subsumed wives in the names of their husbands. Widows' role in continuing to apprentice boys after their husbands' deaths was so long established that their company paperwork reflected their position more accurately. Richard Court, apprenticed to Elizabeth Marsh, widow of a blacksmith, was indentured with a form pre-printed for a citizen's widow, which described her as working 'in the same Art which her late husband used' (Figure 3.2). Women's assumption of their husbands' trades was institutionalised in print.

Indentures rarely named married women as mistresses, but other records were more likely to do so. Nearly half the girls suing out their indentures at the Mayor's Court had husbands and wives named in their

---

[19] Daryl M. Hafter, 'Female Masters in the Ribbonmaking Guild of Eighteenth-Century Rouen', *French Historical Studies* 20, no. 1 (1997): 1–14; Clare Haru Crowston, *Fabricating Women: The Seamstresses of Old Regime France, 1675–1791* (Durham, NC: Duke University Press, 2001), 302.

litigation, often giving an occupation. Some companies, such as the Clothworkers, also listed many of their girls as bound to both husband and wife. Thomas and Elizabeth Couse, milliners in the Clothworkers, took five apprentices between 1676 and 1686, only one of whom, the sole boy, was registered to Thomas alone.[20] Some records named both husband and wife: in a typical entry in the Clothworkers' Company registers, Joan Powell was apprenticed to 'John Stuckey and his wife Alice'. Alice's name had in fact been written first, then deleted, and the designation 'in Coleman street woostead [worsted] seller' in the margin could have applied to both of them.[21] It may make more sense to understand these kinds of occupational references as applying to couples rather than individuals, given the evidence of women's involvement in some way in their husbands' businesses. In other documentation, women's businesses were clearly marked out as separate. Susanna and John Dalbye, in the Goldsmiths' Company, took girls as apprentices together in the 1680s. Elizabeth Bell, a gentleman's daughter from Maidstone, was apprenticed to John 'also to Susanna his wife useing the sole Arte of a Sempstress'. The phrase 'sole art' invoked the status of feme sole trader, enabling Susanna Bell to keep her debts and income separate. John took no apprentices himself, but he bought himself into the Goldsmiths' Company by redemption shortly before they took their first apprentice. He died around 1693, and Susanna took three more girls into apprenticeship as a widow.

The marital relationship was pivotal to the association between people and company. Guild masters were not just men, but husbands, and married couples were the pillars of the guild system. A semi-satirical apprentice petition of 1641 expressed a familiar anxiety about mistresses' role in relation to male apprentices: 'whereas we are bound in our Halls, onely to our Masters, yet of late have our Mistresses gotten such predominancy over us, as if that we were bound to them, not to our Masters.' Binding, again, was marked as significant evidence.[22] In the individual life cycles of men in the guilds, as in the idealised version of the artisanal life story, masters were husbands with their own households. The years of establishing a family were often also the time of establishing a workshop, and the labour of wives was essential in a working

---

[20] ROLLCO, apprenticeships to the Couses, and of Elizabeth Bell; Michael Scott, ed., *Apprenticeship Disputes in the Lord Mayor's Court of London, 1573–1723* (London: British Record Society, 2016), see, for example, entries for Elizabeth Lane, Jane Silvester, Anne Cox. The Mayor's Court cases also occasionally list couples for boys.

[21] Clothworkers' Company, Apprenticeship Registers (28 November 1661).

[22] *The Petition of the Weamen of Middlesex ... with the Apprentices of Londons Petition* (1641), Thomason Tracts E. 180 [17].

household. Marriage brought women into companies, but they lost any previous company affiliation. Nevertheless, their work was not subsumed by their husbands' labour identity. The sector of female apprenticeship supports the extensive evidence for married women's independent work.[23]

Like their company identity, mistresses' relationship to artisanal training was also different to that of masters. The traditional understanding of guild work is as a community of practice, transmitted from generations of workshops, ensuring continuity through imitation, whilst leaving some room for innovation.[24] That pattern did not hold for women. While most freemen had attained the freedom by apprenticeship, most freewomen had gained it through widowhood or patrimony. The majority of mistresses were wives, and the number of female apprentices means that only a few of them would, like Ann Kent, have received any formal training before their marriage. So most of the men who trained boys had been apprenticed themselves, and most of the women who trained girls had not.[25] Spinsters' careers were more like those of men: around half the unmarried mistresses in the guilds examined here had been apprenticed. This changed later. By the eighteenth century, Amy Erickson found, the majority of spinsters taking apprentices in the guilds had acquired their freedom through patrimony: it may be that apprenticed women paved the way for their successors to become single mistresses without training.[26] Finally, the balance of continuity and innovation that typified artisanal training took a particular form for seamstresses, whose relationship with the guild system was at best a generation old. As trends grew and collapsed, and particularly with the spread of ready-made goods and more changeable fashions, continuity of skills was necessarily balanced by significant adaptation to change.

Dependent as guild ideology had always been on masters being married, guild rhetoric also had a history of treating marriage as problematic in relation to craft transmission, because girls and women who had worked at a craft might marry outside it. Thomas Delony's 1595 complaint to the London Dutch and French churches, on behalf of the Weavers' Company, had a pointed claim about the malpractices of Dutch and French refugees. Amongst other grumbles, it alleged that

---

[23] For more evidence of this, see Erickson, 'Married Women's Occupations'.
[24] S. R. Epstein, 'Craft Guilds, Apprenticeship, and Technological Change in Preindustrial Europe', *Journal of Economic History* 58, no. 3 (1998): 684–713.
[25] Around 80 per cent of masters had been freed by servitude in the late seventeenth century, based on data from ROLLCO.
[26] Amy Louise Erickson, 'Eleanor Mosley and Other Milliners in the City of London Companies 1700–1750', *History Workshop Journal* 71 (2011): 147–72.

women spread the secrets of the trade to outsiders. The French, they complained, 'set Women and Maids at work' at the looms. When they became 'perfect in the Occupation', they married men in other trades – 'and so bring that which should be our livings to be the maintenance of those that never deserved for it, and these likewise increase an infinite number'.[27] This vision of women as enabling skills to escape from guild control assumes that women learn and teach craft skills to their husbands, making women a significant vector of skills transmission and a risk to the monopoly that was the essential aim of guild organisation. Ideas like this were part of guilds' self-representation. They often conflicted with actual practice, but they signposted the formal exclusion of women from guild discourse.

In many ways, then, mistresses training girls did not fit the model of guild work, both as it was understood by contemporaries and as it has been modelled by historians. Mistresses and girls were effectively operating in a parallel system, one which drew on the credit of guilds, but could access their resources only within limits.

Married and Single Mistresses

The capacity of women for independent work was well established, but marital status was one of the key determinants of the shape and nature of women's work as mistresses. For women like Ann Bell, marriage made apprenticeship possible; for others, it undercut existing arrangements, undermining the freedom they had acquired independently. Widows' continuation of their husbands' business could, likewise, be tenuous.

Wives, widows and single women taking apprentices shared some characteristics but also had distinctive patterns of work. In apprenticeships of boys in London at this point, Patrick Wallis has shown, the majority were trained by a small number of masters who each took several apprentices.[28] Mistresses training girls were not generally running this kind of business, particularly if they were single or if they were only training girls. Amongst both couples and single women, female apprentices were fairly evenly distributed in small numbers with little overlap. Most girls were their mistress's first and only female apprentice, and most mistresses only took one girl in their working lives. However, most married mistresses were members of working couples who were training boys in larger numbers as well.

---

[27] Frances Consitt, *The London Weavers' Company* (Oxford: Clarendon Press, 1933).
[28] Patrick Wallis, 'Apprenticeship in England', in *Apprenticeship in Early Modern Europe*, ed. Maarten Prak and Patrick Wallis (Cambridge University Press, 2019), 247–81.

Table 3.1. *Mistresses of female apprentices, 1640–1700*

	One female apprentice only	2+ girls only	One girl, one or more boys	More than one girl and any number of boys	Total
Single women (both spinsters and widows)	47 (72%)	15 (23%)	3 (all widows)	0	65
Couples and men	56 (27%)	17 (8%)	95 (47%)	33 (16%)	201
Total mistresses	**103 (38%)**	**32 (12%)**	**98 (37%)**	**33 (12%)**	**266**

Source: Data from ROLLCO.

Table 3.2. *Numbers of apprentices to married couples taking boys and girls*

	1	2	3	4	5	6	7–17
Total 201 apprentices	56	35	30	27	15	13	24
Cumulative percentage	*27*	*45*	*60*	*74*	*79*	*87*	*100*

Table 3.1, which includes couples who took both male and female apprentices as well as couples and single women who took only girls, allows us to examine the careers of married and single mistresses in ten major companies. Marriage made a difference, less to the number of female apprentices, than to the overall numbers. Married couples were likeliest to take one girl and several boys; single women and widows were overwhelmingly likely to take just one female apprentice, although a quarter of them took more than one girl, and a quarter of married women also took a girl as their only apprentice.

Table 3.2 reveals the wide spread of apprentice-taking amongst couples who took female apprentices. For one in four married mistresses, the girl they trained was the only apprentice their household had. However, significant numbers – 44 per cent – took more than three apprentices, and 14 per cent took more than seven, eight of those taking ten or more. These were not large, proto-industrial workshops with multiple apprentices, but long-lived working households in which two or three apprentices overlapped, the established skills of the older boys supplementing and supporting those of the younger apprentices. Young women, it seems, so rarely overlapped with each other in apprenticeship that mistresses' relationship with their apprentices was likely to be intense. Married or single, mistresses mostly took only one or few female apprentices. This data reflects only those girls recorded in apprenticeship registers: given the number of unrecorded girls discussed in Chapter 2, some of these mistresses probably took more than are listed.

The early ending of so many contracts for boys as well as girls means it is not possible to trace the apprenticeship cycle exactly, but the start dates, and sometimes the freedoms awarded at the end, reveal persistent patterns. The point at which girls were taken on by married couples indicates the times when mistresses were actively supervising, and thus gives some idea of the relationship between men's and women's work in the trading household.

The most productive end, the households that took between seven and seventeen apprentices, balanced their girls and boys in various ways. William Mayne (and presumably his wife) in the Tallow Chandlers' Company took fourteen boys between 1679 and 1719; two girls were enrolled in 1687 and 1692. The girls probably did not overlap, given the likelihood of apprenticeships ending early, but the boys tended to, especially in the 1680s when William was taking on apprentices every year or two. This was not always the case: in other larger-scale households, girls were apprenticed with only a year or two between them, or sometimes two together. Elizabeth and Hewett Ram, coat-sellers and tailors in the Barbican, took a young male relative first in 1654, then three girls in quick succession, and then just boys. Their occupational descriptors in the Clothworkers' Company reflect either a wide-ranging business or its development over time. In 1657, one girl was apprenticed to Elizabeth and Hewett, 'silkweaver in Redcross Street'; in 1658, the master was Hewett, 'tailor in Redcross Street'; in 1659, he was 'coate seller in Barbakin', and from 1661, after which point his apprentices were male, he was a tailor in the Barbican.[29] Elizabeth was still alive, though she was to die in the plague outbreak of 1665, but the later period saw a solidifying of Hewett's occupational title as 'tailor' and a corresponding end to the girls learning silkweaving or coatmaking.[30]

In a larger house and shop near St Paul's, the merchant Captain William Hulls and his wife, Mary, took thirteen apprentices from 1680 to 1708. The boys were generally spaced two or three years apart (Figure 3.3). Girls were clustered in two periods: two in 1688 and 1690, and another two, who were sisters, in 1697 and 1698. It looks as if the girls worked together in parallel to the boys. The Hulls' shop had £100

[29] ROLLCO, Hewett Ram.   [30] LMA, P69/GIS/A/002/MS06419/006, p. 146.

Managing the Trade: Women as Mistresses 113

Boys 1680 1682	1685 1687 1690 1693		1699	1702	1708
Girls		1688 1690	1697 1698		

Figure 3.3 Mary and William Hull's apprentices

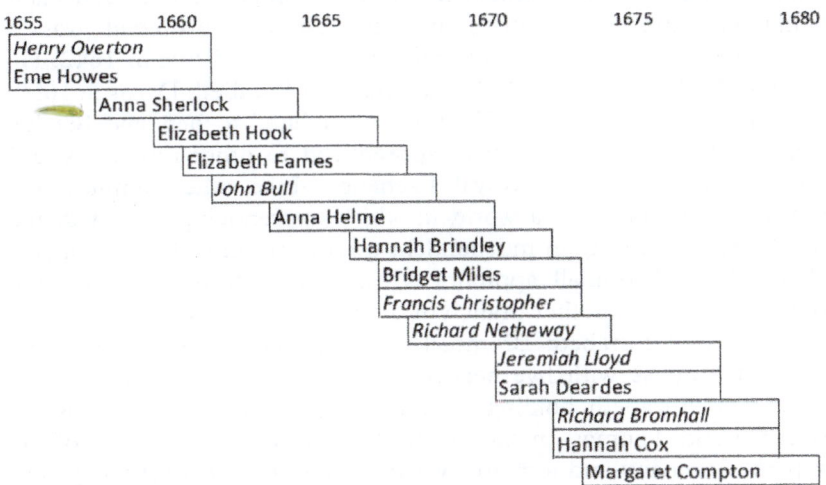

Figure 3.4 Elizabeth and Thomas Bromhall's apprentices

worth of stock in 1691, and in 1695 their household included four children, two male apprentices, two female apprentices (both of whom had completed most of their terms and one of whom went on to become free) and another two girls who may have been servants.[31] As with the Mayne household, the female side of the business is more contained, as if William was continually training apprentices while Mary took them occasionally.

A few households of company members took a balance of male and female apprentices. Elizabeth and Thomas Bromhall in the Drapers' Company, running shops alongside several other occupations, took on a steady flow of both. Figure 3.4 depicts the chronology, assuming the unlikely case that all apprentices completed a seven-year term. The Bromhall apprentices suggest a household business sustained by both boys' and girls' labour. It begins with two-year intervals between each apprentice, starting with one of each sex and continuing with girls; in the

---

[31] LMA, COL/CHD/LA/04/009, p. 3; ROLLCO.

later years, girls and boys are taken on at the same time, suggesting complementary roles. There is often a potential overlap of three or four apprentices, even if they left early. At the same time, there were periods with no boys apprenticed at all, where the active business seems to have been in Elizabeth's hands. Only two of the boys and none of the girls took up the freedom.[32] The backstory to the Bromhall household connects it to national and metropolitan politics. Thomas Bromhall was a Shropshire gentleman's son, apprenticed in 1634 and free in 1642. He fought for Parliament in the 1640s and married Elizabeth Dards in 1650. Their later apprentice Sarah Deardes was related to her, and Sarah's sisters, Rebecca and Mary, were apprenticed to other mistresses and went on to work in the Royal Exchange. Like other families, the Deardeses were creating a world in which apprenticing girls with the aim of setting them up in independent trades was an ordinary strategy. Others of the Bromhall apprentices came from Shropshire like the Bromhalls or from another branch of the family in Dorset.

Thomas and Elizabeth Bromhall's establishment was considerable: they kept a house with five hearths in 1666. They also had separate shops, with Elizabeth holding a shop on the west side of the Royal Exchange and Thomas on the north. Thomas was a liveryman of the Drapers' Company and a churchwarden, later accused of Anabaptism; he also published the *City Mercury* and wrote a treatise on ghosts.[33] In the 1670s, his profiteering tenure of Warden of the Fleet Prison caused financial and political trouble. At Thomas's death, he left Elizabeth several houses in Shropshire and leases on thirty properties in Fenchurch Street, as well as three shops on the Exchange.[34] Other Dissenting merchants had ties to female apprenticeship too. Robert Blaney, like Bromhall a subscriber to the Dissenters' loan to Charles II in 1670, aimed at influencing his religious policy, was guardian to one of the seamstress apprentices who used the Mayor's Court.[35] Apprenticeship was one of the ways that London Dissenters, powerful in the City, were bound together: we can see from this one group that those connected in this way included young and established women in

---

[32] ROLLCO.

[33] Thomas Bromhall, *An History of Apparitions, Oracles, Prophecies, and Predictions* (London, 1658).

[34] Edwin Freshfield, ed., *The Vestry Minute Books of the Parish of St. Bartholomew Exchange in the City of London* (London: Rixon and Arnold, 1890), 131; Gary S. De Krey, *London and the Restoration, 1659–1683* (Cambridge University Press, 2009), 133; Donald Francis McKenzie and Maureen Bell, *A Chronology and Calendar of Documents Relating to the London Book Trade 1641–1700: Volume II: 1671–1685* (Oxford University Press, 2005), p. 187; TNA, PROB 11/360 (1679).

[35] De Krey, *London and the Restoration*, 130; LMA, CLA/024/05/318.

business. On the other hand, political ties were not necessarily dominant, and in any case the political alliances of 1650–80 were often in flux. Eme Howes, one of the first Bromhall apprentices, was sponsored by a Levant merchant from her home town of Wisbech, Cambridgeshire, who was an Anglican and a Royalist.[36] Elizabeth Bromhall's life and work were evidently enmeshed in a web of political and trade ties. Her husband's connections to Robert Antrobus added another layer. A social-network analysis of the female partnerships of the Exchange puts her solidly in the centre, connected through kinship and business ties with the key figures of London's fashion trade. Being a mistress made her a patron and a shaping influence, and her work appears to have been relatively or entirely autonomous from her husband's.[37]

Frances and John Spillett used apprenticeship in a similar way through the Mercers' Company, based in a house near the City wall and the Exchange, with an estate rated at £600, two shops in the Exchange and £150 of stock.[38] With them lived their children Frances, aged eighteen, John in his early teens, six-year-old Elizabeth, and five young apprentices and servants, Elizabeth Medon, Elizabeth Tyth, Kate Smith, Mary Hinton, and William Oswin. Hinton and Oswin were bound to John Spillett in 1691 and 1692, and both later became free. Over the period 1680–99, John and Frances Spillett took on at least eleven apprentices, five of them girls (Figure 3.5).

The long life of this thriving working household reveal some of the interconnections of family and work in business London. John had come to London in 1668 from Kent, three years after the death of his father, who had been mayor of Faversham. He was apprenticed to a mercer at seventeen, became free of the company at twenty-four and shortly after married Frances, establishing a business household whose reliance on female skill and labour was typical of the new middling class. At John's death in 1733, when his estate included land in Essex and Hertfordshire, as well as jewels, he left Frances to distribute it as she thought fit: 'in consideration that she (by Gods blessing) on her care and industry hath

---

[36] www.marinelives.org/wiki/John_Buckworth; ROLLCO, Eme Howes; Steven Pincus, *Protestantism and Patriotism: Ideologies and the Making of English Foreign Policy, 1650–1668* (Cambridge University Press, 2002), 242.

[37] LMA, P69/STE1/A/002/MS04449/002, 5 January 1648. Thomas Bromhall and Robert Antrobus carried out the inventory for Herbert Allen's Exchange shop in 1668: LMA, CLA/002/02/01/0570, no. 215.

[38] Derek Keene, Peter Earle, Craig Spence and Janet Barnes, 'City of London, Broad Street Ward, All Hallows the Wall', in *Four Shillings in the Pound Aid 1693/4: The City of London, the City of Westminster, Middlesex* (London: Centre for Metropolitan History, 1992), *British History Online*, www.british-history.ac.uk/no-series/london-4s-pound/1693-4/broad-street-ward-all-hallows-the-wall.

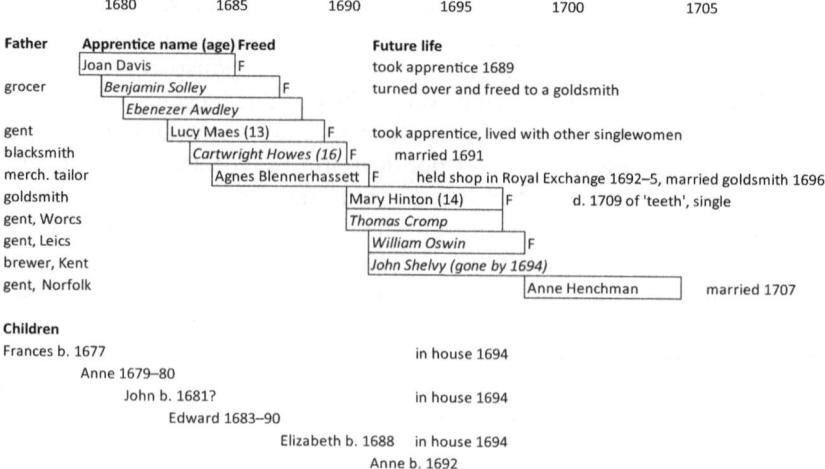

Figure 3.5 Frances and John Spillett's apprentices and children

gotten the Major part of my estate'.[39] Frances's work as a mistress, shopkeeper and investor was evidently central to their successful lives.

When Frances and John took their first apprentices, within a few years of their marriage, they already had two small children. That their first apprentice was a girl indicates again that childbearing and training apprentices were not perceived as contradictory, especially with domestic servants to help. Their next girl, Lucy Maes, was bound when Frances's fourth child was two months old. The short birth intervals between Frances' children suggest she may not have breastfed them herself; wealthier city households were still sending babies to be wet-nursed outside London, or employing a live-in nurse, and her youngest child, at two, is missing from the household listings of 1694.[40] Conversely, the oldest children in their late teens were still at home in 1694.

Most of the Spillett apprentices, and all but one of the girls, ended up taking the freedom, so they would have stayed the whole seven years. Their origins also indicate a shift from London citizens to rural gentry, although many of those gentry would have had London homes or connections too. Lucy Maes had been born in Church Alley off Fetter Lane, the youngest of three sisters, and had recently lost her father:

---

[39] TNA, PROB 11/659 (1733).
[40] Gill Newton, 'Infant Mortality Variations, Feeding Practices and Social Status in London between 1550 and 1750', *Social History of Medicine* 24, no. 2 (August 2011): 260–80.

apprenticeship was a sensible option, although she had some inheritance waiting.[41] Maes's indenture is inscribed on the back with a note: 'This apprentice must serve bona fide and really and not colourably only or else lose her freedom.'[42] This unusual addition refers to a persistent concern that apprentices were not actually serving but rather using a fictive contract to establish the right to freedom. However, in the tax lists of the 1690s, all the apprentices who should have been in the Spillett household were recorded there, and like most of them, Maes worked out her seven years and became free, later taking an apprentice into her own shop in the Exchange alongside her erstwhile master. Agnes Blennerhassett, the next girl enrolled, was the daughter of William Blennerhassett, a merchant tailor and lieutenant colonel in the Parliamentary army whose grave survives in Bunhill Fields. It is Blennerhassett who gives us a little more sense of Frances Spillett's background. Her father's will left money to 'my niece and nephew Spillett'.[43] Frances Spillett, this will reveals, was a Blennerhassett herself, her father one of ten children of this Norfolk family, and her apprentice, Agnes, was her cousin. The web of merchants involved countless such ties, the essence of the bonds of credit that made the middling class, but the difficulty in tracing women's maiden names often masks the extent to which marriages and service made the connections. Frances's gentry background, like many of London's businesswomen, helped provide a network of connections from which to build apprenticeship, providing both labour and premiums to invest in the business.

The Spillett household was not only an exceptionally productive training environment, but also unusual in the number of girls Frances trained and the proportion who stayed the course and became free. The Spilletts had apprentices from 1679 to 1706, with particularly busy points in the mid-1680s, when they had five apprentices and three young children, and the early 1690s, when they had another crop of four apprentices and three children between the ages of two and thirteen. In the end, the Spilletts trained at least six female and five male apprentices, of whom four of each took up the freedom of the City and mostly went on to trade alone. The record suggests little difference in the careers of the boys and girls: about half took an apprentice within three to five years after becoming free, most took their own shops and most married shortly after becoming free. In the longer run, many of the women's careers become invisible after marriage. Agnes Blennerhassett took the freedom

---

[41] LMA, P82/AND/A/001/MS06667/004, 22 November 1670; TNA, PROB 11/370/394 (1679), will of Daniel Maes.
[42] LMA, COL/CHD/FR/02/0040 no. 83.   [43] TNA, PROB 11/454 (1699).

and a shop in the Exchange and three years later gave up her lease when she married Valentine Barrington, a goldsmith on Cheapside and son of an Essex draper, who had just gained his own freedom after apprenticeship.[44]

Frances and John Spillett took their last apprentice, Anne Henchman, in 1699. They moved out to Hackney, where John became a vestryman, and died a year apart in their eighties in the 1730s. Frances's will distributed her goods among their three surviving children, one of whom had married a connection of one of the male apprentices, and five grandchildren. Her estate included property, jewels and stock worth £600 in the Bank of England, an investment not mentioned in her husband's will. She had become one of the generation of early investors whose careers have been traced by Amy Froide: active participants in the capitalisation of the Bank and other enterprises.[45]

There were connections of influence between households too. The parishes around the Royal Exchange were full of shopholders and their apprentices. Further down the occupational rankings, two other serial apprentice households in the 1690s were next-door neighbours in Smithfield. Samuel Withers, a hemp dresser, continued his father's tradition of taking girls as well as boys into apprenticeship; his parents had begun their careers as master and mistress with two girls in 1656 and 1658. His neighbour, Thomas Burrell, and his wife, Elizabeth, were in the same trade of preparing flax for spinning, and they took four girls as apprentices between 1682 and 1687, including their own daughter, who went on to become free.[46] Hemp-dressing was both housewives' work and a trade, enabling daughters to work in the main family business and then use the City freedom to trade alone.

Households with many girls in apprenticeship like the Spilletts and Bromhalls were the minority. In most couples where both took apprentices, wives took fewer than husbands, over a more limited period of time. This suggests both flexibility in and constraints on women's enterprise; only a larger or enlarging business had both a need for apprentices and the capacity to train them. The life events of marriage and widowhood visibly shaped women's lives as mistresses. Alice Guidot took apprentices over a period of over twenty years. The daughter of a London leather seller who had his own stall in the Exchange, she married

---

[44] Mercers' Company, Gresham Registers 1678–1722, p. 278; Ancestry.com, *England, Select Marriages 1538–1973* [online database]; Ambrose Heal, *The London Goldsmiths* (Cambridge University Press, 1935), 89.
[45] TNA, PROB 11/666 (1734); Amy M. Froide, *Silent Partners: Women as Public Investors during Britain's Financial Revolution, 1690–1750* (Oxford University Press, 2016).
[46] GL, MS 34038/16–17; 1692 Poll Tax.

Managing the Trade: Women as Mistresses

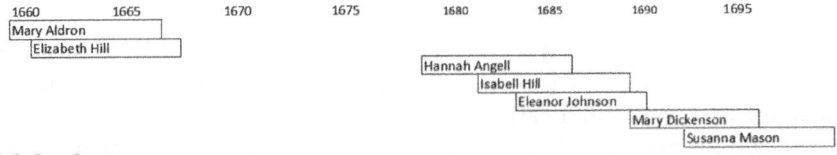

Figure 3.6 Alice Guidot's apprentices. B = birth. The two Hills do not seem to be related

John Guidot, a gentleman in the Girdlers' Company, in 1655; their banns read out as the Commonwealth jurisdiction required in Leadenhall and Cheapside Market.[47] Their children were born in 1658, 1659, 1660 and 1663. In the same period, in 1660 and 1661, they took on two girls as apprentices (Figure 3.6). Twenty years later, widowed, Alice was holding her own Exchange shop and took on four apprentices in quick succession: the daughters of a lawyer, a silkman, a gentleman and a clergyman. By then, Alice Guidot's son John had an Exchange shop too, and she was working in partnership with her daughter Margaret's husband. Guidot probably only had two apprentices at a time, and like other married mistresses, her apprenticeships co-existed with her pregnancies, supported by domestic servants.

The impact of childbirth and childrearing was surprisingly minimal. Married couples regularly took on female apprentices, whose training would be the wife's responsibility, in the same years they were having their first children. Apprentices were often providing premiums to invest in shops at precisely the same time as new babies were joining the household and younger children were toddling about the house. Lower-status apprentices and servants probably helped; gentry daughters were unlikely to expect to. The short birth intervals of women like Alice Guidot, delivering a child every year or two, suggest that at least some such households used wet nurses in the early years. However, households with several children and many female apprentices were rare, and the likelier scenario is that women moved out of training as their families grew, keeping their shop work more flexible. Taking apprentices is best seen not as an index of business success, for women's businesses continued far outside the periods in which they took apprentices. It was particularly useful at one point: the beginning of a shop. Premiums of £5–£30 were enough to augment or even supply the stock of a small

---

[47] LMA, CLA/062/04/16; P69/HEL/A/002/MS06831/001 (29 January 1633/4); P69/HEL/A/001/MS06830/002 (September 1658).

shop, where an apprentice could later work alone. Taking apprentices intermittently, supported by domestic service and wet-nursing, enabled women to structure their work lives flexibly around marriage, domestic management and childbearing.

At the lowest end of the apprenticeship market, arrangements were vulnerable to the risks of bankruptcy and poverty. Ann Jackson petitioned the Westminster sessions in 1696 for the discharge of her granddaughter, who was apprenticed to a couple in St Martin in the Fields: they had beaten her, fallen into financial trouble and left their house, leaving her with their sister at Limehouse, 'who being poor herself would keep her no longer'; Ann had 'enquired after' the couple but failed to find them. The contract of apprenticeship was sufficiently binding that she felt the need to have it formally dissolved before finding another person to teach her granddaughter 'an honest livelyhood'.[48] In another case, a mistress's responsibility was undercut by her husband's violence. Ann Masters petitioned that her husband, through his 'wilfull and malitious humour', had driven her and their apprentice, threatening them with violence; he refused to let them back in, risking them becoming dependent on the parish, and Ann petitioned that he should be made to 'indempnifye the parish and to make provision for your petitioner and family'. Here, the apprentice had become part of the family, mistreated and excluded alongside the woman who trained her.[49] A petition from a Cooper's wife in 1688 suggests the ways that apprentices might be expected to sustain families under pressure. Ann Tyler's husband, abroad for several years, had left her 'very poor and having totally lost her Trade was unable to support her self and family'. She still had an apprentice, Jeremiah, and she requested the court who governed the company for permission to let him out to another freeman so that he could be better instructed and she could earn from his labour. Apprentices, while under contract, were part of the family resources.[50]

While single women, like wives, took apprentices in small numbers, their careers as mistresses fit interestingly into the argument that places them, across Europe, as a significant economic force in a period of late and relatively infrequent marriage.[51] Around one in four of the girls apprenticed through London's companies were bound to single women, of whom more were spinsters than widows. This is unsurprising in a city

---

[48] LMA, MJ/SP 1696/10/016.   [49] LMA, WJ/SP 1691/07/006.
[50] GL, Coopers' Company, MS 056026A.
[51] Tine De Moor and Jan Luiten Van Zanden, 'Girl Power: The European Marriage Pattern and Labour Markets in the North Sea Region in the Late Medieval and Early Modern Period', *Economic History Review* 63, no. 1 (2010): 1–33.

where nearly one in five households were headed by independent women, but it contrasts with the masculine model of artisanal households: to be a master had long been understood to require a wife.[52] Residential tax records show no signs of apprentices living and working with single men. Instead, men who had completed apprenticeships and become free worked as journeymen before they set up households and businesses of their own. Single women did so too, but, in a reversal of assumptions about the marital economy, women in City companies were actually more able than men to establish themselves in business without being married. Single women holding their own shops, some of whom had been apprenticed themselves, were an important group in the City, and their domestic and business arrangements ranged from the apparently marginal and temporary to the weighty and long lasting. Both depended on and created networks of kin and fellow workers.

When the actual occupations of single women in companies were recorded, by the Clothworkers' Company and at the Mayor's Court, nine out of ten were making clothes. Seamstress was invariably the largest occupational descriptor, with other women calling themselves coatmakers (particularly children's coats, which were loose and untailored), milliners and exchangewomen. Widows had a wider range of occupations, reflecting their capacity to continue their husbands' trades, though the habit of describing widows as 'late wife of John Smith tailor' blurs definitions still further. The quarterage books of the Merchant Tailors' record widows and spinsters in the company working across London as seamstresses; but also as bodice-makers, button-makers and a slop-seller, producing cheap ready-made clothes, at Charing Cross. Others listed include a victualler in Smithfield, a mop-maker in Southwark, a bookbinder in Fleet Street and a carpenter in Cloth Fair; some or all of these were widows continuing their husbands' businesses.[53] This concentration on sewing is not an accurate reflection of the range of work single women were actually doing in seventeenth-century London, but it does reflect the kinds of retail occupations for which a company membership was necessary. The street sellers of London's food economy, hawkers and the whole service industry are largely invisible.

While company identity seems to have had little impact on married women's work, because they came to their companies through their husbands, single women's company membership had a more recognisable effect. There are noticeable differences between companies. Nearly

---

[52] Craig Spence, *London in the 1690s: A Social Atlas* (London: Centre for Metropolitan History, 2000), 179.
[53] GL, MS 34,042.

a third of the twenty-eight girls in the Fishmongers were apprenticed to women, compared to only 13 per cent in the Clothworkers. Most of the Fishmongers' girls had gentry parents, and the company was a prestigious one which evidently made room for single women's businesses. At the other end of the scale, the Glovers, a lower-status company whose artisans still largely practised its craft, also had high numbers of mistresses. In their case, mistresses were more likely to be widows, admitted as mistresses specifically during the period of their widowhood, than spinsters. Some were daughters freed after serving their mothers or fathers.

Mistresses were particularly popular with parishes placing pauper girls in apprenticeships: 35 per cent of these indentures were to women. Their occupations were divided between housewifery, seamstresses and, more specific, lower-status textile occupations which also appeared in company records: 'stocking mender', 'wiremaker and rolls', 'trimming gloves', 'winding and twisting silk' and 'buttonmaking'. The lowest number of single mistresses can be seen in the sample of girls suing to dissolve their contracts at the London Mayor's Court. These disputes reflect not only a useful problem-solving mechanism but a wider training structure that was flexible and open-ended; perhaps it was less so for single mistresses. The figures suggest that spinster mistresses were more oriented towards freedom and city careers for their apprentices. Single women's apprentices were apparently more likely to complete their contracts, even if they did not then become free.[54] In the archive of freedoms kept by the Chamberlain, a third of those claimed by women went to those who had been apprenticed to single women mistresses, although this group represented only 22 per cent of female company apprentices overall (Table 3.3).

Spinsters constituted about a third of the single mistresses of girls in companies whose marital status can be traced; they had gained the freedom in roughly equal proportions as apprentices or through patrimony via their fathers. The rest were widows, using their husbands' freedom. Although the numbers are small, single mistresses working in companies had a recognisable profile which was more likely to lead their apprentices to freedom (Table 3.4).

While there is a clear pattern of small apprentice numbers across all women taking apprentices (around three-quarters of mistresses took only one apprentice), where single mistresses' history can be traced, those

---

[54] On flexibility, Patrick Wallis, 'Labor, Law, and Training in Early Modern London: Apprenticeship and the City's Institutions', *Journal of British Studies* 51, no. 4 (2012): 791–819; apprentice dispute figures from Scott, *Apprenticeship Disputes*.

Table 3.3. *Girls apprenticed to single women*

	Apprenticed to single women, as a proportion of all
Girls in company apprenticeships 1640–1700	270 of 1229 (22%)
Girls in parish apprenticeships 1660–1700	25 of 71 (35%)
Girls suing at Mayor's Court	37 of 285 (13%)
Girls free after company apprenticeships 1670–1700	33 of 99 (33%)

Sources: ROLLCO, LAA, LMA Freedoms, *London Lives*, Scott, *Apprenticeship Disputes*. Single women means women not currently married.

Table 3.4. *Apprenticeships and their outcomes in ten companies, 1640–1700*

	Bound to single women and widows	Bound to men or couples	Total
Girls apprenticed	83 (22%)	297 (78%)	380
Girls taking freedom after apprenticeship	7 (28%)	18 (72%)	25

Source: ROLLCO, representing approximately 12 per cent of all company apprentices.

who had been apprenticed themselves were also more likely to take multiple apprentices, and widows were most likely to take only one (Table 3.5).

Single women with multiple apprentices were most likely to be found in the companies associated with fashion and the Royal Exchange, such as the Mercers and the Merchant Taylors, and in the prestigious Fishmongers. The most prolific single mistress in the Merchant Taylors' Company, Rachel Erskine, a seamstress with a linen shop on the Royal Exchange, had been apprenticed herself, becoming free in 1670. One of three sisters, she had inherited £150 from her father, a higher clergyman.[55] She went to take at least seven apprentices between 1673 and 1693, their origins from Scotland to Gloucester a testament to the wide-ranging networks of apprenticeship, though at least one was a relation (Figure 3.7). None of Erskine's apprentices seem to have become free,

---

[55] TNA, PROB 11/267 (1657); GL MS 34018/5 (1670), 9 March 1669/70. Erskine's work on the Exchange is discussed in Chapter 1.

Table 3.5. *Mistresses and their female apprentices, 1640–1700*[a]

	Taking one female apprentice	Taking 2 or more female apprentices	Total
Widows of freemen	20 *80%*	4	24
Spinsters freed by servitude	8 *57%*	6	14
Spinsters free by patrimony/redemption	10 *73%*	4	14
Total single mistresses	**39** *73%*	**14**	**52**
Married mistresses	132 *73%*	47	179
Total taking apprentices	**172** *71%*	**68**	**240**

[a] *Source*: ROLLCO, LAA.

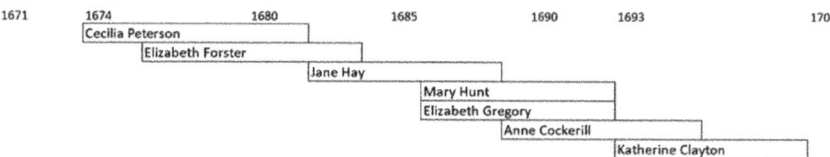

Figure 3.7 Rachel Erskine's apprentices

but tax records show Anne Cockerill, apprenticed in 1689, still living with her in 1695, as well as the more recently apprenticed Katherine Clayton, suggesting that the residential training lasted at least a good portion of the seven years. Erskine continued to run an Exchange shop, living with other exchangewomen nearby, until around 1710, at which point she bought several annuities. Erskine's widowed sister, who lived in Westminster, bequeathed her estate to her in 1712, and Rachel Erskine herself died in 1718, planning to share her sister's grave.[56]

Erskine was one of a few mistresses in the formal record with numerous, overlapping apprentices; her long career was unusual. Elizabeth Kingsman was another prolific mistress. A single woman who had claimed freedom by her father's right in the elite Grocers' Company, she enrolled five girls between 1692 and 1696, three of them the daughters of gentry in Surrey and Middlesex (Figure 3.8). Her apprentices overlapped even more than Erskine's, but in the 1695 tax records, only

[56] GL, MS 34038/16–17; LMA, COL/CHD/LA/04/058, p. 10; TNA, PROB 11/547, 565 (1715, 1718); LMA, MS 11316/31 and 34. Erskine's sister's will mentions a 'niece Hay'.

Managing the Trade: Women as Mistresses 125

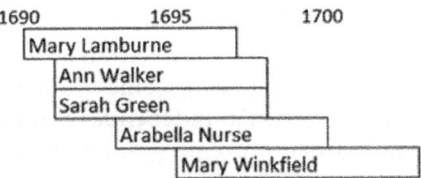

Figure 3.8 Elizabeth Kingsman's apprentices

two of the four who should have been living with her were listed, suggesting short and interrupted contracts. Kingsman was a lodger herself, and her business has left no other records except the household tax list which describes her as partners with Mrs Mary Daniels.[57] More typical were the many single women who took a few apprentices for short periods of their lives with gaps of one to three years between them; their businesses were either short-lived or not large enough to require apprentices. For some, marriage was a significant disruption. Margaret Drury, a mantua-maker in St Martin in the Fields, married in the middle of her apprentice's time: the apprentice petitioned for a discharge because her new husband, 'John Turin, a Scotchman', ill-treated her.[58]

Apprenticeship, it seems, could fit the many different circumstances in which women found themselves in a world where marriage defined legal and economic identity, but most women spent part of their adult lives single or widowed, and a significant proportion never married. The distinctive autonomy of mistresses also made them vulnerable to the risks of trade collapse. In 1692, Katherine Cole complained to the Middlesex sessions that her daughter, apprenticed with a £20 premium, had been abandoned by the milliner she was apprenticed to in Covent Garden: the mistress, Bridget Lazenby, had left her house, taken her goods and taken refuge in Blackfriars.[59]

Spinster mistresses were part of the group of single women in late seventeenth-century cities who, segregated from the marital economy, found room to develop independent work. Edinburgh had a similarly strong apprenticeship economy, with seamstresses established in the city shops.[60] A testimony in the London church courts reveals brief details of a girl who travelled with her mistress between the two. Katherine Hill, born in Newcastle around 1667, was apprenticed to an embroiderer when she was around twelve; she began in Jermyn Street in London

---

[57] LAA; 1692 Poll Tax; LMA, COL/CHD/LA/04/032, p. 14.
[58] LMA, MJ/SBB/524, p. 20 (1695).   [59] LMA, MJ/SBB/499, p. 18 (1692).
[60] Elizabeth Sanderson, *Women and Work in Eighteenth-Century Edinburgh* (Basingstoke: Macmillan, 1996).

but then moved with her mistress to Edinburgh for five years.[61] In the Glovers' Company, girls were taken on as journeywomen with certificates of their training outside London, having come from Cardiff or Nottingham.[62] In other places, women's independent trading was obstructed, with provincial authorities preventing single women from accessing the privileges of civic freedom. In late seventeenth-century Southampton, bodice-maker Mary Shrimpton was just one of those evicted from the town. Portsmouth, Liverpool and Nottingham also prosecuted single women for trading the town for trading (as, for example, drapers and grocers) without the freedom.[63] London's corporation also pursued women who traded without being free, but with a difference: it offered a route to enable them to become so. From the 1650s and more markedly from the 1670s, single women took up the freedom after apprenticeship, or through patrimony (drawing on their father's rights) or redemption, paying a fee. Southampton followed something of the same route from 1700, moving towards licensing single women traders rather than penalising them.[64]

Neither apprentice numbers nor the size of shops predicted the stability of a woman's business. Elizabeth Fazakerley took only one apprentice, in 1694, but she was still an active member of the Drapers' Company in 1712, when she paid the quarterage tax, and her apprentice also became an Exchange shopkeeper. Another single mistress, Elizabeth Rand, was born a few months after her father's death in 1660. While her older brother became an apprentice, she took up the freedom by patrimony when she was twenty-two, using her father's old membership of the Joiners' Company. By the 1690s, in her thirties, the poll tax described Rand as a sempstress, and she took on a distant kinswoman, Ann Dryden, 'to learn her trade'. In 1695, the two were living in lodgings with a goldsmith's family in the parish of Christ Church. There was one maidservant in the household whose services they may have shared. Rand may have taken other apprentices, but Ann Dryden is the only one whose records survive, because she too took up the freedom after completing her training. Elizabeth Rand's years of London work established her on a sound social and financial footing. At her death in 1715, she left instructions for ten bachelors and ten maids to lead her funeral procession with

---

[61] LMA, DL/C/ 242, p. 253 (10 February 1688).   [62] GL, MS 4591/1.
[63] Amy M. Froide, *Never Married: Singlewomen in Early Modern England* (Oxford University Press, 2005), 93.
[64] On the marginalisation of never-married women compared to wives and widows, see Amy Froide, 'Marital Status as a Category in Early Modern England', in *Singlewomen in the European Past, 1250–1800*, ed. Judith Bennett and Amy Froide (Philadelphia: University of Pennsylvania Press, 1999).

scarves, gloves and favours. She requested the parish clerk of Christ Church to sing the last four verses of Psalm 73 ('For, lo, they that are far from thee shall perish: thou hast destroyed all them that go a whoring from thee'). And she left to her executor's wife her best black silk gown of paduasoy, her silk stitched petticoat and her best hood and ruffles.[65]

Once established, single women could be the origin of generations of female apprenticeship. Anne Tirrey was the eldest of three children of a London goldsmith. In 1666, when she turned twenty-one, she took up her right to the freedom through patrimony. In the next four years, she took two apprentices, of whom one, Rebecca Deards, the daughter of a grocer in Bedfordshire, went on to complete her apprenticeship and become free herself. In 1679, Rebecca Deards became a mistress by taking her own fifteen-year-old sister as apprentice. By the early 1690s, in her late thirties, she had a shop in the Royal Exchange, had taken on at least one other apprentice and was living with another sister as a lodger in the parish of St Christopher le Stocks, close to the Exchange.[66] The combination of sibling and professional ties in Rebecca's career was typical and laid a pattern for seamstresses and milliners in the eighteenth century.[67] Sisters and aunts created a parallel system to the patrimonies that only fathers could pass on. Anne and Bridget Flowerdew, from a Norfolk gentry family, followed a similar route, with Anne, who had become free of the Weavers' Company, taking on Bridget in 1679, followed by Ann Stone in 1681 and Elizabeth Burrough in 1684. All of them became free. At least two more of Bridget's own apprentices, Ann Hall and Emblem Stamper, took the freedom in 1691 and 1720 respectively.[68]

One of the ways that single women survived in a household-oriented economy was by partnership and shared accommodation, and apprenticeship records also leave some evidence of these arrangements. In St Martin in the Fields in 1688, two seamstresses, Mary Kent and Barsheba Dynes, took Anne Dyott as an apprentice for five years for a £30 premium; the next year, Clare Guttridge, aged fourteen, was apprenticed for seven years with a £15 premium to learn the trade of milliner and embroiderer from Penelope Batchelor and Ann Ithall in Pall Mall.[69] These were business partnerships that were meant to last. Whether they

---

[65] LMA, COL/CHD/LA04/9, p. 30; LMA, COL/CHD/FR/02/0219, no. 63; TNA, PROB 11/550/232 (1716). Ann Dryden's mother was an Austin, and Austin cousins were among Rand's legatees.
[66] LMA, COL/CHD/LA04/026, p. 3.
[67] For another example of this pattern, see Erickson, 'Eleanor Mosley'.
[68] LMA, COL/CHD/FR/02/0024, no. 46, 146; /0055, no. 16; 0171, no. 34; 0394, no. 9.
[69] LMA, MJ/SBB/B/0048 (book 495, p. 18); MJ/SBB/B/0046 (book 479, p. 65).

were living as well as working together is not clear, but spinster couples were well established in the urban economy.[70] In 1659, Suzanna Glascock, widow of a clothworker, took Luce Farmer as an apprentice in partnership with her daughter to teach her buttonmaking. Four years earlier, she had used her husband's trade of a joiner to enrol a male apprentice.[71] Her freedom by courtesy, as a clothworker's widow, enabled her to take apprentices both in the continuing business of her dead husband and, later, a trade more manageable for two women.

The distinctiveness of single women's participation in some London companies suggests they established some kind of company identity that married women, free through their husbands, did not; in the 1650s and 1660s, this may have been as simple as a knowledge of which companies formally enrolled women, and which did not, as this was the first hurdle to the freedom. Equally important were younger female relatives to join them as apprentices, inheritances to allow investment or retirement and the availability of accommodation near a shop. Like the French seamstresses whose guilds gave them a new kind of gendered economic identity, London women, both married and single, were developing a professional identity based on working for themselves.[72] The domestic side of apprenticeship, in which mistresses had to act to some degree as parents, also meant that single women could be better placed to take apprentices than single men. Perhaps it was not surprising that when Ann Gray's mistress proposed to marry, her brother demanded that her husband-to-be provide security for the apprentice.

Widows, commonly described as 'consorts' of their husbands' companies, had a long-standing position in London guilds. It was common for them, often supported by journeymen or older apprentices, to continue their husbands' trade. Some also took new apprentices, although this was as rare as girls being apprenticed: only 1.4 per cent of the boys apprenticed across ten companies were indentured to women, including in the Founders, Girdlers and Goldsmiths. Almost all these women took only one apprentice. They partook, if briefly, in both the freedom and the artisanal competence of their husbands, and their continuing roles help illuminate the partnerships of working marriages.

Widows in companies worked, as single women rarely did, in trades that were typically male, and often took on boys. In the Clothworkers' Company, one of the few companies which recorded actual occupations,

---

[70] Amy M. Froide, 'Hidden Women: Rediscovering the Singlewomen of Early Modern England', *Local Population Studies* 68 (2002): 26–41.
[71] Scott, *Apprenticeship Disputes* no. 4331 (1659); ROLLCO, Suzanna Glascock.
[72] Crowston, *Fabricating Women*, 219.

the balance of sectors in which widows took apprentices was the same as it was for men: around half in textile manufacturing and the rest equally split between making clothes, shopkeeping, food provision and manufacturing non-textile goods. Within the textile sector, widows had access to a wider range of trades than single women, including silk stocking-making, silkweaving, packing and flax dressing. Even those described as seamstresses occasionally took on male apprentices. Outside textiles, widows' trades included cabinet-making, wheel-making, shoemaking and a tobacconist. Seventeen per cent of the Clothworkers widows were in the food and drink trades, including victuallers and food suppliers like Bridget Ford in Leadenhall whose husband was a cheesemonger and who took an apprentice as a bacon-seller after his death.[73] In the Goldsmiths', Mary Chalicombe continued her husband's flourishing business for twenty years after his death, taking nine apprentices. In the Stationers' Company, widows had long established a place in carrying on their husbands' workshops. Elizabeth Purslowe took over her husband George's business in 1634, taking on two more apprentices and printing pamphlets under her name. Anne Purslowe, printing in the 1660s, may have been their daughter.[74] However, widows' work generally preserved a set of gender distinctions. Mostly, they took boys, not girls, and passed on their trades of box-making, distilling or packing to them.

Widows' work offers another side to the independent work of many married women: businesses where husbands and wives worked together and widows continued it. One milliner's widow, in court when her apprentice attempted to claim back his premium after leaving early, offered a detailed testimony of how women learned their trades from their husbands. Anne Eaton's husband was often abroad at fairs, buying commodities; Anne managed the shop in his absence. She was, said a fellow merchant, well experienced, with great insight in the trade and was able to manage it at home and abroad. He recalled her husband 'hath taken her Approbacon in the buying of silk' and that he 'within a short tyme after his being first married to her did begin to bring her up to the management of his trade and to Experience her therein'. After his death, she went to the fairs herself, taking her brother with her. Her defence is a rare glimpse into the quotidian experience of married women and widows learning a trade.[75]

A different case, brought by the widower and debtors of Elizabeth York in 1662, demonstrates the autonomy and responsibility that widowhood could involve. York had married twice, and both husbands seem to

---

[73] ROLLCO; Scott, *Apprenticeship Disputes*.   [74] ROLLCO.
[75] LMA, CLA/024/05/364 (1678).

have been silkweavers. Her first husband was said to have earned at least £100 a year and to have left her £150 in ready money at his death, as well as £150 worth of goods, including 'a good quantity of silk ready to work'. When she married again, she had enough money to lend it out at interest. She kept a tight control of her own affairs, telling friends she 'did not desire that her husband should have any knowledge of her affairs and dealings'. Another friend said she was 'a person very able and capable to tell and count money', so that her first husband trusted her with his whole business: 'selling his wares, buying comodities to work upp and receipt and payment of his moneys'. Her second husband, another witness reported, had so much love and respect to her that he 'was more like a servant then a husband to her and did leave very much the management of his trade and buying and selling his wares and taking and paying his moneys into her care'.[76] Few widows had their business roles tracked in such detail, but York's friends' observations testify to women's close attention to each other's economic activities and to the range of partnerships that were possible.

There is occasional evidence of the strains as well as the successes of widows continuing in a trade. Margery Hickman explained she had been forced out of the cooper's trade she had inherited from her husband because the merchants who employed her would not allow her to keep him in her service, although he was 'well instructed'. It was his habit of theft rather than her management that was the issue, it seems, but there is a sense in the witness's phrase 'would not consent' that suggests the merchants who had previously employed her husband had an overseeing hand in her affairs in widowhood.[77] Rather than arguing she was capable of instructing her apprentices as well as her husband had, Hickman's attorney pointed out that she had another apprentice who was nearly out of his time and was able to do the teaching. The hands-on involvement on training was much less available to her than to a woman working in millinery or another retail trade.

Anne Gardner, a cutler's widow, was described as inheriting 'a plentiful trade and stock' on her husband's death. She tried to continue the business of selling and sharpening knives herself, but 'having noe skill therein herself & hir two apprentices ... being yong & unable to manage the trade' had to give up after three months.[78] She sold the business and went into lodgings. Witnesses for the apprentice's parents felt that had Anne had the skills, or had the apprentices been older, the business would have been viable; it was their shared inexperience that made it

[76] LMA, CLA/024/05/145.   [77] LMA, CLA/024/05/364 (1678).
[78] LMA, CLA/024/05/436 (1685).

impossible. Another cutler's widow managed very well until she took on a male partner. Several men came to testify that Elizabeth Clayton, having worked with her first husband, was 'very well experienced in the trade of a cutler and very well able to manage such a trade'. After his death, she continued to deal in knives, scissors, elephants' teeth, iron and steel, and her second husband joined her as a novice, taking Anthony Drabble as an apprentice. Drabble had served five years when the second husband died, and at his request Elizabeth took him on as a journeyman on wages of £20 a year. She later agreed to take him into partnership, which cost her the sale of a lease and some money from her son to invest in the renewed business. When Anthony Drabble himself fell ill, he asked Elizabeth Clayton to continue the partnership to benefit his kin, but she sensibly refused to sign a contract with a dying man. Frances Cobden, a fellow widow in her fifties, gave the most pointed account of Anthony Drabble's relations with Elizabeth. Requested to give his accounts to her, he had refused, sometimes offering 'indifferent good words', but at other times falling out with her. He would 'very much and grossly abuse her with ill language and did call her old trot and say she should never have any account from him'.[79] Frances Cobden's testimony is painfully familiar from other misogynistic depictions of widows with economic power.

Binding Networks

With these complex relationships with the institution of apprenticeship, matching mistresses and apprentices was not necessarily straightforward. Single women and widows would appear to be particularly vulnerable to the risks of their business being undermined by remarriage, yet plenty of parents trusted in their capacity to take on a five- or seven-year apprenticeship. Recommendations spread with city gossip, and by letters. Guilds, for women, seem not to have provided anything like a social network; for many, their access to guild privilege came through husbands or fathers affiliated to, and sometimes practising, a trade that was not theirs. Sometimes the company can be seen helping. The Drapers' Company clerk recorded in 1659 that Dorothy Barber, a 'poor woman of the Company', who had nine children, wanted her daughter to be placed as an apprentice but lacked the premium; the Warden was ordered to place her to 'Mrs Ward a seampster or any other fit person', providing £5 from the company coffers.[80]

---

[79] LMA, CLA/024/05/74 (1654).   [80] Drapers' Company, MB 41, 234 (1659).

Mistresses in one company do not seem to have had particular connections with each other. More significant were the ties of common work, patronage, family and neighbourhood. Gentry families often had city ties: Ann Gray's brother described how he had arranged her contract with Sarah Cleave, who he had known for several years, with a premium paid partly by a Mrs Elizabeth Peyton and partly by himself.[81] For the Hulls/Whinnicks and the Spilletts/Blennerhassetts, apprenticeship drew on and furthered family bonds, leading to further legacies. Marital networks had a long reach through time: Marmaduke Bludder, a girdler, and his third wife took on two girls with the surname of his first wife, Susanna Impey.[82] Provincial gentry families often had regular business in London, which would make it easier to find mistresses for their daughters, but the networks of artisans outside the city are harder to detect.

A collection of personal papers, that of the Temple family of Stowe, contains the record of an apprenticeship arrangement made apparently on the family's behalf. Conquest Taylor and Marie Gascoigne were cousins and both related to the Temples; Marie's father was a Huntingdonshire gentleman, and Conquest, based in Covent Garden, seems to have regularly run London errands for John Temple. In a set of 'articles of agreement' in 1649, Conquest Taylor, himself only twenty, arranged with Thomas Bull, a member of the Merchant Taylors' Company, and his wife Abigail, a button-maker, that they would take Marie as an apprentice for five years, after which she would be made free of the City of London, 'according to the custom of the said City'. Abigail's trade was clearly the dominant one. The contract was witnessed by Abigail, Hester Berry and Nathaniel Howes, the women signing with initials only: full literacy was not critical to participation. Contracts like these, the paperwork that bound girls into new households but was meaningful only to those involved, rarely survive. This one, despite referencing the custom of London, was directly contrary to the rule that required seven years' apprenticeship, and Marie was not enrolled with the company. Marie's training did not assure her future; eleven years later, still single, she was writing to Richard Temple to request him to relieve her hardship by paying her the £20 legacy that his grandmother had left her in 1656, the lack of which was causing her brother and her 'great distresse'.[83]

---

[81] LMA, CLA/024/05/493 (1689). [82] ROLLCO.
[83] Huntington Library, Temple Papers, STT 820, Mary Gascoigne to Sir Richard Temple, and STT Personal Box 10 (14) for the agreement. My thanks to Catherine Hinchliff for these finds. Hester Temple's will is TNA, PROB 11/257/457 (1656).

Connecting girls with mistresses drew particularly on the networks of women that both business and family life fostered, but men were involved too. Mary Huetson, 'instrumental in placeing' Dorothy Stable with Ann Kent, was a Haberdasher's wife who had known the Stables all her life. When Ann died, Dorothy's father directed Anthony Smith, a London gentleman who had known the family only four years, and others of her friends to try to find 'another fitting person of the [same] trade with whom to place her'.[84] Sensibly, some girls would be placed 'on liking' with a mistress for a period before the contract was made.

Descriptions of mistresses' character are much rarer than those of apprentices: it was no one's job, at court, to attack their industry, their morals or their skills. Hester Pinney, who held a shop in the New Exchange in the Strand selling lace, and her sister-in-law Mary left more personal records of their search for a mistress. The Pinney archive records a dispute between Hester Pinney and a Mrs Reeves after an apprentice that Pinney placed with Reeves died. It certifies that Mrs Reeves agreed with 'Madam Peny', after the death of her apprentice A.B., to return to Pinney all the wearing apparel of the apprentice, as long as Pinney defrayed her funeral expenses. She had, however, refused to return it, claiming that Pinney had not fully repaid 14 pence for rosemary, 10 shillings for nursing, 6 pence for the gravedigger, 4 pence for the affidavit that she had been buried in wool as the law required, 4 shillings for king's tax and an apothecary's bill for 40 or 50 shillings.

The identity of A.B. is kept secret. However, the Pinney letters record a long set of negotiations and subsequent conflict about a 'Mistress Wallop', for whom they had assumed responsibility. Henrietta Wallop had eventually been apprenticed to Margaret Reeves, a seamstress in the Haberdashers' Company who took a series of apprentices after her husband's death, starting with her own daughter in 1682. The Pinneys were already finding lodgings for Henrietta Wallop in summer 1693, when Mary Pinney described her difficulties: 'I have had a sad time with Mr Beele and his wife aboutt Mrs Walope he stood mightily on 4s 6d for her board'. The Beeles had haggled over her costs, claiming that Hester had said she'd left £12 with Mary to bind the girl to them. Business was in trouble, and food was becoming very dear, with bread at 3s for a peck loaf. Eventually Mary removed the girl and her things – 'which will be better for the Child'. She proposed to take her to 'the French woman' for a fortnight on trial, but the French woman wanted £15 with her; she thought she might put her in a school at Chelsea, but they had no room

---

[84] LMA, CLA/024/05/449 (1685).

for her on half-board. The letter ends with Mary sending love to her son back in Bristol with the family. (Mary's husband had been transported to Nevis for his part in the Monmouth Rebellion. Her own place in the Pinney family was awkward; Hester's father referred to her persistently as 'the Scot' and claimed she made trouble, but she was also recognised to be a canny and successful worker.)

Eighteen months later, Hester, who at this time was living partly in London and partly in Bristol, heard from Mary again, with a better idea for Henrietta Wallop. She suggested: 'Mrs Reess hass a minde to take aprintess.' She would take no less than £20, but Mary was convinced it would be much better for her there. Mrs Reeves, Mary said, was an ideal mistress, 'the best & most Ingenious of her tread makes & draws all her own patterns works only to people of the greatest quality & for these six years that I have known her she hass binn more like a mother then a mistress to her printess & to her humor & life & conversation I never in my holl life observes eny person of more holliness & scircumspction'. She was sure it was best for the girl: 'I know she will be happy ... genteel & well', and at the end of her apprenticeship, Mrs Reeves paid her journey-people well. Finally, Mary said, 'the child will be safely brought up & in the puerest doctin she being a member of Mr Silvfesters'. (Matthew Silvester's church at Blackfriars would echo the Pinneys' own Non-conformist background.) Mary offered to add 'something towards it myself' to get the girl bound. The letter is now sadly torn, but in the middle of it was a heartfelt phrase: 'if I had a daughter I loved as I love my Life I would binde her to her and go satissfied to Nevis.'[85]

The Haberdashers' records show that Mary's plan came off, and Henrietta Wallop was indentured to Margaret Reeve, a widow who took two other apprentices, in March 1695.[86] Whose was this daughter Henrietta that Mary imagined loving as her own ? The Haberdashers' apprenticeship register lists Henrietta as the daughter of 'Henry Wallop esquire of Downhusband, Hampshire'. The Wallops were county neighbours of the Pinneys and had financial entanglements with them; Henry was the eldest surviving son, an MP, and apparently single. But Henrietta's birth was registered, in 1681, in the parish of St Bride's Fleet Street: 'Henrietta Wallop daughter of Henry Wallop by

---

[85] Bristol University Special Collections, Pinney Papers, Red Box 2 folder VII, Mary Pinney to Hester Pinney, 7 February 1695. The full final phrase of this letter is cited in Pamela Sharpe, 'Lace and Place: Women's Business in Occupational Communities in England 1550-1950', *Women's History Review* 19, no. 2 (2010): 283-306. I'm very grateful to Prof. Sharpe for generous discussions of the Pinney evidence.

[86] GL, MS 15860/007, p. 354 (March 1695).

Hester'.[87] Every other mother on those pages was described as 'his wife' or, in one case, with a different surname, indicating illegitimacy. But the Hester who was Henrietta's mother had no last name. Henry Wallop and Hester Pinney were in their mid-twenties in 1681, both in London away from their families. Hester was a relatively uncommon name. Henrietta Wallop was clearly the responsibility of the Pinneys for at least eighteen months in the early 1690s. The deep concern expressed by Mary Pinney to her sister-in-law about 'the child', and her slip into thinking as a mother, suggests that the Henrietta that Hester and Mary were trying to place was actually Hester's illegitimate child by Henry. Henry died in Covent Garden in 1691, intestate, and the next year Hester sued his family for a debt of £500 that she claimed to have lent him.[88]

The relationship between the Pinneys and Margaret Reeve ended sourly, with the dispute about the costs of 'A.B.' In 1701 Mary Pinney, by this time in Nevis with her husband, was writing to Hester expressing her sorrow that Hester and Mrs Reeves had had a difference; they were selling goods for her in Nevis. Mrs Reeves, she said, had written to her about Henrietta's clothes not being provided as had been promised, but 'I took little notice of it but referred to the indenture knowing I did nothing of my own head'. The indenture was by this time in the hands of Hester's brother Nathaniel. The whole affair seemed to have led to gossip and abuse, with accusations amongst a 'cabal' of other women who had wronged Mary Pinney and were fomenting scandal about reputation and financial losses, 'but all these things is over now the poor girl is dead I think the strife should end'. The 'A.B.' whose death caused the dispute must, in fact, have been Henrietta Wallop, and Hester had been embroiled in arguments over the costs of her daughter's clothes and death until 1700.

Despite its unusual secrets, this story records the kind of care for both work and personal reputation that family and friends put into finding a mistress. Mary Pinney's careful and useful assessment of Mrs Reeves, a haberdasher's widow who had apprenticed a series of girls including her own daughter, emphasised a respectable house and a pious, maternal mistress, but also the future earnings of a wage labourer. Others, with more to invest in their wards or children, were more interested in the chance to set up independently. Details like this survive most often for apprentices with premiums, often substantial ones; how plans were made between poorer families is harder to establish. The expectations that came with high premiums involved a sense of investment, value and

---

[87] LMA, P69/BRI/A/005/MS06540/002 (7 August 1681).
[88] TNA, C10 403/40; C24/1160; C381/1; C24/1158.

gentility, and different rules applied where apprenticed girls were perceived as bringing little value. But given the density of communications and social knowledge in early modern London and the migration-based networks between London and the provinces, we might expect the understanding of apprenticeship as a contract to be nurtured and safeguarded, requiring family and friendly involvement, to apply there too.

The rules of City custom and coverture made women's transitions through the cycle of apprenticeship, freedom and marriage considerably more complex and unpredictable in its advantages than those of men. Mistresses were strikingly independent from both husbands and guild authority: in contrast to the assumptions that often underpin economic history, women appear to have been more necessary to the work of training apprentices than men, and single women could be mistresses in a way that single men were unlikely to be masters. Becoming a mistress was a life-cycle moment but not a single one; women were likely to cycle in and out of the work of running shops and training girls. Marginalised from the social networks of guilds, women used apprenticeship, family bonds and neighbourhood or Exchange contacts to build up networks that benefitted both their businesses and their families. Despite their differences, married and single women partook of a common culture of apprenticeship. Being a mistress itself encouraged the habit and networks of apprenticeship. Mary Bickerstaff's first experience, as far as we know, was in training Hester Hudson as a seamstress in 1650, but when she died in 1687, she left money to have her grandchildren, boys and girls alike, 'put forth … apprentice to some honest callings and imployments'.[89]

---

[89] TNA, PROB 11/389/93.

4 What Girls Learned

Mary Jones and Frances Carey

'Do you know,' demanded the libel that initiated a Mayor's Court case in 1666, 'how long the defendant Frances Carey before the said Mary was bound to her as her Apprentice had kept shop as a sempster, and whether she was not very desirous to have her bound to her and for what reasons?'[1] Mary Jones had been apprenticed to Carey to learn her trade 'as a sempstresse & to wash and starch Linnen & to sell wares in ye shop'. In retrospect, Frances Carey's importunate desire to have Mary Jones as her apprentice was a bad sign. It suggested, Mary's guardian alleged, that she was not sufficiently well established to train her properly, but rather that she needed the premium she brought.

Mary's case was presented by Robert Blaney, the clerk of the Haberdashers' Company, later to establish himself as a leading Nonconformist lawyer. He must have had experience of the apprenticeship of girls into city shops. In the event, as the family told it, his misgivings were justified. Carey did not have enough trade to keep her shop going; she and her husband used Mary Jones's premium as the investment the business needed, and because there was not enough trade, or enough money, to expand the shop, Mary spent her time doing household labour instead of learning the skills of trading that were meant to help her establish herself in life. She left her apprenticeship and got married, and her family sued for the return of her original premium. In the family's eyes, apprenticeship was an education for work, inculcating a hierarchy of skills that gave women a lifelong access to flexible, marketable and sometimes prestigious labour. This artisanal education for girls, notably absent from the contemporary and historical literature on apprenticeship, is the subject of this chapter. Despite the minimal historical and contemporary discussion of female apprenticeship, legal testimonies and apprenticeship documentation reveal an established set of

---

[1] LMA, CLA/024/05/198B.

specialised skills and shared understandings of what, and how, young women learned. Beginning with Mary Jones, the chapter goes on to reconstruct the range of trades to which girls were apprenticed across differences of background and status. The most common occupation, seamstress, involved a hierarchy of competences, from wielding the needle to giving out change. Those skills both enabled economic autonomy and reflected codes of gendered work and behaviour.

Mary Jones's case exemplifies one route to becoming a seamstress, and it illuminates the skills, investment and networks that apprenticeship involved. The dominant trade of girls in apprenticeships in late seventeenth-century London, seamstry encompassed both shop work and manual craft. Mary had been apprenticed to Frances and Richard Carey, based in Whitechapel, in the early 1660s. Frances Carey was running a shop in partnership with Ann Washington, which she rented from Mary Baker for £10 a year, until she left and moved her stock elsewhere. Although Richard Carey is mentioned in the case, all the references to the shop present it as run by Frances with other women. In keeping with this female world, Mary's widowed mother was keen on her apprenticeship, but her uncle and her guardian had made enquiries about the Careys and 'could not understand them to be in such a condicon as they alleged themselves to be'. Rather, they were 'but new Beginners in the world and had not any considerable stock & trade whereby the said Mary might be instructed'. It turned out Frances had only had the shop for six weeks before taking Mary on. Robert Blaney told Mary's mother that he feared the money he was going to give with Mary's apprenticeship would be 'but cast away'. His misgivings clarify the financial implications of kinship. Whether Blaney was kin to Mary Jones or a friend, in the fullest early modern sense, he was bound to support her by investing in her future. The apprenticeship would give her somewhere to live and the skills to support herself, or to bring both skill and business opportunity into a marriage. Such arrangements worked as service did for other young women, as a means of transition from natal family to adult life, and perhaps they were particularly useful when, as in Mary Jones's case, widowed mothers had remarried. Like service, apprenticeship was a life-cycle experience, and more explicitly than service, it trained young women in marketable, non-domestic skills.

Robert Blaney also helped Mary and her mother manage the risks of apprenticeship, drawing up a contract in which the Careys received £10 in hand and the promise of £15 more in three years' time, but only if Frances Carey offered the correct training. This was summarised: 'Provided that she the said Frances kept open shopp & continued in th'art of a sempstresse and to wash and starch Linnen and to sell wares in ye shop.' This is one of the few phrases that outlines a seamstress's actual work, but it still leaves the 'art of a sempstresse' a little obscure. What Mary Jones and her peers were meant to learn was a trade which included sewing; washing and starching; and selling goods from a flourishing, well-stocked shop. It was a combination of skills that meant they could work independently, in their own shops, or for others.

After a year, the arrangement was proving unsatisfactory to Mary's family. Her uncle, William Roberts, himself a merchant tailor, testified that Frances and Mary were both 'but as servants' to another woman who had been established in trade by Ann Washington, Frances's original partner. Frances's trade was 'in a declining condition', and Mary 'could not in all likelyhood be taught her trade'. William Roberts demanded part of the £10 premium back, and the bond for the further £15, but Frances refused, saying that if she did not get the full amount, Mary could go and learn her trade where she liked. Mary left, and her mother hired an attorney to sue out her indentures. Ann Washington was described as bankrupt, and Frances lost her business and 'never again kept open shop', working instead from a private room. Frances Carey had moved from sole trader to partnership to serving another woman, and with every step away from autonomy her capacity to be an effective mistress was undermined.

Mary Jones's mother, Elizabeth Wolfe, gave more detail about these confrontations. Elizabeth, who signed her deposition only with a 'W', described herself, not her brother, as the active party in challenging the failed apprenticeship. Frances, Elizabeth said, had told her that they needed the premium money to open a new house and shop. Frances had explicitly told her that she would keep her daughter out of the shop itself (and its trade) until she got the extra £15, saying 'that the said Mary should not do a stitch of work in her trade and that she would make her a drudge to do the work about the house and that she should not come in the shop till such time the 3 years were expired'. Shop work, in this story, is a mark of esteem, and Mary was not granted enough of it: her mother said that when she left, she was 'little the better for her trade'. Mary was a London girl from birth, with family connections in the Inns of Court and companies. Literate and numerate, her move into the sewing trade must have seemed like a sensible plan to increase the value she took with her into the world. Instead, her uncle said he feared she would be 'distroyed', because of the 'ill examples given in the said house by men of a wanton life'. No one expanded upon this suggestion, but it resonated with the literary association of millinery with ill repute, a trope which throughout the seventeenth and eighteenth centuries laid a malicious undercurrent to women's work in fashion shops.

Witnesses for the mistress in this case, Frances Carey, naturally had a different version, as they defended her to help her keep the premium that Mary Jones's family had paid. Reflecting Frances's defence of her capacity to train Mary, they revealed a little more of what was expected of apprentices and their mistresses. All of them had worked with Frances. Elizabeth Brackley, wife of a leather seller, and Susan Streeter, whose husband's status of esquire denoted a higher rank, employed Frances to do sewing work for them. Mary Baker, a seamstress herself, leased part of her shop to Frances for £10 a year. Ann Washington, Frances's original business partner, described herself as a gentleman's wife living in Whitechapel. She had lived and worked with Frances for a year, observing her to be 'well skilled in the art of a Sempstress whereby the said Mary the Apprentice might have bine well skilled in her art'. Mary had 'attained to some skill in that time', enough to be 'serviceable to her'. Even here, the exact process of transmitting skill from mistress to apprentice remains opaque, as artisanship always was: apprenticeship was demonstration.[2] Within a year of working side by side, the student had sufficient art to add value to the mistress's trade. The loss of Mary's last few years of skilled labour to her mistress was estimated by Ann Washington at £30; similar sums in other cases suggests this was not an unreasonable price for two years' work from a newly minted seamstress. These careful calculations record both the economic value of apprenticeship, readily imperilled by apprentices who left early or mistresses whose trades were unstable, and the expertise of women of business, practised in careful observation of shop work and girls' value.

The connections between the working women of Mary Jones's world evidently sustained both apprenticeship and trade. Frances Carey's witnesses had used her to do work for them and their friends. Susan Streeter trusted Frances's seamstry skills and the extent of her business, because she had bought several white bands and shirts and other linen from her. She had recommended Frances to others: 'she hath helped her the said Frances to severall Customers which have bought Linnen of her.' Finally, she also bound an apprentice to Frances herself for seven years, who 'doth live very well with the said Defendant Frances & she this deponent questioneth not but that she [Frances] will make her a good workwoman & that she will be well instructed in her trade'. The Jones/Carey case, like others, is rooted in a female world of work and decision-making.

---

[2] LMA, CLA/04/198 (1666); on artisanal apprenticeship, Pamela H. Smith, *The Body of the Artisan: Art and Experience in the Scientific Revolution* (University of Chicago Press, 2004) and Bert de Munck, Steven L. Kaplan and Hugo Soly (eds.), *Learning on the Shop Floor: Historical Perspectives on Apprenticeship* (New York and Oxford: Berghahn Books, 2007).

The passing mention of this other apprentice also reveals something of the larger market of apprenticeships in early modern communities. Several court cases suggest the role women played in helping each other to apprentices: it is a system somewhat reminiscent of the 'brokering in maidens' that roused complaints in the sixteenth century, when women acted as agents in putting girls into service, but suggesting a functional, rather than exploitative, network for girls' training.[3] Frances, despite the reduction of her trade, was apparently still able to take an apprentice. The apprenticeship market for girls was much larger than the companies, and essentially diverse and informal, but that wider market also abode by some constant rules.

Mary Jones left her service sometime in 1665, leaving no evidence whether or not she carried on her trade. By the time the lawsuit began, she had married Richard Fudge, and she came back to see Mary Baker, the shop owner, and tell her that she had married and had a child. She had at least five more children in the next thirteen years but died in 1681; her widower remarried the next year. Frances Carey lost or sold most of her stock and reduced her trade. Their connections demonstrate a business network in which the acquisition of skills went hand in hand with an open shop and a proliferation of personal recommendations and obligations.

The scraps of evidence for young women's training in trade range across the spectrum of apprenticeship, from Mary Jones, apprenticed to learn to run a seamstress's shop for an substantial premium of £25, down to Bell Clement, a 'poor foundling' of St Clement Danes apprenticed to learn housewifery in 1694, costing the parish 40 shillings. Their domestic and labour arrangements differed enormously, as did the scope of their futures, but all belonged to a national system which included both boys and girls, though the terms of that inclusion varied widely by status, place and trade, as well as by gender. Its operating assumption was that girls, like boys, were subject to and protected by the discipline of the apprentice system, its responsibilities and its benefits, and that if this worked, they would emerge independent, capable of earning a living and having recompensed their masters and mistresses with labour and, often, some money. We have already seen how flexible women's sewing careers could be; apprenticeship provided, at best, a portfolio of shop and craft skills to which they could return after marriage if they did not continue as single workers or shopkeepers. Our most detailed evidence comes from the seamstresses and milliners at the higher end of the trade who went to

---

[3] Eleanor Hubbard, *City Women: Money, Sex, and the Social Order in Early Modern London* (Oxford University Press, 2012), 26–7.

court over their premiums. But the model of residential apprenticeships had a much wider social and occupational range, encompassing the poor citizens' daughters apprenticed from Christ's Hospital, the orphans and indigent girls placed out by their parishes and the daughters of artisanal and middling families who made private apprenticeship arrangements. The training of girls was part of the fabric of city life and of families, and it provides another dimension to how girls learned to be women and to how women's labour fitted into the urban economy.

The Range of Trades

Across Europe, the late seventeenth century has been identified as a 'watershed for the creation of new projects to train and employ girls', often outside guilds and typically involving sewing. Sometimes this involved state support, as in France where Jean-Baptiste Colbert, as Controller-General of Finance, encouraged girls into the lace industry and embroidery.[4] Learning to sew fitted girls into a wider market of women's work as well as a narrower concept of appropriate female occupations. Most girls learned to sew; middling girls in the eighteenth century were expected to sew for the family as well as making fancy work. Outside the home, those skills were taught at a higher level both at school and in formal and informal apprenticeships. An education in sewing was part of the provision families with resources gave to their daughters. In 1668, a lawsuit about unequal inheritance compared the various advancements three children had received. The son was apprenticed to a silversmith. His sister Elizabeth was sent to a boarding school 'to learne needleworke & starching': both 'education and provisions' were a 'great advancement' to both children. The last daughter, Frances, was left 'unadvanced' at her father's death: she had been 'a dutifull & obedient child to [her father] & did all his houshold worke in place of a maide servant'. Her father frequently proclaimed his good affection for her for her 'obedience and doing of his business about the house', but he died intestate and left her unprovided for.[5] Frances, no doubt, would have done the plain domestic sewing; her sister Elizabeth had received the investment of learning decorative needlework and starching, skills which could be used both in and out of the household.

---

[4] Clare Haru Crowston, 'Engendering the Guilds: Seamstresses, Tailors, and the Clash of Corporate Identities in Old Regime France', *French Historical Studies* 23, no. 2 (2000): 339–71.

[5] LMA, CLA/024/05/223 (1668).

The emphasis placed on the needle trades across the social spectrum meant, of course, that women who could sew were soon far too plentiful to make it a source of decent pay.[6] While some seamstresses, like those training the girls who sued out their premiums at the Mayor's Court, had shops or access to them, many more provided increasingly cheap labour for ready-made clothes shops. Although sewing was the foundation of the 'genteel' trades that eighteenth-century trades manuals recommended to middling daughters, to make money from it required running a shop, more than plying the needle. The Mayor's Court evidence tells us most about the early years of an apprenticeship, and in these years, girls were learning to sew the goods their mistresses sold; other evidence suggests shop work and managing the trade came later. The inventories of shops in the Royal Exchange and elsewhere provide further evidence for what women were doing in the sewing trades. Alongside 'suits' for both men and women, shops were selling ready-made shirts and sleeves, shifts, aprons, gloves, hoods, cuffs, linen bands and every kind of lace. Larger shopkeepers were buying linen, holland cloth and other textiles in quantity to put out to seamstresses to make up garments; in other shops, women both sold and made garments and accessories. Apprentices paying higher premiums were set to learn fancy sewing, make lace, cut patterns and sell in shops. Court cases also describe them starching, hemming and mending garments such as petticoats, part of the perpetual work of finishing and maintaining clothes. At the lower end, apprentices were mending stockings, making buttons, and cutting fur. All this testifies to the importance of accessories, trimming and remaking in the world of fashion, which allowed seamstresses to take an important part in the innovations and specialisation that London's wealthy consumers encouraged.[7]

Sewing was by far the main category of trade girls learned in apprenticeship, although there are risks in generalising across the gaps in indentures and apprenticeship registers, and the difference between company trades and what mistresses were doing.[8] Finding women's trades is complicated further by the uncertain extent to which married women worked independently from their husbands, and in indentures which

---

[6] Margaret R. Hunt, *The Middling Sort: Commerce, Gender, and the Family in England, 1680–1780* (Berkeley: University of California Press, 1996).
[7] John Styles, 'Product Innovation in Early Modern London', *Past & Present* 168 (2000): 124–69.
[8] Michael Scott, ed., *Apprenticeship Disputes in the Lord Mayor's Court of London, 1573–1723* (London: British Record Society, 2016) finds one in three masters practising trades that differ from their company; in the same sample, amongst mistresses of girls, only the Fruiterers are practising the same trade as their company.

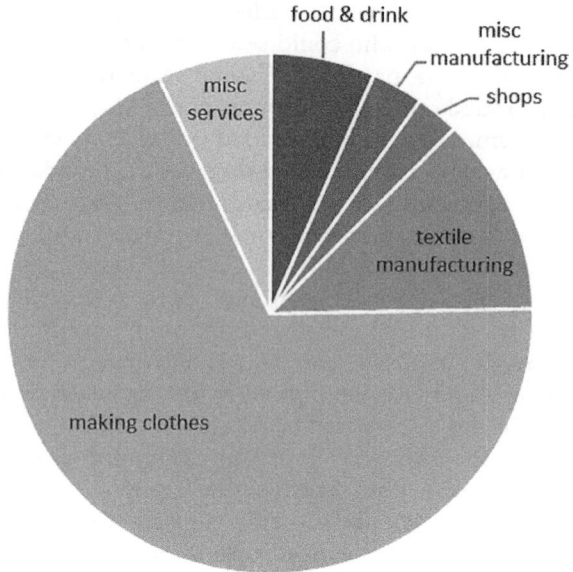

Figure 4.1 Named occupations in girls' apprenticeships
Source: 187 records which name occupations separate from company from Scott, *Apprenticeship Disputes*; ROLLCO, Clothworkers; Merchant Taylors' Company, GL, MS 3438/16-17

apprenticed girls to men rather than to the wives they were actually working with. However, enough reference to separate trades survives to list the range to which girls were apprenticed, without a guarantee that that was what they were actually learning.

Figure 4.1 shows the occupational sectors to which girls were apprenticed. It draws on the few records that give separate occupation details for women in guilds: the Clothworkers' and Merchant Taylors' apprenticeship registers and the Mayor's Court apprenticeship disputes. In all of them, making clothes was dominant. In the Clothworkers, apprentices were more likely to be bound to masters and mistresses with the trades of gloving, buttonmaking and subsidiary occupations like flax-dressing and silver-spinning; in the Merchant Taylors, seamstresses and milliners dominated, with bodice-makers, periwig-makers and coat-makers. Coats, and particularly children's coats, were well established as women's sewing work, on the understanding that they required less tailored cutting. There is also at least some evidence of non-textile work. The printers, leather-guilders and writing master in the Merchant Taylors may not have been teaching their trades to the girls apprenticed to them, but there are enough herbwomen to suggest this was a recognisable trade for women and girls. Fruiterers seem to have regularly apprenticed girls, and confectionery was another possibility. An unusual surviving indenture early in the eighteenth century records Isabella Dixon, an orphaned tailor's daughter, being bound 'of her own free will & the good liking of her friends' to Christopher Cobson of Aldersgate Street, a needlemaker, and to Alice, his wife, 'To Learn the Art & Mistery of a Pastry Cook, which the said Alice nowe Exercises and follows'.[9] Unusually, too, they guaranteed to give her a set of clothes fit for Sundays.

The more precise list of occupations to which apprentices were bound provides further details of the textile trades. The mistresses whose apprentices sued to dissolve their contracts at the Mayor's Court included a fringe-maker in the Shipwrights, button-makers and a wood-shavings hat maker in the Clothworkers, a coney-wool cutter in the Feltmakers, and a Clockmaker 'spinning silver and gold thread and flatting the same'. The clothes market was a specialised one, and the delineation of particular crafts suggests that the gendered distinction between tailors and seamstresses was not the only or perhaps even the main one at work. By the mid-eighteenth century, guidebooks like Joseph Collyer's *Parent's and Guardian's Directory* offered a compendium of apprenticeship possibilities, noting gendered skills in passing. Making bodices, buttons, fringes, fans, caps and quilting for petticoats and bed quilts were all identified as women's work; hat-making had become a women's trade, while tire-makers to dress women's hair had fallen out of fashion.[10] Cutting rabbit fur to trim hats or clothes demanded girls with great dexterity 'first to pluck off the long straggling hairs, and then to cut off the fine wool that grows underneath' without damaging the fur's integrity. The delineation of trades here invokes gender differentiation based in part on the nature of the object – women's and children's goods, and ornamentation like fringes, were suited to female manufacture – but also on the type of skill: dexterity, or the 'good eyes and a dry hand' and 'fancy and genius' required for gold and silver buttons. Gold and silver thread-spinning, another trade frequently offered to the apprentices of the late seventeenth century, likewise demanded a dry hand. Many of these trades involved working in workshops, on machines such as the wheel that flattened gold and silver wire. Pinmaking, still done by hand, involved predominantly female apprentices and many other women

---

[9] LMA, COL/CHD/FR/02/184/35.
[10] Joseph Collyer, *The Parent's and Guardian's Directory, and the Youth's Guide, in the Choice of a Profession or Trade* (1761), 114.

outside the guild: they would have been cutting wire and coiling the head using a pinner's bone and sharpening the pins. A tradesmen's guide of 1747 noted 'no hard Labour, some Nicety, yet dirtyish'.[11] The range of apprenticeship trades in the later seventeenth-century evidence provides a valuable reference point between the better-recorded occupations of the later eighteenth century and the specialised dress-related occupations of the earlier seventeenth. Female apprenticeship was expanding, and it was being integrated both into potentially genteel and lucrative millinery and seamstress shops and into the lower, poorer paid work manufacturing the raw materials of fashion.

Table 4.1 uses legal and company records to track the gendered crafts taught to female apprentices in the London companies in the later seventeenth century. The sample includes registers from two companies particularly associated with textiles, but the more representative records from the Mayor's Court reflect a similar balance of clothing and non-clothing work for women. The table includes only occupations that are listed separately from guild membership, with the exception of fruiterers who were consistently practising that trade, and the second column indicates occupations ascribed to single mistresses, which provide the most reliable guide as to whether a woman was actually practising and teaching them. It can be seen from these figures that only a few trades were identifiably practised by women on their own: seamstresses, coat-makers and children's coat-makers predominate. The tire-women (all married) would have been making headgear, part of women's sewing work that spread from the theatrical world of the sixteenth century into private households and shops.[12] Exchangewomen and men trained girls to both work in shops and sew for them. Women's labour also included heavier manual tasks. Flax-dressers, who broke down the fibres for weaving, can be found in the Merchant Taylors' Company and others, and while most girls apprenticed to it were from artisanal families, one had a father identified as a gentleman. Flax- and hemp-dressing had domestic origins, like silk-spinning and weaving. Through the medieval period, while women were excluded from the wool trade, weaving and other textile work were symbolic of the virtuous wife. The apprenticeship of girls into flax-dressing was suggestive rather of routine work with minimal technology and low reward. Strikingly, none of this textile work risked the ill repute that was associated with brewing, as it became a male

---

[11] *A General Description of All Trades, Digested in Alphabetical Order*, 166.
[12] Natasha Korda, *Labors Lost: Women's Work and the Early Modern English Stage* (Philadelphia: University of Pennsylvania Press, 2011), 34.

Table 4.1. *Gendered occupations*

Occupations given (different to company title except where noted)	Total girls apprenticed	Girls apprenticed to single mistresses (widows and spinsters)
Button-maker	21	2
Bodice-maker	2	2
Child's coat-maker	6	2
Coat-maker	11	0
Coney-wool cutter	3	0
Exchange	8	5
Flax-/hemp-dresser	8	2
Gloves	4	0
Gold and silver wire/lace	10	1
Linen draper/seller	3	2
Mercer	2	0
Milliner	21	1
Periwig-maker	6	1
Seamstress	27	11
Tailor	29	1
Tire-woman	2	2
Other clothing	11	2
Total clothing	*143*	*23*
Gardener	3	
Herbman/woman	4	3
Fruiterer (in company)	11	3
Bookbinder	3	
Victualler	3	
Other non-clothing	20	1
Total non-clothing	*44*	*4*

Source: As Figure 4.1

trade.[13] Ruth Karras points out the significance of marital status in the reputation of medieval textile crafts: single women weaving were attacked, married women encouraged.[14] The distinction between married women's labour, which could be seen as contributory to a domestic economy, and single women's independent work continued

---

[13] Judith M. Bennett, *Ale, Beer and Brewsters in England: Women's Work in a Changing World, 1300–1600* (Oxford University Press, 1996).

[14] Ruth Mazo Karras, '"This Skill in a Woman Is By No Means to Be Despised": Weaving and the Gender Division of Labor in the Middle Ages', in *Medieval Fabrications: Dress, Textiles, Clothwork, and Other Cultural Imaginings*, ed. E. Jane Burns (New York: Palgrave, 2004), 89–104.

in the intermittent challenges to women 'working at their own hand' in the late sixteenth and early seventeenth centuries.

Marriage, as much as gender, had an influence on occupational options: while clothing work dominated for all women, single women were most associated with sewing and particularly with the occupation of seamstress. The more ambitious range of trades detected amongst female apprentices by the pioneering London research of Dorothy George and Alice Clark in the early twentieth century, which included carpentry, butchering and weaving, seem to have reflected company names rather than trades in practice.[15] Lois Schwoerer's more recent research into gunmaking, though, does indicate that the twenty-five women practising the trade were taking both girls and boys as apprentices.[16]

Parish apprenticeship drew on some of the same trades, with a heavy reliance on seamstresses and less appearance of choice. Across England, parishes followed the guidance of the Elizabethan poor law in apprenticing orphans and children of poor parents to masters and mistresses, generally with low or no premiums, and with limited if any choice. Until 1692, they could force children onto unwilling masters, and after 1692 the connection between apprenticeship and legal settlement gave churchwardens and overseers a motivation to find masters outside their own parish. In the first half of the seventeenth century, pauper families could be dismantled by poor law authorities removing their children into apprenticeships and reducing pensions for those parents who did not comply; in the 1620s, some of London's poor children were shipped to Virginia.[17] By the late seventeenth century, hundreds of young women and men a year were being indentured, pressed or 'spirited' into Atlantic servitude, using forms that drew on the same formulae as those of apprenticeship, including the consent of the servant. Around a quarter were women, making up 524 between 1683 and 1686 alone.[18] As Sonia Tycko argues, their initialled but uninformed consent on indentures marked them out as servants, not slaves, whose period of contracted work without pay had poor conditions and abuses but a closure. In

---

[15] M. Dorothy George, *London Life in the 18th Century* (London: Capricorn Books, 1965); Alice Clark, *Working Life of Women in the Seventeenth Century*, ed. Amy Louise Erickson (London: Routledge, 1992).

[16] Lois G. Schwoerer, 'Women and Guns in Early Modern England', in *Challenging Orthodoxies: The Social and Cultural Worlds of Early Modern Women: Essays Presented to Hilda L. Smith*, ed. Sigrun Haude and Melinda S. Zook (Farnham: Ashgate, 2014), 33–52.

[17] Patricia Crawford, *Parents of Poor Children in England 1580–1800* (Oxford University Press, 2010).

[18] John Wareing, *Indentured Migration and the Servant Trade from London to America, 1618–1718* (Oxford University Press, 2016), 263.

Virginia, this 'contributed to a specious logic' that privileged indentured servants over enslaved Africans and Native Americans.[19]

In late seventeenth-century London, the high levels of parental mortality continued to leave children at the mercy of parish provision, and apprenticeship was also used to provide for illegitimate children. A typical order against the alleged father of an illegitimate child ordered him to pay 2 shillings weekly from birth to the age of twelve and then to pay £10 to put the child forth as an apprentice. The parish acted as mediator in the apprenticeship and had the father and his guarantors bound to protect them from its costs.[20] Overseers had the responsibility of putting out orphans, illegitimate children and paupers, though some indentures described young people as 'putting themselves' as apprentices in just the same way as private and company apprentices did, and some apprentices at least signed their agreement. The consent that was incorporated in the standard parish indenture was, in practice, very variable.[21]

Housewifery always featured heavily on parish apprenticeship indentures for girls, making up over half the trades described, and in some parishes much more.[22] The other main occupations were agricultural labour and making clothes. In seventeenth-century Bristol, as Ilana Ben-Amos has shown, girls were increasingly bound into both housewifery and craft: the two categories, for girls, were becoming blurred.[23] In London, housewifery was also the main single occupation for parish girls; while elite apprentices' families did all they could to protect their daughters from the more menial end of domestic labour, housewifery was a valuable range of skills. Several indentures amplify it by adding 'reading', 'sempstry' or, in one case, 'doing and performing all manner of household work and business'.[24] Martha Edwards promised to teach her apprentice to knit and sew 'at times when she had no other household work to do'.[25] Some overseers sent London girls out to rural households, like Jane Jennings, apprenticed in 1698 from All Hallows Lombard Street to George Goose, a husbandman in Hook, Surrey, to learn 'reading

---

[19] Sonia Tycko, 'Bound and Filed: A Seventeenth-Century Service Indenture from a Scattered Archive', *Early American Studies* 19, no. 1 (2021):186.
[20] LMA, MJ/SP/1691/01/009, Petition of Christopher Harrison (1691).
[21] James Fisher, 'Inventing a New Form of Labour: Early Indentures for Parish Apprentices, 1598–1630', *University of Exeter History of Economy Research Blog* (January 2021).
[22] Steve Hindle, '"Waste" Children? Pauper Apprenticeship under the Elizabethan Poor Laws, c. 1598–1697', in *Women, Work and Wages in England, 1600–1850*, ed. Penelope Lane, K. D. M. Snell and Neil Raven (Woodbridge: Boydell, 2004), 15–46.
[23] Ilana Krausman Ben-Amos, 'Women Apprentices in the Trade and Crafts of Early Modern Bristol', *Continuity and Change* 6, no. 2 (1991): 227–52.
[24] LMA, P69/GIS/B/049/MS08476/001(1696).   [25] TNA, C6/386/47 (1679).

knitting sewing and other works of huswifery'.[26] In Hanwell, Middlesex, Rebecka Roane and her three sisters and brother were apprenticed into housewifery by a local charity, using large and elegant indentures that described 'brewing washing carding spinning and such like'.[27] While high-premiumed apprentices complained about being made to do housework, housewifery had an established value.

Across the country, occupational gender distinctions were marked by status: Keith Snell identified a sharp gap between the wider range of less clearly gendered trades, including shoemaking and carpentry, to which parish apprentices were put, and the more female-specific millinery and mantua-making that appeared on family or guild apprenticeships. Similarly, Joan Lane found poor girls being apprenticed to heavy manual labour.[28] In Edinburgh, a form of apprenticeship for paying orphaned girls' debts focused specifically on perling lace.[29] In London, the distinction between parish and family or company apprenticeships was less pointed, with less housewifery and a universal engagement with manufacturing and finishing textiles or making clothes, reflecting the dominance of textile trades in urban women's work.[30] Provincial pauper apprenticeships would follow the same pattern in the eighteenth century.[31] Behind this textile dominance was a hierarchy of skills, but very few trades were specific to parish apprenticeships.

The surviving indentures for a few London parishes in the 1680s and 1690s demonstrate the range of apprentice girls' occupations.[32] London parish apprentices were set up fairly well, with premiums, ranging from 14s to £3, and a standard term of seven or eight years, similar for both girls and boys, with some longer contracts to compensate for a low premium.[33] Their masters and mistresses were expected to provide

[26] LMA, P69/ALH4/B/045/MS18976.   [27] LMA, ACC/0933/031/015-019.
[28] K. D. M. Snell, *Annals of the Labouring Poor: Social Change and Agrarian England, 1660–1900* (Cambridge University Press, 1987); Joan Lane, *Apprenticeship in England 1600–1914* (London: Routledge, 1996), 34.
[29] Cathryn R. Spence, 'A Perl for Your Debts?: Young Women and Apprenticeships in Early Modern Edinburgh', in *Children and Youth in Premodern Scotland*, ed. Janay Nugent and Elizabeth Ewen (Woodbridge: Boydell, 2015), 31–46.
[30] Alexandra Shepard, *Accounting for Oneself: Worth, Status, and the Social Order in Early Modern England* (Oxford University Press, 2015), 219. On local differences, see Penelope Lane, Neil Raven and K. D. M. Snell, *Women, Work, and Wages in England, 1600–1850* (Woodbridge: Boydell, 2004), introduction.
[31] Snell, *Annals of the Labouring Poor*, 286.
[32] The following discussion is based on 115 indentures from the parishes of St Botolph's Aldgate, St Clement Danes, St Giles-without-Cripplegate, St Dionis Backchurch, St Mary Bothaw, All Hallows Lombard Street, St Martin Outwich and St Katherine Coleman in the late seventeenth century. Slightly over half were girls.
[33] In contrast to the more variable terms of girls in rural apprenticeships: see Snell, *Annals of the Labouring Poor*, 287.

clothes, defined as 'double apparel' 'suitable for her station'. Many were bound with pre-printed indentures like those of guild apprentices, prescribing training and occasionally even offering the potential of the freedom: the metropolitan apprenticeship market extended to parish officers as well as the companies.

The London parish records are particularly illuminating about girls' training. Their paperwork echoes that of companies, often using printed indentures, similar to those of companies but without company arms, and adding some precision about whose craft was being taught. Sarah Shackbolt's indenture, unusually, records that she was apprenticed to Simon and Elizabeth Crouch to learn the trade of a weaver and fringe-maker 'which the master now useth', while Mary Ellis was bound to John and Mary Phibbs to learn 'the trade of sempstresse which she now useth'.[34] Elizabeth Emerton was bound to Thomas Helpe in Whitechapel to learn 'the arte mistery or occupation of buying and selling all sorts of things that his wife now useth'.[35] These extra details were a bulwark against parish girls being taken up by drudgery and also suggest that the company clerks who drew up the less precise company indentures were obscuring women's role out of administrative habit, as much as a wider social practice of subsuming women's work in that of their husbands. The overall picture supports the trend of recent research on the extent and independence of married women's urban work. Precisely what girls were learning, paid for by parishes, mattered.

Amongst the many girls indentured by their parishes to make clothes and care for them, the commonest description was 'seamstress' or 'learning all sorts of plain work'. Plain work was structural sewing, which had both domestic and trade uses, as opposed to embroidery or specialised stitching. It was a uniquely female trade. Children's coat-making was another standby for parish apprentices, as well as others. Described in 1761 as a very suitable skill for those 'a little above the vulgar', in the late seventeenth century it was one of the trades which crossed the boundary of parish, family and company apprenticeships.[36]

The descriptions of work given for other parish girls reflect the multitude of tasks that went into trimming Londoners' clothes and dressing their feet, hands and heads. Stocking work appeared several times:

---

[34] St Botolph's Aldgate Apprenticeship Indentures, *London Lives* GLBAIA107000071 (6 August 1691); St Clement Danes Apprenticeship Indentures, *London Lives* WCCDPA364000005 (2 August 1688).
[35] St Botolph's Aldgate Apprenticeship Indentures, *London Lives* GLBAIA107000077 (16 May 1698).
[36] Joseph Collyer, *The Parents' and Guardians' Directory* (1761), 101, quoted in Snell, *Annals of the Labouring Poor*, 293.

making them out of flat knitted worsted, mending them and 'sizeing and seaming' silk stockings. One of the stocking-making apprentices in St Mary Bothaw, a foundling naturally named Mary Bothaw, was indentured with the proviso that, at the end, she be made free of the Company of Framework Knitters. Unusual for a parish apprenticeship, this indicates the degree to which, in London, such contracts had a potential overlap with guild apprenticeships.[37] Apprentices put forth from Christ's Hospital sometimes received the same opportunity, being placed with freemen's wives. Button-making was another common option: Mary Ackelom in St Giles Cripplegate, an impoverished gentleman's orphan, was apprenticed to a labourer to learn 'his wife's art of button-making'. Buttons were made of such a range of materials that their creation ranged from the fancier objects made with silk and gold to those made in mass by girls getting 'a poor living' paid by the dozen.[38] The large proportion of girls from ordinary backgrounds in the Glovers' Company was reflected in gloving work outside the company: several parish apprentices were bound to masters in other companies to learn to trim gloves with metallic embroidery or lace. Johana Luke was apprenticed to learn from her master the trade of a periwig-maker, a trade also practised by several women in the Merchant Taylors' Company.[39] There were limits to the work women were given: making shoes was a particularly male preserve, though, by the early eighteenth century, girls were learning to make 'children's pumps' and pattens. As with coats, shoes for children were perceived as appropriate work for women.

Better represented in the parish apprenticeships, as in some companies, were the specialised arts of manufacturing textiles and trimmings for clothes. Mary Long's father had been a painter. Orphaned and poor at thirteen, she was apprenticed by the parish of St Giles Cripplegate to a member of the Coopers' Company to learn 'winding and doubling cone and wrought silk'.[40] Abigail Bothaw and Elizabeth Coleman, their names marking them out as foundlings from St Mary Bothaw and St Katherine Coleman, were set to the notoriously dextrous task of cutting fur for hats: 'Pulling and Cutting of Beavor and Conney Wooll and Such Like'.[41] Millinery, coat and mantua-making, bodice-making and button-making set girls up for working for the sewing trade and, in some cases, for independent businesses: foundling apprenticeships were not distinctive

[37] LMA, P69/SWI/B/019/MS03369 (1683).
[38] LMA, P69/GIS/B/049/MS08476; *A General Description of All Trades, Digested in Alphabetical Order* (1747), 47–8.
[39] *LL*, WCCDPA364000030 (20 September 1688).
[40] LMA, P69/GIS/B/049/MS08476/001/117.
[41] LMA, P69/SWI/B/019/MS03369 (1693); P69/KAT1/B/032/MS07740 (1705).

but part of a wide range of textile trades. Christ's Hospital, just by St Paul's, offered a similar range of trades to the daughters of poor citizens, apprenticing them out around the age of fourteen after teaching them to read and write. The later seventeenth century saw its girls apprenticed to more precise occupations in sewing and retail, often to the wives of freemen across the City who were practising their own trade, or of artisans in the suburbs: their products included bone lace, quilting, black-work embroidery, caps, knitting, mantuas and coats. Their terms were usually shorter than seven years, often four, and they were not generally offered the chance to become free.

At the top of the apprenticeship spectrum were the high-premiumed seamstresses and milliners' apprentices, bound with premiums from £15 to £50 and destined for elite shops and marriage. At the lowest level, pin-makers who would graduate into wage labour. Between them, girls across the range of institutional, parish, family and company apprentices learned skills from a common set: dressing flax and winding silk; washing and starching; making bone lace, buttons, fringes, periwigs and silk stockings; making pastry; selling fruit and herbs; and keeping shop. Spinning gold and silver thread and making bone lace are rare examples of trades that appear only in company and Christ's Hospital apprenticeships, but even mending stockings was not exclusive to paupers. The changing world of sewing and fashion opened up 'interstices' in the textile crafts, in many of which women were heavily involved.[42] Non-textile trades had sharper distinctions. In one boy's apprenticeship case, a different aspect of gendered skilled labour is revealed, taking us into the workshop. A silversmith's apprentice was set to do the laborious side of the work, scouring and nailing – all except the burnishing, which 'they usually were wont to have women' doing.[43] Polishing by hand remained women's work well into the nineteenth century.[44] Apprenticeship's gender divisions offer only a partial view of gendered labour; particularly after marriage, what women did was likely to be widely variable, and most women were not apprenticed. It offers, though, a useful view of the interaction between craft rules and artisanal practice.

How Girls Learned

The marginalisation of women in guilds involved both ideological exclusion from many areas of artisanal training and a structural impact on how

---

[42] Mary Prior, 'Women in the Urban Economy', in *Women in English Society 1500–1800*, ed. Mary Prior (London: Methuen, 1985).
[43] LMA, CLA/024/05/276 (1671).
[44] Philippa Glanville and Jennifer Faulds Goldsborough, *Women Silversmiths 1685–1845* (London: Thames and Hudson, 1990).

skills were passed on. The freer controls of London had their own impact, impeding the development of a collective occupational identity amongst the seamstresses who were seeded across companies. As we have seen, girls in guilds were only sometimes learning from women who had been taught as apprentices themselves, so the sense of apprenticeship as generational and the idea of skills transmission through continuous replication had little purchase for women. Yet if company membership did not offer seventeenth-century women the same world of associations it did men, it did build connections between trading families and single women. The expertise apparent in Mary Jones's case offers a glimpse of the female initiatives and patronage that accompanied the transmission of skills in London's retail world.

For boys, apprenticeship was a long-established part of the civic life cycle. It was flexible, and often broke down by intent or design, but for 40 per cent of them, it led on to an established independent trade and becoming a master in their own right.[45] For girls, that life-cycle model is hard to trace. It was not rehearsed in prescriptive sources or descriptive print literature, which almost never mentioned apprenticing of girls; when authors did discuss female apprenticeship, they saw it as another form of service. Yet life-cycle apprenticeship for girls clearly existed in practice, and girls' apprenticeship and freedom continued to be referred to in guides to London custom, before the apprenticeship of girls was more fully discussed in the eighteenth-century trades directories. Despite the comparatively small number of female apprentices through the seventeenth century, girls' training had a recognisable pattern, focusing on specific trades. Most were making clothes or the materials for them; many were learning skills they could use as journeywomen or outworkers, or in shops outside the City; a minority would become free and establish their own City businesses as seamstresses and milliners. To become a seamstress meant cutting and sewing clothes and accessories, selling to customers, getting and keeping contacts and, for the most successful, looking and acting the part. Marriage to a man who was not free of the City of London, as we will see, might imperil women's capacity to use that training in business, but learning to sew for the market provided a degree of both short- and long-term labour autonomy for many women.

Learning a trade did not, of course, exclude book learning, which for most girls probably preceded their trade training. The high proportion of girls signing their indentures suggest they were often already literate at

---

[45] Patrick Wallis, 'Apprenticeship and Training in Premodern England', *Journal of Economic History* 68, no. 3 (2008): 839.

fourteen; even pauper apprentices sometimes signed their names, though not all their mistresses did. If they could not, they may have learned in service, but there is no evidence of mistresses actually teaching it. When Mary Bignell was apprenticed as a framework knitter to John and Sarah Spencer in 1696, her manuscript indenture included being taught the trade, provided with clothing and given an hour a day to learn to write, but the writing was clearly a separate cost.[46] In contrast, the better-provided Hester Hudson, apprenticed as a seamstress in 1650, was described by court witnesses as 'as well educated as any mans daughter in London'.[47]

Numeracy must have been an essential, but there are few clues as to where, when and how it was learned. Mathematical skills were being taught and learned not just ad hoc but in formal schools. Bathsua Makin's school prospectus, in 1672, planned to offer mathematics as well as geography and astronomy; she had tutored a princess and aspired to teach the middling sort of London.[48] Other women advertised schools of writing and arithmetic.[49] In the same decade, the anonymous female author of *Advice to Women and Maidens* urged women and girls to learn to calculate, with a specific eye to trade, and the examples it gives help flesh out the mathematical life of consumers as well as shopkeepers. This work imagined first a woman keeping her domestic accounts, recording sums of 18s for a hood, apron and gloves; £1 13s for a petticoat; and £1 for the maid's quarter wages. The next stage of the booklet outlines the potential accounts of a shopkeeper or exchangewoman. Their detail offers a precise picture of the transactions required to start a shop: buying silk to make hoods and linen to make handkerchiefs, cravats and cuffs; putting out the making to seamstresses. She makes 4 pence profit on each hood, paying the seamstress 6 pence each to make them up. At the end of a week, she is imagined to be £6 in profit. The accounts includes the house as well as the shop, and demand balancing every farthing, but only once a year. Perhaps an apprentice who made off with a handkerchief or kept the change for ribbons was not unreasonable in hoping to get away with it.

The author of the *Advice* recalls her parents teaching her writing and arithmetic to enable her to practice trade and bookkeeping: 'though *Arithmetic* set my brains at work, Yet there was much delight in seeing the end, and how each question produced a fair answer and informed me of things I knew not.' This is an explicit reflection, akin to those of

---

[46] LMA, COL/CHD/FR/02/111/8.   [47] LMA, CLA 024/05/72 (1654).
[48] Bathsua Makin, *An Essay to Revive the Antient Education of Gentlewomen* (1673).
[49] Amy Froide, 'Learning to Invest: Women's Education in Arithmetic and Accounting in Early Modern England', *Early Modern Women* 10, no. 1 (2015): 3–26.

Bathsua Makin and Mary Astell, on the psychology of learning and its impact on the sense of self. Once the writer was older, her father engaged her to keep the housekeeping books, to call all the family to account every night for what they had spent, reimburse them and note it down. It presents bookkeeping as a potential career: 'This is the way to make one a Cashier, as they are termed.' Not only is this an excellent record of how a girl learned to keep accounts but its publication from the Exchange in 1678 demonstrates the appeal a lesson for women in bookkeeping was expected to have. Notional or actual objections were forestalled in the text:

Methinks now the objection may be that this art is too high and mysterious for the weaker sex, it will make them proud: Women had better keep to their Needlework, point laces, &c and if they come to poverty, those small Crafts may give them some mean releif.

To which I answer, That having in some measure practiced both Needle-work and Accounts I can averr, that I never found this Masculine Art harder or more difficult than the effeminate achievements of Lace-making, gum-work or the like.[50]

Bookkeeping would enable a seamstress to run her own shop, leaving someone else to keep to the 'small Crafts'. *Advice* reminds the advocates of feminine crafts that making money from them requires the 'masculine' arts of bookkeeping, too: gendering skills can only go so far.

Hannah Woolley's *Guide to Ladies* (1668) makes intriguing reference to another connection between apprenticeship and education: girls being apprenticed into schools. This is the rarest of Woolley's works, with only one copy surviving. Her advice to girls offers several pages directed, uniquely, at 'young Maidens, who are desirous to go to be apprentices, either in Schools or to any Trade'. It is almost the only surviving work of the period to make any reference to skilled female apprenticeship, and the connection between apprenticeship in schools and in skilled trades is also novel. Little information about girls' work in schools survives. Woolley herself may have been a school apprentice: she describes herself elsewhere as being put in charge of a school before the age of fifteen, around 1637, and she worked in schools for much of her life. Writing with the experience of running a school in Essex with her first husband until his death, Woolley saw apprenticeship in a small girls' school as a sensible route to adulthood and independence, alongside being a

---

[50] *Advice to the Women and Maidens of London Shewing, That Instead of Their Usual Pastime, and Education in Needlework ... It Were Far More Necessary and Profitable to Apply Themselves to the Right Understanding and Practice of the Method of Keeping Books of Account* (Benjamin Billingsley, 1678).

chambermaid, a housemaid in a great house or a scullery maid. 'Maidens,' she advised, 'if it be your lot to be in a School your parents or friends have provided well for you.' There is one household in the 1695 tax listings that looks like it might fit this model. Margaret Rutter, a widow, was a householder in the parish of St Edmund, Lombard Street; she lived with two children, four or five young female boarders, a lodger, a servant and an apprentice, Anne Trigg.[51]

The readers of Woolley's *Guide to Ladies* were advised to be diligent to please their mistresses, presumably the head, or only, teacher. As apprentices, they were also set in opposition to the pupils: should 'any of the boarders rail against her, or combine anything, you are bound to tell her of it, that she may by her discretion help it'. Much of the direction concerned manners at table and around the house, and suggest the subtleties of an apprentice teacher's position. She should help to clear the table, but might have liberty to walk in the garden after meals; she might have liberty to sing a song or tell a story; she should help dress the gentlewomen pupils and go well dressed herself. Woolley urged young women to miss no chance to learn from the teachers; the pupils might have estates and so could afford to waste their learning, but the apprentice, 'if you neglect your time, you undo your self, for it must be your portion'. Apprenticeship, she pointed out, offered a girl the chance to teach the children of nobles or work in their household, or to be a teacher or run a school herself. Without educating herself, her best preferment would be 'but a common Chambermaid'.[52] Model letters in the same volume offered more details of the imaginary school apprentice: 'Since it pleased God to take my Father away,' she writes to her mother, 'you could not have shewed a greater care for me, than in providing me so good a place for my education as I find this to be.' Her mistress is kind and allows her time to learn as the rest do, and she wishes that her sister could also find a place there, to avoid being made a drudge. A second letter asks an aunt to send a little money to buy some silk to do her own work, reiterating the centrality of sewing to both leisure and labour.[53]

For Woolley, writing in 1668 and perhaps looking back to her own youth in the late 1630s, the relationship between education and apprenticeship evidently made sense, but it appeared in no later editions or revisions of her work. The advice to apprentices was amongst the material that disappeared when her publisher, Dorman Newman, allowed someone else to edit the work for republication as *The Gentlewomans*

---

[51] LMA, COL/CHD/LA/04/030.
[52] Hannah Woolley, *A Guide to Ladies, Gentlewomen and Maids* (1668), 39–42.
[53] Woolley, *Guide to Ladies*, 87–8.

Companion.[54] Woolley's complaint about this in her last book returns to the seam of self-representation as a woman turning her work experience to advice for youth, noting in particular that she had important advice for young women who risked falling into bawdry or poverty. 'There are very many at this present time who want service, both Gentlewomen and others.'[55] Amongst much else, this useful advice on apprenticeship as a viable path for young women was removed from her book, though it certainly continued to be an option.

Historians of the guild system in England and Europe have described a practice by which artisanal labour skills were transmitted by imitation, but studies of women in guilds have mostly focused on exclusion from a more general social capital of work rather than on the mechanics of skill acquisition. The records of skills transmission are scarce for all crafts. Craft was understood to be learned by hand, not by word or print, and apprentices swore to keep their masters' secrets.

Girls learning to sew were moving into the changing, but still gendered, world of fashion. Across Europe, tailoring was established as largely a masculine prerogative, and women worked on its margins. Margins were, of course, critical to the innovations of seventeenth-century fashion. Immigrant women were employed extensively in making for the London stage, working with buttons, feathers and sequins and bringing in new knowledge and techniques.[56] The making and remaking of ruffs, which had to be done every time they were worn, was dependent on the skill of starching, brought to Elizabeth I's court by Dutch women and soon practised by London women as a trade. A woman in 1624, her husband claiming the rank of gentleman, told a court clerk that she 'getteth her lyving by starchinge of bands to shopps'.[57] Commentators described the gender division of Dutch labour as peculiarly egalitarian, with women managing business, travelling as merchants and keeping accounts. French and Dutch immigrant women were also reputed for making and selling periwigs, tires and bone lace. Satires on fashion in the early seventeenth century mocked the specialised accessories worked by tire-women, including French bodices, farthingales, ruffs, curled periwigs and shoe linings. By the later seventeenth century, these objects and the craft of making them were part of fashion's mainstream. The trade in technical hair accoutrements provided independent work for women like

---

[54] Hannah Woolley, *The Gentlewomans Companion* (1673).
[55] Hannah Woolley, *A Supplement to the Queen-Like Closet, or, a Little of Everything Presented to All Ingenious Ladies, and Gentlewomen* (1674), 94.
[56] Korda, *Labors Lost.*
[57] Alexandra Shepard, 'Crediting Women in the Early Modern English Economy', *History Workshop Journal* 78 (2015): 13.

Bridget Park, a tire-woman in Bartholomew Lane who took an apprentice in 1686, and Anne Loveday, a tire-woman living with her husband, a refiner, near Goldsmiths' Hall, who took an apprentice to learn to make periwigs.[58]

The skills to make such objects underpinned the clothes market of the later seventeenth century, with fine starching becoming the work of specialised servants or seamstresses, and girls apprenticed specifically to learn to work lace and needlework. Sewing itself was already in the seventeenth century a trade which extended far beyond the skills and structure of the domestic sewing that was conceived of as suitable, virtuous and pragmatic.[59] While the expansion of women's sewing work to making loose gowns and mantuas from the 1680s was certainly significant in the London market, much of what seamstresses were making and selling in the late seventeenth century seems to have been their long-established realm of linen undergarments and an increasing range of ready-made accessories. In 1688, Randall Holme's compendium of occupations delineated the line between tailors and seamstresses: tailors dealt with the body and seamsters with the hands, head and feet. He did not, interestingly, align the distinction with gender. Seamsters made shifts and smocks, the basic garments of men and women, whose white folds showed beneath their outer garments.[60] 'Shapes for mantuas' were just one element in a long list of production. They sewed the extensive range of linen that was worn throughout society: shirts and separate half sleeves, kerchiefs, aprons, childbed linen and baby and children's clothes, bibs and biggins (caps). For the middling and elites, they made bands, ruffs and cuffs; gorget and cravats for the neck; and the newly fashionable whisks. Most of these could be made from squares, rectangles or triangles of linen; the trick was in the cutting and seaming.

Seamstresses, as Randall Holme noted, also made 'Womens Head Dresses', a category which includes fillet and snood, ruffled coifs and hoods. Women covered their heads outdoors, and one of the tasks of shopkeeping and sewing women was to furnish the hoods of gauze, alamode, lutestring, sarsnet, India silk and so on, as well as coifs and the forehead cloths that went beneath them. Holme's list includes 'head rolls' to shape the hair, so tire-makers were closely connected to seamstresses. Here, the seamstress's craft involved knowledge of fabrics and fashion and the use of trimmings.

[58] Scott, *Apprenticeship Disputes*.
[59] Judith G. Coffin, 'Gender and the Guild Order: The Garment Trades in Eighteenth-Century Paris', *Journal of Economic History* 54, no. 4 (1994): 783.
[60] Randall Holme, *The Academy of Armory* (1688), 97.

Holme is a good deal less precise on seamstresses' than tailors' skills. His account of the construction of men's and women's clothes allows the reader to effectively follow the tailor's needle. The 'Petticoat Breeches', for example, are 'short and wide Coats with Waist bands, having no petition, or sowing up between the Legs; but all open like a short Peticoat, from whence they are named'; a Jacket has sleeves 'which reach to the Wrist having the turn-up sometime round, then with Hounds Ears, and an other time square'.[61] The seamstress's art in making multiple kinds of headgear, lace or cuffs and ruffs is left vague: the tailor is the one endowed with technical mastery.[62] A more utilitarian guide of 1696, *The Plain Dealing Linnen-Draper*, gave forty pages' alphabetical catalogue of types of linen to assist drapers and details to seamstresses on how to cut out shifts, whilst castigating pedlars and hawkers who sold bad cloth.[63] Susan North's magisterial reconstruction of the seamstress's labour, and the evidence of pattern books, fills out the picture of what seamstresses had to learn. Seamstresses' work combined cutting and a relatively small range of stitching. Shifts had to be flat and smooth when worn under clothes, which meant an extremely narrow seam allowance, often less than an eighth of an inch. To keep this accurate meant measuring stitches against the warp or weft threads of the linen itself, which had to be cut 'on the thread'. Sometimes seamstresses hemmed the sleeves separately first so they could be removed for laundering – a classic example of attending to what showed rather than what did not.[64] Seamstresses also learned to vary their stitches to the range of linen weights they used for different garments, and to reinforce wearing linen at the points of stress, shoulders and necklines. 'The seamstress's art,' writes North, 'was perfectly crafted to accommodate the properties of her raw materials, to cut the pieces required for body linens as sparingly as practicable and to stitch them together securely, ensuring that they withstood, as long as possible, the friction of wear under early modern clothing, and the strains of their use and care.'[65] Other tasks finished garments, either when they were made or after laundering or for repairs. Frances Angel, at work for her mistress,

---

[61] Holme, *Academy of Armory*, 96.
[62] For a full discussion of sewing work in London, see Sophie Pitman, 'The Making of Clothing and the Making of London, 1560–1660' (PhD thesis, University of Cambridge, 2017).
[63] Margaret Spufford, *The Great Reclothing of Rural England: Petty Chapman and Their Wares in the Seventeenth Century* (London: A & C Black, 1984); J. F., *The Merchant's Ware-House Laid Open: Or, the Plain Dealing Linnen-Draper* (1696).
[64] Susan North, *Sweet and Clean?: Bodies and Clothes in Early Modern England* (Oxford University Press, 2020), 192.
[65] North, *Sweet and Clean?*, 207.

was given a petticoat 'to bind around the top', sewing filleting along the edge to keep the pleats in.[66]

Another set of marketable artisanal skills characterised fine needlework, distinct from domestic sewing. While the parish of St Giles Cripplegate apprenticed Sarah Cole, an impoverished Joiner's daughter, to a widow who would instruct her in 'making all sorts of plain work', other young women learned more elaborate sewing.[67] Tailors had an extensive range of stitches, such as 'fine drawing', sewing two pieces of cloth together invisibly, and 'Raveling', loosening threads from a piece of silk or cloth. Randall Holme listed thirty-six different 'terms of art' for sewing work, from backstitch and Irish stitch to Virgins Device and Bread work, as well as finger work with silk, pearls and wires.[68] In 1622, Katherine Dickinson, a gentleman's daughter, was apprenticed to learn seamstry from Katherine Farnaby, a Joiner's wife, for four years for £10. The manuscript indenture described what Farnaby would teach her, a compendium of early seventeenth-century embroidery techniques: 'white work and black work, all sorts of net work, purse work, tent stitch, Barbary work, frost work, silk flowers, bugle work and hair tires'.[69] These elaborately differentiated stitches, beads and plaits would fit her for creating garments and accessories of fashion and the head dressings that Philip Stubbes had castigated at such length forty years earlier; it might also lead her into work on theatrical costumes.[70] In apprenticeship disputes, girls complained of failing to learn marketable skills that would differentiate their work from ordinary sewing. In 1674, Elizabeth Mason testified, supporting another apprentice's complaint, that the result of her apprenticeship was that she was 'rather made worse than better in her skill in sempstry work' in her apprenticeship. They were barely instructed, she said, but spent their time 'employed upon stitching of stomachers and making coarse shirts': plain, domestic sewing on coarse linen which did not require the tiny stitches of finer goods, or stitching stomachers which was hard but not, apparently, skilful.[71] Plain work, that domestic mainstay, could actively deskill a seamstress. In a similar vein, one of Frances Bickley's witnesses deposed 'she could never have learned her trade of a milliner because she was for the most parte employed in making of poynt which doth not relate to [her] trade'. Other seamstress apprentices expected to learn making point lace, but for

[66] LMA CLA/024/05/509B, 509A (1689).
[67] LMA, P69/GIS/B/049/MS08476/001/10; Norah Waugh, *The Cut of Women's Clothes: 1600–1930* (Abingdon: Routledge, 2013).
[68] Holme, *Academy of Armory*, 99.
[69] William Salt Library, M1024/2/1, courtesy of Mark Jenner.
[70] Korda, *Labors Lost*, 30–2. [71] LMA, CLA/024/05/318 (1686).

Frances it was not germane to sewing garments she could sell or running a business.[72]

With sewing came cutting. Christiana Hutchins was indentured to learn, according to witnesses, 'the trade of a seamstress and to cut out and to buy and to sell'.[73] Seamstresses and tailors depended on patterns, which were available in reduced form in print, passed between seamstresses, or the most skilled developed their own. Shifts and shirts were cut to the fixed width of bolts of cloth, but a good pattern enabled a seamstress to get more out of her linen.[74] Hester Hudson, apprenticed in 1650, vowed to strike out on her own when she had had enough of her mistress, telling a friend 'she was able to manage the same trade her selfe if she were free & had but some paternes'.[75] Margaret Reeves, the 'ingenious' seamstress who took on Henrietta Wallop in the 1690s, 'makes and draws all her own patterns'. After their training, her apprentices became journeywomen earning 12s a week, doing markedly better than those working for the Exchange.[76]

The linen seamstresses provided was integral to cleanliness and health. A clean and wholesome body, in the seventeenth century, was one clothed in 'sweet and clean' linen, well made from fine and hard-wearing fabric that was laundered, bleached white and ironed. Frances Carey's training involved 'the art of a sempstress and to wash and starch linen'.[77] While laundering was an occupation for many women outside apprenticeship, and part of maids' labour as well as wives' work, specialised washing and starching was closely tied to the world of sewing. The untailored gowns and under-petticoats sewn by seamstresses, without boning or lining, pleated or bound with tape, were made to be washed. Sometimes this involved taking garments apart by unpicking the single seam that bound sleeve to body, so sewing and laundry skills were intimately linked.[78] Hester Pinney's work as a lace trader included, according to her brother, working 'dayly hard Early and late at her needle for her living which she gets by that, and putting out lynnen and laces to wash': she was at once managing a trade, working with the needle and acting as the middlewoman for the specialist washing of linen and lace.[79]

Randall Holme's compendium of useful information describes laundering, like other trades' arts and mysteries, in 'terms of art'. They

---

[72] LMA, CLA/024/05/509A (1689). [73] LMA, CLA/024/05/318 (1686).
[74] North, *Sweet and Clean?*, 186. [75] LMA, CLA/024/05/72 (1654).
[76] Bristol University Special Collections, Pinney Papers, Red Box 2 folder VII, Mary Pinney to Hester Pinney, 7 February 1694/5.
[77] LMA, CLA/024/05/198B (1666). [78] North, *Sweet and Clean?*, 212.
[79] Geoffrey Nuttall, ed., *Letters of John Pinney, 1679–1699* (Oxford University Press, 1939), 67.

included sorting and soaping; scalding; wrenching or bouking; 'beating the Cloths to get the Bucking Stuff out'; starching and wringing.[80] Hannah Woolley noted that girls aspiring to be chambermaids to gentlewomen should learn to wash and starch tiffanies, lawns, points and laces, as well as mending them; laundrymaids needed to learn to take care of linen, points and laces and to wash the finest linen swiftly to prevent it from stinking and going yellow.[81] The struggle to keep linen white was particularly challenging in the city, where access to the sun was limited. While starching was no longer such a prominent part of the urban economy, and such a consumer of wheat, as it had been in the earlier heyday of starched ruffs, it remained a trade of prestige for women as well as domestic labour, and it featured in apprenticeships.[82] A few of the freemen's daughters leaving Christ's Hospital were apprenticed to starchers, such as Jane Glover, bound in 1694 to Elizabeth Ames, starcher, the wife of a draper, for five years.[83] Complaints to the Middlesex sessions from apprentices' parents include girls apprenticed to washing point lace and gauze, and apprentices at the Mayor's Court had been bound to trades such as 'sempster and starcher' and 'starcher and cutter out of linen'.[84] Sewing, washing and starching were overlapping skills whose connections put the seamstress and her apprentices at the centre of bodily propriety as well as elegant frippery.

Learning to sew and cut, like most crafts, was imitative: an apprentice needed to work alongside a woman who was practising frequently and whose work was accounted reputable. Direct instruction was also important. Mary Baker's description of Mary Jones being 'instructed and advised in the art of a seamstress' indicates the verbal side of teaching: mistresses explained and demonstrated. Susan Streeter assessed the value that Frances Carey had imparted to another apprentice in her training. After three years, she said, the girl was 'for her time very well instructed in the art of a sempstress and to wash and starch linen'. Time was of the essence in measuring the acquisition of skills; over and over, witnesses referred to the amount of time spent and the value of labour accrued in the process of training.

Running a shop, seamstresses used their sewing experience to judge the goods they bought and had made up. By the time linen reached a

---

[80] Holme, *Academy of Armory*, 98.   [81] Woolley, *Guide to Ladies*, 37.
[82] On starch shops earlier in the period, see Natasha Korda, 'Sex, Starch-Houses, and Poking Sticks: Alien Women's Work and the Technologies of Material Culture', *Early Modern Women* 5 (2010): 201–8; for later, Erickson, 'Married Women's Occupations'.
[83] LMA, CLC/210/F/003/MS 12818/006 (August 1694).
[84] For example, LMA, MJ/SB/B 493, p. 49. Scott, *Apprenticeship Disputes*, nos. 13120, 8535.

shopkeeper, cut into lengths, it might have lost the identifying marks of packaging, binding and coloured ribbons of its manufacturer. Retailers needed to be able to judge and attest to its quality themselves.[85] The exhaustive range of weights of linen, and their origins, listed in *The Plain Dealing Linen Merchant* gives a sense of the knowledge involved, as well as the importance of brand. The author lists the (allegedly) best makers of holland and their marks; the types of calico in use for shirts; the sizes of diaper from which tablecloths and napkins could be made; silks, Indian muslins and calicos are analysed for value and good wearing. In *Advice to Women and Maidens*, the shopkeeper's key role is purchasing and selling fabric and commissioning goods like gloves to be made by the seamstress. This was the work at which apprentices training to keep shops would be aiming. The expertise they needed drew on their artisanal knowledge of how to cut and sew garments and accessories from different weights and types of textile, but also required an expert understanding of what, and how, to buy from dealers.

Managing customers was a higher-order skill, likely to be withheld until the end of apprenticeships; apprentices were not expected to cope alone in shops early on. Learning to run a shop where prices were negotiable, goods were easily moveable, and credit was expected required proper supervision. Mary Jones's agreement included being instructed in 'the selling of wares in the shop', but she told her family that they had little trading and that her mistress neglected her business, leaving Mary alone in the shop for a week at a time so that she 'feared she should not learn her trade because the said Frances her mistress did soe neglect to teach and instruct her'.[86] Mary Baker, however, who rented part of her shop to them, countered that Frances had a sufficient trade and deliberately encouraged Mary's independence, giving 'her liberty to sell in the shopp sometimes by her selfe for the better encouraging & entrusting her in her art'. Dorothy Stable's mistress described a rather tighter supervision. Frances Kent said she did her 'best endeavour' to instruct her in the trade and to 'further her therein all she could', putting her connections and knowledge behind her. She set her to buy and sell goods in her shop 'and gave her full directions touching the same'. At her hands, Dorothy was 'as well taught as any of the trade' and 'by the instruccons & skill she had attained in the said service was well able by hir work to gett 18 d. or 2 s. a day'. Two shillings a day, the estimate of what Dorothy could make on her own, was about two-thirds of the day wages set for the masons and carpenters rebuilding St Paul's

---

[85] North, *Sweet and Clean?*, 168.   [86] LMA, CLA/024/05/198 (1666).

Cathedral.[87] In another case, a young male apprentice's testimony reveals the kinds of tasks that were expected of shopkeepers. At question was whether Katherine Venner had taken up her own shop with Hester Wright; she was alleged to be acting, without the right to do so, as Wright's partner in business. The apprentice deposed

> he hath seene her about buying of goodes for accomodacon & supply of the said shopp wher she now is & once going himselfe to receive some money that she owed him she the said Katherine went freely to the mony box in the said shopp (the said Hester Wright being presente) without asking leave or saying any thing to her & took out of the said box soe much money as to pay him, and the said shopp goeth more in the name of the said Katherine then of the said Hester.[88]

Such autonomy was the mark of a woman trading for herself, with practice in buying goods wholesale as well.

The word 'occupation' has a spatial meaning that remains significant in seventeenth-century apprenticeship. While many apprentices lived and worked with their mistresses, particularly in smaller businesses, the seamstresses' shop was often not the traditional household-based shop of artisanal workshops but a place away from home, in a shopping gallery like the Exchange, in the prestigious shopping street of Cheapside or further out in Shadwell or Whitechapel.[89] Mary Jones worked in a part-shop rented by her mistress from another seamstress; others spent at least part of their working lives in the small stalls of the Royal Exchange, where their masters and mistresses had shops, and so their work and training was mobile. Many shops were small and could only contain two people, while others had room for several workers, probably not all there at once. Accounts of Herbert and Katherine Allen's shop on the Exchange referred to at least three shop apprentices and another woman working in it.[90] Apprenticeship remained a residential contract, but many single mistresses lived in lodgings and rooms, working elsewhere. In late seventeenth-century France, Clare Crowston has argued, men's guild identity remained fundamentally familial, while women's became increasingly individual, representative of an autonomous trade.[91] The gendered workspaces of London involved a comparable transition,

---

[87] Judy Z. Stephenson, '"Real" Wages? Contractors, Workers, and Pay in London Building Trades, 1650–1800', *Economic History Review* 71, no. 1 (2018): 115.
[88] LMA, CLA/024/05/131A (1662).
[89] Waugh, *Cut of Women's Clothes*, 42–7; Marjorie McIntosh, *Working Women in English Society, 1300–1620* (Cambridge University Press, 2005), 245–8. See also Béatrice Craig, *Women and Business since 1500: Invisible Presences in Europe and North America?* (London: Palgrave Macmillan, 2015).
[90] LMA, CLA/024/05/131A (1662).   [91] Crowston, 'Engendering the Guilds', 341–2.

separating the domestic scene from the workplace; apprentices and mistresses made complaints about both.

Networks of shops and seamstresses like those in Mary Jones's case reveal a working world in which young women could move swiftly towards independent trade, manoeuvring around the regulation of the City. Dorothy Stable, as we saw in Chapter 2, aimed to run her own shop aged eighteen, after five years' training, though her own mistress had left her apprenticeship after a year. She ended up back in Pontefract, where she died, single, in her thirties.[92] Hester Hudson had been given the same arrangement, a four-year contract which her father apparently still expected would lead to the freedom of the City at the end of it.[93] These were pragmatic arrangements which seem to have been specific to girls, most of whom did not become free after apprenticeship and so did not necessarily need to serve the full seven years that custom required. Some went on to work for others; others married, in which case they could use their husbands' freedoms to trade. These manipulations of set terms of service suggest that the trade was learned fast and that shopkeepers needed to take advantage of apprentices' skills before they left. Hannah Woolley's imaginary letter from a girl apprenticed to a trade, to her mother fleshes out how that felt from the other side: requesting her mother to remind her mistress that she had promised to impart 'all the secrets of her trade' to enable her to set up by herself, she writes, 'I have now but a year and half to serve, and it is time that I understood how to manage my business.'[94] Woolley's imaginary letter writer was a good deal more patient than the girls in court who were determined to rush into their own shopkeeping before their terms were out.

The best way courts had to measure what apprentices had learned was how much they were deemed worth. Apprenticeship was traditionally understood by historians as a relationship which began with loss-leading training and ended in valuable free labour; as Patrick Wallis has shown, though, the training and the useful work were more likely to be distributed together across the years.[95] Seamstresses and their families, nevertheless, calculated their worth based on time and apparently on a trained sense of what a girl with one, two or three years' training should have learned (Tables 4.2 and 4.3). Like those who calculated their own worth in court, seamstresses and their families cultivated the skill of appraisal: not just of goods but of the labour that made them.[96] Katherine Venner's

---

[92] West Yorkshire Archive Service, D40/4, 9 December 1698, www.ancestry.co.uk.
[93] LMA, CLA/024/05/72A, Interrogatory (1654). [94] Woolley, *Guide to Ladies*, 90.
[95] Wallis, 'Apprenticeship and Training in Premodern England', 832–61.
[96] Shepard, *Accounting for Oneself*, surveys the appraisal of self-worth by court witnesses.

Table 4.2. *Valuing seamstresses*

Dorothy Stable's labour's worth after three years' apprenticeship, estimated by her mistress	10d–2s per day
Training Christiana Hutchins to learn point from a gentlewoman, 1668	5s a week
Rent of a part-shop for Frances Carey	£10 p.a.
Premium demanded to take on the untaught Christiana Hutchins	£12 plus clothes
Turnover premium for Frances Bickley, 1689	£20
Premium paid by Katherine Venner's family to a Royal Exchange seamstress for five (or seven) years	£50
Premium paid for Sarah Gibson to a mantua-maker in Holborn for four years, 1715	£4
Cost of physick for Ann Gray's two fits of sickness, according to her apothecary	£3 8d
Wages of Miss Goreing's maid, 1697[a]	£2 p.a.
Paid by Miss Goreing for scouring a coat and petticoat	7s
A year's diet, washing, fire and candles for Miss Goreing and her two servants, 1697	£52
Ralph Josselin's annual income c. 1660[b]	£150

[a] TNA, C114/182/32, 'Miss Goreing's Account Book'.
[b] Lorna Weatherill, *Consumer Behaviour and Material Culture in Britain, 1660–1760* (London: Psychology Press, 1996).

Table 4.3. *Costs of shop goods*

1 yard point Venice lace	14s
Cap and linen	16s
Woman's whisk[a]	3s
Gauze pass from Sarah Frost's shop	14d
Pair of gloves bought for Elizabeth Ward	1s 6d
Pair of bodies for Elizabeth Ward	1s 6d

[a] LMA, CLA/002/02/01/0570, no. 215; other items from Mayor's Court cases cited here and Elizabeth Ward in LMA, CLA/024/05/91 (1656).

final two years were estimated as being worth £20 to £40 to her master and mistress – if she behaved. Indeed, her master and mistress were offered £60 with another apprentice but refused it 'meerly because Katherine was well able to manage their business'.[97] Ann Gray was described by her mistress's witnesses to be 'very capable' because she

[97] LMA, CLA 024/05/131B (1662).

had served over two and a half years. Katherine Bobart said she would have happily taken her on herself for wages as well as lodging and diet, but for her poor behaviour.[98]

The emphasis on learning business skills is borne out in another case in which Alice Cryer sued Elizabeth Jenaway over debts from the shop they ran together. Recalling their dealings as they formed a partnership, Margaret Cooper, a fifty-four-year-old spinster who sold them tea, described how Alice was the more established in trade, and Elizabeth said that she would give her a guinea 'to have instructed her in the said way of tradeing and to goe along with her to Gentlemens houses to observe her way of dealing'. Nothing like an apprenticeship, this transaction nevertheless represents the kinds of skills that were considered worth paying to learn.[99] Ways of dealing involved the display of goods, the bargaining and the management of credit that underpinned new consumption. Those who came shopping were not just individual customers; habitually, women staying or living in London were commissioned to buy for provincial family and friends, and some professional shopkeepers were also proxy shoppers. Hester Pinney's archive contains a letter from a friend, Thomas Rose, beginning:

Dear Mrs Easter, My wife receivd yours and gives you her thanks for your kinde offer, which she does willingly embrace and desires you to buy two capps for my Girles and a plaine silke Girdle for her self and whatever they cost shall faithfully be repayd.[100]

Hester's extensive shopkeeping experience would have given her a good eye as well as bargaining expertise. Both formal and informal learning provided the foundations of the active participation of women in business throughout the next century.[101]

Part of the skill of shop work was appraisal, bargaining and giving credit. Apprentices learned to wait on customers politely but with firmness. Thomas Rumsey, a grocer's apprentice, was complained of by his master in 1670 for sending customers away without serving them if they did not have ready change.[102] They were expected to know the price of goods and, of course, to account for everything they sold. Keeping money or change back, or letting goods get 'lost', was a regular issue.

---

[98] LMA, CLA/024/05/498 (1689).   [99] LMA, CLA/024/05/462 (1685).
[100] Bristol University Special Collections, Pinney Papers, Red Box 2.
[101] On the range of women's business activity, see, for example, Nicola Phillips, *Women in Business, 1700–1850* (Woodbridge: Boydell & Brewer, 2006); Pamela Sharpe, 'Lace and Place: Women's Business in Occupational Communities in England 1550–1950', *Women's History Review* 19, no. 2 (2010): 283–306.
[102] LMA, CLA/024/05/258 (1670).

Mary Mason, a sixteen-year-old apprentice working in a shop with the younger and unreliable Christiana Hutchins, testified that she had gone to ask her master a price, leaving Christiana and an 'ancient woman' customer in the shop; when she came back, some cloth was missing, and Christiana suggested the customer had taken it.[103] Frances Bickley's master and mistress alleged that she had been untrustworthy in house and shop. Elizabeth Dunn, who had lodged in the household along with several others, observed Frances give a mask, a fan and a yard of green ribbon to a nurse in the house and sell two quilted caps for 22 pence, of which she gave her mistress only 18 pence. Elizabeth took a ring from her cousin, wrapped it in paper and tucked it in her room's window frame; later, she found it down the stairs, wrapped in a handkerchief of Frances's with a sixpence that she had seen in Frances's hand. She gave Frances the keys to her trunk, asking her to go and fetch her hood and gloves, and Frances took a ring from it; charged with it, she offered a crown in exchange but never gave Elizabeth either the money or the ring. This saga of domestic labour and exchange mirrors shop bartering and suggests how girls might learn to cheat as well as deal honestly.[104] Katherine Venner was involved in similar confrontations over a hood and a scarf, which she insisted she had taken openly from the shop, witnessed by her fellow servants, and with a promise she would 'make satisfaction' for them. Anne Chanor, a servant in the same household, reported hearing her mistress saying 'in a passion that Katherine was a theif and had stolen the same hood and scarf'. Mary Roe, Katherine's mistress's sister, had been in the shop too, and that evening the girls who worked there talked with her privately. Katherine asked Mary Roe why she had pretended to her sister that she had taken the scarf 'privately without giving notice when she as well knew of her taking thereof and bine paid 14 shillings for the scarf'; Mary answered, 'Yes it is trewe I knew yow did tell me of it and did pay me 14 shillings for the said scarf but [my sister] coming on me of a sudden and questioning me touching it I had it not then in mind and had denyed that I knew anything of them ... and having soe denyed it I dare not now confess it.'[105] It was evidence of the confusing transactions of a millinery household as well as the power of Katherine's mistress, Mrs Allen, an Exchange seamstress with several apprentices and an elite clientele.

In the increasingly genteel trade of millinery, business and artisanal skills went hand in hand. The hands of seamstress apprentices attracted attention: mistresses watched their skilfulness, relatives looked out for

---

[103] LMA, CLA/024/05/010 (1674).   [104] LMA, CLA/024/05/509B (1686).
[105] LMA, CLA/024/05/131A (1662) – lightly edited to remove repeated clericalisms.

their appearance. Eighteenth-century commentators observed women's use of their hands to 'tumble over goods' in shops, unravelling textiles and browsing with their hands as well as their eyes. Kate Smith has shown how these sensory engagements helped consumers conceptualise their material worlds.[106] The hands of shopkeepers also embodied a haptic skill, one that had to be learned: not just sewing, but displaying goods. Milliners' and seamstresses' hands were a commodity as well as a tool.

The ways apprentices used their hands was indicative of the status of their apprenticeship. The stories of litigation sometimes dwelt on the minutiae of such distinctions. The interrogatory to witnesses in Frances Bickley's case posed some telling questions: did her master keep any maidservant besides Frances? Was she not forced to do all the work of a servant, 'as washing the house, scouring of pewter and brasse potts, fetching of bread from the bakehouse as farr as Aldersgate?' Elizabeth Morrelly, who had lodged in the Johnsons' house, was a confidante of Frances Bickley, and after she left the house, she continued to see the apprentice about the neighbourhood 'in a very dirty and nasty condition'. She asked her 'how she came so', and Frances told her that John Johnson no longer had a maidservant and was making her do the 'servile work'. Mrs Johnson made her 'carry a great boy of hers about with her upon a Sunday'. They misused and mistrusted her, she said. On the other side, Mrs Johnson's witnesses accused Frances of theft. They described the mask and ribbon she had taken, the money she had pocketed after selling the quilted caps, and a petticoat she had been given to sew, which was mislaid when she left it lying around the shop. Frances left, and her uncle arranged for her to be turned over to Mary Barton, another milliner with a shop on the Exchange, paying £20 for the final five years of her apprenticeship.[107]

The fetching of bread and other errands of which Frances Bickley complained suggest the risks of being drawn into housework, echoing the evidence of tax records that female apprentices were substantially more likely than male not to be living alongside domestic servants. Anne

---

[106] Kate Smith, 'Sensing Design and Workmanship: The Haptic Skills of Shoppers in Eighteenth-Century London', *Journal of Design History* 25, no. 1 (2012): 1–10; see also Helen Berry, 'Polite Consumption: Shopping in Eighteenth-Century England', *Transactions of the Royal Historical Society* 12 (2002): 375–94, and Claire Walsh, 'Shopping at First Hand? Mistresses, Servants and Shopping for the Household in Early-Modern England', in *Buying for the Home: Shopping for the Domestic from the Seventeenth Century to the Present*, ed. D. E. Hussey and Margaret Ponsonby (Aldershot: Ashgate, 2008), 13–26.
[107] LMA, CLA/024/05/509B, 509A (1689).

Crispe, witnessing in another Mayor's Court case, described her work as a servant as 'tending of the Complainant's child & sitting in his shopp and doeing of semstry work'.[108] Of these tasks, only childcare was clearly not part of an apprentice's work. Apprentices complained of being set to household work. At the Westminster Sessions in 1691, Isabella Lamb petitioned to be discharged from her mistress Elizabeth Wood on the grounds that instead of teaching her to make bone lace, as she was meant to do, she had put her to do 'household work and other Business'. Her mistress, Isabella argued, 'cannot perfectly instruct your Petitioner in her trade whereby your petitioner may gett her Living herafter', and she requested to be discharged from her indenture so she could be placed instead with 'some skilfull person using the same Trade' for the rest of her term. This document makes quite clear that the trade specified in Isabella's indenture was understood precisely and that the aim of her seven-year apprenticeship was to enable her to get her own living through a trade. Rather than paying a premium, Isabella was supported by her friends, who had engaged themselves to provide not only her clothes but also food, washing and lodging: it was an investment in her future earning capacity.[109] Gertrude Kirby, apprentice to Angellat Patilla in St Martin in the Fields, made a similar complaint of failure to instruct, this time in washing point lace. She was given back £3 of her premium to place herself elsewhere.[110] Sarah Gibson, bound for three years in 1715 to learn to be a mantua-maker from Joanna Worthington in Holborn, a contract which was made for £4 and paid by her brother, petitioned that instead she had been employed in 'comon household worke, cleaning and washing Lodgers Rooms and attending them'.[111]

The slippage between domestic labour, service and skilled work was significant enough to feature in the basic agreements of apprenticeship, verbally if not on paper. Dorothy Penny, witnessing as part of a lawsuit to recover the premium paid with her daughter Christiana Hutchins in 1674, described how her daughter's mistress Mary Haslam had agreed 'to employ Christiana wholly in the trade of a sempstress and that she should not bee imployed in service and drudgery work in the house but would keep a Maid servant to do the same'. Within three-quarters of a year, Christiana was complaining to her mother and their friends that the Haslams had 'put away their maidservant and made the said Apprentice Christiana doe the drudgery work about the house as washing thereof making fyres and washing clothes and fetching water'. Christiana was one of three orphaned

---

[108] LMA, CLA/024/05/91 (1656).   [109] LMA, WJ/SP/1691/07/009.
[110] LMA, MJ/SB/B 493, p. 49.
[111] Middlesex Sessions, *London Lives* LMSMPS501450002 (1 April 1715).

daughters of a haberdasher from Marylebone; her mother had remarried, to a gentleman in St Giles in the Fields. Like Mary Jones, Christiana Hutchins had strong company connections; the orphan of a fishmonger, her case was prosecuted by her uncle Robert Hutchins, a wealthy member (and later liveryman) of the Clothworkers' Company. With her mother, he had overseen the 'agreement making', in which Christiana was bound to a barber-surgeon's wife for £20, her clothes provided by her family.

The other side of Christiana's story cut straight to the challenges an unwilling apprentice might pose. Mary Haslam and her husband brought two witnesses who testified that Christiana, so far from being forced into drudgery, had actually preferred it to sewing. Mary Mason was an apprentice in the house with Christiana and described how, when Mrs Haslam told her off for doing her work amiss, Christiana fought back, telling her not to look at it if she didn't like it: 'she did it well enough to serve her own turn and would not do it better'. She told her mistress 'that she never intended to follow her trade but when her time was out she would be a chambermaid And if she never worked again her uncle would give her an Estate to live on without working'. Finally, she said 'she would not nor could she sit constantly pricking of a Clout', picking up a mocking phrase for tailoring. She asked her mistress instead to let her do work about the house. Alice Smith, who had put her own child out to Mrs Haslam, told the same story: Christiana would leave her work in the shop and go to the kitchen and do the work of the house, wandering off to fetch water (precisely the kind of job that other apprentices complained of as drudgery) instead of sewing as her mistress told her to. Christiana's resistance to sewing left her only two other options, it seemed: hoping her uncle would provide better for her, or becoming a chambermaid, another of the options that Hannah Woolley offered in 1668 as a good career for young women.[112] Christiana was only eleven or twelve at this point; she had been apprenticed, apparently, at nine, which was one of the problems. Her mistress complained that she cut up the silk and lace from the shop to make herself 'babies'. But in the four years of her apprenticeship, she gained an astute grasp of the limited opportunities ahead.[113]

Mary Haslam's response to Christiana's intransigence was to send her out to another teacher: she boarded her out in Holborn to learn point with 'a gentlewoman that was rarely expert therein', paying the teacher 5s a week. Christiana behaved so 'rudely and wantonly' that her teacher feared she would spoil her other scholars and declared she would not have her for more than twice the money. This enterprise indicates some

---

[112] Woolley, *Guide to Ladies*, 25.
[113] LMA, P69/MRY7/A/002/MS04997 (7 January 1658/9).

of the other ways that specialist sewing and lacemaking was being taught to young women in the city. Mrs Haslam herself took boarders as well as apprentices and claimed in her libel that she treated Christiana as well as a boarder who paid £20 a year for 'boarding and teaching'. Christiana then left the Haslams and was turned over to Mary Culpepper, who testified that when she arrived, she was 'very little instructed in the trade of sempstress'. Her skills remained basic: 'for fine work she could doe nothing therein or had any skill in Sempstry other then to hem an ordinary thing.' Mrs Culpepper refused to take her without a premium of at least £12 (and her clothes), indicating that all Christiana's previous service had left little value in her hands. The Haslams found Christiana, they said, surprisingly young and ill prepared for apprenticeship. A witness described her as 'very little of growth for her age and in a manner a child and not able to dress herself'; her mistress had to comb and dress her hair for her for the first few months, when she was still only ten.

Overseeing Christiana's apprenticeship, her female relatives and her fellow servant scrutinised her hands, which had become hard. They judged that, like her clothes, they had been 'spoiled'; her aunt observed that she could tell that 'she did do all the drudgery work in the house not relating to the trade of a sempstress, for that her hands did very much evidence the same, being made very unfit to handle and work with a needle'. She told Christiana's mistress that the apprentice 'looked as if she did make the fires and dress the meat', and Mrs Haslam replied in her defence, 'they had all their meat from the cooks and dressed none at home.'[114] Hands were a key marker of female gentility in the eighteenth century.[115] Those distinctions may have been less culturally established in the late seventeenth, but judging the work that a hand did, and what it was capable of, was evidently part of the supervision of apprenticeship. Elizabeth Mason, another fellow apprentice, said that when Christiana's aunt complained of the lack of a maidservant, Mary Haslam responded 'that durty Girle does all that'.

Mary Haslam's skill as a mistress, like Frances Carey's, also came under scrutiny. Dorothy Bowyer, a bodice-maker aged twenty-five, testified that 'she knoweth the defendant Mary is a very industrious woman and one that takes a great deale of paine in the world for a livelyhood and the like care and paines to teach and instruct her Apprentice'. Dorothy's testimony of industry and livelihood, and their attendant pains, is also

---

[114] LMA, CLA 024/05/318 (1674).
[115] Kate Smith, 'In Her Hands: Materializing Distinction in Georgian Britain', *Cultural and Social History* 11, no. 4 (2014): 489–506.

notable because, unusually for a female witness, the court documents record her occupation. Many courts did not record occupations for anyone, plaintiffs or witnesses, but church courts and equity courts like the Mayor's Court wrote down miniature biographies for their witnesses, detailing age, place and details of occupation or status. Men were ascribed an occupation and no marital status; women were given the status of wife (for example, 'wife of William Culpepper, citizen and fishmonger'), servant (assumed to be single), widow or spinster. Of all the Mayor's Court female witnesses, only Dorothy Bowyer had an occupation and no marital status, suggestive of the new place of industrious women in London's labour market. Bowyer's trade of bodice-making was another piece in the jigsaw of the urban garment trade. Bodices were integral to ordinary women's clothing as well as part of more elaborate outfits. Originally they were made of two sections laced together, including boned stays and a partial or full sleeve so that they could be worn on top of a smock to shape the upper body. By the 1680s, stays were emerging as foundation garments in their own right and were mostly made by men, although women were employed to stitch them; bodices became a separate garment, and making them became a female trade, characteristically employing pauper apprentices and women.[116] Dorothy Bowyer's training is invisible, but by twenty-five years old, she had become an independent worker. She lodged for a while in the same house as the Haslams and worked 'sometimes' with them in Mary's shop; without a shop of her own, but with a trade.

For Dorothy Bowyer, watching mistress and servant together, teaching was something that involved care and pain rather than the seamless transmission of skill that seemed to have been assumed between Frances Carey and Mary Jones. She saw Christiana 'make sober good plain work', when she was in the humour for it, though when she was cross, she would spoil it. Dorothy had a sharp eye, too, for the emotional and physical conflict between Christiana Hutchins and her mistress. She defended Mary's teaching methods against the Hutchins family's allegations of violence, testifying that she saw no unreasonable correction 'save now and then her Mistress gave her a patt with her hand for neglecting or spoyling her work as often she did doe'. Dorothy recalled Christiana saying to her that her mistress threatened to put her away, but 'if she knew not when she had a good servant, she (Christiana) knew when she had a good mistress, and would stay with her'. The regard, however forced, was meant to be reciprocal; if these words seem precocious for a

---

[116] Lynn Sorge-English, *Stays and Body Image in London: The Staymaking Trade, 1680–1810* (London: Pickering & Chatto, 2011).

ten- or eleven-year-old, perhaps they came from Dorothy's own sense of fit working arrangements.[117] A fellow apprentice described a much less amenable relationship, and the capacity of fellow workers and servants to offer such different stories suggests the wide difference between the experiences of apprentices and co-workers. The detail both sides gave, prompted by but amplifying the clauses of the libels crafted for each side, also record the stories and values that were shared about workplace malpractice and good or bad teaching. Elizabeth Mason had moved on to work for a sailor in Ratcliffe but had been an apprentice alongside Christiana for three years. Together, she said, they did 'all the work about the house ... washing thereof making fyers and fetching water and scowring the pewter and trenchers'. They were expected to sit up late to let Mr Haslam in, whereupon he raged at them and sent out to light his friends home. Mary, she said, often beat and misused them and hit Christiana's head 'sometimes with a stick and with a pair of Sizers (what was next hand)'. There would always be scissors to hand in a seamstress's workplace: this, along with Dorothy's description of the 'pats' that the mistress gave her servant to correct her work, conveys a working relationship imbued with physical discipline and at least the potential of considerable violence. William Haslam was violent too: Elizabeth Mason said he threw Christiana upon the ground, kicked and stomped upon her and pinched her. Christiana's mother reported that her daughter had a broken, swollen head, a bruised shoulder, arms that were black and blue, and an injury on her side that made her swoon when she tried to lace her bodice. Frances Bickley alleged that she had been 'beaten til she was black with bruises'. Immoderate correction was a standard plea for the dissolution of indentures for both girls and boys; its appearance in legal records conveys both its perceived legitimacy and its limits.

Both Christiana's family and her mistress complained of her flawed appearance. She did not match the requirements of a girl working with patterns of fashion. Her aunt, visiting her, expressed shock at her clothes: she was 'in a poor and ragged condition (as if she had gon abegging) with her clothes all rent and torne and stockings all too peeces with addling and shoes on her feet too big for them that this deponent was ashamed to see her'. She bought her shoes and stockings, pattens, petticoat, a black hood and several aprons. Sarah Hutchinson, another relative, described what she found when she visited in evocative and emotive terms: 'her clothes very ragged & torne & in a perilous durty condicon like unto a sinder girle that sifts sinders on a dunghill'. Cinder girls in early modern

[117] LMA, CLA/024/05/318.

cities sifted ash to find any remnants of value – bones, paper or metal – before it was taken off to be used as fertilizer. Scavenging jobs were often allotted to women, and they were also readily aligned with sexual dishonesty.[118] Sarah Hutchinson's words brought to the surface the proximity of the rubbish heaps and dirty channels of the city, and the finery sold in milliners' shops. Stinking dunghills were everywhere. The importance of female apprentices being seen to do the right work, wear the right clothes and be well treated in the household involved a struggle to be differentiated from pauper apprentices and maidservants. A seamstress's trade was not servile work, or drudgery, but it could come perilously close to them. Anxiety about clothes and appearance reflects the ideal of neatness that was coming to be associated with the millinery trade: by 1747, a trade directory described millinery as 'a most genteel business for young Madams that are good Proficients at their Needle, especially if they be naturally neat, and of a courteous behaviour'.[119] Wayward apprentices and poorly managed clothes brought the high expectations of genteel parents and the drudgery of so much women's work face to face.

For girls from parish dependents to gentry, apprenticeship offered a precarious structure for non-domestic labour. As both life cycle and training, it helped make the norms of the gendered artisanal workplace and the gendered skills of the working life of women, both as apprentices and as mistresses. At the higher end, sewing and shopkeeping remained prominent. In between, a somewhat wider range of training options came into play. The means by which herbwomen, fruiterers, button-makers and pin-makers transmitted their trade remain largely invisible, as do the expectations of girls apprenticed to them and their families. Court testimonies offer a selective account of how girls learned, biased towards divergences of approach that could be blamed for contractual breakdown. The vast majority of apprenticeships were more harmonious, though many were uncompleted. The shape of court cases was determined by the only kinds of complaint that were acceptable in equity: contraventions of the indenture, itself a very old convention written for boys in craft workshops. Seamstresses' disputes reflect life in shops and households that took on girls with high premiums and were expected to provide proportionate skills; the large numbers of seamstresses and milliners enabled networks of reputation and expertise and strong

---

[118] See, for example, *The Gossips Braule, or the Women Weare the Breeches* (London: Printed in the Year of Womens honesty, 1655).

[119] *A General Description of All Trades, Digested in Alphabetical Order* (1747), 149.

occupational identities. They also nurtured a sense of sewing and shopkeeping as female trades, which demanded female discipline.

In seamstress apprenticeships, the journeys to craft proficiency and to performatively submissive femininity went hand in hand, just as city boys learned to be men and artisans together. Apprenticeship, the transition to adulthood and independent work, might usefully be seen not only as training for artisanship but as the crafting of gender.

5 Making Havoc: Discipline, Demeanour and Resistance

Katherine Venner

On a Sunday afternoon in November 1661, Katherine Venner found herself shut out of the house where she lived as an apprentice. She had been invited to dinner at Mrs Buckhurst's house, several doors away, and had gone without asking permission: when her master and mistress, Herbert and Katherine Allen, missed her, they told the rest of the household not to let her in again, calling her idle and determining to get rid of her for good. This was the story her family presented to the Mayor's Court, when her brother tried to regain some of the large premium her father, now dead, had paid down six years earlier. Lawsuits over premiums followed set patterns, not unlike marital separations, in which the irreconcilable differences of master or mistress and apprentice were rehearsed along established lines: the broken obligations of food, clothes, training, obedience and reliability. They reflected the rules of indentures as much as real incidents, following the requirements of apprenticeship for both boys and girls. Within those predictable outlines, witnesses and litigants presented convincing and familiar stories of the dilemmas of service. Gestures, acts and words were reported in detail, with particular attention to evidence of behaviour, obedience and disposition, as competing sides argued over whose behaviour had undermined the apprenticeship contract. In the context of genteel seamstress shops, civility and demeanour were particularly significant, and the Mayor's Court witnesses were good at describing them.

Katherine's exclusion was preceded by a series of confrontations. Mrs Allen had accused her of theft after she had taken a hood and scarf without permission; Katherine Venner's parents said this defamed Katherine's credit. Some witnesses mentioned a scuffle. The other apprentices and servants were divided: two girls testified for Katherine Venner, a boy for the other side. As in other cases, these stories noted the gestures and demeanour of the parties. Samuel Richards, another of the apprentices, offered acute observations on Katherine Venner's general attitude: 'this deponent certainly knoweth that the said Katherine was of a very proud peremptory & stubborn nature & disposicon & when ever the defendant or his wife being moved did speake anything high or hastily to her she the said Katherine did constantly returne the like or other scurvy words & behaviour to them with very much pride & insolence without any manner of submission.' Richard Manwaring, a young gentleman and soldier from Nantwich in Cheshire, reported coming to intervene after being told that Katherine's mistress had struck and abused her. Mrs Allen 'declared noe other cause or reason but that upon some question asked of her she [Katherine] had in returning an answer stood in a malapert manner & looked her in the face with her hands before her'. And Francis Hunlock, a painter-stainer whose wife, Martha, was an Exchange seamstress, had been involved in the Venners' initial appearance before the Chamberlain of London, when Katherine's contract was dissolved. There, he said, the Allens offered to take her back, but when the Chamberlain presented this option, Katherine 'utterly refused' and 'did behave herselfe somwhat proudly & with more confeidence then was fitting'.[1]

Francis Hunlock's appraisal of Katherine Venner as too proud and confident when she appeared before the Chamberlain of London pinpointed precisely the awkward gap between the subordination of apprenticeship and youth in a domestic hierarchy and the standing of the children of gentry and clergymen who were at ease with magistrates and aldermen.[2] Katherine Venner and her peers used the Mayor's Court because they had substantial premiums to recover and families who could back them. For such families, mercantile apprenticeships provided both girls and boys with advancement and security, helping to build the foundation of the new middling sort. The meeting of provincial gentry families with City trade sheds light on the integration of artisanal training into the lives of girls and women whose families put money by to apprentice them well, and for whom apprenticeship was a means of securing a future for girls as well as boys. Despite the lawsuit over her premium, Katherine claimed the freedom of the Haberdashers' Company in 1663, suggesting she went on to become a seamstress herself.

Hunlock's deposition also reveals something of how court proceedings worked for the young women involved in them. Litigation was brought by fathers or guardians on behalf of these apprentices, but they certainly attended court proceedings and mediation: when the conflict between the Venners and the Allens went to the Court of the Chamberlain of

---

[1] LMA, CLA/024/05/131 (1662).
[2] Henry French, '"Gentlemen": Remaking the English Ruling Class', in *A Social History of England, 1500–1750*, ed. Keith Wrightson (Cambridge University Press, 2017).

London, Katherine was asked for her own opinion and gave it with forthright conviction.

Katherine's stubborn spirit was fostered in an atmosphere of religious and political debate. Her father, Richard Venour, minister of St Mary's, Warwick, was one of a circle of godly ministers and scholars around Warwick Castle who were discussing Puritan and Presbyterian ideas in the 1640s.[3] Katherine's master and mistress, Herbert and Katherine Allen, ran a shop in the Royal Exchange selling shirts, suits, scarves, hoods, lace and childbed linen. By the time of the court case in 1661, they had at least three other apprentices and servants, and Herbert's will in 1668 refers to 'shop-maid-servants' as well as house servants, suggesting the extent and variety of labour they used. Their servants and apprentices both sold in the shops and sewed for them; they also used outworkers. Their apprentices, especially the girls, came from an interesting set of families, many of them gentry and including some significant contemporary figures. The premium of £50 paid by Katherine, with £70 suggested for another, put them at the top of the apprentice market. After her, the Allens' apprentices included Helen Dugdale, the daughter of the antiquarian and royal herald William Dugdale and Mary Babington, from a Staffordshire gentry family. Katherine went on taking apprentices after Herbert's death, including Penelope, daughter of the physician Robert Waller.[4] Helen Dugdale, Katherine Venner and Mary Babington were the children of the Commonwealth, born between 1642 and 1648. They had lived through war and regime change; they were apprenticed under Cromwell and freed, or left their apprenticeships, in the first months and years of the Restoration, as London's new regime established itself. Their fathers, though, came from rather different political backgrounds; the Allens' networks were clearly not driven by memories of the divisions of the Civil Wars.

Herbert and Katherine Allen took Katherine Venner on at the start of their business life together. With no experience as parents or employers, they were learning on the job. The Allens had married in London in 1655, Katherine Roe a Londoner and Herbert, the grandson of James I's surgeon, from Sussex. Herbert had been apprenticed into the Haberdashers and freed in 1650. Six months before Katherine's apprenticeship, Herbert's father, Isaac, had died in circumstances that left sharp

---

[3] Ann Hughes, 'Thomas Dugard and His Circle in the 1630s – A "Parliamentary-Puritan" Connexion?', *Historical Journal* 29, no. 4 (1986): 771–93.
[4] LMA, CLC/L/HA/C/011/MS15860/006, pp. 121, 200; William Salt Library, WA1/1/2/645/991 for Mary Babington, courtesy of Mark Jenner. Dugdale put both his daughters and his granddaughters into apprenticeships: see Chapter 2.

memories. His memorial brass in their Sussex church recorded that he died in the King's Bench Prison in Southwark, following a prosecution for defamatory words: 'most falsely & Maliciously, by One single Witness sworne against Him, as he had often-tymes, & on his death-bed Protested & Declared to severall Friends'.[5] Like most gentry and middling families, the Allens were familiar with lawsuits, grievances and libellous words. Herbert and Katherine's business life together was short: Herbert died just seven years after Katherine Venner's lawsuit, still in his thirties. Their two children died in the next ten years. Katherine Allen's life as a shopkeeper and mistress outlasted all this. Living in St Martin in the Fields, she maintained her Exchange shops and kept taking apprentices, mostly girls but two of them boys, until 1690, when she turned the shops over to the milliners William and Mary Barton (Mary Barton later took on another litigious apprentice, Frances Bickley). Between them, Herbert and Katherine Allen trained at least thirteen apprentices. Katherine Allen's mother, who lived with or near her in her widowhood, recognised her daughter's material success by leaving her only two silver porringers ('extremely too litle considering her verie great kindnesse to me') and passing on her estate to another, less secure daughter.[6] Herbert's probate inventory leaves a rich picture of the family style. The Allens had moved out of the City by the time the inventory was taken in 1668, but many of the furnishings must have been known to Katherine Venner. The maid's chamber contained striped curtains, two old rugs and striped hangings; the parlour had a Spanish table, turkey-work chairs and carpet, three pieces of tapestry and a picture hanging over the chimney; the cupboards contained best and second-best child-bed linen. There was a small Bible and 'several other books', valued at only 20s, and looking glasses in most rooms including the kitchen.[7] London tradespeople were often the leading buyers of new consumer goods, their probate inventories recording particularly high numbers of dishes for entertaining, curtains and looking glasses. The Allens' customers included gentry and aristocracy. Katherine's move from provincial clergy home to city merchant's house meant a material and social transition, and her place in the domestic order of her new life was not entirely straightforward.

---

[5] Herbert Haines, *A Manual of Monumental Brasses: Comprising an Introduction to the Study of These Memorials and a List of Those Remaining in the British Isles* (J. H. and J. Parker, 1861), 214.
[6] TNA, PROB 11/353/320 (1675).
[7] LMA, CLA/002/02/01/0570 fo. 215, 3 October 1668.

Stories like these make claims about the appropriate demeanour of young women amidst the complex social and hierarchical dynamics of life in city households. More broadly, they offer some insight into the patterns of discipline, work and manners that helped to form femininity in the years of adolescence, which so many girls spent away from home. This chapter examines the behavioural conflicts of apprenticeship disputes, ranging from gestures, words and violence to food and clothes. It argues that across the spectrum of occupations and status, apprenticeship was a corporeal and disciplinary experience, taking place critically at a time of life when girls were meant to be learning gender norms but might be resisting them. In a culture and city of changing manners and habits, the workplace was one of the places, and the relationship between girls and mistresses one of the dynamics, through which social identity was established. The evidence of apprenticeship disputes radically expands what it meant to be a young woman, presenting work not just as labour but also as identity and selfhood. Katherine Venner and her peers were learning about power, performance, authority and independence.

The Body in Service

The Allens' complaint that Katherine Venner failed to show appropriate submission speaks to the work of the body in conveying respect and obedience. In households as in society, hierarchy was embodied in manners and gesture. The politics of gesture were integral to early modern social order, from Quaker battles over 'hat honour' to the bared bottoms that sometimes featured in protest. Such moves were deliberate violations of the contained, courteous body that young people throughout the social scale had, in different ways, learned. Pierre Bourdieu's sociology of class theorised the way people learn cultural and social capital as 'habitus', the way of 'knowing the game'. Apprenticeship helped the young acquire that, as well as technical learning, and in the world of shop and house, the bodily aspect of habitus ('bodily hexis') was critical.[8] Bodily habits were in flux, both in historical time and for individuals. Adolescents were likely to be working out their own bodily manners in a new situation; and in the years between the 1650s and the 1690s, civility and manners were themselves subject to copious definition and redefinition, as the norms of a new politeness were elaborated.

Bodily decorum was the subject of frequent printed, and doubtless also verbal, advice. Manners books prescribed appropriate levels of contact

---

[8] Pierre Bourdieu, *The Logic of Practice* (Stanford University Press, 1990).

and deference; one study of rhetoric detailed the hand gestures that made it effective. Norbert Elias's model of the invention of civility used manners codes to track the internalisation of constraint and shame through the early modern period to the modern: eventually, people knew not to spit.[9] Many such codes were directly aimed at the young. Apprentices and servants, quintessentially socially aspirational and with high levels of literacy, were the ideal readers of advice; part of their training was to fashion themselves into the likeness of masters and mistresses. Male apprentices were also, collectively, a perennial problem of urban order, licensed to engage in a certain degree of misrule, such as the notorious attacks on bawdy houses, and regularly castigated for their incivility. For male apprentices, the process of self-fashioning might involve both an internalisation of the rules of demeanour and civility and a performative resistance to them. The drinking and fighting proscribed by civic ideals was also necessary to civic life. The subordination expected of male apprentices was, moreover, temporary: at its end, the successful youth became a master in his own right, ruler of his own household.[10] He would grow out of deference, into patriarchal authority. This dynamic was different for girls. The subordination required of them was less clearly temporary: it might, rather, be the pathway to the convention of wifehood. Performing respect, for girls, was related to the project of internalising modesty that started young. However, as Ilana Ben-Amos argued, the autonomy that apprentices learned, and the skills of work that young women learned in other forms of service, provided the foundation of independent work in their adult lives.[11] The model wife was less useful than the model businesswoman.

The manners books of the seventeenth century are largely focused on men, providing a primer for aspirational masculinity and assuming a male norm.[12] In practice, women's civility, as Sara Mendelson has shown, had its own variable paradigms. For Dame Sarah Cowper, reflecting on her own practice in 1702, civility was part of 'the knowledge

---

[9] Norbert Elias, *The Civilizing Process* (Oxford: Blackwell, 1969).
[10] Paul Griffiths, *Youth and Authority: Formative Experiences in England 1560–1640* (Oxford University Press, 1996); Steven R. Smith, 'The London Apprentices as Seventeenth-Century Adolescents', *Past & Present* 61 (1973): 149–61; Lyndal Roper, 'Blood and Codpieces: Masculinity in the Early Modern German Town', in *Oedipus and the Devil: Witchcraft, Sexuality and Religion in Early Modern Europe* (London: Routledge, 1994), 107–24.
[11] Ilana Krausman Ben-Amos, *Adolescence and Youth in Early Modern England* (London: Yale University Press, 1994), chapter 6.
[12] Susan North, *Sweet and Clean?: Bodies and Clothes in Early Modern England* (Oxford University Press, 2020), chapter 2; Anna Bryson, *From Courtesy to Civility: Changing Codes of Conduct in Early Modern England* (Oxford University Press, 1998).

how to live', involving offering politeness, but with distinctions to avoid levelling. Incivility might come from roughness or, worse, pride. Both, it would seem, were a risk for wayward apprentices. Plebeian women's sense of what was incivil can be glimpsed in legal records of disputes over defamatory words or places in pews, where age, marital status and social rank all played a part in determining what was due to whom, and neighbourly conflict was regularly played out through gesture and demeanour.[13] In a fight over pew places in Somerset in 1634, one woman accused another: 'she comes into church like a lyon stareing, 'twas good her pride was pulled down.'[14] The navigation of decorum in a largely oral culture, Mendelson argues, was particularly complex and ambiguous.

Katherine Venner's world of gesture had more in common with Sarah Cowper than the pew quarrellers, but the vivid imagery of pride and overconfidence that was used to undermine women appears in her case too. Apprenticeships like hers were premised on social differentiation; the products she was creating and the place where she sold them helped to create it. The apprentices themselves were required, it seems, both to perform subordination and to help create the edifice of fashion and civility. Venner's behaviour reflected what girls learned as they grew into their adult selves: how to look at their seniors, how to act with men, how to speak and how to assert the appropriate level of pride and dignity at home, on the street and even in a courtroom. The move of gentry girls into city apprenticeships created a set of new stresses, which the tone of Mayor's Court depositions reflected.

In the late seventeenth century, as the focus of the literature of manners shifted to politeness rather than civility, authors began to concern themselves more explicitly with the presentation of the female body. *The Gentlewomans Companion*, first published in 1673, proposes manners for elite women, describing how to sit straight at the table, not gobbling food and walking to the left of your superiors. It also attempts to pin down the ever-present danger of a 'loose carriage': 'wanton gesticulations', wayward feet and a 'stragling disposition of the eye'. A loose body denotes uncertain chastity.[15] At the start of the eighteenth century, Bernard Mandeville's satire on views of human nature, *The Fable of the Bees*, pointed out in passing that while boys were expected to lift their

---

[13] Sara Mendelson, 'The Civility of Women', in *Civil Histories: Essays Presented to Sir Keith Thomas*, ed. Peter Burke, Brian Harrison and Paul Slack (Oxford University Press, 2000).
[14] Somerset Archives, D/D/cd/71, Bale als Culliford c. Garvin (30 May 1634).
[15] Hannah Woolley, *The Gentlewomans Companion; Or, a Guide to the Female Sex* (1673), 34–41, 65–72.

coats and piss in public, at three, 'Miss' had already learned to hide her legs. A modestly educated girl, Mandeville observed, would watch and imitate the care with which her elders covered their bodies before men. She had absorbed 'civility' while her male peer had learned to perform his bodily functions without constraint.[16] The ideal of politeness demanded feminine containment and bodily modesty. For apprentices, these prescriptions were to be aligned with another set of ideals: those of the occupational hierarchy into which they had enrolled themselves.

Apprenticeship had its own decorum. While there was an established tradition of complaint about rude and bawdy young men learning the artisanal trades, the gentle origins of many of London's seventeenth-century apprentices, particularly in mercantile contexts, added a different dimension to the hierarchy of apprentice households. In 1671, Caleb Trenchfield, an ejected Nonconformist minister in Kent, published instructions to his apprentice son as *A Cap of Grey Hairs for a Green Head*. In the prescriptions that convey a middle-aged man's wisdom to youth, hard work goes hand in hand with humility. An 'industrious officiousness' is recommended: take commands with a pleasant cheerfulness and avoid sullen murmurs. Above all, 'take care to be a servant now, as that you may be a master hereafter … come off the stage with the clear applause of having acted the part of a Servant well'.[17] This instruction to act the part encapsulates the problem with apprentice behaviour: submission can only be performed. The subject, constantly labouring with his promotion in mind, must be ready to stop serving and become a master.

Twenty years after Trenchfield's advice was published, the son to whom it was addressed was at odds with his own apprentice. In 1689, Caleb Trenchfield the younger was a citizen and mercer, with a household of servants, apprentices and journeymen. One of his apprentices, James Ellis, sued out his indentures and instigated litigation at the Mayor's Court. Ellis accused his master of kicking him while he was washing his hands and face, and threatening him with a rope. Caleb Trenchfield's witnesses described a model employer, civil and generous with privileges, allowing his apprentice to sit at the table with him. James, they testified, was a youth of 'turbulent disposition' who was 'high and surly' in his manner, impertinent to a journeyman, and threatened to stab

---

[16] Bernard Mandeville, *The Fable of the Bees, or, Private Vices, Publick Benefits*, ed. Frederick Benjamin Kaye (Oxford: Clarendon Press, 1924), 71–2; 69.

[17] Caleb Trenchfield, *A Cap of Gray Hairs for a Green Head: Or, the Fathers Counsel to His Son, an Apprentice in London* (Glasgow, 1692), 44, 22.

his master 'to the heart's blood'.[18] The contrast with the model apprentices and masters described in Trenchfield's personal guide to virtuous youth was palpable. At an arranged meeting in a coffee house in Paternoster Row, James Ellis was brought to apologise, which he did 'in a very submissive manner', saying his words were spoken 'in his passion'; but Trenchfield insisted he had not showed sufficient remorse.

Apprentice behaviour was a topic of discussion, reflection and contest in print, in court and in households. In the earlier seventeenth century, those discussions took place largely in the context of patriarchal households; by the later seventeenth, they refer more generally to norms of civility and politeness relating to age and social rank. Thomas Wilson, another Mayor's Court litigant, brought a case that illuminates the ambiguous relation of bodily manners, social status and domestic hierarchy. His hat featured prominently in it. Thomas Wilson had broken his apprenticeship contract because his master's trade was in decline. At the same time, Thomas had found himself heir to a good estate on the sudden death of his brother. This reversal in circumstances upset household relations, to Thomas's discomfort. His master asked him to take the daughter of the house home from church, hoping to lure him into marrying her. He allowed him to wear his hat in the workshop, admitting that Thomas's changed circumstances had made him 'give him a liberty to wear his hat before him'.[19] Both shop business and inheritance prospects could be volatile.

Advice to girls was less readily available than that to boys. The one writer who offered direct advice to girls in apprenticeship, Hannah Woolley, had her recommendations removed from her work in a later unauthorised edition, but they are resonant with concerns about manners, dress, food and hands. Woolley's advice 'to all young Maidens who are desirous to go to be apprentices, either in Schools or to any Trades' is both generic and autobiographical. In Woolley's pages, apprentice girls are navigating a complex social hierarchy of a household of teachers, mistress and boarders. Food loomed large, its provision and placement at the table an index of power relations and table manners, drawing on their prominence in Erasmus's advice to youth.[20] 'Eat not in fear', she warned, but do not talk at table; do not put a whole piece of bread in your mouth at once; do not put your knife to your mouth, do not gnaw the bones; if you carve for yourself, take no meat that your mistress

---

[18] LMA, CLA/024/05/521 (1691).
[19] LMA, CLA/024/05/120. See also Penelope J. Corfield, 'Dress for Deference and Dissent: Hats and the Decline of Hat Honour', *Costume* 23 (1989): 64–79.
[20] Desiderius Erasmus, *De Civilitate Morum Puerilium* (1534).

or anyone above you would like. And, tying together manners and humour with a sharp flourish: 'Dip not your fingers in the dish for sauce, for that will render you saucie and liquorish.' A sweet tooth was a danger, and girls were warned never to use the keys they were trusted with to take fruit or sweetmeats. A curtsey to the table was prescribed at the start and end of every meal, and girls were reminded to take their plates away, having shaken the crumbs off it first. Bodily functions were to be contained by social rank: do not blow your nose, spit or pare your nails before anyone above you, and give or take nothing with your left hand, 'especially to your betters'. Woolley specialised in anatomising awkward gestures, as she did badly written letters: 'Use no ridiculous or unhandsom actions, as tittering your stool or chair, keeping a noise with your feet, or playing with your lips, scratching your head, making of faces, thrusting your feet in the fire, treading upon cinders, pulling your eyes, gigling or laughing too loud, leaning on your elbows, or otherwayes: For all these are rude and deforming'. Her account is one of the adolescent body, fidgeting under the eye of adult scrutiny, and she pointed out, too, that a young woman's visage should be open to her betters: 'Never go muffled up with many Hoods and Scarves into the presence of any Noble Person, nor wear a Mask in their light.' Dress marked respect: dirty linen, loose hair, holey stockings and long nails were all noted. Speech should be carefully contained, avoiding unseemly laughter, calling out or lascivious and lewd talk. Girls were to learn how to talk to their betters: 'Answer them with such language as becomes their quality, which you may learn from others, who you hear speak to them'.[21] Mouth, hands and limbs were all trained into mimicry, the key to habitus.

Woolley's advice offers the aspirant young woman a route to raise herself via service, gaining respect through effective emulation. Her apprentices are 'below' their mistresses, apparently in status as well as in age, and this reflects both the environment of a boarding school of young gentlewomen and the service in a gentry household that she had also experienced. It must have echoed the prescriptions that countless mistresses gave to their apprentices. Girls like Katherine Venner, whose social status was at least equivalent to her mistress, and who was invited out to Sunday dinner with a neighbour whilst she was still working as an apprentice, were in a somewhat different position, the hierarchy of age and occupation in tension with those of social status. Venner, like others who worked in the Exchange, was also at work outside the household; the

---

[21] Hannah Woolley, *A Guide to Ladies, Gentlewomen and Maids &c* (1668), 40–5; the later, unauthorised edition is *The Gentlewomans Companion*.

spatial separation of domestic and work authority posed another challenge to mistresses.

Katherine Venner's physical insubordination was described precisely: she looked her mistress in the face with outstretched hands. To look someone in the face was a loaded act. While a downward look was often read as characteristic of evasiveness and laziness, it was also an appropriate pose for inferiors, servants and women. In the performances of femininity, mothers were meant to enjoin their modest daughters to look downwards bashfully, and young girls might resist with boldness and wit.[22] Outstretched hands were not the gently clasped hands of modest maidens or wives in portraits but suggestive of violent resistance to authority. While girls in service and apprenticeship were training to be mistresses themselves, they were also expected to demonstrate a kind of submission that marked their roles as subordinate, featuring modesty, lowered eyes, few words and a careful carriage. Manners were a significant part of how, and what, girls learned, and apprenticeship happened at just the point that resistant girls were being moulded into women.

Strikingly, girls were not accused of unchastity. Immodesty was a more general bodily concept. Fornication was rarely specifically forbidden in their contracts, though one indenture from early seventeenth-century Norwich specifies that a woman, if caught fornicating, is 'to double the term of her service'.[23] It may be that seamstress apprentices were too busy, well regulated or well behaved to toy with the young men with whom they lived and sometimes worked, or that their high premiums protected them from harassment. But it's also unlikely that such complaints would feature in this particular legal process.

Male apprentices' bodies mattered too, but their incivility tended to be more externally focused, and modesty was not the measure of their conformity. At the Mayor's Court, William Loefeild was said to have drunk too much and 'behaved himself very wildly and incivilly in the said house in singing drunken songs and catches'.[24] Francis Ince tempted a maidservant 'to attempt that which was incivil' and persuaded her to naughtiness; the agency was all his.[25] Others loitered on the quays

---

[22] As in the joke in *England's Merry Jester ... Done by a Lover of Merriment* (1694), 26–7; on adolescent girls as sites of resistance, see Jennifer Higginbotham, *Girlhood of Shakespeare's Sisters: Gender, Transgression, Adolescence* (Edinburgh University Press, 2013), 62–5.

[23] Norwich Record Office, AB1 171X1 (Helen Dallyson, 1624). Medieval indentures were more precise about fornication, with some making stricter rules for girls: Kim M. Phillips, *Medieval Maidens: Young Women and Gender in England, c. 1270–c. 1540* (Manchester University Press, 2003), 83.

[24] LMA, CLA/024/05/115 (1661). [25] LMA, CLA/024/05/150 (1662).

looking at the Thames instead of working; lay too long in bed in the morning and were too friendly with a servant maid; stayed out all night; slept in the shop at nine or ten o'clock of a summer's morning; and went out to a tavern one night in 'Womans Apparell like a Country Gentlewoman'.[26] According to indentures, alehouses were, like gaming, out of bounds for both sexes of apprentice, but the indenture of one pauper in St Clement Danes, Elizabeth Keyser, set to learn housewifery, suggests there was some flexibility: she was bound not to visit alehouses except on her mistress's business.[27] Lawsuits suggest that male apprentices' training allowed a greater range of movement, and the models of incivility and misconduct were markedly broader than those available to young women learning to sew. For both young men and women, though, the relationship with master and mistress was an important arena of manners codes. In the shop, in schools and at home, apprentices were learning how to bear their bodies and use their hands with civility, politeness and authority. Hannah Woolley saw this and imagined apprenticeship as one of the ways a girl might shape herself into a woman.

Woolley's text alerts readers to the significance of food in domestic order. Taking a place lower down the table, or eating later, would be a shock to the gentry daughters entering the hierarchy of a city household. Hannah Woolley reminded her apprentice readers not to take the best meat at table; at both ends of the apprentice market, some were complaining of unwholesome meat or lack of provisions. One lace-making apprentice recorded that her indenture required her friends to provide her food and drink, as well as lodging and clothes.[28] Other accounts suggest dinner tables were a predictable flashpoint for relations between the inferiors of the household. Nicholas Hall, a clothworker's apprentice described by a neighbour as stubborn, 'saucy in his carriage' and 'rude and quarrelsome in the family', picked a quarrel with the maidservant over dinner, on a 'very slight matter' and put a knife to her chest, swearing a great oath.[29] For Edward Barlow, in his brief apprenticeship in Manchester in 1656, the table arrangement provoked grumbling resentment. The whole household sat together, but at the upper end of the table – where the master, dame and children sat – there was 'a great difference of victuals, namely a pudding with suet and plums'. At the lower end, where he sat, a plain pudding. At the upper end a piece of fat beef, at the lower 'a piece of surloin next the horns'; 'there was always

---

[26] LMA, CLA/024/05/415; CLA/024/05/416; CLA/024/05/521; CLA/024/05/258.
[27] St Clement Danes Parish Apprenticeships (1689), *London Lives*, WCCDPA364000050.
[28] LMA, WJ/SP 1691/07/009 (Isabella Lamb).   [29] LMA, CLA/024/05/312 (1674).

something or other which we had not'.[30] Ely Walwyn, apprentice to a merchant tailor, reported that his fellow apprentice refused to eat beef on Friday that had already been served on Thursday, 'although the beafe was indeed very good and sweete'.[31] Even the high-premiumed London apprentice girls said they were kept from the good food. Frances Bickley was said to have been prevented from eating breakfast, 'nor could she come at either butter or cheese the same being allwaies locked up'. Elizabeth Mason, eighteen-year-old apprentice to Mary and William Haslam, complained that her master and mistress left the apprentices often short of food, because they bought most of their dinner at the cook's and ate their fill themselves, leaving for the four apprentices 'only a quarter of a pound of salt butter a farthing worth of beere and such bread as the [master and mistress] were pleased to cut them'.[32] Elizabeth's younger sister, Mary, took the opposite side and said there was plenty of food: they just needed to ask. Mrs Haslam herself had been heard to complain that Christiana would 'make havock of her victualls … flinging the same up and downe in severall places of the house'.

Food was an issue between Christiana and her mother, too. The mother complained that Mary Haslam fed Christiana 'so unreasonably that she was growne out of shape and that she wondered [she] had no more reason and told her she would not have her daughter to eat so much'.[33] This is an unusual constellation of adolescent battles over food, domestic order and discipline. Food control mattered to early modern girls, but rarely took this form, and is generally not related explicitly to appearance; their best-attested food issues are self-starvation, often with a spiritual context.[34] Christiana, now fourteen or fifteen, had been an apprentice for five years, and her mother, remarried and still living in London, could only observe her changing body on her visits. She was, apparently, so angry at her daughter's mistreatment and out-of-shape body that she called Mary Haslam 'slutt' and other insults. Christiana herself complained that her mother had 'almost starved her': she was determined to stay in her apprenticeship rather than return to her. Christiana Hutchins's troubles, and the scraps of her words that emerge

---

[30] Edward Barlow, *Barlow's Journal of His Life at Sea in King's Ships, East & West Indiamen & Other Merchantmen from 1659 to 1703*, ed. Alfred Lubbock (London: Hurst & Blackett, 1934), 575.
[31] LMA, CLA/024/05/82 (1655).
[32] LMA, CLA/024/05/509 (1686) and CLA/024/05/318 (1674).
[33] LMA, CLA/024/05/318 (1674).
[34] Nancy A. Gutierrez, *'Shall She Famish Then?': Female Food Refusal in Early Modern England* (Aldershot: Ashgate, 2003); Sasha Garwood, *Early Modern English Noblewomen and Self-Starvation: The Skull Beneath the Skin* (London: Routledge, 2019).

in others' accounts, suggest an embattled journey from childhood to adolescence. Kate Chedgzoy's analysis of the conversion narrative of the young Sarah Wight, another London girl, traces a young woman struggling against the assimilation of cultural norms to become adult and the embodied power structures of the household.[35] Wight's battle against temptations began with issues familiar to young women in and out of service: 'her superiour bid her doe a small thing' which she felt was unlawful; then she lost a hood and lied about it. Later, she broke her earthen drinking cup throwing it against the wall.[36] Eating too much, wasting food and complaining about it were the tools by which Christiana negotiated bodily autonomy, in the same way as the more familiar starving girls did.

The apprentices of the Haslams' shop, as well as the neighbour whose daughter also worked there, reported on these fights in detail, filling out the litigants' claims about food, discipline and clothes. Servants, apprentices and their parents were close observers of the dynamics of disturbed working households, and the Mayor's Court depositions capture the particular strains of gentle apprentices in the households of seamstresses, drapers and merchants. The testimonies, recorded by court clerks in response to questions crafted with the assistance of court attorneys, deploy the language of civility and politeness to address the world of work: it is a cultural encounter that should inform how we understand London's middling women and their world.

In houses like this, clothes more than bodies were the currency of work and identity, and the stuff of argument. Traditionally, apprentices' clothes were provided by their employers: a typical provision was that in the contract made for Frances Niccols in 1688, who was bound aged twelve to Mary and James Lambert to learn Mary's trade as a cook, on condition that the Lamberts provided 'sufficient wholsome and necessary lodging washing diet and apparell'.[37] The indentures of seamstress apprentices in London companies tend to have this provision deleted, and witnesses in court cases often noted that seamstresses or exchange-women expected their apprentices to provide their own clothes, perhaps in keeping with the importance of good clothes. Petitions for discharge ordered mistresses to return both indentures and apparel. The cost of clothes constituted a substantial part of the charges of supporting an

---

[35] Kate Chedgzoy, 'Other Maids: Religion, Race and Relationships between Girls in Early Modern London', in *Literary Cultures and Medieval and Early Modern Childhoods*, ed. Naomi J. Miller and Diane Purkiss (Basingstoke: Palgrave Macmillan, 2019), 187–201.
[36] Henry Jessey, *The Exceeding Riches of Grace Advanced by the Spirit of Grace* (1647), 6, 11.
[37] LMA, MJ/SB/B 479, p. 69 (17 December 1690).

apprentice, and they might also be capital for an apprentice. In Shadwell in 1697, Elizabeth White was accused by her mistress, a mantua-maker, of 'pawning her own wearing clothes and spending the money in wicked company'. The mistress, who was a 'poor widow' with two small children, was worried her apprentice would steal the 'severall goods of great value releateing to her Trade' that she kept in the house, imperilling her capacity to work.[38]

Apprentices were typically supplied with suits, comprising a bodice or waistcoat on top and petticoats below, or a gown and petticoat combination. Under this they wore shifts and sometimes drawers.[39] Aprons, stockings, caps and hoods, neckerchiefs and pattens to pick through the London streets were also necessary. Legal records provide an indication of what was expected for the higher 'quality' seamstresses. Dorothy Stable's family provided her with 'all sortes of clothes and necessaries fitting and convenient for an Apprentice of her quallity', including three gowns and two petticoats, all of which she apparently wore out in her two years of service. Best and ordinary sets of clothes were expected. Christiana Hutchins's family agreed to provide her initial clothes, followed by another new suit two years later, on condition that her mistress would maintain her in the same style: 'as she was used to go, so would they keep her and use her as their owne'. Christiana started off with a new suit, petticoat and linen worth £4, alongside 'an old suit for everyday', four shifts, four aprons, sleeves, caps, hose and shoes. A month into her work, her master and mistress said she needed more, and her friends provided a new worsted 'farandine' silk and wool gown and a striped silk 'tabby' (taffeta) petticoat. This combination of gown and petticoat sounds more fashionable and smart, with the petticoat good enough to show. Another witness noted that, whilst in service, Christiana had been given '3 indifferent good waistcoats, 6 shifts whereof three are new, several scarves and hoods'. The combination of used and new was perhaps not good enough for the looks of the Haslams' household. Her mother complained they were worn out by her daily drudgery and her master and mistress's failure to replace them. When she left their service, Christiana was in a 'very ragged mean & Lowsy condicon', with her clothes so full of vermin they had to be thrown away. Poor housekeeping and hard work could transform a wardrobe, if not its wearer, from gentility to rags. The Haslams would have been responsible for the

---

[38] LMA, MJ/SP 1697/07/009.
[39] Danae Tankard, *Clothing in 17th-Century Provincial England* (London: Bloomsbury, 2019), 130, 147; Sarah Bendall, *Shaping Femininity: Bodies and Farthingales in Elizabethan and Stuart England* (London: Bloomsbury, 2021).

expensive task of having their apprentices' linen washed: unlike maidservants and apprentices in housewifery, genteel seamstress apprentices would not be doing the laundry, and the failure to manage linen appropriately was known to encourage lice and cause disease.[40]

Judgements of appropriate quality were part of the work of both employer and family. Frances Bickley's master took away the fine handkerchiefs given her by her grandmother, thinking they were too good to be hers.[41] Elizabeth Hudson, visiting her sister Hester during her apprenticeship, judged that 'she wanted necessaries to keep her handsome & in cleanly in such manner as might become a servant of far meaner quality'. Hester's family and friends had, they said, provided her with 'at least four severall suites of Apparell and all sortes of Lynnen' so that she was 'very well furnished of all necessarye befitting her condicon'. Ann Joyner was in service alongside Hester and said, on the contrary, that the apparel Hester had brought with her, 'both woollen and linen' – outer and inner wear – was 'verie poore and meane'. She had only two woollen gowns, one of which she was ashamed to wear and the other that she had already had for a year; and her linen, her undergarments, was also 'very mean'. In the household, Ann said, it was appraised as worth about 40s all told, and she was given no others. This description of 'mean' describes value, look and feel, the qualities that seamstresses were trained to evaluate. The linen would be coarser, would wear poorly and might not bleach as white as better goods would.[42] Ann Joyner's testimony conveys high expectations of a seamstress apprentice, and a household culture that was well used to appraising the value of clothes and their wear, in the house and out. Hester Hudson's poor clothes were offset by her frivolity: she spent 'much money in pies and tarts and such other things' and on 'needles and superfluous things'.[43] Perhaps frivolous spending was the parallel of the gaming and drinking boys were accused of, but it was also an appropriate part of learning to be a consumer: superfluous things were what many shops dealt in.

Like Hester, Frances Angell was accused of vanity and waste. She insisted on wearing her best clothes to work in, and her mistress, Appollonia Maddox, 'being not able to endure to see the extreame spoyle she made therof', reproved her and said her father (who paid for them) had complained too. She advised her 'not to wear her best everyday but to be saving thereof'; Frances told her she would wear what she wanted. Frances's own sister testified that Frances was 'very wasteful and a

---

[40] North, *Sweet and Clean?*, chapter 3. [41] LMA, CLA/024/05/509 (1686).
[42] North, *Sweet and Clean?*, chapter 5. [43] LMA, CLA/024/05/72 (1654).

slatterne in her clothes'.[44] A girl who could not maintain her own clothes could hardly hope to be employed to make, clean or refurbish those of others, and perhaps most tellingly her failure to properly assess the value of what she wore undermined her as a potential businesswoman.

Apprentices also, as we have seen, wanted to spend on clothes, to be consumers themselves. Thefts were always of scarves, hoods or gloves from the shop. One servant girl's case included a detailed account of the goods she had been provided with by her master. Elizabeth Ward's master claimed he had spent £7 in six months on clothes and accessories for her from his shop. Most of it went on accessories and trimmings: 18 yards of satin and silver ribbon to trim gloves, a sarsnet scarf, a green apron and string, a large alamode hood, a knife sheath, a necklace and black ribbon, and gifts of gloves for 'Nurse Wilson her husband and daughter' and another maidservant. Ward's social circle evidently extended outside her master's house. She also had money to go to the Lord Mayor's show, to mend her shoes and to have her clothes made up.[45] Mistresses understood the need to spend. In Mile End, Susan Shippey petitioned to be discharged from her dishonest apprentice, explaining with frustration that she had 'allwayes allowed her six pence a week for spending money, as an incouragement not to wrong her'. Despite a good start, the girl had begun to cheat and defraud her by selling lace and linen without accounting for it; 'all the Indulgence that can be shewed her will not reclaym her, and bids defiance to your peticoner when ever she asks her the reason of it'.[46]

The management of appearance was integral to the mistress–servant relationship, because one of the apprentice's jobs was to represent the business.[47] Christiana Hutchins's poor clothes suggested to her family that her mistress was not investing in her as a milliner's apprentice but treating her as a lowly servant. From at least the early eighteenth century, discourses about millinery described it both as a genteel profession and a costly trade, dependent on keeping up appearances and at risk of leading to prostitution.[48] Girls were selling gentility and discrimination: there was a perfectly clear business logic behind the worries about raggedness, mean dress and dirt.

Problems with clothes were intimately related to those more integral to the body: bedwetting, illnesses and vermin. Clean linen was one of the

---

[44] LMA, CLA/024/05/249 (1670).   [45] LMA, CLA/024/05/91 (1657).
[46] LMA, MJ/SP/1690/01/006, and MJ/SB/B/471 (January 1690).
[47] LMA, CLA/024/05/315.
[48] Elizabeth Kowaleski-Wallace, *Consuming Subjects: Women, Shopping, and Business in the Eighteenth Century* (New York: Columbia University Press, 1997).

essential keys to a clean person; dirty clothing spread disease. The concerns of apprentice parents and mistresses echo this well-established conviction. Seamstresses' shops sold scarfs, coifs and lace, but they also sold the underlinen that ensured a clean, healthy body. Hester Hudson's case reveals how care of the body might become a concern, as young women moved from the regimen of their parents to those of their mistresses and, eventually, themselves. Her 1652 apprenticeship to William and Mary Bickerstaff of the Barber-Surgeons' Company was interrupted by an unspecified illness. Since Mary Bickerstaff was about to give birth, Hester's sister Elizabeth arranged for her to be moved. She took her to the once grand wooden-fronted house on Bishopsgate known as Paul Pindar's house, whose frontage is now in the Victoria and Albert Museum, where her mother nursed her (Figure 5.1). When Hester recovered, the Bickerstaffs refused to take her back.

Illness was not uncommon in apprentice disputes; the costs of apothecaries and physicians were a trouble, as well as nursing. Margaret Pelling has argued that these cases sometimes indicate apprenticeship could provide a way to find care for children with physical or learning difficulties.[49] Hester Hudson's lawsuit does not elucidate the nature of her sickness, but her employers (who, as members of the Barber-Surgeons, may have had medical roles) complained sharply about her behaviour, her belongings and her bodily state while she was in service. The Hudsons claimed their daughter was made ill by her poor living conditions; the Bickerstaffs argued she was already disordered. Illness, here, was suggestive of infection, corruption and infestation. Hester arrived, they said, full of vermin 'by means of a very scabby head'. She had lice and was 'very nastie'. A fellow servant gave the fullest details. Hester's verminous head was compounded by her 'other ill qualities insomuch as it was a maid's work every morning almost (if not altogether) two hours to comb and clean her head besides her other nastinesses'. Other apprentice disputes raised the same issue of vermin. Elizabeth Fenner testified in 1654 that Thomas Piggott, apprentice to a barber-surgeon, was 'very lousy in the defendant's service'.[50] Interrogatories in the case of Thomas Weekes, a dyer's apprentice, included the question 'was he lousy or ill apparelled', which was only answered by the female witnesses.[51] It was likely to be a woman's work to comb the lice out.

---

[49] On the medical problems of these apprentices, see Margaret Pelling, 'Apprenticeship, Health and Social Cohesion in Early Modern London', *History Workshop Journal* 37 (Spring 1994): 33–56.
[50] LMA, CLA/024/05/70B (1654).   [51] LMA, CLA/024/05/291 (1672).

Figure 5.1 F. Shepherd, *Sir Paul Pindar's House*, 1812. 38 × 27 cm. London Metropolitan Archives (City of London)

Combing hair for lice was a standard part of domestic life and care in the early modern household. It is often depicted in Dutch genre paintings as a quotidian household scene, generally between mother and child, but sometimes involving the whole family; in other versions, it is an erotic interchange.[52] In a witchcraft case in Northumberland twenty years after this London scene, a servant named Anne Armstrong

---

[52] Pierre-Patrice Cabotin, 'Le pou à travers la peinture hollandaise du XVIIe siècle', *Histoire Des Sciences Medicales* 28 (1994): 381–8.

described how she was sent by her mistress to buy eggs from another woman, Anne Forster, but could not get them cheap enough; instead, Anne Forster told her to sit down, and she would 'look her head'. Then they reversed the roles, and Armstrong searched Forster's head for lice in turn. A few days later, an old man told Anne Armstrong that the woman who looked her head would make a horse of her spirit and lure her into witchcraft, and a lurid tale of Sabbath feasts ensued; but it all began with the looking of the head that was offered as a compromise for a failed attempt to bargain.[53]

So picking through another woman's hair was not exclusively the work of a servant, but rather a mutual exchange. It was embedded in friendly and neighbourly relations, but far from neutral. For Anne Armstrong, telling stories of witches, a woman looking her head, was loaded with power and fear. Such looking would probably also include judgements about bodily care. If some lousiness was to be expected, too much was appalling, and Hester's scabbed head must have been particularly offensive in a household that lived by the look and touch of fine goods. In the Bickerstaff household, in commercial London, vermin was a serious threat not only to appearances but also to domestic economy. It was most likely Ann Joyner's work time that Hester's troubles took up and who provided the alleged two hours daily to comb her hair and squash the vermin. In another case, the presence of vermin was the result of a lack of underwear, the 'necessaries' always mentioned in clothing lists. Hannah Wilkin's father petitioned the sessions to get her discharged from her apprenticeship to a seamstress in St Martin in the Fields, on the grounds of mistreatment and lack of clothes. His petition was accompanied by a certificate from five neighbours (female and male) in St Martin's Lane, testifying that Hannah had been 'Barbarously used' and 'wanted necessaryes both for the Back and Belly soe that she is in Danger of being Devowred by verment not having shifts fitting for a Christian'.[54] Apprentice bodies were a public concern, and the othering that Mr Wilkin invoked added another dimension to the language of civility.

The threat of infestation reflected an early modern body that was still somewhat unbounded, in which vermin could be spontaneously generated, a symbol of both moral and environmental corruption. Children were particularly susceptible to producing lice; younger apprentices

---

[53] James Raine, ed., *Depositions from the Castle of York, Relating to Offences Committed in the Northern Counties in the Seventeenth Century* (Durham: Surtees Society, 1861), 192 (February 1673). I am indebted to Miranda Chaytor's analysis of this case at a seminar over twenty years ago.

[54] LMA, WJ/SP/1696/10/11 (1696).

might still require adult management of their bodies and hair.[55] More generally, the body's open pores and fragile boundaries required clothes to protect it. The responsibility for managing apprentices' clothes, hair and bodies was not always clear, and it was of especial significance for marking out the distinction between girls who worked at household drudgery and those who served in elegant shops.

Hester Hudson's ill-governed body had other issues too. Like some of the male apprentices whose contracts fell into dispute, she was said to have night-time incontinence, another marker of moral failure as well as poor hygiene: Anne Puckeridge, a widow who lived in Hampshire and knew both families, reported that Hester 'did by her nastiness much wet and spoil the defendants' bedding'. Hester's sheets would have been carried to be laundered outside the house, in communal facilities, by the servants. The cost of replacing a mattress and bedding might be more than that of the bed itself. Menstruation would be another issue: girls started to menstruate between fourteen and sixteen, so most apprentices and servants would experience their first period away from home.[56] Hester Hudson's case, like that of Christiana Hutchins, is a reminder that early adolescence overlapped with the neediness of childhood and that young or immature apprentices might be too burdensome for their new households. Hester's mistress, it was claimed, refused to take her back after she recovered after her two months' illness, and she apparently said she would not provide a nurse for her: 'she would make her earn her bread' first. Apprenticeship in adolescence had important implications for the management of the body.

Fighting Talk

In apprenticeships, authority was negotiated through the verbal exchanges of daily work. Katherine Venner's 'scurvy' and 'uncivil' words demonstrated her pride.[57] Words were often treated as a touchstone for female behaviour, and apprentice disputes drew on a long tradition of advice to women to talk less, and more modestly. Katherine's failure to show appropriate submission transgressed gender, age and occupational hierarchy. The sheer number of words, as well as their incivil or scurvy nature, was a feature of other complaints about girls. It was particularly

---

[55] Robert Pennell, *De Morbis Puerorum, or, a Treatise of the Diseases of Children* (1653), chapter 2.
[56] Sara Read, *Menstruation and the Female Body in Early Modern England* (Basingstoke: Palgrave Macmillan, 2013), 57.
[57] LMA, CLA/024/05/115A (1662).

pointed in relation to their youth: they assumed an authority they did not yet have. Frances Angell was described by a neighbour as 'peremptory and sawcy' to both her father and her mistress; she 'gave them word for word and sometimes 2 or 3 words for one'.[58] She responded to orders with taunting and saucy answers or told her mistress she would do what she pleased; witnesses suspected she was deliberately goading her mistress to get rid of her. Boys spoke rudely too: Thomas Piggott, apprenticed to a barber-surgeon, was described as returning 'incivill answers' to his master.[59] But incivil speech had a special significance for girls on the road to a womanhood that was so often the target of advice to curb their tongues or to speak no more than a parrot would in echoing their husbands' words. Frances's particularly provocative speech was reminiscent, too, of the familiar figure of wayward female speech, the scold: one witness said she had 'so vile and lewd a tongue as was not endurable'. Christiana Hutchins was 'apt to abuse people with affronting and unseemly language'. Her abusive language to both neighbours and customers lost her mistress several clients. Words were strong weapons for frustrated girls.

At the heart of these conflicts was the refusal to submit. Frances Angell was heard several times to say 'she would be burnt ere ever she would submit herself' and 'she could maintain herself quite well without them'.[60] Her master and mistress's statement encouraged witnesses like her fellow apprentice Edward Wills to describe her as 'growne to that sullen stubborne and evell disposicon that she would only doe what she listed'. Christiana Hutchins was 'very cross and stubborn and saucy in her behaviour to her mistress & when that her mistress had reproved her stood and laughed at her as if she had no regard what she said and was of a slothful and nasty nature'. Told to work in the shop, she ignored her mistress and went to work in the kitchen instead 'and told her mistress let her say what she would she had no mind to do it and would do it and stand and laugh at her mistress when she had been angry with her for it'. This maddening defiance accords with many historical and contemporary descriptions of adolescent resistance, but in court it was pathologised to describe girls as impossible to teach.

Rage characterised the worst conflicts. Hair-combing was a flashpoint for Christiana Hutchins, whose fellow apprentice said that 'when her Mistress had bin combing of [her] head she would ly all along the floare and cry out murder and cause tumult about the doore to the disgrace of the defendants'. All the good words and endeavours possible could not

---

[58] LMA, CLA/024/05/249 (1668).   [59] LMA, CLA/024/05/70B (1654).
[60] LMA, CLA/024/05/249 (1669).

calm her down, and she would not get up until her 'cross fit' was over.[61] This habit of 'crying out murder' seems to have been a familiar one; two male apprentices were also accused of doing it. The young men were responding to the allegedly mild correction, or the threat of it, that was an apprentice's lot; Christiana, too, had received 'small correction' from her mistress. Several boys were also 'surly', 'abusive' and 'saucy'; Caleb Trenchfield's apprentice was 'of a very high turbulent disposition', the language evocative of humoural terms.

Confrontations ranging from saucy or peremptory talk to fitful rage were, and are, characteristic of adolescent authority conflicts. Apprentices were not explicitly identified as adolescents, the concept being too uncertain at this point. They were, though, clearly in the midst of the critical years of transition from dependent youth to semi-autonomous adulthood. The average age of the young women apprenticed across livery companies was fourteen and a half, ranging from eleven to eighteen, with most aged fourteen or fifteen. Girls tended to both start and finish their apprenticeships earlier than boys, in keeping with the belief that young women matured before their male peers; starting a seven-year apprenticeship before the age of fourteen was also less problematic if they were not expected to take up the freedom, which was not possible before twenty-one. Because of this limit, exact age mattered. It was also possible to be too young to serve. Christiana Hutchins's master and mistress sought to prove that she was only nine when she was indentured, and the uncertainty over her actual age is a telling reminder of the difficulty of establishing chronological age exactly.[62] The late age of marriage in early modern Northwestern Europe, in the mid-twenties, made for a surprisingly prolonged transition from childhood into adulthood; the term 'youth' could extend until the early twenties, as did 'boy', though 'wench' was used particularly for girls in their earlier teens. Apprenticeship and domestic service were the typical life-cycle experiences in the years from fourteen to twenty-one, and the assumption of quasi-adult roles in apprenticeship came in the last few years.[63] Apprentice girls do not, though, seem to have shared the collective rituals and identity that have been observed in the London apprentices of the seventeenth century.[64] Domestic service, a widespread female experience, was more likely to lend itself to collective identity, but

---

[61] LMA, CLA/024/05/318 (1674).
[62] Corinne T. Field and Nicholas L. Syrett, 'Introduction' to Forum on 'Chronological Age: A Useful Category of Historical Analysis', *American Historical Review* 125, no. 2 (2020): 371–84.
[63] Ben-Amos, *Adolescence and Youth in Early Modern England*.
[64] Smith, 'The London Apprentices as Seventeenth-Century Adolescents'.

its characterisation was of continued subordination, ending in marriage, rather than the eventual autonomy of apprenticeship.

The individual experience of adolescence was recognised as a time of transition and turbulence, and here there are more references to the female experience. In the classically derived model of bodily humours that drove mainstream medical thought, teenage girls, like boys, were bursting with heat, diametrically opposed to the cold, damp humours of older women. Green sickness, the disease of unsatisfied desire, was an archetypally pubertal disorder.[65] Its identification by early modern medics drew on Galenic ideas of excessive blood and agitated humours at the time of puberty. Caroline Bicks argues for a positive side to this: in the words of Thomas Willis's 1684 medical handbook, adolescence was a time when 'the gifts of Body and Mind begin to show themselves'. The activation of lust might also be seen as a quickening of imagination. With the late age of marriage that characterised the period, 'vehement adolescence' could be seen as a time not only of developing sexuality but also burgeoning thought, planning and self-realisation.[66] The space for that in apprenticeship was limited. Aristotle's *Rhetoric* formulated male youth in terms of conflict with authority, recognisable both to modern readers and to early moderns: prone to anger, vehement, cannot brook contempt, impatient at injury, downright and confident.[67] The descriptions of wayward apprentices, both male and female, draw on established understandings of the difficult years between leaving home and marriage or autonomy.

These kind of arguments, characterised by what masters and mistresses perceived as overreaction to the slightest word or deed, may also reflect processes that neuroscientists have attributed specifically to the adolescent brain. The amygdala is swiftly activated in response to expressions, words or gestures, putting adolescents into 'fight or flight' mode; the more controlled, rational response of the higher cortex comes with maturity.[68] Adolescent brains, current research shows, are in the process of being remodelled, with the regulation of impulse and emotion in a particularly labile state as the prefrontal cortex works to integrate brain,

[65] Helen King, *The Disease of Virgins: Green Sickness, Chlorosis and the Problems of Puberty* (London: Routledge, 2009).
[66] Caroline Bicks, 'Incited Minds: Rethinking Early Modern Girls', *Shakespeare Studies* 44 (2016): 180–99.
[67] Aristotle, *Aristotle's Rhetoric, or, the True Grounds and Principles of Oratory* (London, 1686), 123.
[68] K. Suzanne Scherf, Joshua M. Smyth and Mauricio R. Delgado, 'The Amygdala: An Agent of Change in Adolescent Neural Networks', *Hormones and Behavior* 64, no. 2 (July 2013): 298–313; Daniel J. Siegel, *Brainstorm: The Power and Purpose of the Teenage Brain* (London: Scribe, 2014).

body and social world. To project this into the early modern experience requires a leap of faith. There are important reasons that adolescent brain development might be different 350 years ago: diet, nurture, parental presence and caring style, and a historically specific sense of the self, are all likely to have impacted how the brain changed, and when, and the way adolescents experienced those internal shifts. Considering brain development helps to parse the gender-specific stories of those conflicts. It suggests the conflicts of apprentices and mistresses were less closely related to their specific relationship and more to a generic conflict, whose shape was common to boys as well as girls. However, while girls and boys were both impulsive and argumentative, the social construction of gender emphasised inward control for girls more than it did for boys; it also encouraged witnesses to describe girls' resistance in slightly different terms to that of boys. The social and economic dynamics of apprenticeship also made a difference: to a degree, they legitimated argument. Servants, in a more explicitly subordinate role, working for money rather than paying to be trained, are not recorded as fighting like this.

Apprenticeship was one of the ways that early modern society dispersed the responsibility for disciplining youth. In other circumstances, parishes stepped in to divest indigent parents of their familial roles, sending children to Virginia or apprenticing them out. The French state, Julia Gossard has shown, assumed the authority to discipline wayward adolescents whose parents proved unable to keep them in order, with Parisian detention centres attempting to rehabilitate the rebellious youths of artisan and poor parents.[69] Apprentices generally had mothers, siblings and aunts, as well as friends, to keep an eye on them; relatives watched out for their clothes, food and general health. Enough of the patriarchal model of household order survived to preserve the sixteenth-century ideal that apprentices owed their masters a similar duty of obedience as they did their parents, just as subjects did to their rulers.[70] Parental relationships were hardly straightforward either. Christiana Hutchins and Frances Angell both had conflicts with their parents as well as their mistresses. Frances Angell's father complained of her indiscipline, as did her mistress. Frances's mother, also named Frances, had died of quinsy shortly after giving birth to twins, when the young Frances was fourteen months old.[71] She had given birth at least four times in six

---

[69] Julia M. Gossard, 'Breaking a Child's Will', *French Historical Studies* 42, no. 2 (2019): 239–59.
[70] Gordon J. Schochet, 'Patriarchalism, Politics and Mass Attitudes in Stuart England', *Historical Journal* 12, no. 3 (1969): 413–41.
[71] LMA, P69/GIS/A/002/MS06419/005 (18 October 1653).

years, and the short intervals between them suggest she used a wet nurse. Such contexts added to the authority battles between girls like Frances and their mistresses and parents.

The stresses of apprentice households also made themselves felt in conflicts between male apprentices and maidservants, who had an inconvenient domestic authority. William Ravenscroft was described as carrying himself 'very lofty and imperious towards the servants and [did] often miscall them & use other improper terms and expressions towards them no way befitting an apprentice or any other'.[72] In conflicts like this, apprentices perceived maidservants as threats to their autonomy. Margaret Fletcher, in service in the same household as the apprentice Edward Powell, bumped into him in Moorfields on Sunday afternoon, when he should have been in church; he threatened her that if she told their master, 'he would be the death of her, live where she would'. Nevertheless, once she had left, she went back and told her mistress.[73] Elizabeth Watts, another domestic servant in a mercer's household, testified that the unruly male apprentice there was so unreliable, regularly getting drunk at night, that it became her job to wait on him, going downstairs to light him back to bed and locking up the shop behind him.[74] Alice Holland had a disciplinary role over the apprentice she worked with in an apothecary's shop; she reminded him 'in a friendly manner' to do the business left for him but found he 'slighted her words' and spent his time idly playing about the door.[75] Mary Herald, servant of a scrivener in 1663, testified that she had reproved his apprentice for lying, with no effect; the apprentice also persuaded her into 'naughtiness' and attempted 'that which was incivil' with her.[76] Maidservants, like apprentices, were only temporary subordinates, or so they hoped, but the two groups were by no means natural allies. Employers endorsed the divisions; one complained that his apprentice was 'idle and remiss and too friendly with the servant maid'.[77] The expectation that young women would supervise and reprove their peers may have helped lay the foundations for the roles adult women played as moral regulators in the household and community.[78]

---

[72] LMA, CLA/024/05/314 (1661).   [73] LMA, CLA/024/05/308 (1673).
[74] LMA, CLA/024/05/269A (1671).   [75] LMA, CLA/024/05/136 (1661).
[76] LMA, CLA/024/05/150B (1663).   [77] LMA, CLA/024/05/416 (1684).
[78] On those roles, see Bernard Capp, *When Gossips Meet: Women, Family and Neighbourhood in Early Modern England* (Oxford University Press, 2003), chapter 5, and Laura Gowing, 'Ordering the Body: Illegitimacy and Female Authority in Seventeenth-Century England', in *Negotiating Power in Early Modern Society: Order, Hierarchy and Subordination in Britain and Ireland*, ed. Michael J. Braddick and John Walter (Cambridge University Press, 2001), 43–62.

Another familiar conflict was between male apprentices and their mistresses, in re-enactments of the classic drama of adolescent boys in sexually charged conflict with their female superiors. Jacobean household drama and popular pamphlets had rehearsed such plots extensively, fantasising about apprentice boys and their lustful mistresses; Restoration drama had shifted its emphasis towards comedies of manners. Apprenticeship disputes suggest it was still a source of tension in domestic hierarchy, while the nature of that hierarchy itself was being remade, and this gave apprenticeship disputes a cultural resonance. William Trussell, apprenticed to a dyer, 'carried himself with very little respect to his mistress and was not so observant and dutiful as an apprentice ought to have been'. His employers accused him of striking his mistress 'so that the blood came from her'.[79] In two cases male apprentices were accused of causing miscarriages by upsetting their mistresses.[80] Mary Walker, the servant in one of these houses, described how she had stayed up late for the apprentice to return home, as he had the key. When he came home, the master confronted him, they had a 'skirmish' about the key, thrust up against a counter in the warehouse where the hot-pressing work was done; the heavily pregnant mistress came down and was frightened and gave birth a week later to a child who died shortly after.[81]

Mistresses of apprentices had their own power to discipline. Violence was, we have seen, inherent to the model of teaching; the notion of 'moderate correction' licensed a mistress, like a master, to hit or beat her apprentice or servant. The 'pat with her hand' cited in Chapter 4, used by a mistress to discipline her apprentice into attending to her work, suggested the physical discipline that was embedded in learning to sew.

At the sessions courts, dealing with matters of criminal rather than civil law, violence prompted apprentices and their families to plead for discharge and sometimes led to prosecutions. Most brought their own complaints or were represented by their mothers, resulting in a series of complaints pitting women against women. Immoderate correction was sometimes a formulaic complaint to get apprenticeships easily dissolved, but legal records also provide more detail on the range of violence of which parents or apprentices complained. Bridget Dalby, a seamstress in Stepney, and her husband had their three female apprentices discharged in 1690, after being accused of immoderate correction and a failure to provide food. They managed to convince the magistrate that they should keep the premiums, and while two girls were freed to serve any other

---

[79] LMA, CLA/024/05/303 (1673).   [80] LMA, CLA/024/05/82 (1655).
[81] LMA, CLA/024/05/314 (1674).

mistress, Margaret Blackman was ordered to live with her father and continue serving Bridget Dalby for a further month, 'provided the said Bridget do not beat or abuse her'. Physical abuse did not dissolve the financial obligation of apprenticeship.[82] Anne Tutchbury, apprentice to a tobacco-pipe maker in Whitechapel, took a more effective line, having her master bound over to appear at the sessions charged with tying her to a beam and beating her 'unreasonably'.[83] Hanna Lovering, a widow in Westminster, found a scrivener to write a petition to the sessions in 1646 about the treatment of her 'poor fatherles child' Elizabeth, who had been apprenticed for 40s to be taught the art of a sempstress by James Fuller and his wife. She had been 'used as a drudge to do the worke about the house and fetch in water'. Moreover, Fuller's wife 'not therwith content', 'most cruelly abused the said Apprentice and beate her with a candlestick about her shoulders', leaving her black and blue. Elizabeth ran away in fear of her life, and eventually the Fullers were compelled to return her clothes and repay half her premium.[84] Another petition came from Anne Dyott, who had run away from the two seamstresses she was apprenticed to in 1688: she begged to be discharged because they had not instructed her in their trade and had 'severely beaten' her and 'dragged her by the hair of her head'; but she had no witnesses to prove it, and they said in return that she had purloined their money, wasted and damaged their goods and spent her time in loose and idle company. The court agreed with them and declined to refund her premiums, though they were ordered to return her clothes.[85] The legal regulation of apprenticeship at least enabled young people and their parents to pursue abuse through the courts, though the best they mostly achieved was the dissolution of a contract.

In cases of extreme violence and murder, the idea of reasonable correction for poor work persisted. The inquest on an apprentice named Hester Que in 1677 found a history of being beaten by her mistress because 'she had not cleaned the house so clean as she would have it'. Hester ran away from her mistress to a barber-surgeon, her face black and blue, and told him her mistress beat her with an iron rod and 'laid rods in piss' for her. Her sister and nine other women swore that they heard her scream 'with such skreeks ... as would peirce ones heart'. John Greene, who had placed her with Joane and William Shute, persuaded her to return. Eventually, she escaped out of the attic window by climbing from a piece of black farrindon tied onto the casement. It broke, and she fell to her death.[86] At the Old Bailey, the most brutal cases of

---

[82] LMA, MJ/SB/B 476/51.   [83] LMA, MJ/SB/B 487/691.   [84] LMA, WJ/SP 1646/1.
[85] LMA, MJ/SB/B 495/18.   [86] LMA, CLA/047/LJ/13/1677/001.

violence to apprentices still refer to the idea of correction. Ann Hollis's 'sickly' fourteen-year-old apprentice died with consumption, after Hollis had beat her with a birch rod: 'The Prisoner's defence was, that she only Whipp'd her for several Faults, as Lying, and Slutishness, and the like, and she gave her but moderate Correction.' The consumption was found to be the cause of death; 'moderate correction' was still portrayed as a reasonable response to 'faults' like these.[87] In a notorious murder case in Wapping in 1681, Elizabeth or Lettice Wigenton and John Sadler, her lodger, were convicted of the violent killing of her apprentice. Versions of the story varied across printed and legal accounts. In one, Wigenton is a 'School-Mistris, or Sempstris', but in the Old Bailey's printed story, she is a coat-maker, and she beat her apprentice 'greviously' because 'having set the Girl upon a Piece of Work, she had not done it so well as she required'.[88] Rarely did any witness mention intervening. As Susan Amussen has argued, state-licensed violence was integrated into the household; in these cases, it was also legitimated by a literal discipline of labour.[89]

In the higher-premium cases at the Mayor's Court, a different level of detail was provided, but they reflect the same assumption, that discipline was part of learning, and physical conflict part of turbulent domestic life. Katherine Venner's fellow apprentice Samuel Richardson described her as having 'some scuffle together' with her mistress, who complained that Katherine had hurt her; at another time, when Mrs Allen tried to strike her, Katherine 'opposed and resisted'. She should, presumably, have accepted the discipline.[90] Christiana Hutchins's family accused her mistress of discouraging her by striking her often with 'unlawful weapons'.[91] Boys complained more explicitly of beatings and not always from masters: in 1671, a servant, Judith Neale, deposed that her master beat her fellow apprentice William Knight himself, let his sister beat him and sometimes beat him 'merely to satisfy his sister's humour'.[92] These stories of discipline through violence represent the other side of the education of body manners.

This cumulative picture of the requirements of appearance, the threatening hands of correction, and the sullen, difficult nature

---

[87] *Old Bailey Proceedings Online* (www.oldbaileyonline.org), Ann Hollis, 20 May 1686 (t16860520-2).

[88] *The Last Dying Speeches and Confessions of the Three Notorious Malefactors* (1681); *Old Bailey Proceedings Online* 17 January 1681/2 (t16810117-1); for more on this case, see Randall Martin, *Women, Murder and Equity in Early Modern England* (New York: Routledge, 2008).

[89] Susan Dwyer Amussen, 'Punishment, Discipline, and Power: The Social Meanings of Violence in Early Modern England', *Journal of British Studies* 34, no. 1 (1995): 1.

[90] LMA, CLA/024/05/131. [91] LMA, CLA/024/05/318.

[92] LMA, CLA/024/05/271 (1671).

attributed to girls who failed to learn well demands an expansion in what training and skill involved. Seamstresses were subject to a particular breed of discipline, meant to shape them into models of elegant dress as well as neat craftswomen and competent shopworkers. Its integration into girls' domestic training left Mary Wollstonecraft raging in 1792 at the contraction of faculties produced by too much attention to 'making caps, bonnets, and the whole mischief of trimmings'.[93] Sewing was a regime that notoriously tried girls' patience. A Victorian moralist reflected on the bad habits that poorly supervised girls acquired, such as clicking the needle against the thimble, biting the thread and sticking the needle into the front of her dress. 'Unladylike' habits are historically specific: the survival of bodkins with ear-wax scoops on them, enabling the user to seal thread-ends, suggests the different norms of the seventeenth century.[94]

Criminal records of seamstresses gone wrong leave us some practical details of how the moral imperatives of needlework translated into practice further down the social scale. The female criminals of the Newgate Calendar were often seamstresses gone wrong: typical was Mary Wilder, who 'once wrought Plain-work which she sold at the Exchange' but grew idle, left off her prayers and fell into bad company and was convicted of burglary in 1693.[95] A cluster of women coiners in 1695 told the same story, all five of them trained to work with their needles: the formulaic life stories of the Calendar described them each as idle at their work. Mary Pyne, apprenticed to a silk-throster, 'left her service being Idle and Ungovernable'; Jane Pattison, 'brought up to handle her Needle that she could embroider', had become idle; Elizabeth Hartley 'did not work hard at her needle'.[96] Governance and hard work were the tests of success and virtue, in contrast to the focus on chastity and its appearance that dominates advice literature and the language of discredit.

The refusal to submit featured, too, in higher status apprentice disputes. We have already seen how the young Christiana Hutchins determined she would not be a seamstress, 'pricking clouts', and insisted on doing kitchen work or fetching water instead, in a complete reversal of aspirations. The saucy, sullen words attributed to her and the other apprentices here depict girls who did not want to learn, would not be taught and refused to do their work better. Some were keen to complete

---

[93] Mary Wollstonecraft, *A Vindication of the Rights of Woman* (1796).
[94] Mary C. Beaudry, *Findings: The Material Culture of Needlework and Sewing* (New Haven, CT: Yale University Press, 2007), 66.
[95] *Old Bailey Proceedings Online* Ordinary's Account, 23 October 1693, ref. OA 169310239310230002.
[96] *Old Bailey Proceedings Online* Ordinary's Account, 18 September 1695, ref. OA 16950918.

their training and run shops on their own. Christiana Hutchins had the dream that her uncle would give her an estate. For most of the young women in apprenticeships, other options were minimal; they shifted mistresses but less often trades. Pauper girls had the least choice, and the records of their defiance are few but sometimes dramatic. Ursula Abchurch, a foundling, was apprenticed to Anne Pomfret in the 1690s to sell fruit; Anne claimed that Ursula had threatened to murder her for a gold chain that she wore. She agreed with Ursula to turn her over to a weaver in the same parish.[97] Frances Hogg ran away from her master in Wapping; he was discharged from his obligations to her on the grounds that 'it is proved that the said Frances is a notorious, idle, disorderly, and incorrigible girl, who kept company with soldiers' and ran away with her clothes, and she was sent to Bridewell.[98] There, the discipline would have involved both beating and work.

These various kinds of resistance to the discipline of apprenticeship are an important reminder of its limits. Apprenticeship involved limited choice; for parish apprentices and girls in Christ's Hospital, it was their only option. There is almost no evidence that girls were consulted on their trade, and the predominance of sewing is everywhere evident. At the higher end, the millinery or seamstress trade appeared the only option that would give girls a chance at autonomy before, or in place of, marriage, and its prominence as a choice in fathers' wills suggests both a clear grasp of the need for girls' occupational training and a sense of its limits. In the scraps of complaints from proud, sullen or peremptory girls, we get a sense of how unsatisfactory the life of the needle might be.

[97] City of London Sessions Papers, *London Lives* LMSLPS150100165 (15 May 1699).
[98] LMA, MJ/SB/B 563, p. 51 (1692).

6   Freedoms and Customs

Mary German

Apprenticeship had a long afterlife. Successfully completed, an apprenticeship guaranteed a man's membership of the body of freemen of London. Inheriting the right to the freedom of the City through patrimony had the same effect, of a continuous, permanent entitlement. The same was not true for women. An archive of petitions filed at the end of the seventeenth century illuminates the distinctive experiences of women in the institution known as the Freedom.

Mary German petitioned the aldermen of the City in 1700. It was over twenty-five years since her apprenticeship: she had completed her term but had never taken up her right to the freedom. Belatedly, in her early forties, she had decided she needed it. Her petition pleaded:

That your Peticoner was bound an apprentice to Daniel Williamson Cittizen and Haberdasher of London for the Terme of Seven yeares and served her said Master the said Terme. But may it please this honorable Court that your Peticoner was bound by a foreigne Indenture which is mislaid or lost for which reason your Peticoner is refused her freedome by Service

Your Peticoner therefore humbly Prayes that by the favour of thy honorable Court she may be admitted into the freedome of this honorable Citty by Redemption

And your Peticioner shall pray &c

Not only had Mary lost her indenture in the years since her apprenticeship, but it was 'foreign': made outside the Company Hall and hence not formally recorded by the company.

Two aldermen were sent to investigate. They went directly to her old master and mistress to examine them and reported

we have Examined the matter to us referred and finde upon the Examinacon of Daniel Williamson Citizen and Haberdasher and his wife the petitioner's Master and Mistris that the petitioner did serve them as an apprentice for the space of seaven yeares but was bound by foreign Indentures about 26: yeares since and sayth yt the reason why she was bound by such Indentures was because she was a Gentleman's Daughter and as her friends then said should never want a freedom/ But since being much reduced would follow the Employ of a Symstresse within this City and therefore prayes to be admitted by Redemption upon a moderate fine.

Her petition was granted, and she was admitted to the Freedom on the payment of 46 shillings and eightpence.[1]

Mary German's story brings the City's customary laws to life. Her qualification to work within the City walls required a personal investigation going back a quarter of a century to resolve the flaws of her original indenture by personal interview with her old master and mistress. The story of her 'foreign indenture' describes her friends – the kin, parents and associates who helped plan her future at about fourteen – deliberately not enrolling her apprenticeship, because they thought she would not need to earn her own living, and perhaps did not imagine the uses of a shop. Accordingly, she was not registered in the Haberdashers' Registers with the Williamsons' other apprentices. For most of her life Mary German managed otherwise, but in middle age she wanted the freedom to trade for herself. The aldermen's investigation of German's claim emphasises, too, the archival basis of the freedom. To be in the freedom meant to be listed in the sets of printed indentures and other proofs of freedom spiked and preserved by the office of the City Chamberlain; when the archive failed, personal inquiry was the answer. This chapter explores the relationship of women to the freedom, with its associated institutions of citizenship, custom and patrimony. Returning to city women in their middle age, we will see a civic life cycle in which gender and marital status defined the terms on which women engaged with the key institutions of civic life and a set of strategic manoeuvres by which City officials and working women negotiated women's place in market, company and city.

Petitioning for Freedom

Mary German's description of herself as a well-born young woman whose family did not anticipate her needing the freedom was not shared by the hundred or so female apprentices who claimed the freedom of the City in the last two decades of the seventeenth century. For her, the economically stressful 1690s, in which she reached the middle age that

---

[1] LMA, COL/CA/05/01/0005; COL/CHD/FR/02 153/19. On these petitions, see Hilda L. Smith, '"Free and Willing to Remit": Women's Petitions to the Court of Aldermen, 1670–1750', in *Worth and Repute: Valuing Gender in Late Medieval and Early Modern Europe, Essays in Honour of Barbara Todd*, ed. Kim Kippen and Lori Woods (Toronto: Centre for Reformation and Renaissance Studies, 2011), 279–309.

often marked a downgrading of women's work opportunities, may have made the difference, but for other female apprentices, the freedom was firmly in view as a possible end to their training. Freedom was the central plank of the customs of the City of London. It bestowed both citizenship, in the form of rights to participate in the selection of aldermen and other officials, and the privilege of trading within the City walls.

The political side of citizenship was not generally extended to women: there is no evidence that they voted in City elections in the seventeenth century, although the lack of records and the subtleties of gendered political participation in the early modern period make it hard to tell. Publicly engaged politics were, increasingly, predicated on an idea of active male citizenship. The extensive verbal, spiritual and popular political authority claimed by women in the Civil Wars and the English Revolution functioned, by the 1660s, as a reminder of the dangers of a world turned upside down. In the realm of political thought, social contract theory paradoxically treated female subordination in marriage as part of the natural order. Economically, though, women claimed and required the privileges of citizenship. In order to do business within the walls, in key trading sites like the Royal Exchange or Cheapside, women were required to have the freedom either in their own right or through their husbands. Apprenticeship in a City company was the main route to freedom for men, but a minor route for women. Wives of citizens shared in the freedom of their husbands and kept it after widowhood; daughters of citizens, like sons, had the right to a freedom by patrimony. In the later seventeenth century, as many women became free by patrimony as through apprenticeship. Freedom achieved by marriage outnumbered both options. All these routes, though, risked running into difficulties with custom. The relationship between women and the freedom was not straightforward, and the archive of petitions to the Mayor and aldermen reveals the complexities of City custom as it applied to women.

Histories of the City have often mentioned women's capacity to become free, but the relation of women to the freedom was deliberately complex. Moreover, access to the freedom was one of the traditional keystones of urban masculinity. Becoming free at the end of apprenticeship was not universal, even for boys; apprenticeship was increasingly a short-term affair which was disrupted before completion, its flexibility its strength.[2] Girls, though, seem to have been more likely to have missed out on the opportunity for freedom at first, returning to it later. Women's petitions to the Chamberlain also described a range of obstacles that kept

---

[2] Patrick Wallis, 'Labor, Law, and Training in Early Modern London: Apprenticeship and the City's Institutions', *Journal of British Studies* 51, no. 4 (2012): 791–819.

them from becoming free. Their pleas were largely accepted, sometimes conditionally; the City was happy to extend at least part of the privilege of freedom in exchange for fees. The customs that impeded full membership remained.

At the other end of the genre of petitions in this archive is a smaller, scrappier piece of paper. Mary German's was copied out on foolscap, folded and annotated on behalf of the aldermen. Mary Spark's petition (Figure 6.2) looks to have been written in her own hand. The widow of a grocer, with a young child, she described how she had been 'left in a mean condition'. She was, she pleaded, 'very willing to work for bread for her selfe and poor fatherles Child but is denyed the Liberty by the masters of the company of tobackapip makers of which traid she is one'. She begged them to allow her the right to work despite not being free of the City:

> now she being a poor widow of this honourabull City of London humbly begs your honours will be plesed to commisserate the deplorabull condishon of your poor petishonour and give her an order weareby she may have leave to work for a poor Livelyhod or else they must perish for they turned her out of her work by reason they threetin to arest who so ever shall set her a work therefor she humbly begs your pety to her destrised condition.

Pipe-making was rather different from sewing, offering a 'poor livelihood'. London's riverbed still throws up the clay pipes that were produced for centuries as disposable smoking utensils. A pamphlet of 1653 classes tobacco-pipe makers with the lowest, smallest-scale trades, who needed minimal fuel for their work: alongside tailors, bone-lace makers, button-makers, washwomen and 'scolding oyster wives', pipemakers were part of a 'beggarly rabble' of artisans.[3] Many of these trades were associated with lower-paid women's work. Pipemakers were estimated by a petition of 1695 to make a profit of 2 or 3 pence per gross (144).[4] The same petition described pipe-making as a trade done by families, with women and children helping men to carry it on.[5] It was a trade for the poorest, and a woman named Mary Spark is on the poor relief list in St Clement Danes in 1687.[6] Mary Spark's personal petition brings this archive of pleas much closer to the humble petitions that

---

[3] William M. Cavert, *The Smoke of London: Energy and Environment in the Early Modern City* (Cambridge University Press, 2016), 126.
[4] Anon., *The Humble Petition and Case of the Tobacco-Pipe-Makers of the Cities of London and Westminster* ... (1695).
[5] Alice Clark, *Working Life of Women in the Seventeenth Century*, ed. Amy Louise Erickson (London: Routledge, 1992), 193.
[6] Westminster Archives, St Clement Danes Vestry Minutes 1686–99, *London Lives*, WCCDEP358020035, p. 25.

feature in almost every level of seventeenth-century government, and that offered a relatively accessible means for women to make complaints and requests.

Despite their apparent differences, Spark's and German's petitions are part of the same process. Many of the petitions in the aldermen's archive look similar to German's, suggesting that they were restyled for the formal record. Like most petitions, these are formulaic ones, crafted to reflect the institution's requirements, and either written or rewritten by scribes. Ostensibly, they present a challenge to the City customs, forcing the admission of women into the Freedom. In fact, their requests to be made free or to be given the liberty to trade offered useful fees and reinforced, in a rhetoric sanctioned by the aldermen and their clerks, the continuing power of the customs of London.

The freedom of London was traditionally the mark of civic membership of the adult male population. Across medieval and early modern Europe, apprenticeship led to freedom of a company, which was required to trade, and citizenship, the freedom of a city which entailed political participation. In London, the two kinds of freedom were separate but connected. Apprentices were registered with companies and made free of the company when they completed their contracts; they were also required to be enrolled with the Chamberlain, though many were not, and women seem particularly likely not to have been enrolled. Once free of the company, they could apply for the freedom of the City, which brought political privileges as well as the right to trade there. Fewer than half got this far, because so many apprentices left before completing their contracted terms, and women, again, were much less likely to become free than their male counterparts. The overall number of freedoms being claimed were falling somewhat in the seventeenth century, both in absolute terms and as a proportion of Londoners. Estimates put the proportion of adult male Londoners who were free at around 75 per cent in the mid-sixteenth century and 50 per cent in the mid-seventeenth.[7] While the city had expanded far outside its walls, the restriction of the right to trade to freemen was less expansive, since it traditionally applied within the walls only. By the seventeenth century, though, at least some guilds were expanding their remit into the greater metropolis. By the later seventeenth century, the proportion of Londoners who needed the freedom to trade had significantly decreased, and corporate control generally was losing its grip. Nevertheless, the language of corporatism was still lively and remained part of political participation, as it became more

---

[7] Steve Rappaport, *Worlds within Worlds: Structures of Life in Sixteenth-Century London* (Cambridge University Press, 2002), 53.

focused on party in the later seventeenth century. As the proportion of adult men who were free of the City decreased, its meaning as an index of inclusion was eroded, but it still mattered. At a time when women's political participation was also a point of contest, the place of women in the urban freedom is significant.[8] Much work on the City has mentioned the nominal inclusion of women in the freedom, but very little has examined the specific customs and practices that, over time, ruled women in and out. Women were always a small proportion of those who held the freedom, but their place in it and its meaning to them was historically variable.

As the meaning of the freedom altered, the place of the livery companies in the City and national polity was shifting too. Despite intellectual and practical challenges to companies' role in controlling trade, they continued to have a political significance in the late seventeenth century. Livery halls were mostly rebuilt after the Fire, and the overlap of City and company political roles was still very apparent. By the late seventeenth century, the power of the livery companies was shifting away from the control of all trades towards a more social and economic role. Membership, for men at least, provided connections and access to credit, as well as sociability and feasts for those holding company office. They remained significant to urban life. Although London by this stage stretched far beyond the walls, and the companies were shaken by political changes, they maintained a tight hold over the right to trade in the City of London itself, which was still very much a place of shops, stalls and standings.

Freedom also bestowed the right of political participation. Freemen ratepayers elected the City's leaders, the Common Council and the aldermen. Hilda Smith has argued that this aspect of guild membership obscures women's participation in guilds, by allowing the symbolic political side, from which women were excluded, to overshadow the daily labour of craft, in which women did participate. The symbolic and political aspect of guilds, though, is enlightening on its own terms. Guilds still occupied significant roles in the political and economic world of the City. Citizenship remained urban and local, but eventually its civic

---

[8] Perspectives on guilds' decline are offered in J. R. Kellett, 'The Breakdown of Gild and Corporation Control over the Handicraft and Retail Trade in London', *Economic History Review* 10, no. 3 (1958): 381–94; Michael Berlin, 'Guilds in Decline? London Livery Companies and the Rise of a Liberal Economy, 1600–1800', in *Guilds, Innovation, and the European Economy*, 1400–1800, ed. R. Epstein and Maarten Prak (Cambridge University Press, 2008), 316–42; Mark S. R. Jenner, 'Guildwork', in *Guilds, Society & Economy in London 1450–1800*, ed. Patrick Wallis and Ian Gadd (London: Centre for Metropolitan History, 2002), 163–70.

aspect would become the foundation of the post-Enlightenment understanding of citizenship as national political participation.⁹ The path from this civic citizenship to a national one came gradually. In 1700, the vision of citizenship as participation in the nation was beginning to come into focus, but it was also superimposed upon the older, civic model. The significant part that City politics continued to play on the national stage also meant that urban politics were more than local.

The place of women, and indeed gender, in these changing ideas of citizenship was often, perhaps deliberately, opaque. Few records specified precisely when, how or why women were included or excluded; the model citizen was male. Medieval guilds had a defined place for women, tending to depend on their marital status. They paid lower rates, were occasionally entitled to wear livery and were generally excluded from voting for wardens and alderman.¹⁰ In the sixteenth and seventeenth centuries, women's role was less clearly defined. Many guilds imposed particular restrictions on women's work, but few left any record of their participation in the political side of company life. Ceremonially, 'wives' continued to feature in feasts, often with their own tables. At the same time, women's capacity to hold the freedom independently was well established. Across ten City companies between 1650 and 1700, ninety single women took the freedom in their own right through apprenticeship, patrimony and occasionally redemption, with the highest numbers in the last two decades. In the same companies, around 900 widows took apprentices using their husbands' freedoms. In the City Freedoms archive from 1680 to 1700, indentures survive from at least ninety female apprentices claiming the freedom after apprenticeships in companies from the Scriveners' to the Ironmongers'.¹¹ Alongside these free single women were all the widows who used the freedoms of their deceased husbands to take apprentices of their own: around 1,000 did so across the ten companies. As with apprentices, women were a small proportion of freemen, but there were enough of them to be well established.

The way company records described women in their midst conveys something of how they fitted in. Helen Smith, analysing the sixteenth-

---

⁹ David Harris Sacks, 'Freedom to, Freedom from, Freedom of: Urban Life and Political Participation in Early Modern England', *Citizenship Studies* 11, no. 2 (2007): 135–50.

¹⁰ Maryanne Kowaleski and Judith M. Bennett, 'Crafts, Gilds, and Women in the Middle Ages: Fifty Years after Marian K. Dale', *Signs* 14 (1989): 474–501. Hilda L. Smith, *All Men and Both Sexes: Gender, Politics, and the False Universal in England, 1640–1832* (University Park: Pennsylvania State University Press, 2002), 85, takes a more generous interpretation.

¹¹ This is a conservative count, based on searching for women's names. LMA, Freedom Admissions Papers COL/CHD/FR/02, www.ancestry.co.uk.

century Stationers' Company archive, finds widows treated not as a separate group of freewomen but 'subsumed within categories of citizenship and trade identity', with descriptions such as 'citizen and stationer' or 'widow late of London stationer deceased'.[12] By the seventeenth century, printed forms were using the term 'widow consort' when widows took on new apprentices, establishing a precise guild identity for the widows of citizens. As a collective term, citizens might include women who partook of the status of citizen, and sometimes women with the freedom were specifically described, like men, as, for example, 'citizen and draper of London'. They were not, as far as we know, entitled by this description to the same rights of political participation as men. Hilda Smith suggests that the repeated but imprecise definition of citizenship and freedom as male allowed women to be both included in the concept of freeman and excluded from it. As with the broader picture of gender, office, rights and participation, the ways in which words are used are indicative of the ambiguous political meanings of the category 'woman'. Patricia Crawford pointed out in 2001 that women's rights in mid-seventeenth-century England depended sharply on context and marital status: the legal dependency of married women applied only to a minority of women.[13] By the later seventeenth century, legal opinion at a national level was articulating rationales for the legal marginalisation of women as a group. Their incapacity to vote, or to hold local office, was held to stem from the nature of womanhood and to apply even to maidens or widows as well as to the more obviously dependent wives. In London, though, customs retained a set of peculiar specifics without much generalisation. Commentaries explained feme sole trader status, which enabled married women to trade as if they were single and independent.[14] William Bohun's defence of City custom in 1702, *Privilegia Londini*, noted that women were included in the category of citizens and freemen included in Edward I's charter relating to the tax on wine. Discussing apprenticeship, the same text noted the particular rules that applied to girls and women: a 'Maid Apprentice' could be enrolled 'in like manner as a Youth', but a freeman's wife must have her apprentice bound to her husband, not herself. At other points, as in the quotation of an Act of Common

---

[12] Helen Smith, *'Grossly Material Things': Women and Book Production in Early Modern England* (Oxford University Press, 2012), 95–6.

[13] Patricia Crawford, '"The Poorest She": Women and Citizenship in Early Modern England', in *The Putney Debates of 1647: The Army, the Levellers and the English State*, ed. Michael Mendle (Cambridge University Press, 2001), 216.

[14] See Nicola Phillips, *Women in Business, 1700–1850* (Woodbridge: Boydell & Brewer Ltd, 2006), chapter 3, for a discussion of custom in relation to feme sole trader status.

Council from 1526 about fraudulent apprenticeship, the text addresses, equally, 'any Freeman or Freewoman of this City'.[15] The place of women in the freedom depended on a combination of vague inclusivity and specific exclusions.

The political rights that accompanied freedom were an index of urban belonging, but they were dependent on another precondition: being a householder, defined as paying the tax of scot and lot. Freemen householders selected aldermen, elected them to common council and participated in governing the ward. Women seem not to have participated in this work. Throughout the early modern period, there are a few records of women claiming the right to participate in parliamentary elections, and one case where single women's having voted was described as dishonourable.[16] At critical points in the seventeenth century, the visible inclusion of women in the political roles of guilds might have been a liability.[17] By the later eighteenth century, though, the social cachet of political power was such that the political rights accruing to freemen's daughters in incorporated towns like Bristol were celebrated and sought out.[18]

Amongst those claiming the freedom in seventeenth-century London, women were a tiny proportion of the whole. They took up all the means of becoming free – apprenticeship, patrimony through their fathers' right and the additional possibility of 'redemption' by paying a fee – but all of them were unusual. Numbers increased somewhat, both proportionally and absolutely, in the eighteenth century, when more women were taking up freedom by patrimony; in the early nineteenth century, there were even more women doing this, mostly as seamstresses. Throughout the early modern period, though, women's relationship to the freedom was more likely to involve a range of roles: as mothers of apprentices who hoped to become free, as wives and widows of masters and as mistresses in their own right. Men encountered companies as individuals who gained their own right to be free. Women moved, depending on life stage, between individual identities and roles that were defined by their husbands or fathers. Their conjugal status could either qualify them for

---

[15] William Bohun, *Privilegia Londini* (1702), 105, 152–3, 307.
[16] Simonds D'Ewes, discussed in Sara Mendelson and Patricia Crawford, *Women in Early Modern England 1550–1720* (Oxford University Press, 2000), 396–7; Charlotte Carmichael Stopes, *British Freewomen: Their Historical Privilege* (London: Swan Sonnenschein, 1894); Hilda L. Smith, 'Women as Sextons and Electors: King's Bench and Precedents for Women's Citizenship', in *Women Writers and the British Political Tradition*, ed. Hilda L. Smith (Cambridge University Press, 1998).
[17] Smith, *All Men and Both Sexes*, 103.
[18] Elaine Chalus, *Elite Women in English Political Life c. 1754–1790* (Oxford University Press, 2005), 40–2.

participation in companies or keep them out of the freedom. Petitions to the aldermen reveal a set of complex rules, enforced by custom and complaint, against which women who needed to be free appealed.

Petitions are some of the most compelling documents of the early-modern archive. The conventions that structure many of them seem to testify to a conviction that the voices of the 'humbull', weak, fatherless, 'destrised' and poor would be heard by someone in power and would receive a response. The listening ears of authority offered the chance of elevating an ordinary problem and solving it. This understanding was integral to early modern government, and it also featured in the City's governing processes. There, though, petitions drew on the established language of pleading to address more institutional issues. People petitioned the Lord Mayor and aldermen for favourable treatment in relation to companies, building regulations, charitable institutions or injuries while in the service of the City.

Petitioning for special mercy, advancement or relief was an integral part of the state–subject relationship, which both qualified and demonstrated the authoritarian power of local and national authorities. The language of praying and favour that petitions and responses expressed were long established in public discourse. David Zaret has argued that petitioning was changing in the seventeenth century from a private act to a political claim, and printed petitions of political complaint changed the form.[19] Others are more sceptical. Brodie Waddell points out that the political import of petitioning was not novel or unique to the mid-seventeenth century.[20] Rather, the political significance of private or personal complaints can be traced in numerous contexts. The collective petitions of the Civil War period, many of which came from groups describing themselves as 'women' or 'wives', were part of that shift, and they helped inaugurate a public 'women's voice'.[21] They had precedents in other women's collective petitions, such as those on behalf of sailors captured in Barbary.[22] All these uses of women's collective voice drew on an idea of 'women' and 'wives' which cast them as responsible

---

[19] David Zaret, *Origins of Democratic Culture: Printing, Petitions, and the Public Sphere in Early-Modern England* (Princeton University Press, 2000).

[20] Brodie Waddell, 'Was Early Modern England a Petitioning Society?', *The Many-Headed Monster* (blog), https://manyheadedmonster.wordpress.com/2016/11/07/was-early-modern-england-a-petitioning-society/.

[21] Ellen A. McArthur, 'Women Petitioners and the Long Parliament', *English Historical Review* 24, no. 96 (1909): 698–709; Ann Hughes, *Gender and the English Revolution* (London: Routledge, 2011).

[22] Judith Hudson, '"2000 Wives": Women Petitioning on Barbary Captivity, 1626–1638', *The Many-Headed Monster* (blog), https://manyheadedmonster.wordpress.com/2016/11/11/2000-wives-women-petitioning-on-barbary-captivity-1626-1638/.

for family provision and national peace, countering any suggestion that women were wholly excluded from the public sphere. Most petitions, after all, were made to a public authority: overseers, justices of the peace, governors of hospitals. They functioned as a conduit between personal need and public responsibility. In that context, women's voices drew authority particularly from their role as mothers and providers. In the freedom petitions, some of the same rhetoric came into play, with women describing the needs of their dependents. Most of them, though, also struck a different note: the right to work at a skilled trade. While the freedom petitions were essentially individual requests, they also had a public meaning. Many were necessitated purely by the City's customs regarding women, all of them were in some way granted, and the over-representation of women in freedom petitions suggests that aldermen, guild members and other traders saw women as an awkward but necessary group within the freedom.

The precise relationship between women and their petitioning words is rarely easy to make out. These ones feel particularly performative, but even the most straightforward petitions in seventeenth-century culture are clearly shaped by a well-established rhetoric, typically featuring a nicely judged balance of hard work, entitlement, humility and special pleading. Women often predominate among petitioners, particularly in relation to the poor law. Their carefully crafted phrases suggest a learned skill at negotiating the law, as well as the capacity to deploy the concepts of 'weak' and 'humble', endorsing inferiority in order to win a cause. The process helped solidify a supplicatory role in relation to governing and charitable institutions. Cordelia Beattie's work on medieval petitioning delves deeper into language and identity in these formulaic documents. Petitioning, Beattie argues, does not display a prelinguistic self but is itself a process of identity formation. The work of telling a story to a scribe, choosing details and shaping a narrative to suit convention and law helped make female selfhood.[23] In a legally informed world, it encouraged legal and institutional knowledge, whilst often requiring the petitioner to disavow the very expertise with which she presented. The female voice these documents represent is performative and symbolic, a kind of ventriloquism. Read out at the aldermen's court, the petitions of women helped constitute public female identity in relation to the freedom. Rather than being refused, women were given a means to buy into

---

[23] Cordelia Beattie, 'Your Oratrice: Women's Petitions to the Late Medieval Court of Chancery', in *Women, Agency and the Law, 1300–1700*, ed. Bronach Christina Kane and Fiona Williamson (London: Pickering & Chatto, 2013), 17–30.

the freedom that limited its privileges, so the petition itself looks like a formalised request, one which was specially tailored to working women.

Ignorance was a classic petitioner's tool. When Jane Wallis petitioned the aldermen to prevent a man building alongside her house, she pleaded female ignorance: 'your petitioner being a widow woman and unacquainted with the method that ought to be taken'.[24] In the same way, some women petitioning for the freedom stressed their ignorance of the City customs that determined membership. In 1691 Susanna Newlin was working as a seamstress in Castle Alley, by the Royal Exchange, without a freedom to allow her to trade. She had been apprenticed to a Clothworker in 1682, but after six years of service he had allowed her to leave, 'remitting' her the final year of labour she owed him. Her petition described herself as 'ignorant of the custom of this honourable city' because she had not found another master to complete her time and so could not gain the freedom by service; she requested to pay for freedom by redemption instead. She brought her indenture with her to plead, and it survives, pinned inside her petition. The paperwork of apprenticeship was preserved with care. Susanna was a gentleman's daughter from Iffley, and her use of the rhetoric of ignorance alluded more to being an outsider than humble. Her gender was, however, intrinsic to her words: so few men found themselves in this position that comparable pleas are unlikely.

After being examined by the Lord Mayor about her apprenticeship, and paying the redemption fee, Newlin was admitted into the Broderers' Company, reflecting their continued interest in regulating their trade. The Clothworkers, in which she had been apprenticed, seem to have had no tradition of freeing their female apprentices. Over a year later Newlin took on an apprentice, a Hertfordshire clergyman's daughter, and in 1693 she had a shop in the Exchange itself and a house worth £4 annual rent in the winding lane of grand timber houses, Great St Helen's, Bishopsgate.[25] The disruptions in Newlin's procession from apprentice to mistress testify to some of the uncertainties that remained in female apprenticeship. Patience Lee, another would-be seamstress, explained that she had been apprenticed to a widow in the Pewterers' Company, but only for five years instead of seven.

And may it please this honorable Court that your Peticoner at the expiracon of her said time hopeing to obteine her freedome by her said service was informed

---

[24] LMA, COL/CA/05/01/0001 (1672).
[25] LMA COL/CA/05/01/0003 (1691); LMA, MS 14657/1, 8 July 1692; 4 Shillings in the Pound Tax, UK Data Archive, *London Lives* (Susanna Newlyn); LMA, MS 11316/6, 1693. ROLLCO (Susanna Newland).

she could not be made free in that capacity for that she was bound but for five yeares (Of which your Peticoner was wholly ignorant at the time of her binding) Which will be your Peticoners Utter Ruin if not Releived by this honorable Court.[26]

The question at issue in Patience Lee's petition was, in fact, well established, although she may still have been ignorant of it. As we saw in earlier chapters, while seven-year contracts were well understood to be the minimum to achieve freedom, five-year contracts were in common use for women apprentices, particularly those working at the Royal Exchange. Shorter terms often cost parents more, because they allowed apprentices to leave servitude sooner, depriving employers of their acquired skills. Short contracts allowed women to treat apprenticeships with even greater flexibility than men did, but also added some key constraints, impeding the right of completed apprentices to the freedom and creating a potential obstacle for women who remained single and worked for themselves. Whether or not this was intentional, it had an obstructive effect on women trying to trade.

In practice, for several women like Susanna Newlin, access to the freedom proved manageably flexible. Ann Cleverly, apprenticed as a gentleman's daughter from Hampshire in 1694, petitioned after five and a half years' service that her mistress, a milliner in the Shipwrights' Company, had left off her trade but was happy to remit her the remainder of her time. She too attached her original indenture. She was granted the freedom by redemption in 1700 and paid quarterage to the company for several years, ultimately in Covent Garden; in 1724, still in London, she married a widower. For both Cleverly and her mistress, intermittent shopkeeping and a loose relationship to the freedom were useful.[27]

Alongside claims of ignorance, the common passive voice of petitions may make women petitioners sound disengaged from the customs of London. They were 'informed' by others of the rules. This seems to undermine Londoners' references elsewhere to the customs of their city as a well-known body of law and to counter the evidence from elsewhere that women were generally proficient in customary law. Nicola Whyte's work on rural women litigants has shown women displaying notable expertise in custom. Widows knew their property rights; wives knew their place in church pews; older women testified about their knowledge of ancient tradition.[28] Andy Wood finds women's testimonies strikingly

---

[26] COL/CA/05/01/003 (1692).
[27] LMA, COL/CA/05/01/0005 (1700); C. H. Ridge, *Records of the Worshipful Company of Shipwrights* (London: Phillimore, 1939), vol. 1, 43.
[28] Nicola Whyte, 'Custodians of Memory', *Cultural and Social History* 8, no. 2 (June 2011): 153–73.

assertive about customary rights; self-deprecations like 'being a woman she marked not' are unusual.[29]

Custom mattered a good deal in London too, but it was cast in different terms than in the landscape-bound customs of rural areas. City custom was laid out in print and discussed in diaries as a matter of interest. Its subjects were mostly born outside the city, and they would have been more likely to learn custom from their London employers and friends than their families or natal communities. Women involved with companies were likely to understand custom quite differently from the rural and provincial plebeian women who dealt so often with custom in the courts elsewhere. Many of them were gentry-born, not custom's natural defenders. London custom largely addressed not land or property but the market, and it was organised around transactions. Descriptions of the City's laws and customs tend to feature women collectively in one of several ways: as traders, as wives and as the targets of sexual insult. *Privilegia Londini*, the account of the privileges of the (female) City, follows a full description of the custom of feme sole trader with a point about the insult of 'whore' being actionable.[30] Women whose fathers had the freedom, some of them native Londoners, would probably have become aware of the different ways that patrimony extended to women compared to men. City wives would learn the way that custom modified the impact of coverture on married women, to the benefit not just of them but of their husbands, freed from responsibility for their debts. The commentaries' general disinclination to feature distinctions of gender may indicate an assumption that citizenship was fundamentally a male affair. The rarity of claims of female ignorance in petitions suggests that London women were expected to know the rules.

There were, however, plenty of cases where women found they did not know how things worked. Petitioners described themselves as 'being informed' they needed the freedom or that they could not have it. Those who did the informing were sometimes officials employed by guilds to pursue the regulation of craft: the Merchant Taylors' Company was still doing this intermittently in the 1680s. They might also be other shopkeepers, women and men, who had followed the system and paid for their freedom and whose interests lay in excluding outsiders. Petitions provide direct evidence of how the freedom excluded people and which people acted as its agents. Elizabeth Thomas's

---

[29] Andy Wood, *The Memory of the People: Custom and Popular Senses of the Past in Early Modern England* (Cambridge University Press, 2013), 297–315.

[30] Bohun, *Privilegia Londini*, 123–7.

elegantly copied petition for a licence to trade described how she had served a seven-year apprenticeship as a tailor to the draper Nicholas Westfield.

That your Petitioner did formerly serve Seaven Year's apprenticeship to the trade of a Taylor, with Nicholas Westfeild late cittizen & draper of London deceased, and hath, ever since the Death of her first husband John Hodwell late cittizen & merchant Taylor of London deceased used, carryed on, and exercised the said Trade of a Taylor in the Citty of London, and by her Industry therein hath hitherto maintained her aged Mother and Two Children, who, without her supporting them, must of necessity fall to the charge of the Parish of St Nicholas Acons London, where she and they now dwell.

That your Petitioner hath of late been often molested in her said Trade by the Officers of the Chamberlain of London, upon the information of envious persons unknown to your Petitioner, in respect Your Petitioner's said Husband Jenkin Thomas hath not as yett taken up his freedom, altho' he doth intend to do the same at his return from Cadiz, to which he hath good right, having serv'd an Apprenticeship unto Mr Robert Woodcock now one of the Livery Men of the said Company of Clothworkers.

It was the 'envious persons unknown', in Elizabeth's plea, who had prompted the Chamberlain's officials to prevent her from trading. Like Mary German, her apprenticeship was unformalised: she was not registered in the company records alongside Nicholas Westfield's male apprentices. While her work had previously been protected by her first husband's freedom, her second husband's failure to take his up left her vulnerable, until the aldermen granted her 'liberty to follow her trade' in his absence.[31] Elizabeth Thomas's petition is particularly striking for its claim to having been trained as a tailor by her master, probably in the 1650s: only very occasionally were women described as tailors in occupational records.

Pheby Young's scrappier petition also described her 'livelihood' being 'molested' by another woman. Pheby was a freeman's daughter who had been in service for many years. She fell 'lame', a disaster which her petition describes with typically defensive language: 'your petitioner ... hath sought for cure but could not attain any.' It may have been a stroke, or another disability, or literal lameness; it left her, she said, unable to put her own clothes on, and her husband was weakened by consumption. Her lameness prevented her from continuing to work as a servant, and instead she took a stall selling apples and oranges by St Dunstan's church, where 'by her care' she made an 'honest but poor livelihood'. She sold fruit for nine years, acquiring 'the good will of all the

---

[31] LMA, COL/CA/05/01/003 (1691).

Neighbourhood': her economic place was secured, in her story, by the combination of her father's freedom and her own hard labour.

Pheby Young's endeavours were undercut by another, more righteous woman: Mary Rolles. Rolles 'outed' Young – in other words, she had her removed from her stall – 'on pretence that your petitioner's husband was no freeman'. Mary Rolles knew who fitted in where; perhaps she had her own business, and perhaps she was related to the Gertrude Rolles who held a shop in the Royal Exchange and whose will commended her two daughters for their industry.[32] Pheby, though, also had her own supporters, a group of officials and parishioners who signed her petition to testify to the truth of her circumstances. Only one of them, Katherine Marshall, was a woman. Pheby's petition makes clear the localism of reputation. Only that stall by St Dunstan's church would do, for the neighbourhood's goodwill kept her in place; anywhere else, she would be 'forced to beg her bread in a strange place'. This is a weighty reminder of the continuing power of local ties, specific to a parish, in a rapidly expanding city. The economic woes of the later seventeenth century may have given them still more grip, but it may also be that locality had particularly strong meanings for women without access to the other credit assets that the freedom brought.

Like Pheby Young, other women sought to obtain permission to trade freely in the City, usually by means of entrance to the freedom by redemption, sometimes with reduced fees. Sarah Wolsley explained that her husband had gone to serve in Ireland, leaving her poor and helpless 'with one small child and big with another'. Her friends and relations offered to help her buy into the freedom for 'a moderate price' so she could run a business to maintain herself.[33] Her account suggests the long interest that those 'friends' who helped set girls up in apprenticeship could hold over a working life time. Many petitioned with laborious explanations of their disenfranchisement from the City privileges. Lettice Freeman had no freedom of her own. She had been employed for several years in a shop on Cheapside, working for a freeman selling coats and acquiring 'sufficient skill in that trade'. When he discharged her, she wanted to take her own shop on Cheapside, 'being otherwise destitute of subsistence'. Without having served an apprenticeship, she 'presumes not to set up within the city' and requested to pay the redemption fee to become free: here, apprenticeship was clearly recognised as the appropriate route into independent business. Elizabeth Moore had

---

[32] Margaret R. Hunt, *The Middling Sort: Commerce, Gender, and the Family in England, 1680–1780* (Berkeley: University of California Press, 1996), 143.
[33] LMA, COL/CA/05/02/003.

been 'bred a Sempstress' and wanted to use her skills in widowhood, but her husband had not taken up his own freedom. She had a clear view of the larger economic causes of her problems: her husband had been apprenticed as a framework knitter, but the war with France from 1688 meant that the silk he needed was no longer available, and he 'betook himself to a seafaring life', where he died, leaving her with a small child. She could not follow her trade without being admitted to the freedom 'which she is no waies able to purchase nor otherwise in any hopes but by the favor of this honorable Court'. Her fellow parishioners (all male) testified that she was 'a diligent and industrious woman, and humbly recommend her to your honor and Worship's favour'.[34]

Another set of petitioners explained how they had been apprenticed themselves but had not become free. While this was a common outcome of female apprenticeship, it did not hamper women from practising their trade as long as they worked for someone else or married a freeman. Those who did not, and wanted to trade independently or take apprentices, ran into trouble. The petitions of these ex-apprentices indicate some of the futures of those apprenticed. Mary Howsley had been apprenticed in her youth but had not taken up the freedom. Her husband, an immigrant, had not been given indentures by his master, even after he was naturalised, and had applied to become free by redemption but had died before taking it up. Left 'very poore with two children to maintaine', she was unable to pay the £6 13s 4d fee to become free in his stead. On her petition explaining her prior freedom, the aldermen's court reduced her fee to 40 shillings.[35] The freedom would enable her to practice the trade she had learned and might also entitle her to company charity. Mary Poynter's petition reflected another set of complex circumstances. She had served a seven-year apprenticeship to Frances Browne of the Painter-Stainers' Company; she then married a member of the Barber-Surgeons, 'who had a right to the freedome of this honorable city both by service and Patrimony but liveing altogether in the Countrey never tooke up the same So that yor Peticioner is informed she cannot be admitted into the freedome of this City by service'.[36] She pleaded to be allowed to pay the fee for admission to the freedom by redemption, so that she could 'follow some imploy whereby to mainteine her selfe and Children'.[37] Accounts like this suggest the number of women who lost the advantages of their apprenticeships.

---

[34] LMA, COL/CA/05/01/0004 (1697).
[35] LMA, COL/CA/05/02/004; COL/CHD/FR/02/69/122.
[36] LMA, COL/CA/05/01/0005 (1699).   [37] LMA, COL/CA/05/02/004.

Patrimony and Matrimony

Alongside petitions about interrupted and unrecorded apprenticeships and requests for the right to work sat pleas relating to patrimonial freedom. Both daughters and sons of freemen were entitled to apply for the freedom. As part of the custom of London, patrimonial redemption allowed the children of freemen to pay a small sum (two shillings) to be admitted to the company (and the City freedom) in their own right. Nevertheless, daughters' rights to do so could be eroded by marriage, another complication of freedom in practice. Patrimonies offer a new perspective on women's relationship to the city world of trade and business. Research by Margaret Hunt and Richard Grassby on women in seventeenth- and eighteenth-century businesses has illuminated the important role played by wives, and the key place of marriage in the networks that determined access to markets, agents and suppliers.[38] Pamela Sharpe and Amy Froide have reconstructed the dimensions of single women's careers in the early modern urban environment, showing the new opportunities for independent shop work from the late seventeenth century.[39] Patrimonies reveal the continuing power of the natal family, with women using their paternal inheritance in a variety of ways to progress, to connect or to survive.

Mary Taylor petitioned the court for help in acquiring the freedom by patrimony after her father, an ironmonger, went bankrupt and ended up in prison. His wife and six children were left penniless. Mary's relations were 'willing to put your Petitioner into a way of Trade and to set up a Shop for her', drawing on her right to freedom by patrimony: but she was under twenty-one, and the plea was refused.[40] Mary Taylor's relations were picking up on an increasingly common practice in the late seventeenth century: women's use of patrimonies to trade. The archive of freedoms preserved by the Chamberlain's office provides a record of how women used this opportunity.

Like men's, women's patrimonial freedoms were recorded on printed forms. As with Anne Allison's patrimony (Figure 6.1), calculations were worked in the margin to establish that they had been born after their fathers were free (in this case from 1720, the year of her father's freedom,

---

[38] Hunt, *The Middling Sort*; Richard Grassby, *Kinship and Capitalism: Marriage, Family, and Business in the English-Speaking World, 1580–1740* (Cambridge University Press, 2001).

[39] Pamela Sharpe, 'Dealing with Love: The Ambiguous Independence of the Single Woman in Early Modern England', *Gender & History* 11, no. 2 (1999): 209–32; Amy M. Froide, *Never Married: Singlewomen in Early Modern England* (Oxford University Press, 2005).

[40] LMA, COL/CA/05/02/003.

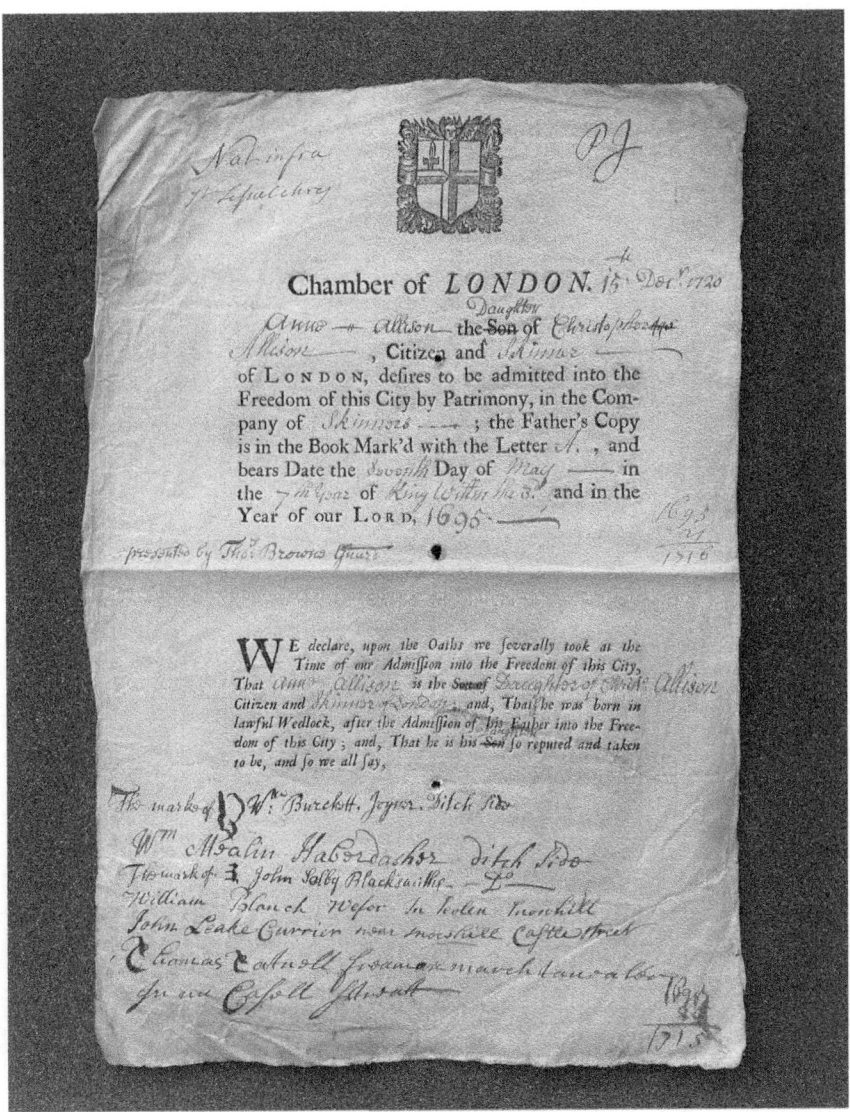

Figure 6.1 Patrimony form for Anne Allison.
London Metropolitan Archives (City of London)

1695, plus her twenty-one years making 1716). The procedure of requesting a patrimony involved returning to the archive and noting down the year, and sometimes the book, in which the father's freedom (the 'copy') had been recorded. Names and addresses of those, all men,

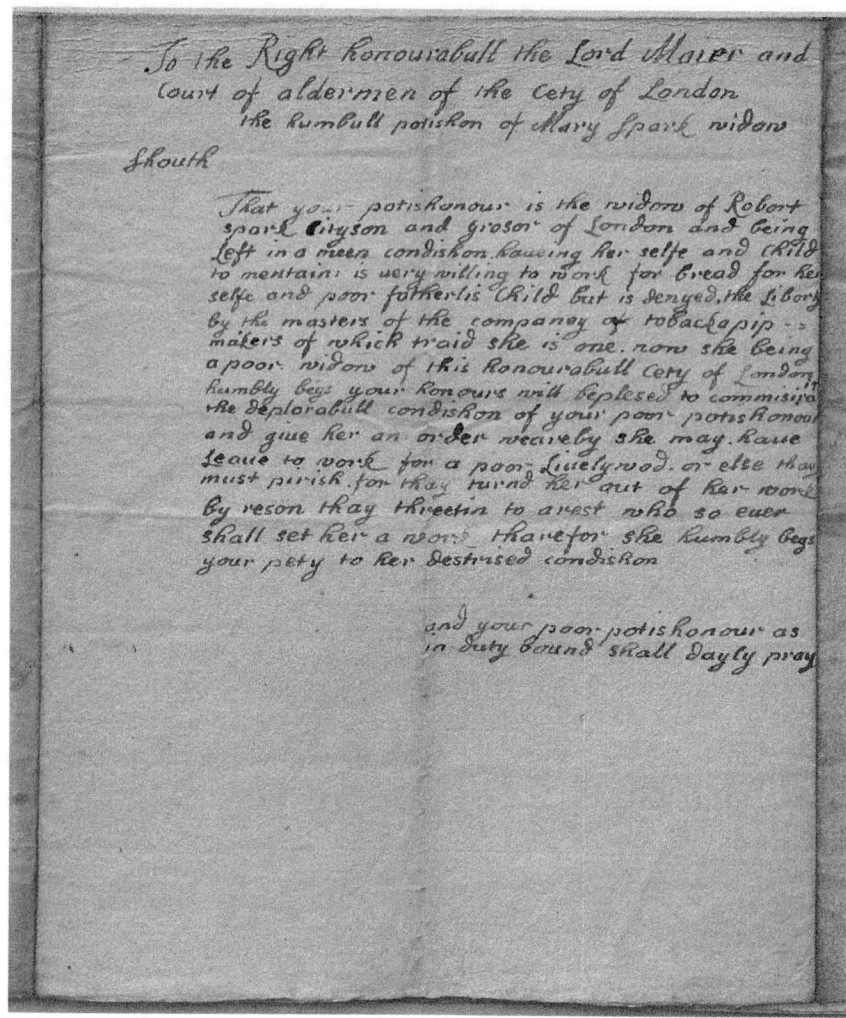

Figure 6.2 Mary Spark's petition.
London Metropolitan Archives (City of London)

who could testify to her birth and legitimacy were provided below. All this was done for both sons and daughters, the only difference being the clerical alterations necessary to turn the 'son' and 'he' of the form into 'daughter' and 'she'. That the printed patrimony forms never included a female version, unlike apprenticeship indentures, may indicate a process less permeable to female initiative, less responsive to it or less driven by the market.

For men, patrimonies were an unusual, but convenient, way of obtaining the freedom. The utility of apprenticeship, particularly for boys, meant that only a small percentage of families took advantage of that opportunity. In the later seventeenth century, only about 13 per cent of freedoms were claimed by patrimony rather than servitude.[41] Redemptions without patrimony, simply paying a fee, accounted for a few more. For women, though, patrimonies increasingly offered another way of accessing freedom's benefits. As many took that route to the freedom as apprenticeship; it was still a very small number, but it was evidently a feasible alternative option towards achieving the right to trade independently. Patrimonies were used in a variety of circumstances by a range of women as diverse as the members of companies. Some were on the poor roll, others were related to wealthy mercers and left extensive wills, but all of them returned to and used the freedom won by their own fathers, sometimes as long as 70 or 100 years before. City custom prescribed particular means of inheritance for women, ensuring that wives were not excluded but also making provision for all children; patrimonies, for a few, offered another means of perpetuating the advantages of citizenship, if only for one more generation.

Over time, women's use of patrimonies seems to have shifted. Forms like Anne Allison's, with their dates of birth, make it possible to trace something of the life histories of these freemen's daughters. Seventeenth-century applicants tended to be in their twenties or thirties. Several requested the freedom soon after reaching the age of twenty-one, as soon as they became eligible for it. This suggests they were aiming at independent trading. Often, their parents were still alive; patrimonies were functioning, apparently, as an alternative to apprenticeship as a route into independent adulthood before or outside marriage. Several women took the patrimony as soon as they could, at twenty-one, such as Elizabeth Baddiley from St Botolph's Bishopsgate, daughter of a member of the Drapers' Company. Baptised on 19 October 1673, she received the freedom on 8 October 1694 and took Susan Templer from Northamptonshire as an apprentice on 24 October, paying quarterage at the Royal Exchange.[42]

---

[41] Sample of 10 companies from ROLLCO 1671–9: 1,528 servitude, 200 patrimony, 99 redemption.

[42] ROLLCO; Drapers' Company, Boyds' Roll, for apprenticeship details; *England, Births and Christenings, 1538–1975* (Salt Lake City: FamilySearch, 2013), 19/10/1673, www.ancestry.co.uk.

Whilst only a few of these women seem to have taken their own apprentices, the main use of a patrimonial freedom was to protect the right to trade independently in the City, and so the age at which women took them up offers good evidence about their working lives and their family circumstances. A woman who worked in her parents' shop, or with a partner (business or marital) who was free, did not need the freedom; a woman buying and selling in a shop in her own right, employing others or training apprentices, did. The late seventeenth-century group of women with patrimonies, then, were mostly expecting to trade independently in their twenties and thirties. Either their parents had died or they were setting out alone to start a separate business from their family's. Most likely, the freedom would give them the chance to take a shop and work as a seamstress.

In many cases, patrimonies were linked to paternal death, constituting part of a family strategy. Ann Povey lost her father, a mercer, at the age of two. His will circumvented the London custom that a third of a man's property went to his widow and at least a third to his children by noting that he had already provided for his wife by a separate settlement. He left her five shillings 'willing her therewith to be content' and the rest to be kept in trust by the Chamberlain for their daughter. In Ann's early twenties, in 1686, she took up her patrimonial freedom of the company, and nine months later married a gentleman of the Inner Temple.[43] Her freedom re-enrolled her in the city networks to which her father had belonged. It would have enabled her to begin an independent working life, and the company membership (if not the privileges of freedom) was perhaps also seen as part of the portion she brought to marriage. In 1694, Catherine Grosvenor and her brother Thomas both took up patrimonial freedoms in the Drapers' Company, ten months before their sixty-year-old father died and a month after he wrote his will, suggesting the family's plans envisaged both children stepping into a future with the company. Sarah Grosvenor, his third child, was too young to become free. John Grosvenor's will followed City custom in giving a third of his estate to his wife and a third to his children, but he divided the final third between his daughters alone, suggesting that Thomas was already well established. Thomas Grosvenor went on to take his own apprentices. A few months later, Catherine married a felt-maker, George Procter. Procter's parish was outside the City, in Westminster, and he does not

---

[43] ROLLCO, Ann and Justinian Povey; death, 4 March 1669, LMA, P69/GIS/A/002/MS06419/007; LMA, TNA PROB 11/329, f. 277; *London and Surrey Marriage Bonds and Allegations, 1597–1921*, www.ancestry.co.uk. (This is a distant relative of the Justinian Povey who was accountant-general to Anne of Denmark.)

seem to have been free; Catherine's use of her patrimony is unrecorded. Widowed four years later, Catherine died in 1732, leaving cash legacies of £20 to £100 to her nieces and nephews, along with material goods including 'my muff and seven crimson cushions', 'my father's picture' and 'my agate fork and knife'.[44] Many of her bequests were to the family of her younger sister, Sarah, who had married their father's last apprentice six years after his death.

Siblings did not always become free in parallel. George and Sara Cullimore were the oldest and youngest surviving children of a sixteenth-century member of the Drapers' Company. George took up his own freedom by patrimony in 1595, aged twenty-two, applied unsuccessfully to be a factor with the East India Company in 1614, paid quarterage at premises in Blackwall and Lothbury, married twice, was taxed as a gentleman and held office as a vestryman in Stepney and died in Mile End in 1644, aged seventy-one. He left sums of £150 to his grandchildren and £5 to his forty-four-year-old sister Sara, perhaps the last surviving of his thirteen siblings, of whom eight had died in childhood.[45] Sara's life up until this point is invisible; after taking the patrimony, she is recorded in the company's quarterage book as 'poor'. For her, patrimony offered a very different footing than for her brother; perhaps it entitled her to some charity.

Eighteenth-century women used patrimonies somewhat differently than their seventeenth-century predecessors. The numbers who did so remain at the same level, but they took up their option of freedom later in life. In the seventeenth century, women freed by patrimony had an average age of twenty-five, ranging from twenty-one to thirty-seven; although few ages were recorded, the longest gap between a father's freedom and a daughter's patrimony was forty-six years. The women who took up patrimonial freedom in the eighteenth century were older, with an average of forty; the oldest was seventy, and several were in their fifties, becoming free many years – in one case, a century – after their own fathers had. The rationale for paying to take up the freedom was less clear by this point; the options to trade outside the City were extensive, and guild membership was not obviously necessary, although controls over trade in the City were restated by an Act of Common Council in 1712.

---

[44] LMA, GL MS 9172/84, no. 291 (John Grosvenor); LMA, GL MS 9172/136B, no. 28 (Katherine Procter). Other family details from *Boyd's Inhabitants of London*, www.findmypast.co.uk.

[45] Draper's Company, Boyd's Roll, Cullimore; 'East Indies: March 1614', in *Calendar of State Papers Colonial, East Indies, China and Japan, Volume 2, 1513–1616*, ed. W. Noel Sainsbury (London: HMSO, 1864), 279–89. Quarterage, a tax paid to the company, indicates active membership.

The concerted attempt to sell the freedom from the 1730s might have brought more women to take up patrimonies as well as the more expensive redemptions.[46] For widows, patrimonies offered another chance to access City privileges. Mary Exelby, daughter of a Stepney weaver, was born in 1692. She married young, at fifteen or sixteen, another weaver in Spitalfields, Benjamin Pellett. She seems to have worked alongside him until he died, and in 1739, when she was in her late forties, she applied for the patrimony. Her husband was not free of the City; Spitalfields was just outside the City's jurisdiction. She may have intended to work in a City shop or to apply for charitable help. She died in 1748, still in Stepney, at sixty-five, the cause listed as 'age'.[47] Another widow, Elizabeth Boult, daughter of the goldsmith Francis Jeyne, took the patrimony aged thirty-four in 1719. None of her several siblings appear in the company records. In 1718, she was living in Falcon Court, off Fleet Street, alongside one of the goldsmiths who signed her claim to patrimony; she was, in some way, part of a company community.

The oldest in this sample, Mary Gosse, was seventy when she applied for freedom by patrimony in 1733. Her position was different again: a well-off single woman looking back to her family connections. Mary's father, Henry, had been freed in the Salters' Company a hundred years earlier in 1633, after his apprenticeship. His death in 1673 left his children, several underage, with substantial estates, and his son Henry appeared in the 1687 heraldic visitation, in which merchants were prominent.[48] None of the children, though, seems to have taken up a freedom or participated in company life until Mary's application for a patrimony at the age of seventy. Mary's will, made ten years later, suggests family tradition held great importance; she was to be buried in the chancel of St Matthew Friday Street, a tiny church rebuilt after the Fire, where her father and uncle were buried and where she had been born. Perhaps her old age brought her back to the company rituals of the livery of her father. In any case, Mary was the last Gosse in the Salters, and although she left extensive legacies to female friends and relatives (and some men), she did not mention the company. Her will is beautifully revealing of the life of a well-off ageing spinster in mid-eighteenth-century London. Like many of the middling sort, she lodged over a shop, on Goswell Road on the

---

[46] Ian Doolittle, 'The City of London in the Eighteenth Century: Corporate Pressures and Their Consequences', in *Revisiting the Polite and Commercial People: Essays in Georgian Politics, Society, and Culture in Honour of Professor Paul Langford*, ed. Elaine Chalus and Perry Gauci (Oxford University Press, 2019), 104.
[47] LMA, CL/CHD/FR/02/608/11 (Pallett); P93/DUN/269, 20 February 1748/9.
[48] *The Visitation of London Begun in 1687* (London: Harleian Society, 2004), ed. T. C. Wales and C. P. Hartley, part 1, 28.

northern borders of the City; the shop was that of a grocer, and his wife who had been her servant. She left them a substantial legacy, and also the standard £5 to her maidservant if she was still living with her at her death. Money for mourning was left for numerous friends and connections, and she ordered escutcheons on her hearse and white feathers on her funeral horses, up to a cost of £10.[49] In the last ten years of Mary's life, the company connection would have given her both social and financial credit. While patrimonial freedoms did not enfranchise women, they may have brought some local political influence.

Women who took up the patrimonial freedom were often the only ones in their family to do so. Their brothers tended, rather, to be apprenticed. Although many had sisters who were also single, it was rare for more than one woman in a generation to take up the freedom by patrimony. This is good evidence for the uses of the freedom, as it enabled sisters to share the benefits of one freedom, gaining the same advantages as a woman married to a citizen. The wealthy Cleeve family, pewterers both by trade and company membership, took a different approach. Alexander Cleeve, the father, died in 1738, when his two youngest children, Richard and Elizabeth, were under age. His will left them £1,000 each and joint tenure of an estate. In 1746, when all the children were over twenty-one, all four of them took up their patrimonies in the Pewterers' Company. The Cleeve sisters were unusual. Most women with patrimonies were the only female members of their generation holding the freedom, suggesting that if they had sisters trading too, they were working together.

Demographic evidence indicates that to be single at this age was to be fairly securely so, with a low chance of marriage after age forty-five: an awareness of this might also structure these older women's choices, with patrimonies becoming a part of the single woman's provision for herself. Married women did not take up patrimonies. If they were married to free men, they had no need to, and if they were married to non-freemen, they were ineligible. Most patrimony applicants were single, still using their natal surname. A few had brothers who did the same thing, taking up their own patrimonies, but most were the only members of that generation who appear in the records of that company, and because patrimonies could not be transmitted by women, the line ended with them. Those few who were widows had 'widow' and both their surnames inscribed upon the forms; freedom petitions also indicate that there

---

[49] TNA, PROB 11/725/322.

was some idea that marriage permanently disqualified women from the patrimony.

One family had, unusually, three sisters taking the patrimony, and their evidence indicates another rationale for its use. Mary, Ann and Elizabeth Tiler were three of the five surviving children of Francis Tiler, a member of the Drapers' Company who had gained the freedom in 1653 after serving an apprenticeship. He had nine apprentices in the 1660s and 1670s and was a liveryman, all suggesting a flourishing trade, but his trade was given as an 'oilman' selling lamp oil. His second wife, Anne Spendlove, was the daughter of Norfolk gentry, and he was the son of a Norfolk clothier; the variable evidence of their status suggests the precarity of livelihoods and occupations in the mid-century. The Tiler sons, and one of their daughters, all died in their first year of life. Three younger daughters, Elizabeth, Anne and Mary, stayed single, though we have no evidence of what they did for most of their lives. In their fifties, within a few months and years of each other, each of the three took out the patrimonial freedom and were described in the records as 'almswomen' or 'poor'.[50]

Patrimonies, which only cost three shillings, seem to have brought women back within the purview of company charity. This would be particularly useful in middle age, when the capacity to do close sewing after a lifetime of working in poor light might be becoming more difficult. Like younger women, those who took up the freedom in their forties, fifties, sixties and seventies may also have been aiming at, or already operating, the 'little shop' so often referenced in freedom petitions. In the eighteenth century, City shops were being replaced by those in the West End, the Exchange's small shops disappeared and freedom was less necessary for shopkeeping. Patrimonial freedoms may also have been useful for protecting the rights of children, as freemen's orphans were entitled to help from the Orphans' Court.

Returning to the petitions reveals the stories of another set of company women: those who missed out on the patrimony. Their pleas suggest another obstacle in the way of women becoming, or remaining, free. Marriage could bring women into the freedom, but it could also take them out of it. Mary Clarke had the benefit of the freedom of two successive husbands, both stocking-frame makers in the Blacksmiths' Company, but then married 'a foreigner' – someone from outside the City. Although he then died, she had lost her right to practice her trade. The aldermen noted that she had always lived outside the freedom's

---

[50] ROLLCO, Tiler; Drapers' Company, Boyd's Roll.

jurisdiction but had two 'very weak' children to maintain and only wanted the freedom to take apprentices 'who may work to help support her and family'.[51]

The case of the Pannier family provides some detail of the strategies women might take in response to mortality or marital breakdown. Unusually, and fortunately, they are traceable across various records, being christened in a foreign church, paying the marriage duty and both taking apprenticeships and petitioning. Sarah Seale was the daughter of a man who belonged to the Skinners' Company: she would have been entitled to apply for patrimony via her father, but she did not. She married first a joiner, who died, and then in 1681 married a man named Daniel Pannier, from Paris, who was described as a gentleman; as an alien immigrant, he had no rights to the freedom. They lived in Spitalfields, perhaps working in the silk trade there, and had a daughter, Henriette, in 1682. The family were still together in 1694 when Henriette was twelve and they apprenticed her to a goldsmith and his wife in the parish of St Vedast Foster Lane. Daniel then left Sarah and went abroad. Sarah was left, she said, 'in a very mean and low condition; and being 'willing to betake herself to something whereby to support her self and family, is informed she cannot, her present husband being no freeman'. The passive construction is from Sarah's petition in 1699, which presents her as an ignorant, deserted wife, subject to the whims of civic prejudice; the customs of the freedom, even to a woman born, brought up and married in company membership, are an external imposition. Nevertheless, she, or a scrivener, constructed herself in relation to her access to the freedom: 'she is daughter of John Seale citizen and skinner and later married to Christopher Cooper citizen and joiner deceased.' In response, Alderman Richard Levett recommended that 'she may be indulged to keep a small seamstress shop during her life, for support of herself and family'. Perhaps her daughter Henriette, then aged seventeen, left her apprenticeship and brought her skills to work with her mother there; in any case, she did not take the freedom herself but married a minister when she was twenty-two.[52]

---

[51] LMA, COL/CA/05/01/0005 (1699).
[52] LMA, COL/CA/05/01/001 (1698); ROLLCO, Henrietta Panier; D. V. Glass, *London Inhabitants within the Walls, 1695* (London: London Record Society, 1966), for Pannier; LMA, P69/BOT2/A/012/MS09230/001, 23 June 1681; TNA, RG4/4643, Chapel of the Hospital, Spitalfields, 5 August 1682; Marriage of Hennareta Panier to William Bissett, 15 November 1704 at St Katherine by the Tower, *England, Select Marriages, 1538–1973*, www.ancestry.co.uk.

Petitions about patrimonies lost as a consequence of marriage suggest a set of rules that were nowhere set out clearly but which laid a set of traps around women's freedoms. Susanna Baldwin petitioned that she

> is the daughter of Ralph Trunkett citizen & cooke of London and being desirous of her fredome she is informed she cannott obteine it by patrimony for that she married an Unfreeman which is since dead
>
> Therfore humbly prayes that this Honorable Court would admit her into ye freedome of this Honorable City by redempcon

For Susanna, as for many others, patrimony had been destroyed by matrimony. She was refused the freedom by redemption but allowed to continue trading. The aldermen's note records that 'she is ... a widow left with 2 children and keeps a small shop in ye old bayley and very pore, hath by favour of this court beene permitted to keepe ye sayd shope, & are of oppinion ye same favor may be continued'.[53]

Some women claimed poverty had prevented them, or their husbands, from accessing the freedom. Joan Hippisly came to the aldermen as the widow of a man who was entitled to the patrimony, but had not claimed it. Her petition requesting the freedom to trade explained:

> That your Peticoners husband both by his fathers Copy & his own Service was intitled to the freedom of this City, but by reason of his poverty was not able to take up the Same. And is since dead & has not made any Provision for your Peticoner And yor Peticoner in respect of her husband not being free as aforesaid cannot follow a trade as the Widow of a Freeman.

The aldermen noted that Robert Hippisly had been too poor to take up the freedom but had served as a journeyman to a silversmith instead. They concluded, 'soe are of oppinion she cannot pretend any right from hir husbands servis, or his fathers copy; yett waying the poverty of your Peticoner she may be by the favor of this Courtt be Lycenced to keepe a littell chandlers shop during the pleasure of this court.'[54]

Joan Hippisly's manuscript petition, a folded piece of foolscap like the rest, included a print object: the apprenticeship indenture of her husband's father, dating back to many years earlier. It must have been handed down to her husband, who had died within a year or two of their marriage, and thence to her.[55] The archive of freedoms was a living resource, but because indentures were doubled, it worked alongside the private archives of citizens.

---

[53] LMA, COL/CA/05/01/0005 (1699).   [54] LMA, COL/ CA/05/01/0005 (1698).
[55] LMA, P69/TRI2/A/008/MS09243, Holy Trinity, Minories, Marriage of Robert Hippisley and Joan Bate, 20 November 1697.

The need to accompany such petitions with original indentures meant women had to either get hold of family documents or go to the Chamberlains' archive and enquire. One found herself going even further back. Elizabeth Mullinox wrote as a poverty-stricken widow, one of the many suffering from the City's calamitous plundering of the Orphans' Fund. Her husband, now dead, had been orphaned as a child when his father died in 1666, perhaps in the plague of that year, but had never received the money invested for him in the fund. By the 1690s, that fund was half a million pounds in debit.[56] Mullinox had sold her curtains, valance, rug and everything except her bare bed; she owed three years' rent to her landlord, 15 shillings to the baker and chandler and 25 shillings for nursing her children. She hoped to get her daughter into Christ's Hospital, the institution for poor freemen's children. But trying to trace her husband's freedom turned out to be impossible. Her petition explained that

> her husband was the son of Joseph Mullinox late citizen and merchant tailor ... But your peticoner cannot find that her husband did take up his freedom by patrimony as he might have done, whether by his neglect or want of money to take up the same, she cannot tell, although he told your peticoner he was free. But finding your peticoners husbands father was made free about the year of our Lord 1658 and died when your petitioner's husband was very young.[57]

Again, freedom's benefits required paperwork and sometimes archival research, an endeavour which in itself demonstrated and reinforced women's investment in the institution of the freedom.

While there were a number of successful claims to the patrimonial freedom from widows, there is also evidence that marriage to an unfree man was believed to impede it, even after his death. The Court of Aldermen received a series of petitions in the 1690s from women who had the right to freedom by their father's patrimony but who had married unfree men who were now dead or at sea, and wanted to trade in their own right. To get back into the freedom, they had to apply all over again by another method, paying a fee for freedom by 'redemption'. At issue here is the understanding of what marriage did for women: it redefined their civic identity. Judith Bennett and Maryanne Kowaleski's point that marriage was the key determinant of women's status in guilds is borne out again in relation to what happened to widows: their bonds with their fathers were overridden by their bonds with their husbands.[58] The

---

[56] I. G. Doolittle, 'The City of London's Debt to Its Orphans, 1694–1767', *Historical Research* 56, no. 133 (1983): 46–59.
[57] LMA, COL/CA/05/01/0003 (1692).
[58] Kowaleski and Bennett, 'Crafts, Gilds, and Women in the Middle Ages'.

238   Ingenious Trade

implications of this add another dimension to the meaning of marriage for city women.

In a series of petitions, widows of unfree men brought their tenuous claims to the freedom to the aldermen for adjudication, most hoping to buy their way into the freedom by redemption at a reduced rate. Susanna Russell petitioned that she

> is the daughter of Lancelott Emmott citizen and cutler of London and that she married John Russell (lately deceased) an unfreeman but had a right to his freedome and being informed she cannott have her freedome by Patrimony by reason of her marriage and haveing severall small Children to mainteine

> Therefore humbly prayes this Honorable Court to grant her her freedome by Redempcon or elce an Order to follow her trade of selling Coates for maintenance of her selfe & Children.

Richard Levett, one of the aldermen, commented that she was indeed ineligible for patrimony but advised that, 'considering her great poverty', she be allowed to continue retailing coats.[59]

Martha Pitt, stricken by poverty like so many others in the 1690s, had been doubly entitled to claim the freedom. Her father had been free, as had her first husband, belonging to the Clothworkers and Tallow Chandlers respectively; but her second husband was not. Her petition of February 1693 explained

> That your Peticoners last husband Charles Edward Pitts was not free So that your Peticoner hath (as she is informed) lost the benefitt of her first husbandes freedome, That your Peticoner is refused her freedome by Patrimony for that she hath Changed her name.

> Now May it please this honorable Court that your Peticoner's last husband having left her in a mean Condicon with One Child, She by the help of some friends might be put into some way to mainteine her Selfe and Child could she obtaine her freedome which she cannot by Patrimony as aforesaid.

The Chamberlain, Leonard Robinson, examined her petition, and added his conclusion:

> she cannot in stricktnesse have her freedome by Patrimony. However Am of Opinion she may have her freedome of this Citty by redemption paying a small fine As this honorable Court hath heretofore allowed of in the like Case (particularly as in the Margin).[60]

In the margin are notes of two earlier precedents, those of Elizabeth Chamberlain in 1690 and Susanna Kerby in 1691, with the fines they had paid for their patrimonies in similar situations: 3s 4d and 6s 8d. The

---

[59] LMA, COL/CA/05/01/0004 (1697).   [60] LMA, COL/CA/05/01/0004 (1693).

Freedoms and Customs   239

problem of married women's interrupted access to the freedom evidently came regularly to the eye of those responsible for regulating it.

Martha's reference to changing her name adds another aspect to marriage's consequences. Susanna Kerby, too, said 'being desirous of her freedome is informed she cannot obteine it by her said Father's Coppy (tho' admitted in the said Company of Haberdashers) for that she has changed her name by Marriage'.[61] Mary Jones's petition, enclosing her father's 'copy of freedom', noted 'your Peticoner having Changed her name by Marriage is refused her freedome by Patrimony by the name of Jones'.[62] At one level this is a factual description of marriage as a change of name, but it also says something about how women saw marriage in relation to the freedom. It impeded the connection with patrimony at a conceptual level – a woman, even if widowed, was covered by her husband. But it also involved the replacement of a father's name by a husband's, a feature of the English regime of coverture that was more routine than elsewhere in western Europe.[63] The actual documents of freedoms were filed by surname: if a woman was no longer known as Jones, her relationship to her father's freedom could be undermined.

This treatment of women who had married unfree men extended even to those who had already bought into the patrimony. Mary Farr, daughter of a haberdasher, took up her patrimony but then went on to marry a non-freeman, who was in the army: 'she has (as she is informed) therby lost ye benefitt of her Freedome of this City'. She prayed for liberty 'to follow the trade of a milliner which she has long used, it being for her own Mainteynance, and her husband not intermedling with it'. Mary Farr's reference to intermeddling was echoed by another petitioner, Elizabeth Cossens. The daughter of a merchant tailor, she had served a full apprenticeship herself to a milliner but had married out of the freedom (to a man in royal service) and hence 'by reason of her marriage is uncapable of her freedom both by patrimony and service'. She requested that the court allow her 'to follow her said trade of a Milliner as they shall think it meet being for her own support her Husband not medling with it'.[64]

The word 'meddling' recalls the terms, enshrined in London's custumal, of feme sole trader status: a married woman whose husband did not 'intermeddle' with her trade could operate as if she was single,

---

[61] LMA, COL/CA/05/02/004.   [62] LMA, COL/CA/05/01/0003 (1691).
[63] Amy Louise Erickson, 'The Marital Economy in Comparative Perspective', in *The Marital Economy in Scandinavia and Britain 1400–1800*, ed. Maria Ågren and Amy Louise Erickson (Aldershot: Routledge, 2005), 11.
[64] LMA, COL/CA/05/02/004 (both).

exempt from the coverture of common law. This did not work exclusively in favour of women's economic autonomy; rather, it could be used to support a family economy by protecting a wife from her husband's debts and allowing women to take over the businesses of bankrupt husbands. In the later medieval period, some women avoided feme sole trader status, preferring the greater manoeuvrability of joint marital responsibility.[65] The wording of these pleas suggests another way of using feme sole trader status: to allow a woman whose marriage had taken her out of the freedom back into it as if she was still free and single.

These stories of freedom lost by marriage reveal families whose connection to the freedom was wrought and undone across several marriages and generations. Women's writing of this, and other, eras often refers to the losses women face in marrying into a new family. Margaret Cavendish's reflections on her autobiographical impulse bring it back to her conviction that should she not write, another Mrs Cavendish, her husband's future wife, might take her place: 'for my Lord having had two wives, I might easily have been mistaken, especially if I should dye, and my Lord marry again'.[66] Propertied women anticipated and faced frequent displacement from the dynasties, land and houses into which they were born. Something of the same process operated for city daughters. The pursuit of freedom by patrimony offers a testament to the extent to which gender differentiated city privilege: whilst it was abundantly clear that women could hold the freedom, it was always held conditionally, and it is not too much of a stretch to envisage the connection between this understanding of citizenship and that which came to explicitly exclude women from sensible participation in civic politics.

The petitions discussed in this chapter seem to present a story of women inadvertently or deliberately disenfranchised from the City's privileges. The Freedom of the City was ostensibly a binary system of inclusion or exclusion, but it was not so for women. Its application to wives and daughters, particularly in relation to patrimonies, exposed its fragility and its flexibility. The cumulative effect of the city customs relating to women, freedom and marriage looks akin to the ancient game of snakes and ladders. Marriage, widowhood and poorly planned paperwork were all liable to let them down. Not so for men, for whom the freedom, once gained, could not be lost. At one level, this imbalance is an accurate representation of the starkly different relation in which

---

[65] Marjorie K. McIntosh, 'The Benefits and Drawbacks of Femme Sole Status in England, 1300–1630', *Journal of British Studies* 44 (2005): 410–38.
[66] Margaret Cavendish, 'A True Relation of my Birth, Breeding, and Life' in her *Natures Pictures* (1656), 391.

women and men stood to the City and its institutions. But there is another way of reading the archive.

The accounts petitioners and clerks constructed, and which were endorsed by officials, represented women as plaintiffs for their rights, frustrated by a complex system that treated men as full subjects of the City and women as conditional ones. Men did not pursue petitions like this: their main cause for petitioning was to be translated from one company to another, a claim which was only once made by a woman in the petition archive. Petitioning might equally plausibly represent a formal structure by which the City compelled women to apply for inclusion, using the fees for redemptions or patrimonies, to buttress funds and perhaps to enhance or underline the role of the freedom itself. It was in some way useful to go through the motions of describing how married women and widows had lost their right to patrimony and restoring it generously. Performance was important to civic life, particularly in the late Stuart era. Guilds' powers had been confiscated and restored; the utility of trade controls was debated.

The process of petitioning was still a meaningful one, causing women to have to represent themselves as pleading citizens, entitled to urban privilege but removed from it largely by the effects of marriage or ignorance. It adds a missing piece to the history of the City: the piecemeal, grudgingly charitable incorporation of those excluded from the freedom as a means of maintaining the freedom's significance. Petitions add, too, to the history of women's work and its relationship with identity. Whether these women's words were transcribed authentically from their own mouths or were produced in the process of petitioning, such documents contributed to the construction of a gendered labour identity. The phrase 'a small shop' was the habitual description of the genuinely tiny stalls in the Royal Exchange's upper pawn, but also reflected the circumscribed aspirations understood to be appropriate for women. Susanna Russell was 'permitted' to keep 'a small shop in the Old Bailey'. Sarah Pannier was 'indulged to keep a small seamstress shop during her life'. Joan Hippisly was 'licenced to keep a little chandlers shop during the pleasure of this court', and Mary Clarke was 'admitted into the freedom' only 'to take apprentices who may work to help support her'. It was the court's officers, rather than female petitioners, who persistently described women's workplaces as circumscribed. And when women's petitions, most of them presumably drafted by a scrivener who knew the right formula, often presented a clear case to request admission to the freedom, the notes presented to the court by the Chamberlain or aldermen seemed to fall over themselves to make it sound difficult and exceptional. The very process of claiming a place in the freedom familiarised women with the City's rules and reminded them of their conditional place in its customs.

It is helpful, too, to consider the broader meanings of freedom in relation to women, cities and custom. London's customs were privileges, protecting City dwellers, by tradition, from arbitrary government. Within those privileges, the entitlement to freedom was a right, earned by labour or inheritance. For women it did not work in quite the same way: the right to freedom was a conditional qualification, bestowed only so long as its holder remained single or married the appropriate man. In a reversal of all the customs articulated here, in 1713, the Clockmakers' Company allowed the free single woman Mary Jevon to transfer her patrimonial freedom to her husband. The well-established position of women milliners in the Clockmakers' Company seems to have changed the rules.[67]

The work that the freedom did for women, both individually and collectively, in the late seventeenth-century City was important. It let them into companies and made their access to the market conditional. As an institution, the freedom's divisive power interacted with coverture to hedge women's place in both polity and market with restrictions. As such, the freedom's rules reflected the City's overall policy in relation to its female traders. Living with and working round those rules reminded women of the legal weight of marriage as well as the potential for using custom and petitioning to negotiate it. It offers a stark contrast to the capacity of both single and married women to make business lives in the wider city. Citizenship included women temporarily and conditionally, recognising their economic contribution, constraining any political implications and reinforcing the consequences of marriage by exercising indulgence. A woman's place in the City was, above all, contingent.

---

[67] Amy Louise Erickson, 'Eleanor Mosley and Other Milliners in the City of London Companies 1700–1750', *History Workshop Journal* 71 (2011): 152.

Conclusion

In 1658, aged forty, Apolonia Browne fell ill with smallpox in London. She made her will and died a week later, to be buried at her request in the vault built by her mother's family in St Michael, Cornhill. Amongst the legacies to her numerous nieces and nephews, ranging from beds, linen undergarments and a mare called Button, to a pepper mill and a diamond ring, she bequeathed to her sister Mary Sterry 'the pin pillow which her Daughter wrought with the Effigies of the King & Queene thereon'. This daughter, named Apolina after her aunt and grandmother, had died sixteen years before, aged eighteen, a lodger in the City. Her pincushion, embroidered with the king and his wife, which must have been made while Charles I was still king, and cherished by her aunt, went back to her mother. Apolonia Browne had two other nieces with the same name, daughters of her brothers. To one she left a bequest of a feather bed and £50. The other became a seamstress, married John Maddox, a silk-dyer, and in 1667 took on an apprentice named Frances Angell, the young woman whose story began this book.[1]

In families like this, the goods made by needlework circulated along with family names, clothes, stocks and debts. Apolonia Browne died in London, but her house was in Staffordshire, and her nieces, like her, moved between London and provincial England, carrying with them the skills of urban life and a sense of belonging to the churches and companies of the City. Sempstry, running shops and training apprentices were part of their social and economic capital.[2]

---

[1] TNA, PROB 11/290/203 (Apolonia Browne, 1658). Browne, who was single, had been the executor for her mother Appollonia Browne, previously Farfax (who had been twice widowed, and earlier in her life courted by Simon Forman), TNA, PROB 11/226/380 (1653); death of Mary Sterry's daughter, LMA P69/GRE/A/002/MS10232 (13 July 1642); Appollonia Maddox's birth, Derbyshire parish registers 1538–1812 (19 November 1640), www.ancestry.co.uk.

[2] LMA, CLA/024/05/249 (1669). Appollonia's sister Margaret Browne was also living in London and testified.

Frances Angell, Appollonia Maddox's troublesome apprentice, resisted her father's complaints about her wastage of her clothes and her mistress's offers to take her back after their disagreements and set off, she decided, to make her own living. Her subsequent life has left few traces; she may have gone on working as a seamstress until and after her marriage to a Westminster man nine years later. Apprenticeship, however contested and incomplete, gave her the tools to set up as a working gentlewoman. It gave her mistress a premium to invest in her seamstress business, a parallel trade to her husband's occupation. The money, skills and goods of apprentices and their mistresses were woven into the fabric of the early modern consumer revolution.

This book has reconstructed an institution within an institution: female apprenticeship within and around the ostensibly masculine guilds of early modern London. The apprentices who made up so prominent a part of early modern European urban communities modelled a masculine life cycle and work identity. Often represented as disorderly and troublesome, the figure of the apprentice also affirmed the boundaries of artisanal manhood, running up against mistresses and prostitutes or brothel-keepers, as well as maidservants. For apprenticeship to be archetypally male meant that women's work was, by default, outside the affirming structures that transmitted skills, protected quality and wages, and assured charity. Seeing women in apprenticeship shifts women's work into a different register. Apprenticeship gave to the work of both apprentices and mistresses a structure, a set of occupational categories and a route that could both map onto life cycle and adapt flexibly to it. It demonstrates the potential of women's work to be not just extensive and time-consuming but structured, regulated and valued.

Girls had always been apprenticed, both into housewifery and (largely textile) crafts, often outside guilds and sometimes in them. London's guilds, despite or perhaps because of its large contingent of female textile workers, were apparently unwelcoming to women for much of the sixteenth and early seventeenth centuries; single and married, women entered the sewing trade through more informal routes. The specific economic and social dislocations of the mid-seventeenth century made apprenticeship in the city more appealing to artisanal families and to gentry and clergy across England so that a new intake of young women joined city households, and city women took their premiums and trained them. The aftermath of the Fire made it somewhat easier to establish shops and businesses in the City, and from the 1670s, the flourishing upper pawn of the Royal Exchange provided a locale for seamstresses' shops. Outside the companies and the City, families made their own arrangements, often varying the length of service but still making a formal contract with clear shared expectations that could be contested in law, against the risks of violence, bankruptcy and lack of training.

Frances Angell and her peers, bringing high premiums from gentry families and aspiring to run shops, were at the prestigious end of a spectrum of service and apprenticeship. Their clothes and their businesses depended on the work of lace-makers, glovers, flaxdressers, silk-stocking seamers and the cutters of rabbit fur for shoes. The structure of formal apprenticeship was used by private families setting their girls to learn a trade across metropolitan London. It extended to govern the work of poorer girls in pinmaking and gloving, providing a compulsory route towards self-sufficiency, largely through the sewing trades, for orphans and paupers in the charge of parishes and hospitals. A commitment to training girls ran through the social hierarchy, from the families of labourers in Rotherhithe to those of royal heralds in Warwickshire. This was also a geographically extensive network. The provincial background of so many London apprentices, to which some at least returned, helped create a network of connections and tradition that drew girls to the city and into the sewing trades, and that fed knowledge about training, skill and goods back to the provinces. In towns and cities like Bristol, Oxford, York and Edinburgh, women were entering the guilds in similar ways, sometimes with considerable conflict and sometimes, as in York, with the effect of creating a newly female-dominated organisation.

The formal side of apprenticeship, its contracts and rules and the litigation that sometimes ensued when these were broken, unsettles the well-established view of women's work as generally underpaid, unskilled and informal. In companies and, more widely, outside them, young women's labour could be organised and recognised, with an investment in training that anticipated future rewards for both mistresses and apprentices.

The later seventeenth century was a period of general decline in apprenticeship and guild membership, and the decreased economic status of guilds and companies seem to have made it easier for women to find a place in the corporate institution. Women's payments for freedoms helped support both the companies and the corporation of London. This suggests that we should shift the discussion of guild decline into a different register, by looking at who guilds, companies and freedom were serving. Women who were apprenticed, became mistresses and became free benefitted from an institutional belonging which was fractured and contingent but significant both to them and in their economic context. Attempts to contain trading privileges to those who were free of the City and of a company continued into the 1700s, and the women who took up freedom through petitions and redemption suggest they found ongoing advantages in guild membership in terms of charity and civic identity and participation as well as in trade. Being of the City might be associated not with freedom from traditional structures and constraints but with recognised membership of those structures.

Part of that membership involved planning, and this is important for understanding women's life cycles. The dominance and significance of marriage in economic and social histories of women tends to mean that their young life is represented as essentially responsive: agency comes in saying yes, or no, to marriage. But the majority of early modern women did not marry until their mid-twenties, and a substantial minority of them did not marry at all. The evidence of wills and indentures shows the existence of a recognised pathway into independent adult life through apprenticeships that were planned, with care or fortuitous networking, by parents, grandparents, kin and friends, with the idea that artisan skills would make them a living both before marriage and after. Craft and business were part of the working life cycle of many women, and apprenticeship provided a generational structure of skills transmission that scaffolded this.

However work lives were planned, marital status made a critical difference to how women used their apprentices. Single mistresses had a distinctive work life and domestic arrangements, living on their own with apprentices as householders or as lodgers. They took apprentices occasionally and in small numbers. Their significance to the apprenticeship market was less in training numbers of apprentices than in the part they played in creating generations of freewomen, transmitting skills and freedom between women. They constituted an alternative to the patriarchal master–apprentice relationship, which required a married couple to function effectively.

The dramas of apprentices and mistresses have also revealed some of the ways that work was woven into women's identity. This is a critical addition to the work, largely by literary critics, on the nature of the female self in early modern England, which has traced, amongst other themes, embeddedness in family networks, women's role as mediators, and narratives of spiritual humility. In the records of work, we see how girls worked themselves into women, testing the rules of workplace and household decorum as they grew and learning the rules of the game. Alongside them wives and widows created roles for themselves as mistresses, a part of many adult women's lives that brought authority and economic independence.

As girls and wives worked at craft, they participated in the crafting of gender. It was through work, before marriage, that early modern women sent their daughters out into the world. As they laboured in apprenticeships and service, young women learned their adult roles: competence, ingenuity, industry and appraisal paved the way for effective working lives as wives, spinsters or widows. Those lives were shaped by gendered expectations more complex and subtle than those portrayed in popular advice, sermons or the norms of politeness. Repeatedly, though, women were reminded of the contingency of their place in the urban economy, the rewards of their labour and their claims to citizenship.

In the depositions to the Mayor's Court and in petitions of complaint to the sessions court and the Chamberlain, we have glimpsed the language and ideas that both structured and reflected working lives. The cogent articulation of what was, and was not, work by girls and their families suggests that the rights that came with an apprenticeship contract gave some young women the authority to grumble, fight and resist. Tensions with mistresses exploded in resentment and defiance, more than subterfuge. The language of civility and the performance of manners were accompanied by female industry; working women were the creators and the performers of civility. Workplace skills were weighed and appraised by both employers and parents, suggesting a shared culture of expertise in which the speed and skill of a needle could be readily estimated. Ingenuity, care and hard work alike were prized, if not always well rewarded.

The institution of female apprenticeship thus established a capillary network of artisanal training which had both a practical and a cultural impact. It also functioned to disseminate the convention of apprenticeship and freedoms so that girls' and women's participation in skilled training, with formal contracts and paperwork, took roots in the strategies of families from the elites to the poor, and ties of kinship, friendship and neighbourhood became ties of employment.

This networked system of training and skill had an impact on family economies and on London's occupations and markets. The premiums paid by well-off families for their daughters to train to keep shops helped women set up businesses: they were an investment both in women and in trade. The apprenticeship system made it possible for married women, spinsters and widows, most of them without formal training, to be paid for training girls, channelling women's domestic and entrepreneurial skills into productive resources. At the same time, the rules of the freedom and the limits imposed by guilds on women's work helped perpetuate barriers to economic participation in the City, ensuring that the labour market of girls and women was controlled. Women's economic agency was encouraged and constrained. Guilds and companies reinscribed the limits on married women's economic status, making them always subject to their husbands, and problematic in the paperwork.

Like the 'city of seamstresses' described by Clare Crowston in eighteenth-century Paris, the labour of women on seams, lace, trims, shoes and hats was everywhere, and the individual experience of shopping for tailored or personalised goods kept seamstresses' work in the public eye. Relations between customers, artisans and shopkeepers wove the personal and economic together. Women and men knew well how to appraise the quality and manufacture of sewn goods: the seamstress's labour, and that of the button-maker, the pin-maker and the silk-stocking maker, was visible and quantifiable. In the satirical '10 Pleasures of Marriage', attributed (implausibly) to Aphra Behn, the seamstress features as the accomplice of the consuming wife, popping up with predictable regularity. She is an interruption to marital harmony, assisting the wife to make demands for more and finer childbed linen, belly bands, and navel clouts, as well as someone to assist her with the labour of housewifery. When the pleasures of marriage include the delivery of a daughter, she too will be subsumed into sewing: 'you will in time see what a pretty sweet Gentlewoman she'l grow to be; how modestly & orderly she goes to learn to write and read; but most especially to prick samples; which perhaps she'l be wholly perfect in, before she hath half learned to sow: nay its probable that she'l be an Artist at the making of Bone-lace, though she was never taught it'.[3] The coarse double meanings behind all this embed sewing and sex as female vocation. But the surface story also writes the seamstress into marriage like an accomplice, the creator of the intimate garments that shaped womanhood.

Actual seamstresses had close bonds with real women (and with male customers too) but they were also often married women themselves; the fantasy seamstress effectively conceals the place of sewing work in the family economy. The world of early modern work was often less rigidly gendered than the binary oppositions of contemporary rhetoric. Sewing and selling clothes involved women and men in shared businesses and workplaces. But the role of mistresses and female customers, the mothers, grandmothers and sisters of apprentices, helped make sewing a female world of work and patronage.

By the mid-eighteenth century, seamstresses were solidly established on the urban scene, their business cards attesting beautifully to the importance of self-advertisement and the role of businesswomen in the

---

[3] A. Marsh, *The Ten Pleasures of Marriage Relating All the Delights and Contentments That Are Mask'd under the Bands of Matrimony* (1682), 202.

heart of early modern cities.[4] Hogarth's sisters maintained him with their sewing; Charles Gray's mother and sisters, members of the Antrobus family who were prominent at the Royal Exchange, kept a milliners' shop. Fanny Burney's mother and grandmother made fans to support the family.[5] Making a living and running shops was in the blood of eighteenth-century urban family life, and so was the female expertise that went with it. The age of consumption was founded on the groundwork of women sewing, starching, unpicking, laundering, managing shops, arranging apprenticeships and training girls.

In London, the peak of female guild apprenticeship was in the 1690s, though it continued strong from 1720 to 1780, the decreased numbers in companies most likely due to the shift of sewing business and clothes shops out of the City of London, to Westminster and elsewhere where guild membership was not necessary. It is useful to see the developments traced here, of women making a place for formal training, as the foundations of the productive working lives of so many eighteenth-century women; of the increasing identification of millinery with women; and of the clothing-related consumer tasks taken up by women. At the same time, guilds were following the Europe-wide pattern of continuing to limit female autonomy and recognition in artisanal trades. With less outright conflict, London's guilds instead made compromises and charged fines to let women in whilst keeping them to the model of the 'little shop'. The growth of commerce outside the City meant that the place of the Royal Exchange swiftly waned, and many other commercial opportunities flourished. More generally, many women of the middling sort incorporated commerce into their lives as wives, single women and widows.

We get some sense from these records of women's aspirations. Hester Hudson planned to get some patterns and run her own shop; Christiana Hutchins refused to sit on a stool and sew, preferring either to be a chambermaid or to somehow get an estate of her own. Apprenticeship gave girls choices within a constrained world; it helped make single life economically feasible, enabled women to be free of the City in their own right and gave married women money and the practice of supervision. The patterns their work laid out established precedents for labour and reward within a structure of custom, reward, respectability and accountability.

---

[4] These cards have been discussed recently in Amy Erickson's curated exhibition, www.cam.ac.uk/citywomen.

[5] Amy Louise Erickson, 'Esther Sleepe, Fan-Maker, and Her Family', *Eighteenth-Century Life* 42, no. 2 (2018): 15–37.

The new world they helped make had damaging and constraining outcomes too. The energy of shopkeepers drew on the ill-rewarded labour of seamstresses and outworkers. The frustrations of mistresses led to violence and cruelty. The Exchange and its goods were connected to the slave trade; when linen goods were exchanged for sugar, profits from the labour and sale of enslaved men and women led straight to the shop counter.

Early modern London was a city of industrious, ingenious girls and women making a living constructing shirts, ruffs, buttons and pins; starching linen and baking pastry; adapting their work lives to marriage and motherhood; returning to trade in their widowhood; and eventually becoming authoritative mistresses of the next generation of working women. Seeing women in guilds, as mistresses, and in shops changes the picture of work, of the city and of the economic and social structures of the nation.

Appendix   Who's Who

Frances Angell, b. 1652 in London to Robert Angell, gentleman, and his wife, Frances, who died in 1653. Apprenticed to Appollonia Maddox (née Browne), seamstress, and her husband, John Maddox, silk-dyer. Apprenticeship breakdown leads to litigation over premiums in 1669. Accused of spoiling her clothes, rudeness and resistance.

Katherine Allen née Roe. Married Herbert Allen of Lindfield, Sussex, in London in 1655; Herbert was freed in the Haberdashers' Company after apprenticeship to his father. They kept shop in the Royal Exchange, took apprentices from 1656, including Katherine Venner, and had children from 1657. Katherine was widowed in 1668, and both her children died before they were twenty; she kept her shop until the 1690s when she handed it over to Mary and William Barton.

Frances Bickley b. 1669 to Francis Bickley, gentleman, of Hollarton, Warwickshire, and his wife, Mary, with three older siblings and two younger; her sister Sarah was also apprenticed. She was apprenticed in 1686 to John Johnson, dyer, and his wife Mary, milliner, in Poultry. She was accused of theft and complained of poor food and violence and turned over in 1688 to Mary Barton, milliner at the Exchange, with £20; in 1689, she sued, supported by her uncle Robert, for the return of her premium.

Rachel Erskine, c. 1650–1718, one of three daughters of William Erskin DD and Rachel née Kinaston. Erskine or Aerskine became free after apprenticeship in the Merchant Taylors' Company, worked as a seamstress and ran a linen shop in the Royal Exchange. She took seven apprentices in the period 1673–93 and lived with Frances Antrobus in St Mary Abchurch, running the shop until at least 1710.

Ann Gray, daughter of George Gray, barber, who died before 1689. Ann was apprenticed in 1687 with a premium of £40 to

Sarah Cleave, seamstress in the Salters' Company, who had been apprenticed herself, and subsequently married William Frost, scrivener. Ann sued out her indentures two years into her apprenticeship and then sued for her premium, supported by her brother, gaining back £30 of it.

Hester Hudson, brought up in London, apprenticed to Mary and William Bickerstaff, barber-surgeons, in 1650; brother Lawrence and sister Elizabeth helped make an agreement, the length of which was disputed. She sued for her indentures in 1654 after her apprenticeship broke down following illness. Possibly died in 1662, St Bride's Fleet Street. Hester's mistress, Mary Bickerstaff, dying in 1687, left money to apprentice her grandsons and granddaughter.

Martha Hunlock 1624–90 née Osbaldeston. She inherited a shop lease at the New Exchange from her father, married Francis Hunlock, a painter-stainer who had a shop in the Royal Exchange by 1668, and took up a shop lease herself after his death in 1679, taking an apprentice milliner in 1687. Hunlock bequeathed her shop to Martha Stalman.

Christiana Hutchins, b. 1659 at St Mary-le-Bow to Joseph and Dorothy Hutchins, with two older sisters; her father died before 1669, and her mother remarried. She was apprenticed aged about ten in 1669 to Mary Haslam, seamstress, and her husband, William, in the Barber-Surgeons' Company with a £20 premium. She sued out her indentures in 1673 and was taken on by Mary Culpepper. Her uncle Robert Hutchins sued for her premiums at the Mayor's Court, alleging violence and poor training; the Haslams accused her of spoiling her work and her food. Her uncle died in 1680 and left his land in St Giles Cripplegate to be divided between Christiana and her two sisters. Christiana married George Curtis in St Mary-le-Bow, 1703.

Mary Jones, daughter of Elizabeth Wolfe, who remarried after being widowed. Mary was apprenticed to Frances and Richard Carey for £10, with a further £15 after three years, but left after eighteen months. Her mother sued out her indentures, and she married Richard Fudge in 1666; a lawsuit for her premium was prosecuted on her behalf by Robert Blaney.

Hester Pinney, 1658–1740, daughter of Presbyterian minister John Pinney of Bristol. Hester worked in the family lace business and ran a shop in the New Exchange with her sisters,

Jane and Rachel, and her sister-in-law, Mary. She lent money to Henry Wallop MP (1657–91) and arranged an apprenticeship for his illegitimate daughter in 1693.

Frances Spillett née Blennerhassett c. 1650–1734. Married John Spillett, mercer, and they lived on Broad Street with several children. They kept two shops in the Royal Exchange, taking a series of apprentices male and female, including Lucy Maes and Agnes Blennerhassett. John died in Hackney in 1733, Frances in 1734.

Dorothy Stable b. 1668, Pontefract, to Leonard and Dorothy Stable; two younger sisters; mother dies 1682. Apprenticed in March 1683, aged fifteen, to Ann and Giles Bell, Goldsmiths' Company, with a premium of £15 or £20. Ann Bell (née Kent) was freed after apprenticeship in 1681. Ann Bell died in 1685, and Dorothy was turned over to her sister, Frances Kent. Dorothy sued for her premiums at the Mayor's Court in 1685, alleging that she expected to be free after five years. Dorothy died in 1698, single, in Pontefract.

Katherine Venner, b. 1642, Warwickshire, to Richard Venour, clergyman, who died 1662, and his wife Margaret. Apprenticed in 1656 to Herbert and Katherine Allen with a premium of £50. Her apprenticeship was dissolved in 1661, and she went to court to recover her premium in 1662, supported by her brother Thomas. The case involved a short contract, rudeness, theft and lies.

Bibliography

Abbreviations

GL – Guildhall Library
LAA – London Apprenticeship Abstracts, www.findmypast.co.uk
LMA – London Metropolitan Archives
London Lives – *London Lives 1690–1800*, www.londonlives.org (version 2.0 March 2018)
MC – Mercers' Company
ROLLCO – Records of London's Livery Companies Online, www.londonroll.org
TNA – The National Archives

Manuscript Sources

Bristol University Special Collections
Pinney Papers, Red Box 2
Clothworkers' Company
Apprentice Register 1661
Orders of Courts 1665–83
Drapers' Company
Apprentice Books 2–3
Boyd's Roll (manuscript register of apprentices and freemen)
Court of Assistants Books MB 8, 41, 42
Goldsmiths' Company
Guildhall Library (GL)
Barber Surgeons' Company Apprentice Bindings 1657–72 MS 5266/1
Barber Surgeons' Company Court Minute Book MS 5257/6 1689–1701
Broderers' Company Court Minute Book 1679–1709 MS 14657/1
Coopers' Company Court Minute Book 1687–96, MS 56026/6A
Glovers' Company Court Minute Book 1675–79 MS 4591/1
Haberdashers' Company Register of Apprentice Bindings MS 15860/6–7
Merchant Taylors' Company Court Minutes MS 34010/7
Merchant Taylors' Company Quarterage Book MS 34042
Merchant Taylors' Company Register of Apprentice Bindings MS 34038/16–17
Merchant Taylors' Freedom Registers MS 34018/5
Skinners' Company Apprentice Bindings MS 30,719/2

Skinners' Company Court Book 1687–97 MS 30,708
Weavers' Company Court Minute Book 1653–4 MS 4655/2
Weavers' Company Court Minute Book 1666–8 MS 4655/4
Weavers' Company Ordinance and Record Book 1577–1641 MS 4647
London Metropolitan Archives (LMA)
All Hallows Lombard Street Parish Register P69/ALH4/B/045/MS18976
Christ's Hospital, Children's Registers 1659–1704 CLC/210/F/003/MS12818/005-006
City of London Sessions Papers CLA/047/LJ (1649–1700)
Commissary Court Wills GL, MS 9172/102
Court of Aldermen Papers COL/CA/05/01/0001-5
Court of Aldermen Petitions COL/CA/05/02/001-4
Freedom Admissions Papers COL/CHD/FR/02 (Ancestry)
Hobbayne's Charity ACC/0933
Holy Trinity Minories, Register of Marriages P69/TRI2/A/008/MS09243
Inventory of Herbert Allen CLA/002/02/01/0570, no. 215
Inventory of Richard Eardley CLA/002/02/01/0276
Land Tax MS 113616/3-34 (1692–1710) (Ancestry)
Marriage Assessments COL/CHD/LA/04
Mayor's Court Interrogatories 1640–1700 CLA/024/05
Mayor's Court Original Bills CLA/024/02
Middlesex Sessions Books MJ/SB/B (1640–1700)
Middlesex Sessions Papers MJ/SP (1641–2; 1662–1700)
Register of Freedom Admissions COL/CHD/FR/01/003
Royal Exchange: Accounts of money received of tenants CLA/ 062/04/16
St Andrew Holborn Register of Baptisms P82/AND/A/001/MS06667/004
St Botolph Aldgate Register of Marriages P69/BOT2/A/012/MS09230/001
St Bride Fleet Street Register P69/BRI/A/005/MS06540/002
St Dunstan's Stepney Register of Marriages P93/DUN/269
St Giles Cripplegate Apprenticeship Indentures P69/GIS/B/049/MS08476/001
St Giles Cripplegate Parish Registers P69/GIS/A/002/MS06419/005-7
St Gregory by St Paul Parish Register P69/GRE/A/002/MS10232
St Helen's Bishopsgate Parish Registers P69/HEL/A/002/MS06831/001-2
St Katherine Coleman Apprenticeship Indentures P69/KAT1/B/032/MS07740
St Mary Bothaw Apprentice Certificates P69/SWI/B/019/MS03369
St Mary le Bow Parish Register P69/MRY7/A/002/MS04997
St Olave Hart Street Register of Marriages and Burials P69/OLA1/A/002/MS28869
St Paul's Cathedral Peculiar Court Probate Inventories CLC/313/K/C/010/MS19504/007
St Stephen Coleman Street Parish Register P69/STE1/A/002/MS04449
Westminster Sessions Papers WJ/SP (1646–1700)
Mercers' Company (MC)
Gresham Repertories 1626–69, 1669–76, 1678–1722
Acts of Court 1669–75
The National Archives (TNA)
Chancery Depositions Pinney v. *Wallop* C24/1160, *Wallop* v. *Pinney* C24/1158

Chancery Pleadings Hester Pinney v. John Wallop C10 403/40, John Wallop v. Nathaniel Pinney C7 381/1, Baker v. Edwards C6/386/47
Chapel of the Hospital, Spitalfields (General Register Office: Registers of Births, Marriages and Deaths surrendered to the Non-parochial Registers Commissions), RG4/4643 (Ancestry)
Fleet Register RG 7/12 (Ancestry)
'Miss Goreing's Account Book', C114/182/32
State Papers Domestic, James II SP 29
Wills, PROB 11

Westminster Archives
St Clement Danes Parish Apprenticeship Indentures and Registers, CD/PA *London Lives* WCCDPA364000030
St Clement Danes Vestry Minutes, 1 June 1686 – 24 October 1699 *London Lives* WCCDEP358020035
Parish registers, and others where noted, consulted on www.ancestry.co.uk.

Digital Sources

1692 Poll Tax: data created by James Alexander generously provided by Olwen Myhill at the Centre for Metropolitan History
Ancestry www.ancestry.co.uk
London Apprenticeship Abstracts and *Haberdashers Apprentices and Freemen* datasets via www.findmypast.co.uk
Four Shillings in the Pound Aid 1693/4: The City of London, the City of Westminster, Middlesex (London: Centre for Metropolitan History, 1992), *British History Online*, www.british-history.ac.uk/no-series/london-4s-pound/1693-4/broad-street-ward-all-hallows-the-wall.
London Lives 1690–1800 www.londonlives.org (version 2.0 March 2018)
Michael Scott, ed., *Apprenticeship Disputes in the Lord Mayor's Court of London, 1573–1723* (London: British Record Society, 2016), data generously provided by Patrick Wallis and Michael Scott
Old Bailey Proceedings Online www.oldbaileyonline.org (version 8.0 March 2018)
ROLLCO www.londonroll.org. Underlying data from the project was generously provided by Mark Merry

Printed Primary Sources

Place of publication is London unless otherwise stated.
A General Description of All Trades, Digested in Alphabetical Order. 1747.
Advice to the Women and Maidens of London Shewing, That Instead of Their Usual Pastime, and Education in Needlework … It Were Far More Necessary and Profitable to Apply Themselves to the Right Understanding and Practice of the Method of Keeping Books of Account … by One of That Sex. 1678.
An Answer to the Character of an Exchange-Wench, or, a Vindication of an Exchange-Woman. 1675.
Ape-Gentle-Woman, or The Character of an Exchange-Wench. 1675.

Barlow, Edward, *Barlow's Journal of His Life at Sea in King's Ships, East & West Indiamen & Other Merchantmen from 1659 to 1703*, edited by Alfred Lubbock. London: Hurst & Blackett, 1934.

Bohun, William. *Privilegia Londini: Or, The Laws, Customs, and Priviledges of the City of London.* 1702.

Bruce, John, ed. *Diary of John Manningham: Of the Middle Temple, and of Bradbourne, Kent, Barrister-at-Law, 1602–1603.* London: J. B. Nichols & Sons, 1868.

Collyer, Joseph. *The Parent's and Guardian's Directory, and the Youth's Guide, in the Choice of a Profession or Trade.* 1761.

Erasmus, Desiderius. *De Civilitate Morum Puerilium.* 1534.

F., J. *The Merchant's Ware-House Laid Open: Or, the Plain Dealing Linnen-Draper.* 1696.

Freshfield, Edwin, ed., *The Vestry Minute Books of the Parish of St. Bartholomew Exchange in the City of London.* London: Rixon and Arnold, 1890.

Gouge, William. *Of Domesticall Duties: Eight Treatises.* 1634.

Holme, Randall. *The Academy of Armory.* London, 1688.

Jessey, Henry. *The Exceeding Riches of Grace Advanced by the Spirit of Grace.* 1647.

Kind, Ehver. *London's-Nonsuch; or, the Glory of the Royal Exchange.* 1668.

Latham, Robert and William Matthews, eds. *The Diary of Samuel Pepys: A New and Complete Transcription.* London: Harper Collins, 1995.

Makin, Bathsua. *An Essay to Revive the Antient Education of Gentlewomen in Religion, Manners, Arts & Tongues.* 1673.

Marsh, A. *The Ten Pleasures of Marriage Relating All the Delights and Contentments That Are Mask'd under the Bands of Matrimony.* 1682.

Marsh, Bower. *Records of the Worshipful Company of Carpenters I: Apprentices' Entry Books 1654–1994.* Oxford University Press, 1913.

Nuttall, Geoffrey, ed. *Letters of John Pinney, 1679–1699.* Oxford University Press, 1939.

P., T. *A Brief Memorial Wherein the Present Case of the Antient Leasees, the Inward Pawn Sub-Tenants, and the Outward Pawn Present Tenants, of the Royal Exchange.* 1674.

Phillips, Henry Laverock. *Annals of the Worshipful Company of Joiners of the City of London.* Privately Printed, 1915.

Ridge, C. H. *Records of the Worshipful Company of Shipwrights.* Bognor Regis: Phillimore, 1939.

The Gossips Braule, or the Women Weare the Breeches. 1655.

The Humble Petition and Case of the Tobacco-Pipe-Makers of the Cities of London and Westminster in Behalf of Themselves, and the Rest of Their Brethren, through the Kingdom of England and Dominion of Wales. 1695.

Vincent, Thomas, *God's Terrible Voice in the City.* 1667.

Ward, Ned. *The London Spy Compleat.* 1703.

Woolley, Hannah. *A Guide to Ladies, Gentlewomen and Maids &c.* 1668.

Woolley, Hannah. *A Supplement to the Queen-Like Closet.* 1673.

Woolley, Hannah. *The Gentlewomans Companion; or, a Guide to the Female Sex.* 1673.

Young, Sidney. *The Annals of the Barber-Surgeons of London.* London: Blades, East & Blades, 1890.

Selected Secondary Works

Ågren, Maria, ed. *Making a Living, Making a Difference: Gender and Work in Early Modern European Society*. Oxford University Press, 2017.

Amussen, Susan Dwyer. 'Punishment, Discipline, and Power: The Social Meanings of Violence in Early Modern England'. *Journal of British Studies* 34, no. 1 (1995): 1–34.

Archer, Ian. *The Pursuit of Stability: Social Relations in Elizabethan London*. Cambridge University Press, 1991.

Baer, William C. 'Early Retailing: London's Shopping Exchanges, 1550–1700'. *Business History* 49, no. 1 (2007): 29–51.

Bailey, Joanne. 'Favoured or Oppressed? Married Women, Property and "Coverture" in England, 1660–1800'. *Continuity and Change* 17, no. 3 (2002): 351–72.

Barron, Caroline. 'The "Golden Age" of Women in Medieval London'. *Reading Medieval Studies* 15 (1989): 35–58.

Bateson, Mary. *Borough Customs*, vol. 1. London: Selden Society, 1904.

Beattie, Cordelia. 'Your Oratrice: Women's Petitions to the Late Medieval Court of Chancery'. In *Women, Agency and the Law, 1300–1700*, edited by Bronach Kane and Fiona Williamson, 17–30. London: Pickering & Chatto, 2013.

Beaudry, Mary C. *Findings: The Material Culture of Needlework and Sewing*. New Haven, CT: Yale University Press, 2007.

Ben-Amos, Ilana Krausman. *Adolescence and Youth in Early Modern England*. London: Yale University Press, 1994.

'Women Apprentices in the Trade and Crafts of Early Modern Bristol'. *Continuity and Change* 6, no. 2 (1991): 227–52.

Bennett, Judith M. *Ale, Beer and Brewsters in England: Women's Work in a Changing World, 1300–1600*. Oxford University Press, 1996.

History Matters: Patriarchy and the Challenge of Feminism. Philadelphia: University of Pennsylvania Press, 2006.

Berlin, Michael. 'Guilds in Decline? London Livery Companies and the Rise of a Liberal Economy, 1600–1800'. In *Guilds, Innovation, and the European Economy, 1400–1800*, edited by S. R. Epstein and Maarten Prak, 316–42. Cambridge University Press, 2008.

Berry, Helen. '"Polite Consumption": Shopping in Eighteenth-Century England'. *Transactions of the Royal Historical Society* 12 (2002): 375–94.

Bicks, Caroline. 'Incited Minds: Rethinking Early Modern Girls'. *Shakespeare Studies* 44 (2016): 180–99.

Birt, Sarah. 'Women, Guilds and the Tailoring Trades: The Occupational Training of Merchant Taylors' Company Apprentices in Early Modern London'. *The London Journal* 46, no. 2 (2020): 146–64.

Bourdieu, Pierre. *The Logic of Practice*. Stanford University Press, 1990.

Brock, Aske Laursen and Misha Ewen. 'Women's Public Lives: Navigating the East India Company, Parliament and Courts in Early Modern England'. *Gender & History* 33, no 1 (March 2021): 3–23.

Brooks, Christopher. 'Apprenticeship, Social Mobility and the Middling Sort, 1550–1800'. In *The Middling Sort of People*, edited by Christopher Brooks and Jonathan Barry, 52–83. London: Macmillan, 1994.

Chakravarty, Urvashi. 'Bound to Serve: Apprenticeship Indentures at the Folger'. *The Collation*, 5 January 2018, http://collation.folger.edu/2018/01/indentures/.

Chedgzoy, Kate. 'Other Maids: Religion, Race and Relationships between Girls in Early Modern London'. In *Literary Cultures and Medieval and Early Modern Childhoods*, edited by Naomi J. Miller and Diane Purkiss, 187–201. Basingstoke: Palgrave Macmillan, 2019.

Clark, Alice. *Working Life of Women in the Seventeenth Century*. Edited by Amy Louise Erickson. London: Routledge, 1992.

Coates, Ben. *The Impact of the English Civil War on the Economy of London, 1642–50*. Aldershot: Routledge, 2004.

Coffin, Judith G. 'Gender and the Guild Order: The Garment Trades in Eighteenth-Century Paris'. *Journal of Economic History* 54, no. 4 (1994): 768–93.

Collins, Jessica. 'Jane Holt, Milliner, and Other Women in Business: Apprentices, Freewomen and Mistresses in the Clothworkers' Company, 1606–1800'. *Textile History* 44, no. 1 (2013): 72–94.

Consitt, Frances. *The London Weavers' Company*. Oxford: Clarendon Press, 1933.

Cowan, Brian. 'What Was Masculine About the Public Sphere? Gender and the Coffeehouse Milieu in post-Restoration England'. *History Workshop Journal* 51 (2001): 127–57.

Crawford, Patricia. *Parents of Poor Children in England 1580–1800*. Oxford University Press, 2010.

——. '"The Poorest She": Women and Citizenship in Early Modern England'. In *The Putney Debates of 1647: The Army, the Levellers and the English State*, edited by Michael Mendle, 197–217. Cambridge University Press, 2001.

Crowston, Clare Haru. 'Engendering the Guilds: Seamstresses, Tailors, and the Clash of Corporate Identities in Old Regime France'. *French Historical Studies* 23, no. 2 (2000): 339–71.

——. *Fabricating Women: The Seamstresses of Old Regime France, 1675–1791*. Durham, NC: Duke University Press, 2001.

——. *Credit, Fashion, Sex: Economies of Regard in Old Regime France*. Durham, NC: Duke University Press, 2013.

Declauer, Harald and Bibi Panhuysen. 'Dressed to Work: A Gendered Comparison of the Tailoring Trades in the Northern and Southern Netherlands, 16th to 18th Centuries'. In *Craft Guilds in the Early Modern Low Countries: Work, Power and Representation*, edited by Catharina Lis, Jan Lucassen, Maarten Roy Prak and Hugh Soly, 133–56. London: Routledge, 2017.

Doolittle, I. G. 'The City of London's Debt to Its Orphans, 1694–1767'. *Historical Research* 56, no. 133 (1983): 46–59.

Doolittle, Ian. 'The City of London in the Eighteenth Century: Corporate Pressures and Their Implications'. In *Revisiting The Polite and Commercial People: Essays in Georgian Politics, Society, and Culture in Honour of Professor Paul Langford*, edited by Elaine Chalus and Perry Gauci, 101–18. Oxford University Press, 2019.

Draper, Helen. 'Mary Beale and Art's Lost Laborers: Women Painter Stainers'. *Early Modern Women* 10, no. 1 (2015): 141–51.

Dumont, Dora. 'Women and Guilds in Bologna: The Ambiguities of "Marginality"'. *Radical History Review* 1998, no. 70 (1998): 5–25.

Dunne, Derek. 'Sign Here Please: _____ Blank Forms from the Folger Collection'. *The Collation*, 30 March 2017. http://collation.folger.edu/2017/03/sign-here-please/.

Earle, Peter. 'The Female Labour Market in London in the Late Seventeenth and Early Eighteenth Centuries'. *Economic History Review* 42, no. 3 (1989): 328–53.

The Making of the English Middle Class: Business, Society, and Family Life in London, 1660–1730. Berkeley: University of California Press, 1989.

Epstein, S. R. 'Craft Guilds, Apprenticeship, and Technological Change in Preindustrial Europe'. *Journal of Economic History* 58, no. 3 (1998): 684–713.

Erickson, Amy Louise. 'Common Law versus Common Practice: The Use of Marriage Settlements in Early Modern England'. *Economic History Review* 43 (1990): 21–39.

'The Marital Economy in Comparative Perspective'. In *The Marital Economy in Scandinavia and Britain 1400–1800*, edited by Maria Ågren and Amy Louise Erickson, 3-20. Aldershot: Ashgate, 2005.

'Married Women's Occupations in Eighteenth-Century London'. *Continuity and Change* 23, no. 2 (2008): 267–307.

'Eleanor Mosley and Other Milliners in the City of London Companies 1700–1750'. *History Workshop Journal* 71 (2011): 147–72.

'Mistresses and Marriage: Or, a Short History of the Mrs'. *History Workshop Journal* 78 (2014): 39–57.

'Esther Sleepe, Fan-Maker, and Her Family'. *Eighteenth-Century Life* 42, no. 2 (2018): 15–37.

Ewen, Misha. 'Women Investors and the Virginia Company in the Early Seventeenth Century'. *Historical Journal* 62, no. 4 (2019): 853–74.

Finn, Margot. 'Women, Consumption and Coverture in England, c. 1760–1860'. *Historical Journal* 39, no. 3 (1996): 703–22.

Fisher, James, 'Inventing a New Form of Labour: Early Indentures for Parish Apprentices, 1598-1630', University of Exeter History of Economy Research Blog, January 2021.

French, Henry. 'Gentlemen: Remaking the English Ruling Class'. In *A Social History of England, 1500–1750*, edited by Keith Wrightson, 269-89. Cambridge University Press, 2017.

Froide, Amy M. 'Marital Status as a Category of Difference: Singlewomen and Widows in Early Modern England'. In *Singlewomen in the European Past, 1250–1800*, edited by Judith M. Bennett and Amy M. Froide, 236–9. Philadelphia: University of Pennsylvania Press, 1999.

'Hidden Women: Rediscovering the Singlewomen of Early Modern England'. *Local Population Studies* 68 (2002): 26–41.

Never Married: Singlewomen in Early Modern England. Oxford University Press, 2005.

'Learning to Invest: Women's Education in Arithmetic and Accounting in Early Modern England'. *Early Modern Women* 10, no. 1 (2015): 3–26.

Silent Partners: Women as Public Investors during Britain's Financial Revolution, 1690–1750. Oxford University Press, 2016.

Fuentes, Marisa J. *Dispossessed Lives: Enslaved Women, Violence, and the Archive.* Philadelphia: University of Pennsylvania Press, 2016.

Furdell, Elizabeth Lane. *Publishing and Medicine in Early Modern England.* University of Rochester Press, 2002.

Gadd, Ian and Patrick Wallis, eds. *Guilds, Society and Economy in London 1450–1800.* London: Centre for Metropolitan History, 2002.

Garwood, Sasha. *Early Modern English Noblewomen and Self-Starvation: The Skull Beneath the Skin.* London: Routledge, 2019.

George, M. Dorothy. *London Life in the 18th Century.* London: Capricorn Books, 1965.

Gerber, Haim. 'Social and Economic Position of Women in an Ottoman City, Bursa, 1600–1700'. *International Journal of Middle East Studies* 12, no. 3 (1980): 231–44.

Glaisyer, Natasha. *The Culture of Commerce in England, 1660–1720.* Woodbridge: Boydell & Brewer, 2006.

Glass, D. V. *London Inhabitants within the Walls 1695.* London: London Record Society, 1966.

Gossard, Julia M. 'Breaking a Child's Will'. *French Historical Studies* 42, no. 2 (2019): 239–59.

Gowing, Laura. '"The Freedom of the Streets": Women and Social Space, 1560–1640'. In *Londinopolis: Essays in the Cultural and Social History of Early Modern London*, edited by Mark S. R. Jenner and Paul Griffiths, 130–53. Manchester University Press, 2000.

'The Haunting of Susan Lay: Servants and Mistresses in Seventeenth-Century England'. *Gender & History* 14, no. 2 (2002): 183–201.

Grassby, Richard. *Kinship and Capitalism: Marriage, Family, and Business in the English-Speaking World, 1580–1740.* Cambridge University Press, 2001.

Gutierrez, Nancy A. *'Shall She Famish Then?': Female Food Refusal in Early Modern England.* Aldershot: Ashgate, 2003.

Hafter, Daryl M. 'Female Masters in the Ribbonmaking Guild of Eighteenth-Century Rouen'. *French Historical Studies* 20, no. 1 (1997): 1–14.

Women at Work in Preindustrial France. University Park: Pennsylvania State University Press, 2007.

Harding, Vanessa. 'Shops, Markets and Retailers in London's Cheapside, c. 1500–1700'. In *Buyers & Sellers: Retail Circuits and Practices in Medieval and Early Modern Europe*, edited by Ilja Van Damme, Jon Stobart, Peter Stabel and Bruno Blondé, 155–70. Turnhout: Brepols, 2007.

Hardwick, Julie. 'Gender, Credit and Rethinking (Economic) History'. *History Workshop Journal* 81 (2016): 253–60.

Heal, Ambrose. *The London Goldsmiths.* Cambridge University Press, 1935.

Heuvel, Danielle van der. 'Guilds, Gender Policies and Economic Opportunities for Women in Early Modern Dutch Towns'. In *Female Agency in the Urban Economy: Gender in European Towns, 1640–1830*, edited by Anne Montenach and Deborah Simonton, 116–33. New York: Routledge, 2013.

Higginbotham, Jennifer, *Girlhood of Shakespeare's Sisters: Gender, Transgression, Adolescence.* Edinburgh University Press, 2013.

Hindle, Steve. '"Waste" Children? Pauper Apprenticeship under the Elizabethan Poor Laws, c. 1598–1697'. In *Women, Work and Wages in England, 1600–1850*, edited by Penelope Lane, K. D. M. Snell and Neil Raven, 15–46. Woodbridge: Boydell, 2004.

Holford, Christopher. *A Chat about the Broderers' Company*. London: G. Allen, 1910.

Hovland, Stephanie R. 'Girls as Apprentices in Later Medieval London'. In *London and the Kingdom: Essays in Honour of Caroline M Barron*, edited by Matthew Davies and Andrew Prescott, 179–94. Donington: Shaun Tyas, 2008.

Hubbard, Eleanor. *City Women: Money, Sex, and the Social Order in Early Modern London*. Oxford University Press, 2012.

Hudson, Judith. '"2000 Wives": Women Petitioning on Barbary Captivity, 1626-1638'. *The Many-Headed Monster*, 11 November 2016. https://manyheadedmonster.wordpress.com/2016/11/11/2000-wives-women-petitioning-on-barbary-captivity-1626-1638/

Hufton, Olwen H. *The Prospect before Her: 1500–1800*. London: Harper Collins, 1996.

Hughes, Ann. 'Thomas Dugard and His Circle in the 1630s – A "Parliamentary-Puritan" Connexion?' *Historical Journal* 29, no. 4 (1986): 771–93.

Gender and the English Revolution. London: Routledge, 2011.

Hunt, Margaret R. *The Middling Sort: Commerce, Gender, and the Family in England, 1680–1780*. Berkeley: University of California Press, 1996.

'Wives and Marital "Rights" in the Court of Exchequer in the Early Eighteenth Century'. In *Londinopolis: Essays in the Social and Cultural History of Early Modern London*, edited by Mark S. R Jenner and Paul Griffiths, 107–29. Manchester University Press, 2000.

Jenner, Mark S. R. 'Guildwork'. In *Guilds, Society & Economy in London 1450–1800*, edited by Patrick Wallis and Ian Gadd, 163–70. London: Centre for Metropolitan History, 2002.

Karras, Ruth Mazo. '"This Skill in a Woman Is By No Means to Be Despised": Weaving and the Gender Division of Labor in the Middle Ages'. In *Medieval Fabrications: Dress, Textiles, Clothwork, and Other Cultural Imaginings*, edited by E. Jane Burns, 89–104. New York: Palgrave, 2004.

Kaufmann, Miranda. *Black Tudors: The Untold Story*. London: Oneworld, 2017.

Kellett, J. R. 'The Breakdown of Gild and Corporation Control Over the Handicraft and Retail Trade in London'. *Economic History Review* 10, no. 3 (1958): 381–94.

King, Helen. *The Disease of Virgins: Green Sickness, Chlorosis and the Problems of Puberty*. London: Routledge, 2009.

Korda, Natasha. 'Sex, Starch-Houses, and Poking Sticks: Alien Women's Work and the Technologies of Material Culture', *Early Modern Women* 5 (2010): 201–208.

Labors Lost: Women's Work and the Early Modern English Stage. Philadelphia: University of Pennsylvania Press, 2011.

Kowaleski, Maryanne and Judith M. Bennett. 'Crafts, Gilds, and Women in the Middle Ages: Fifty Years after Marian K. Dale'. *Signs* 14, no. 2 (1989): 474–501.

Kowaleski-Wallace, Elizabeth. *Consuming Subjects: Women, Shopping, and Business in the Eighteenth Century*. New York: Columbia University Press, 1997.

Krey, Gary S. De. *London and the Restoration, 1659–1683*. Cambridge University Press, 2009.

Lane, Joan. *Apprenticeship in England, 1600–1914*. London: Routledge, 1996.

Lemire, Beverley, *Dress, Culture and Commerce: The English Clothing Trade before the Factory, 1660–1800*. Basingstoke: Palgrave Macmillan, 1997.

Mansell, Charmian. 'Beyond the Home: Experiences of Female Service in Early Modern England'. *Gender and History* 33, no. 1 (2021): 24–49.

McDowell, Paula. *The Women of Grub Street: Press, Politics, and Gender in the London Literary Marketplace 1678–1730*. Oxford University Press, 1998.

McIntosh, Marjorie K. 'The Benefits and Drawbacks of Femme Sole Status in England, 1300–1630'. *Journal of British Studies* 44 (2005): 410–38.

Mendelson, Sara. 'The Civility of Women'. In *Civil Histories: Essays Presented to Sir Keith Thomas*, edited by Peter Burke, Brian Harrison and Paul Slack, 111–25. Oxford University Press, 2000.

Mendelson, Sara and Patricia Crawford. *Women in Early Modern England 1550–1720*. Oxford University Press, 2000.

Merry, Mark and Philip Baker. '"For the House Her Self and One Servant": Family and Household in Late Seventeenth-Century London'. *The London Journal* 34, no. 3 (2009): 205–32.

Miller, Jonah. 'Review of Shoplifting in Eighteenth-Century England'. *Reviews in History*, no. 2329. www.reviews.history.ac.uk.

Minns, Chris and Patrick Wallis. 'Rules and Reality: Quantifying the Practice of Apprenticeship in Early Modern England'. *Economic History Review* 65, no. 2 (May 2012): 556–79.

Moor, Tine De and Jan Luiten Van Zanden, 'Girl Power: The European Marriage Pattern and Labour Markets in the North Sea Region in the Late Medieval and Early Modern Period', *Economic History Review* 63, no. 1 (2010): 1–33.

Monteyne, Joseph. *The Printed Image in Early Modern London: Urban Space, Visual Representation, and Social Exchange*. Aldershot: Ashgate, 2007.

Morgan, Jennifer L. *Laboring Women: Reproduction and Gender in New World Slavery*. Philadelphia: University of Pennsylvania Press, 2011.

Mui, Hoh-cheung and Lorna H. Mui. *Shops and Shopkeeping in Eighteenth-Century England*. Montreal: McGill-Queen's University Press, 1989.

Muldrew Craig. *The Economy of Obligation: The Culture of Credit and Social Relations in Early Modern England*. London: Palgrave Macmillan, 1998.

'"A Mutual Assent of Her Mind"? Women, Debt, Litigation and Contract in Early Modern England'. *History Workshop Journal* 55 (2003): 47–71.

'The "Middling Sort": An Emergent Cultural Identity'. In *A Social History of England, 1500–1750*, edited by Keith Wrightson, 290-309. Cambridge University Press, 2017.

Muncaster, Jane. '"Six Foote of Shop Roome": Women as Subjects in the Records of the Royal Exchange in the 1690s'. MA dissertation, Birkbeck, University of London, 2003.

Newton, Gill. 'Infant Mortality Variations, Feeding Practices and Social Status in London between 1550 and 1750'. *Social History of Medicine* 24, no. 2 (2011): 260–80.
North, Susan. *Sweet and Clean?: Bodies and Clothes in Early Modern England*. Oxford University Press, 2020.
Ogilvie, Sheilagh. *A Bitter Living: Women, Markets, and Social Capital in Early Modern Germany*. Oxford University Press, 2003.
  'How Does Social Capital Affect Women? Guilds and Communities in Early Modern Germany'. *American Historical Review* 109, no. 2 (2004): 325–59.
Pelling, Margaret, 'Apprenticeship, Health and Social Cohesion in Early Modern London'. *History Workshop Journal* 37 (Spring 1994): 33–56.
Phillips, Nicola. *Women in Business, 1700–1850*. Woodbridge: Boydell & Brewer, 2006.
Pincus, Steven, *Protestantism and Patriotism: Ideologies and the Making of English Foreign Policy, 1650–1668*. Cambridge University Press, 2002, 242.
Pitman, Sophie. 'The Making of Clothing and the Making of London, 1560–1660'. PhD thesis, University of Cambridge, 2017.
Poska, Allyson M. 'The Case for Agentic Gender Norms for Women in Early Modern Europe'. *Gender & History* 30, no. 2 (2018): 354–65.
Prior, Mary. 'Women in the Urban Economy'. In *Women in English Society 1500–1800*, edited by Mary Prior, 93–117. London: Methuen, 1985.
Pritchard, Will. *Outward Appearances: The Female Exterior in Restoration London*. Lewisburg: Bucknell University Press, 2008.
Quataert, Jean H. 'The Shaping of Women's Work in Manufacturing: Guilds, Households, and the State in Central Europe, 1648–1870'. *American Historical Review* 90, no. 5 (1985): 1122–48.
Rappaport, Steve. *Worlds Within Worlds: Structures of Life in Sixteenth-Century London*. Cambridge University Press, 2002.
Read, Sara. *Menstruation and the Female Body in Early Modern England*. Basingstoke: Palgrave Macmillan, 2013.
Roper, Lyndal, *The Holy Household: Women and Morals in Reformation Augsburg*. Oxford University Press, 1991.
  'Blood and Codpieces: Masculinity in the Early Modern German Town', in *Oedipus and the Devil: Witchcraft, Sexuality and Religion in Early Modern Europe*, 107–24. London: Routledge, 1994.
Sacks, David Harris. 'Freedom to, Freedom from, Freedom of: Urban Life and Political Participation in Early Modern England'. *Citizenship Studies* 11, no. 2 (May 2007): 135–50.
Sanderson, Elizabeth. *Women and Work in Eighteenth-Century Edinburgh*. Basingstoke: Macmillan, 1996.
Saunders, Ann, ed. *The Royal Exchange*. London: London Topographical Society, 1997.
Schalk, Ruben, Patrick Wallis, Clare Crowston and Claire Lemercier. 'Failure or Flexibility? Apprenticeship Training in Premodern Europe'. *Journal of Interdisciplinary History* 48, no. 2 (2017): 131–58.
Scherf, K. Suzanne, Joshua M. Smyth and Mauricio R. Delgado. 'The Amygdala: An Agent of Change in Adolescent Neural Networks'. *Hormones and Behavior* 64, no. 2 (2013): 298–313.

Schmidt, Ariadne. 'Women and Guilds: Corporations and Female Labour Market Participation in Early Modern Holland'. *Gender & History* 21, no. 1 (2009): 170–89.
Schochet, Gordon J. 'Patriarchalism, Politics and Mass Attitudes in Stuart England'. *The Historical Journal* 12, no. 3 (1969): 413–41.
Schwoerer, Lois G. 'Women and Guns in Early Modern England'. In *Challenging Orthodoxies: The Social and Cultural Worlds of Early Modern Women: Essays Presented to Hilda L. Smith*, edited by Sigrun Haude and Melinda S. Zook, 33–52. Farnham: Ashgate, 2014.
Scott, Michael, ed. *Apprenticeship Disputes in the Lord Mayor's Court of London, 1573–1723*. London: British Record Society, 2016.
Sharpe, Pamela. 'Dealing with Love: The Ambiguous Independence of the Single Woman in Early Modern England'. *Gender & History* 11, no. 2 (1999): 209–32.
  'Gender at Sea: Women and the East India Company in Seventeenth-Century London'. In *Women, Work and Wages in England, 1600–1850*, edited by K. D. M. Snell, Penelope Lane and Neil Raven, 47–67. Woodbridge: Boydell Brewer, 2004.
  'Lace and Place: Women's Business in Occupational Communities in England 1550–1950'. *Women's History Review* 19, no. 2 (2010): 283–306.
Shepard, Alexandra. 'Crediting Women in the Early Modern English Economy'. *History Workshop Journal* 78 (2015): 1–24.
  Accounting for Oneself: Worth, Status, and the Social Order in Early Modern England. Oxford University Press, 2015.
  'Minding Their Own Business: Married Women and Credit in Early Eighteenth-Century London', *Transactions of the Royal Historical Society* 25 (December 2015): 53–74.
Shoemaker, Robert. 'Gendered Spaces: Patterns of Mobility and Perceptions of London's Geography, 1660–1750'. In *Imagining Early Modern London: Perceptions and Portrayals of the City from Stow to Strype, 1598–1720*, edited by J. F. Merritt, 144–65. Cambridge University Press, 2001.
Siegel, Daniel J. *Brainstorm: The Power and Purpose of the Teenage Brain*. London: Scribe, 2014.
Simonton, Deborah. '"Sister to the Tailor": Guilds, Gender and the Needle Trades in Eighteenth-Century Europe'. In *Early Professional Women in Northern Europe, c. 1650–1850*, edited by Johanna Ilmakunnas, Marjatta Rahikainen and Kirsi Vainio-Korhonen, 137–57. Abingdon: Taylor & Francis, 2017.
Sleigh-Johnson, Nigel. 'The Merchant Taylors Company of London 1580–1645, with Special Reference to Politics and Government'. PhD thesis, University College London, 1989.
Smith, Chloe Wigston. *Women, Work, and Clothes in the Eighteenth-Century Novel*. Cambridge University Press, 2013.
Smith, Hilda L. 'Women as Sextons and Electors: King's Bench and Precedents for Women's Citizenship'. In *Women Writers and the British Political Tradition*, edited by Hilda L. Smith, 324–342. Cambridge University Press, 1998.

'"Free and Willing to Remit": Women's Petitions to the Court of Aldermen, 1670–1750', in *Worth and Repute: Valuing Gender in Late Medieval and Early Modern Europe, Essays in Honour of Barbara Todd*, ed. Kim Kippen and Lori Woods, 279–309. Toronto: Centre for Reformation and Renaissance Studies, 2011.

All Men and Both Sexes: Gender, Politics, and the False Universal in England, 1640–1832. University Park: Pennsylvania State University Press, 2002.

Smith, Kate. 'In Her Hands: Materializing Distinction in Georgian Britain'. *Cultural and Social History* 11, no. 4 (2014): 489–506.

Smith, Helen. *'Grossly Material Things': Women and Book Production in Early Modern England*. Oxford University Press, 2012.

'Sensing Design and Workmanship: The Haptic Skills of Shoppers in Eighteenth-Century London'. *Journal of Design History* 25, no. 1 (2012): 1–10.

Smith, S. D. 'Women's Admission to Guilds in Early-Modern England: The Case of the York Merchant Tailors' Company, 1693–1776'. *Gender & History* 17, no. 1 (2005): 99–126.

Smith, Steven R. 'The London Apprentices as Seventeenth-Century Adolescents'. *Past & Present* 61 (1973): 149–61.

Snell, K. D. M. *Annals of the Labouring Poor: Social Change and Agrarian England, 1660–1900*. Cambridge University Press, 1987.

Sorge-English, Lynn. *Stays and Body Image in London: The Staymaking Trade, 1680–1810*. London: Pickering & Chatto, 2011.

Spence, Craig. *London in the 1690s: A Social Atlas*. London: Centre for Metropolitan History, 2000.

Spence, Cathryn R. 'A Perl for Your Debts?: Young Women and Apprenticeships in Early Modern Edinburgh'. In *Children and Youth in Premodern Scotland*, edited by Janay Nugent and Elizabeth Ewen, 31–46. Woodbridge: Boydell, 2015.

Spufford, Margaret. 'The Cost of Apparel in Seventeenth-Century England, and the Accuracy of Gregory King'. *Economic History Review* 53, no. 4 (2000): 677–705.

The Great Reclothing of Rural England: Petty Chapman and Their Wares in the Seventeenth Century. London: A. & C. Black, 1984.

Stallybrass, Peter. '"Little Jobs": Broadsides and the Printing Revolution'. In *Agent of Change: Print Culture Studies After Elizabeth L. Eisenstein*, edited by Sabrina Alcorn Baron, Eric N. Lindquist and Eleanor F. Shevlin, 315–41. Amherst: University of Massachusetts Press, 2007.

Staves, Susan. *Married Women's Separate Property in England, 1660–1833*. Cambridge, MA: Harvard University Press, 1990.

Stephenson, Judy Z. '"Real" Wages? Contractors, Workers, and Pay in London Building Trades, 1650–1800'. *Economic History Review* 71, no. 1 (2017): 106–32.

Stobart, Jon, Andrew Hann and Victoria Morgan. *Spaces of Consumption: Leisure and Shopping in the English Town, c. 1680–1830*. London: Routledge, 2007.

Stopes, Charlotte Carmichael. *British Freewomen: Their Historical Privilege*. London: Swan Sonnenschein, 1894.

Stretton, Tim and K. J. Kesselring. *Married Women and the Law: Coverture in England and the Common Law World*. Montreal: McGill-Queen's University Press, 2014.
Tadmor, Naomi. 'The Settlement of the Poor and the Rise of the Form in England, c. 1662–1780'. *Past & Present* 236 (2017): 43–97.
Tankard, Danae. *Clothing in 17th-Century Provincial England*. London: Bloomsbury, 2019.
Tickell, Shelley. *Shoplifting in Eighteenth-Century England*. Woodbridge: Boydell & Brewer, 2018.
Todd, Barbara. 'Fiscal Citizens: Female Investors in Public Finance before the South Sea Bubble'. In *Challenging Orthodoxies: The Social and Cultural Worlds of Early Modern Women: Essays Presented to Hilda L. Smith*, edited by Sigrun Haude and Melinda S. Zook, 53–74. Farnham: Ashgate, 2014.
Truant, Cynthia M. 'Parisian Guildswomen and the (Sexual) Politics of Privilege: Defending Their Patrimonies in Print'. In *Going Public: Women and Publishing in Early Modern France*, edited by Elizabeth C. Goldsmith and Dena Goodman, 45–61. Ithaca, NY: Cornell University Press, 1995.
Turner, James G. '"News from the New Exchange": Commodity, Erotic Fantasy and the Female Entrepreneur'. In *The Consumption of Culture 1600–1800: Image, Object, Text*, edited by Ann Bermingham and John Brewer, 419–39. Abingdon: Routledge, 1995.
Tycko, Sonia. 'Bound and Filed: A Seventeenth-Century Service Indenture from a Scattered Archive'. *Early American Studies* 19, no. 1 (2021): 185.
Vickery, Amanda. 'Women and the World of Goods: A Lancashire Consumer and Her Possessions, 1751–81'. In *Consumption and the World of Goods*, edited by John Brewer and Roy Porter, 274–303. London: Psychology Press, 1994.
Vries, Jan de. *The Industrious Revolution: Consumer Behavior and the Household Economy, 1650 to the Present*. Cambridge University Press, 2008.
Waddell, Brodie. 'Was Early Modern England a Petitioning Society?' *The Many-Headed Monster*, 7 November 2016. https://manyheadedmonster.wordpress.com/2016/11/07/was-early-modern-england-a-petitioning-society/.
Wallis, Patrick. 'Apprenticeship and Training in Premodern England'. *Journal of Economic History* 68, no. 3 (2008): 832–61.
'Labor, Law, and Training in Early Modern London: Apprenticeship and the City's Institutions'. *Journal of British Studies* 51, no. 4 (2012): 791–819.
'Apprenticeship in England'. In *Apprenticeship in Early Modern Europe*, edited by Maarten Prak and Patrick Wallis, 247–81. Cambridge University Press, 2019
Walsh, Claire. 'Shopping in Early-Modern London c. 1660–1800'. PhD dissertation, European University Institute, 2001.
'Social Meaning and Social Space in the Shopping Galleries of Early Modern London'. In *A Nation of Shopkeepers: Five Centuries of British Retailing*, edited by John Benson and Laura Ugolini, 52–79. London: I. B. Tauris, 2003.
'Shops, Shopping and the Art of Decision-Making in Eighteenth-Century England'. In *Gender, Taste, and Material Culture in Britain and North America, 1700–1830*, edited by John Styles and Amanda Vickery, 151–77. New Haven, CT: Yale Center for British Art, 2006.
'Shopping at First Hand? Mistresses, Servants and Shopping for the Household in Early-Modern England'. In *Buying for the Home: Shopping for*

the *Domestic from the Seventeenth Century to the Present*, edited by D. E. Hussey and Margaret Ponsonby, 13–26. Aldershot: Ashgate, 2008.

Ward, Joseph P. *Metropolitan Communities: Trade Guilds, Identity and Change in Early Modern London*. Stanford University Press, 1997.

Warhurst, Chris and Dennis Nickson. '"Who's Got the Look?" Emotional, Aesthetic and Sexualized Labour in Interactive Services'. *Gender, Work & Organization* 16, no. 3 (2009): 385–404.

Waugh, Norah. *The Cut of Women's Clothes: 1600–1930*. Abingdon: Routledge, 2013.

Weatherill, Lorna. 'A Possession of One's Own: Women and Consumer Behavior in England, 1660–1740'. *Journal of British Studies* 25, no. 2 (1986): 131–56.

Consumer Behaviour and Material Culture in Britain, 1660-1760. Brighton: Psychology Press, 1996.

Weil, Rachel. *Political Passions: Gender, the Family, and Political Argument in England, 1680–1714*. Manchester University Press, 1999.

Whiting, Amanda Jane. *Women and Petitioning in the Seventeenth-Century English Revolution: Deference, Difference, and Dissent*. Turnhout: Brepols, 2015.

Whittle, Jane and Mark Hailwood. 'The Gender Division of Labour in Early Modern England'. *Economic History Review* 73, no. 1 (2020): 3–32.

Whyte, Nicola. 'Custodians of Memory: Women and Custom in Rural England c. 1550–1700'. *Cultural and Social History* 8, no. 2 (2011): 153–73.

Wiesner, Merry E. *Working Women in Renaissance Germany*. New Brunswick: Rutgers University Press, 1986.

'Guilds, Male Bonding and Women's Work in Early Modern Germany'. *Gender & History* 1, no. 2 (1989): 125–37.

Wood, Andy. *The Memory of the People: Custom and Popular Senses of the Past in Early Modern England*. Cambridge University Press, 2013.

Wrightson, Keith, ed. *A Social History of England, 1500–1750*. Cambridge University Press, 2017.

Zaret, David. *Origins of Democratic Culture: Printing, Petitions, and the Public Sphere in Early-Modern England*. Princeton University Press, 2000.

Index

accessories, 44, 48, 82, 143, 158, 194
accounts, 155
adolescence, 5, 190, 198, 200–2
Advice to Women and Maidens, 155, 164
aldermen, 179, 209, 211–13, 217, 219, 223, 238
Aldermen's Court, 219, 225, 237
alehouses, 189
Allen, Katherine, 40, 169, 206, 251
Allen, Katherine and Herbert, 33, 38, 43, 48, 89, 92, 165, 178, 180–1
Angell, Frances, 1, 199, 202, 243, 251
anger, 199
Antrobus, Frances, 42–3
Antrobus, Robert, 42
appearance, 52, 176
Maddox, Appollonia, née Browne, 1
apprentices
    male, 105, 108, 129, 154, 183, 185, 188, 204, 206
    origins, 85
    parental status, 85
    parents' trades, 86
    parish, 93, 98, 122, 150–1
    range of trades, 144, 153
    working in shops, 165
apprenticeship
    age at, 200
    and marriage, 91
    decline, 82, 245
    discussions of female apprenticeship, 154, 156, 186, 216
    enforced, 148
    fictive contracts, 117
    flexibility, 76, 78, 154
    increase of female apprenticeship, 79, 82, 84, 249
    length, 93
    numbers of female apprentices, 80, 94
    outside guilds, 80
    parish, 148
    residential, 40, 94, 165

short contracts, 38, 92, 101, 153, 166, 221
termination of contracts, 78–9, 213
types of, 95
arithmetic, 155
artisanal identity, 63, 84
artisans, 8, 59, 75, 80, 82, 86

Baldwin, Susanna, 236
bankruptcy, 120, 240
Barber-Surgeons' Company, 70, 86, 195
bargaining, 46
Barton, Mary, 40, 170, 181, 251
Batelier, Mary, 52
bawdy houses, 183
Beattie, Cordelia, 219
Bell, Giles, 105
Ben-Amos, Ilana, 149, 183
Bennett, Judith, 237
bequests, 39, 71, 127, 132, 231–2, 243
Bickerstaff, Mary, 136
Bickley, Frances, 40, 167, 169–70, 251
Bicks, Caroline, 201
Billingsley, Benjamin and Deborah, 46
Billingsley, Elizabeth, 43, 47
Birt, Sarah, 44, 62
birthplaces, 78, 84
black Londoners, 54, 98
Blennerhasset, Agnes, 36, 40, 117
Bobart, Katherine, 11
bodices, 167, 174
bodkins, 207
book-keeping, 47, 156
Bourdieu, Pierre, 182
Bowyer, Dorothy, 173–4
Bristol, 97, 149, 217
Brock, Aske, 45
Broderers' Company, 220
Bromhall, Elizabeth and Thomas, 43–4, 87, 113–15
Browne, Apolonia, 243

269

270 Index

businesswomen, 18, 28, 30, 104, 117, 119, 168, 183, 194
buttons, 152

Callendrine, Rachel, 43, 47
capitalism, 4
caps, 48, 66, 145, 153, 159, 169
careers, 3, 49, 73, 83, 99, 117, 122, 156
Carey, Frances, 137, 162
cash, 46
Cavendish, Margaret, 240
Chamberlain of London, 77, 211
chambermaids, 163, 172
character, 133
Cheapside, 25, 96, 165, 224
Chedgzoy, Kate, 191
childbearing, 100, 116, 120
childbirth, 100, 119, 195
  death in, 202
childcare, 171
children, 32, 34, 90–1, 95, 116, 119, 134, 142, 148
children's clothes, 33, 44, 48, 121, 144–5, 152, 159
Christ's Hospital, 7, 93, 152–3, 163, 237
citizens, women as, 106
citizenship, 59, 61, 63, 213–16, 222, 240
  and politics, 211
Civil War, 9, 81, 211
civility, 183, 186, 191
Clark, Alice, 4, 59, 148
Clayton, Elizabeth, 131
cleaning, 171
cleanliness, 162, 195
Cleave, Sarah, later Frost, 11, 132
clergy, 73, 82
clergymen, 180
clerks, 7, 55, 69, 71, 73, 86, 191
clothes
  apprentices', 38, 176, 191–5
  ready-made, 44, 48, 83, 121
Clothworkers' Company, 73, 80, 89, 108, 144, 172
coats, 44, 121, 144, 153
coffee-houses, 47, 53
coifs, 159
coiners, 207
Common Council, 214, 217
consumer culture, 21
consumer revolution, 3, 11, 244
consumerism, 14
consumers, 21, 82, 170, 193
  apprentices as, 21, 194
corporate identity, 63
corporatism, 213

correction, 200, 204–6
Covent Garden, 49, 84
coverture, 29, 32, 103, 136, 239
credit, 12–13, 31, 46, 164, 168, 214
Crowston, Clare, 60, 165, 248
custom, 31, 59, 61, 76, 91, 102–3, 136, 154, 211, 213, 216, 219, 222, 239–40
custom of London, 61, 68, 97, 103
customers, 12, 164, 168, 181, 199, 248
cutting, 144, 160, 162

Deards, Rebecca, 83, 87, 114, 127
debt, 12, 34, 47–8, 50, 103, 135, 150, 168
Delony, Thomas, 109
depositions, 5–7, 184, 191
Dewell, Ann, 50
dirt, 31, 170, 176, 194
discipline, 177, 182, 202, 204, 207
Dissenters, 44, 114
dolls, 172
domestic service, 95, 120, 200
drama, 204
Drapers' Company, 71, 73, 76, 85
drinking, 183
drunkenness, 188, 203
Dugdale, Lettice, 89–90
Dugdale, William, 89, 180
Duke, Henry, 25

earnings, 140, 162, 164, 169
East India Company, 26, 29, 45
East London, 93
eating, 190–1
Elias, Norbert, 183
embroidery, 65–7, 243
English Revolution, 211
Enlightenment, 63, 215
enrolment, 57, 65, 81, 213
enslaved people, 31, 91, 148
Erickson, Amy, 103, 109
Erskine, Rachel, 40, 42, 123, 251
Evans, Ann, 55
Ewen, Misha, 45
exchangemen, 35
exchangewomen, 18, 25, 32, 35–6, 42, 45, 47, 82, 155

Farr, Mary, 239
fashion, 3, 44, 47, 158
feasts, 215
feme sole trader status, 31, 103, 107, 108, 216, 239
femininity, 68, 177, 188
fighting, 183
Fillis, Mary, 98

Index

financial revolution, 29
Fire of London, 9, 23, 82
Fishmongers' Company, 122–3
Flowerdew, Bridget, 127
food, 186, 189
foreigners, 234
forms, 55–7, 229
fornication, 91, 188
foundlings, 152, 208
freedom of London, 29, 36, 38, 59, 61, 71, 122, 210–42
  by servitude, 83, 211
  numbers of freemen, 213
  numbers of freewomen, 83–4, 215, 217
  offered after the Fire, 24, 82
  political privileges, 214, 217
  shared between husband and wife, 62, 99, 242
  single women, 83, 126
friends, 33, 171, 189, 192–3, 202, 210, 224
Froide, Amy, 118, 226
Fruiterers' Company, 145–6
furnishings, 181

gentry, 8, 38, 75, 82, 84–5, 89, 132, 179, 210
George, Dorothy, 148
German, Mary, 209
gesture, 178, 182, 184
Glaisyer, Natasha, 17
globalisation, 45
Glovers' Company, 74–5, 122, 126, 152
gloves, 143, 167
Goldsmiths' Company, 73, 77, 84, 86
Goreing, Miss, 48, 167
Gosfreight, Anne, 35
Gossard, Julia, 202
gowns, 162
grandparents, 120, 136
Grassby, Richard, 28, 104, 226
Gray, Ann, 11, 38, 167, 251
green-sickness, 201
Gregor, Ann, 40
Gresham College, 23–4
Gresham Committee, 22, 24–5, 27, 32
Grevill, Rowley, 36
Guidot, Alice, 33, 118
guild records, 8, 62, 69
guilds
  and family, 64
  and marriage, 108
  and women, 59–61, 214
  decline, 83, 245
  in France, 63
  increase in female apprentices, 30

  medieval, 215
  privileges, 60

Haberdashers' Company, 25, 57, 77, 80
Hafter, Daryl, 60
Hailwood, Mark, 5
hair, 173, 196, 199
hands, 145, 170, 173, 188
Haslam, Mary, 190
hats, 186
headgear, 84, 146, 159–60
healthcare, 195
hemming, 160, 173
Hippisly, Joan, 236, 241
Holme, Randall, 160, 162
hoods, 44, 143, 159
houseful, 94, 96
householders, 41, 217
households
  complex, 41
  female-headed, 4, 93, 96, 121
  large, 96–7, 112
  shared, 43
  size, 95–8
  structure, 95
housewifery, 7, 97, 149–50
housework, 139, 142, 170–1
Hudson, Hester, 136, 155, 162, 166, 252
Hulls, Mary and William, 89, 112
humours, 120, 206
Hunlock, Francis, 38, 179
Hunlock, Martha, 39, 252
Hunt, Margaret, 104, 226
Hutchins, Christiana, 162, 167, 169, 171, 192, 199, 252

illegitimate children, 135, 149
illicit sex, 188
illness, 195
immigrants, 98, 158, 225, 235
incivility, 183–4, 189, 199
incontinence, 198
indentured servitude, 148
indentures, 55–8, 70–1, 81, 84, 91, 95, 105, 117, 149, 191, 215, 220, 236
  foreign, 209
  lost, 57, 209
  of parish apprentices, 151
industrious revolution, 4
inheritance, 39, 128, 181, 229–30
inventories, 33, 48, 143, 181
investment, 29, 118

Jones, Mary, 137, 164, 252
journeywomen, 65, 74–6, 80, 126, 162

Karras, Ruth, 147
Kent, Ann, later Bell, 99
Kent, Frances, 100–2, 164
Kerby, Susanna, 238–9
kinship, 87, 104, 115, 247
knitting, 153
Kowaleski, Maryanne, 237

labour
  emotional, 52
  gender divisions, 63, 153
  hard, 146
  manual, 146
  value, 166, 173
labour market, 63
labour regulation, 64
lace, 13, 37, 48, 161
lameness, 223
Land Tax, 26, 39
Lane, Joan, 150
laundering, 160, 162, 198
Lee, Patience, 220
legal records, 5
Lendale, Margaret, 35
lice, 195
life cycle, 154, 217, 244
linen, 54, 160
  childbed, 44, 48, 159
  quality, 164
  washing and starching, 139, 162–3
  whitening, 163
linen shops, 24, 123
literacy, 154, 183
litigation, 7, 77, 179, 181
livery companies, 3, 8, 154, 214
  enrolling girls, 57, 71, 128
  not enrolling girls, 67, 74, 76, 79
  numbers of female apprentices, 69–89
lodgers, 41, 95, 97
Lord Mayor, 218
Lord Mayor's show, 194

Maddox, Appollonia, née Browne, 1, 193, 243, 251
Maes, Lucy, 35, 116
Makin, Bathsua, 155
Mandeville, Bernard, 184
manners, 7, 102, 157, 182–4, 186
mantuas, 44, 84, 153, 159
manufacturing, 146, 152
marriage
  age at, 200–1
  and civic identity, 237
  and freedom, 154, 211, 226, 234, 239–40
  and patrimony, 233, 235

legal consequences, 242
married names, 31, 239
of apprentices, 71, 91
to unfree men, 235–9
Marriage Duty, 93
masculinity, 63, 69, 183, 211
Mason, Elizabeth, 161, 173, 175, 190
Mason, Mary, 169, 172
Mayor's Court, 5–7, 76–7, 79, 179
Mendelson, Sara, 183
Mercers' Company, 73, 85
Mercers' Maiden, 69, 71
Merchant Taylors' Company, 25, 80, 123, 152
merchants, 18, 47, 51, 53, 114, 181
middle age, 210, 234
middle classes, 104
Middle Exchange, 16
middling sort, 8, 142–3, 191
migration, 85, 102
millinery
  and gentility, 176
  and reputation, 139
miscarriage, 204
mistresses, 101, 135, 166
modestly, 198
modesty, 63, 185, 188
mothers, 33, 66, 171, 188, 202, 204, 219
Muldrew, Craig, 31
Mullinox, Elizabeth, 237
Muncaster, Jane, 20
murder, 200, 205

needlework, 156, 161
New Exchange, 16, 21, 39, 49, 51
Newlin, Susanna, 220
Newton, Mary, née Hunt, 27–8
Non conformists, 53, 134, 137, 185
non-enrolment, 76–7, 210
North, Susan, 160
numeracy, 155

occupational identity, 64, 154
occupations
  bodice-makers, 121, 126, 145, 173
  button-makers, 80, 93, 121–2, 128, 152
  cabinet-making, 129
  cloth-drawer, 104
  coat-makers, 146, 151
  coat-selling, 112, 224
  cook, 191
  cutlers, 130
  cutting rabbit fur, 145, 152
  flax-dressers, 129, 146
  food-sellers, 23, 121

Index

fringe-making, 83
fruit-sellers, 22, 208, 223
gendered, 146–8
glove-making, 74
hat-making, 145
hemp-dressing, 118
herb-women, 145
knitting, 152
lace-making, 80, 171, 189
laundry-maids, 163
mantua-makers, 62, 82, 102, 125, 171, 192
milliners, 62, 161, 194, 239
of female apprentices, 4, 72, 143–53
of single women, 121
of widows, 129
painters, 49
pastrycook, 145
periwig-makers, 30, 152, 158
petticoat-maker, 102
pipe makers, 212
pipe-makers, 93, 205
printers, 129
shoemaking, 129, 152
silk-weaving, 112, 129
silk-winding, 122, 152
silkwomen, 71–2
silversmiths, 153
spinning gold and silver thread, 153
starching, 163
stocking-making, 129, 151
stocking-mender, 122
tailors, 41, 45, 62, 159
tire-makers, 145–6, 158
trimming gloves, 122, 152
victualling, 129
wiremaking, 122
Ogilvie, Sheilagh, 5, 59
orphans, 93, 95
Orphans' Court, 234
Oxford, 62

Painter-Stainers' Company, 49–50
Pannier, Sarah, 235
paperwork, 8, 38, 57–8, 77, 105, 107
parental relations, 202
partnership, 50, 101, 105, 127, 138, 168
patriarchal authority, 183
patriarchal equilibrium, 5
patriarchal household, 9, 202
patrimony, 28, 109, 127, 209, 215, 217, 226–40
  and charity, 234
  single women, 109
patterns, 134, 160, 162

paupers, 95, 97
Pepys, Elizabeth, 51
Pepys, Samuel, 23
Pepys, Samuel and Elizabeth, 53–4
petitions, 29, 45, 91, 93, 108, 120, 171, 209–12, 241
  conventions, 218
  women as authors of, 218–20
petticoats, 48, 160–2, 192
Pinney, Hester, 37, 49, 133–5, 162, 168, 252
plebeian women, 21, 76
politeness, 9, 185
Poor Laws, 8
poverty, 120, 223, 234, 237–8
pregnancy, 119
premiums, 7, 37, 81, 92, 119, 153, 167, 171, 173, 180, 247
  low, 148

quarterage, 75, 121, 126, 231
Que, Hester, 205
quilting, 153

Ram, Elizabeth and Hewett, 112
Rand, Elizabeth, 126
redemption, 215, 217, 220
Reeves, Margaret, 2, 133, 162
refugees, 109
rent, 31
reputation, 12, 135, 224
Royal Exchange, 3, 13–14, 92, 165, 234, 241
  decline, 83, 249
  growth, 84
  increase in women tenants, 25
  increase in women traders, 29
  layout, 18, 26
  leases, 24, 26, 29–31, 34, 37
  literary fantasies, 21
  rebuilding, 25–6
  shop signs, 19, 21, 27, 31, 34
  shop size, 19, 38
  tenants' living arrangements, 40
  upper pawn, 14, 17–20, 29, 44–5
ruffs, 158

satire, 16, 18, 51, 158
scavenging, 176
school, 142
schools, 156
scolds, 199
scriveners, 58, 80, 92, 241

seamstresses
    and femininity, 207
    and tailors, 8, 44, 62, 145, 159–60
    criminal, 207
    garments made by, 159
    in Europe, 102
    in France, 62–3
    in Paris, 106, 248
    in the eighteenth century, 248
    literary representations, 248
    living arrangements, 8, 41
    modern, 84
    outworkers, 49, 155, 250
    range of skills, 67, 84, 139, 154, 159–60, 162–3, 193
searches, 64–8
servants, 48, 54, 96–7, 162, 170–1, 194, 203, 233
    working in shops, 180
sewing, 121
    and barber-surgeons, 86, 94
    and femininity, 248
    and guilds, 61
    as trade, 143, 159
    earnings, 63, 143
    in girls' education, 142
    in later life, 234
    plain work, 142, 151, 161, 174
    types of, 161
sexualisation, 9, 16–17, 22, 51–2
Sharpe, Pamela, 226
Shepard, Alexandra, 4, 104
shifts, 143
shopkeepers, 18, 21, 155
shoplifting, 46
shopping, 21, 25, 48
    proxy shoppers, 45, 168
shopping galleries, 14
shops, 119
    apprentices working in, 164
    contents, 45, 143
    fittings, 45
    location, 41, 94, 165, 234
    'open shop', 141
    rent, 31, 35
    size, 16, 20, 165
    small, 26, 241
    starting, 155
    stock, 41, 45, 120, 167, 195
    structure, 14
siblings, 33, 102, 231
signatures, 86, 105
Simonton, Deborah, 18
single men, 96, 121, 136

single women, 30, 39, 47, 96, 215, 232
    and companies, 121, 128
    and patrimony, 233
    as mistresses, 57, 83, 123
    careers, 109
    range of work, 121
    taking apprentices, 85, 120–8
sisters, 22, 33, 36, 43, 83, 87, 100, 124, 127, 169, 233
skills, 101, 163, 168
    'feminine', 156
    haptic, 170
    of shop work, 46, 168
    transmission between women, 140, 154, 163
slave trade, 47, 250
slavery, 54; see also enslaved people
Smith, Helen, 70, 215
Smith, Hilda, 214
smocks, 159
Snell, Keith, 150
social contract theory, 9, 211
Southampton, 126
space, 21, 54
Spark, Mary, 213
Spence, Craig, 20
Spillett, Frances, 36, 253
Spillett, Frances and John, 35, 115–18
Stable, Dorothy, 100, 166, 253
stalls, 14, 16, 31, 223
starch, 158, 163
starching, 142, 159
Stationers' Company, 70, 129
stays, 174
stitches, 161
Strand, 16, 49, 51
suits, 192

table manners, 186
tailoring, 44, 158
tailors, 223
teachers, 172
teaching, 174
Temple family, 132
textile work, 4
theft, 155, 169–70, 192, 194
Thomas, Elizabeth, 222
Tiler sisters, 234
trade cards, 248
trades
    suitable for women, 102, 145, 154
    women's, 143
Trenchfield, Caleb, 185
Tycko, Sonia, 148

Index

unchastity, 188
under-garments, 159, 193, 195, 243

Venner, Katherine, 92, 165–6, 169, 178–82, 198, 253
vermin, 195–8
violence, 120, 174–5, 204–5
Virginia, 148, 202

Waddell, Brodie, 218
waistcoats, 192
Waller, Robert, 180
Wallis, Patrick, 64, 110, 166
Walsh, Claire, 21
Ward, Ned, 22
washing, 162–3
Weavers' Company, 64, 109
West End, 84, 92, 234
Westminster Hall, 16, 21, 52
wet-nurses, 116, 119, 203
Whittle, Jane, 5
widows, 30, 32, 39, 47, 62, 105, 215, 237
 and companies, 110
 and patrimony, 233, 237
 as consorts, 128, 216
 continuing husbands' trades, 107, 121, 128–31
 remarriage, 32, 130
Wight, Sarah, 191
wills, 39, 50, 89, 136, 180, 224, 230, 232–3, 243
witchcraft, 196

wives
 and companies, 67, 121
 independent work, 66, 103–4, 109–10
 legal position, 31, 103
 named/not named as mistresses, 81, 105, 144, 216
 number of apprentices, 111–13
 public voice, 218
 taking apprentices, 109, 120, 153
 training apprentices, 119
 work and lifecycle, 118–20
Wollstonecraft, Mary, 207
women's work
 and guilds, 58
 and identity, 241
 challenges to, 147
 continuities, 4
 in Dutch Republic, 158
 in Europe, 142
 in middle-class families, 104
 in textile trades, 3
 recording, 5, 77
Wood, Andy, 221
Woolley, Hannah, 156, 163, 166, 172, 186–7
workshops, 64, 74, 103, 111, 145

York, 62
Young, Pheby, 223

Zaret, David, 218